The Bolivarian Presidents

The Bolivarian Presidents

Conversations and Correspondence with Presidents of Bolivia, Peru, Ecuador, Colombia, and Venezuela

Robert J. Alexander

Westport, Connecticut
London

F
2237
.A44
1994
c.1

Library of Congress Cataloging-in-Publication Data

Alexander, Robert Jackson.
    The Bolivarian presidents : conversations and correspondence with
presidents of Bolivia, Peru, Ecuador, Colombia, and Venezuela /
Robert J. Alexander.
        p. cm.
    Includes bibliographical references and index.
    ISBN 0–275–94661–4 (alk. paper)
    1. South America—Politics and government—20th century.
2. Presidents—South America—History—20th century. I. Title.
F2237.A44 1994
980.03′3′0922—dc20   93–11892

British Library Cataloguing in Publication Data is available.

Copyright © 1994 by Robert J. Alexander

Library of Congress Catalog Card Number: 93–11892
ISBN: 0–275–94661–4

First published in 1994

Praeger Publishers, 88 Post Road West, Westport, CT 06881
An imprint of Greenwood Publishing Group, Inc.

Printed in the United States of America

The paper used in this book complies with the
Permanent Paper Standard issued by the National
Information Standards Organization (Z39.48–1984).

10 9 8 7 6 5 4 3 2 1

To Robert De Maria

Contents

Preface

This is the third in a series of books of conversations and correspondence with Latin American presidents. The first was _Venezuela's Voice for Democracy_, dealing solely with Rómulo Betancourt. The second was _The ABC Presidents_, dealing with the chief executives of Argentina, Brazil, and Chile.

The present volume deals with presidents of the five South American countries which were liberated by Simón Bolívar: Bolivia, Peru, Ecuador, Colombia and Venezuela. The sixth nation which might be labelled "Bolivarian" is Panama, which in the Liberator's time was part of what is today Colombia; however, it will be dealt with in a volume on Central America.

A couple of comments are in order concerning the sequences used in this book. The various presidents are dealt with in the order in which they were presidents of their respective countries. The five countries are presented in what seemed to me a more logical order than a merely alphabetical one. We start with the most southerly of these nations, Bolivia, the one which was named after Bolívar. We then proceed geographically from south to north, through Peru, Ecuador, Colombia and Venezuela.

A word is also called for concerning the way my discussions with these people were conducted. In nearly half a century of interviewing and/or talking with political leaders and others, I have never used a recording device, and have seldom taken notes while actually talking to individuals. It has always seemed to me that a person is more likely to talk freely when he or she is not *confronted either with a mechanical contrivance or a pen or pencil taking down what is being said.*

As a consequence, what I have done is to take as extensive notes as possible as soon after leaving the presence of the individual as possible. Then, as soon as I have gotten to my typewriter, I have recorded more or less in full what has been said. Therefore, in putting down a conversation, I have never used the first person singular, as if the person involved were speaking directly, but rather have used the third person, thus clearly recognizing that what I have written is not a direct quotation. Also, both conversations and correspondence are in the present tense, since they use what the presidents said or wrote at the time indicated in each interview or letter.

Both the conversations and the correspondence have been conducted in Spanish. The translations are my own.

As is always the case with authors, I owe many debts to others. First of all, of course, I am indebted to those people who are dealt with in this volume, who have freely given me their time and information. I am also very appreciative of the continuing interest of Dr. James Sabin in this volume and the series in general. I wish to thank Krystyna Budd and Andrea Morgan, who edited the present book, and other people at the Greenwood Publishing Group who have seen this volume through to publication. Also, I owe special gratitude to Eldon Parker, who prepared the camera-ready copy for this volume, as he did for the previous one in the series.

As is ever the case, I owe thanks to my wife Joan, for her tolerance in bearing with me while I wrote this book. Needless to say, without her support the book would never have been written.

Bolivia

INTRODUCTION

The people dealt with in this section are the men and one woman who presided over Bolivia for twenty-eight and a half of the more than forty years since the Bolivian National Revolution of April 9, 1952. That upheaval was one of the three or four most fundamental transformations to take place in Latin America in the twentieth century. It quite literally gave the land back to the Indians, nationalized the Big Three mining companies, which had dominated Bolivian politics since the turn of the century, extended education to much of the peasant population, and took important steps to foster the country's economic development.

The Bolivian National Revolution was carried out by the Movimiento Nacionalista Revolucionario (MNR-Nationalist Revolutionary Movement). All but two of the people dealt with in these pages were associated with the MNR. One exception is Luis Adolfo Siles who, although a half-brother of the MNR's President Hernán Siles, was consistently an opponent of the Movimiento Nacionalista Revolucionario. The other is President Jaime Paz Zamora.

The MNR remained in power from April 1952 until November 1964, through the administrations of Víctor Paz Estenssoro (1952-1956), Hernán Siles (1956-1960), and the second period of Paz Estenssoro (1960-1964), who had barely been in office a few months of what was supposed to be his third term when he was overthrown by a military coup led by General René Barrientos and Alfredo Ovando in November 1964, and Paz Estenssoro went into exile.

One of the principal characteristics of the second half

of the MNR's period in power between 1952 and 1964 was the splintering of the unity of the party. In its first years in office, it seemed to be generally accepted that an order of succession had been worked out among the four leading figures in the party: Víctor Paz Estenssoro, Hernán Siles, Walter Guevara Arce, and Juan Lechín. This widely accepted agreement was fulfilled in the first transfer of the presidency from Paz Estenssoro to Siles in 1956. However, with the approach of the 1960 election, the expected nomination of Walter Guevara Arce as the MNR candidate did not take place. Rather, Víctor Paz Estenssoro was named once again, while Guevara Arce broke away to form his own party, the Partido Revolucionario Auténtico (PRA).

A further split took place in 1964, when it was widely expected that the labor leader Juan Lechín--who was Paz Estenssoro's vice president in his second term--would be the MNR nominee. However, again Víctor Paz Estenssoro was the MNR candidate, leading to a further schism in the party, with Lechín forming his own party, the Revolutionary Party of the Nationalist Left (PRIN).

In the end, the dissident MNR factions joined with General René Barrientos--Paz Estenssoro's vice president after the 1964 election, and until then head of the military cell of the MNR--in overthrowing the Paz Estenssoro government. Paz Estenssoro gives me his version of that event in some of my discussions with him.

Another factor which undermined the MNR politically in Paz Estenssoro's second term was his government's program (known as the Operación Triangular) to rationalize the operation of the government-owned tin mines administered by the Corporación Minera Boliviana (COMIBOL). This measure aroused opposition among the tin miners, who were therefore eager to support Juan Lechín's defection from the MNR. Paz Estenssoro comments on his program to rationalize the operation of COMIBOL in two of my interviews with him.

After a short period of co-presidency of the generals Barrientos and Ovando, Barrientos was elected president in 1966, with Luís Adolfo Siles as his vice president. Early in 1969, Barrientos perished in an airplane crash and was succeeded by his vice president, who was overthrown by General Ovando, who took over the presidency. However, Ovando's regime lasted less than a year, when a further coup, after some confusion, placed General Juan José Torres in office.

During the year-long Torres government, a wide range of far-left groups appeared to share much of the power--including the pro-Moscow and pro-Chinese factions of the Communist Party, several Trotskyite groups, and particularly the country's central labor organization, the

Central Obrera Boliviana (COB). Early in 1971 a Popular Assembly (Asamblea Popular) was organized, presided over by Juan Lechín, a one-time leader of the MNR but since 1964 the head of his own party, the Revolutionary Party of the Nationalist Left (PRIN), and also head of the COB. Although conceived of by many of those participating in it as a replica of the Russian Soviets of 1917, it never effectively controlled the situation.

In August 1971, President Torres was overthrown by another military coup, this time headed by Colonel Hugo Banzer. It was backed by the curious coalition of the MNR and its bitterest foe, the Falange Socialista Boliviana (FSB), joined in what they called the Nationalist Popular Front (Frente Popular Nacionalista) which at first had ministers in President Banzer's cabinet.

However, this alliance of the dominant faction of the Army, the MNR, and the FSB proved to be short-lived. In less than two years, the MNR withdrew and Víctor Paz Estenssoro went into exile once again. The Banzer regime became a thorough-going military dictatorship.

Banzer stayed in power until 1978. Then faced with a hunger strike in the capital's churches by large numbers of women, he called new elections for later that year, and allowed the political parties, unions, and other groups to reestablish themselves. The "government" candidate in those elections was General Juan Pereda. Pereda was certainly defeated by Hernán Siles, running as candidate of a coalition, the Democratic Union of the People (Unión Democrática del Pueblo), consisting of his own faction of the MNR, the pro-Moscow Communists, the Movement of the Revolutionary Left (MIR) headed by Jaime Paz Zamora, and several peasant groups. However, Pereda overthrew President Banzer and declared himself the victor. He was soon overthrown, and new elections were called.

In the 1979 election, Víctor Paz Estenssoro and Hernán Siles were leading candidates. But when Congress could not decide which of them had won, it chose Walter Guevara Arce as provisional president. He had been one of the leading figures in the MNR in the 1950s but had broken with it in 1960, when he was denied the party's nomination for president in favor of the return of Paz Estenssoro, and had formed his own Authentic Revolutionary Party.

However, Guevara Arce lasted less than three months as president, being overthrown by a coup led by Colonel Alberto Natusch Busch. This coup aroused widespread popular resistance, led by Guevara Arce. But when Busch was finally forced to resign, a political compromise was reached by which Guevara Arce was not returned to the presidency. Instead Congress chose Lidia Gueiler Tejeda, a *member of Juan Lechín's PRIN and a one-time Trotskyite.*

President Gueiler summoned still other elections in 1980, in which Hernán Siles was clearly the leading candidate. His closest rival, Víctor Paz Estenssoro, agreed to have his supporters in Congress support Siles's election. But before this could could happen, a new military coup installed General Luís García Meza in the presidency.

The García Meza regime was the most disgraceful one that Bolivia has had in the twentieth century. Its leading figures were engaged in the cocaine trade, and other kinds of corruption were rife. Finally, in 1982 he was overthrown, and after some hesitation, his successor called back into session the Congress which had been elected in 1980. It chose Hernán Siles as the next president.

Hernán Siles's second administration was an economic disaster. It was under conflicting pressures of the International Monetary Fund and the Central Obrera Boliviana (backed by the pro-Moscow Communist Party, which had ministers in his cabinet, and other far Left groups), and the president admittedly lost control of the situation. As a consequence, he called elections one year early, and in 1985 Víctor Paz Estenssoro was once again elected president.

However, this time, Paz Estenssoro carried out an economic and social program which to some seemed to be diametrically opposed to that which he had had in his earlier periods in office. Faced with an inflation which was totally out of control, he inaugurated a drastic austerity program. As part of this program, he closed down many of the country's money-losing tin mines--tin being the country's main export--and virtually broke the power of the Miners Federation and COB.

At the end of the term in 1989, Paz Estenssoro presided over new elections. In a three-cornered race among General Banzer (the ex-dictator), an MNR nominee, and Jaime Paz Zamora, candidate of the Movement of the Revolutionary Left (MIR), the MIR came in last, but no nominee got a majority. Consequently, Congress, which had to chose among the top three candidates chose Paz Zamora, as the result of a deal between his party's members of the legislature and those of General Banzer's party. Paz Zomora took office in August 1989.

In the pages which follow, we deal with Presidents Víctor Paz Estenssoro, Hernán Siles, René Barrientos, Luís Adolfo Siles, Walter Guevara Arce, Lidia Gueiler, and Jaime Paz Zamora. My acquaintance with each of these varied greatly in terms of time and extent of contact.

Víctor Paz Estenssoro was the Bolivian president with

whom I had the longest and most extensive acquaintance. I first met him in La Paz, a few days after he ceased being president for the first time, in 1956. I met him again in New York City during the period in which he was Ambassador to Great Britain, following his first administration. In 1962 I was invited to the celebration of the tenth anniversary of the Bolivian National Revolution in La Paz, although I did not have a chance to talk personally with him at that time.

I did, however, get a chance to converse with him when he was in New York City late in 1963. At that time, he was kind enough to present me--together with Frank Tannenbaum, Norman Thomas, Lewis Hanke, and Frances Grant--with the Order of the Condor of the Andes. Afterward, we got a chance to talk at some length.

Subsequent to his overthrow in 1964, I met with Paz Estenssoro a couple of times in Lima, Peru, where he was in exile. But my most extensive chance to talk with Víctor Paz Estenssoro was in 1969, when he visited Rutgers University for several days. Our Latin American Institute had received a small grant from the Green Stamps Foundation to bring visiting lecturers to the campus, and our first invitee was Víctor Paz Estenssoro. He lectured publicly on both the New Brunswick and Newark campuses of the University, and I had chances to talk with him at length on a personal basis. All these discussions are presented in what follows.

During the period of Paz's exile in Peru, he on various occasions commented to me on things then going on in that country.

Subsequently, after his return to La Paz, following assumption of power by Colonel Hugo Banzer, I had a chance to talk with Paz Estenssoro at considerable length in the Bolivian capital. Still later, when he had once again gone into exile, I interviewed him once more in Lima. Unfortunately, I did not have an opportunity to see him subsequently, particularly after he had once again returned to power in the late 1980s under strikingly different circumstances from those of his earlier administrations.

Several comments are in order concerning things which Víctor Paz Estenssoro discussed. First, it should be noted that he expounded considerably on the history of his country, particularly on the nature of the Bolivian National Revolution and on the ideology of his party, the Movimiento Nacionalista Revolucionario.

Second, several things Paz talked about and one organization which he mentioned need to be identified. One is the so-called "Catavi massacre." This occurred in connection with a workers' strike in 1942 against very bad conditions in the Catavi mine near the city of Oruro. In a demonstration of the miners, their wives, and their children in connection with the strike, troops opened fire, killing and wounding a number of people, including women and children. This was a major factor in the overthrow the following year of the government then in power, as well as triggering an investigation by the U.S. government, which was then purchasing virtually all of Bolivia's tin exports.

Paz Estenssoro also refers to the Andean Pact. This was an agreement negotiated in the late 1960s among Chile, Bolivia, Peru, Ecuador, Colombia and Venezuela to establish a common market. Although there were provisions in the agreement to give Bolivia special exemptions, permitting it to protect its industries for an extended period of time, Paz Estenssoro obviously felt that these exemptions did not go far enough.

Three people Paz talks about need identification. These are Filomeno Velazco, Víctor Andrade and Eudosio Ravines. Velasco was the head of Argentine President Juan Perón's federal police during the period of Paz Estenssoro's exile in Argentina in the late 1940s. Certainly, anti-Peronistas would not have agreed with Paz Estenssoro's judgment that Velasco was "a fine man."

Victor Andrade was a long-time leader of the MNR who had served as Ambassador to Washington both during the government of Colonel Gualberto Villarroel in the 1940s and the MNR administrations of the 1950s. After the fall of Paz Estenssoro in 1964, Andrade became the leader of one faction of the MNR, that which was recognized by the government of General Barrientos as the "official" Movimiento Nacionalista Revolucionario.

Eudosio Ravines was the founder of the Peruvian Commmunist Party, and for some years was an agent of the Communist International. He quit the Communists in 1942, subsequently had his own political party, and became a professional journalist. By the time that Paz Estenssoro was talking about him in 1969, Ravines was employed by the conservative newspaper pubisher Pedro Beltrán.

Finally, Paz Estenssoro frequently mentions "the Rosca." This is a somewhat ill-defined term for the ruling class in Bolivia before the 1952 Revolution. It broadly means the rural large landholding class and the big mining interests.

Finally, it may be noted that Víctor Paz Estenssoro predicted to me in July 1971 the coup which was to take place in Bolivia in the following month and bring Colonel Hugo Banzer to power. Although he did not mention Banzer's name, he did note that the MNR, the Falange Socialista Boliviana, and the Christian Democrats were conspiring with elements in the military to bring down the government of

Juan José Torres.

I had a chance to confer with President Hernán Siles on only two occasions. The first was when he was vice president under Víctor Paz Estenssoro, in his office in La Paz in 1954. The second was when he and I were both guests at the inauguration of Antonio Guzmán as President of the Dominican Republic in 1978. Guzmán had been elected by the Dominican Revolutionary Party, the Dominican counterpart of the MNR.

Several things should be noted about my conversations with Siles. In the first interview, he talks about the case of the La Paz newspaper _La Razón_. This paper had been the spokesman _par excellence_ of the big private mining interests before the 1952 Revolution. After that event it did not appear. The government didn't prohibit it, but as Siles indicates, it also didn't promise to protect it if it did appear and was attacked from the streets. For several years, the late Jules Dubois, then head of the Freedom Press Committee of the Interamerican Press Association, insisted that the failure of _La Razón_ to publish indicated that there was no freedom of press in Bolivia, in spite of the fact that several other newspapers, including the conservative _El Diario_ and the Christian Democrats' _Presencia_, were strongly critical of the MNR government and suffered no adverse circumstances because of their attitude.

Another interesting aspect of my first conversation with Siles was his apparent reticence to run as MNR candidate to succeed Víctor Paz Estenssoro. Instead, he argued that the ban on presidential reelection ought to be changed, and Paz Estenssoro should thereupon be reelected. My first talk with Luís Adolfo Siles, Hernán's half brother, confirmed Hernán Siles's reticence about running. Of course, when Paz sought reelection in the early 1960s, during Paz Estenssoro's second period in office, Siles was strongly opposed to it.

Two observations are in order concerning Siles's comments in my second interview. First, part of what appears here is what Siles said at a public meeting just before President Guzmán's inauguration. This meeting was sponsored by the Socialist International, to which the PRD belonged, and which had played an important part in blocking efforts to nullify Guzmán's election by arousing wide protests in Europe.

Second, Siles's prediction that if, after stealing the election of 1978, the Bolivian military would call new elections, they would honor their results, proved to be incorrect. We have noted that the upshot of the 1979 election was not in accordance with the ballots cast, but

Congress elected two successive presidents of short duration thereafter. Then in 1980, although Siles was the clear winner, his victory was negated by still another military coup, and it took two more years before his victory was finally recognized.

The third Bolivian president who is dealt with in these pages is René Barrientos. He was one of the speakers at the celebration of the tenth anniversary of the Bolivian National Revolution. I record here a very short conversation I had with him at that time, as well as a summary of what he said in the anniversary celebration. In both cases, he certainly did not sound like one who would a bit more than two years later overthrow the MNR regime.

Luís Adolfo Siles, the fourth person who is dealt with in these pages was a half brother of Hernán Siles, both being sons of Hernando Siles, Bolivian president in the 1920s. As the earlier interviews with him show, he was strongly opposed to the MNR regime of the 1950s. He pictures some of the more negative aspects of the revolutionary government. However, my last talk with him, at the inauguration in the Dominican Republic--where he was also an invited guest--indicated that by that time he was supporting his half-brother's aspirations to return to the presidential office.

I interviewd Walter Guevara Arce eight years after he had broken with the MNR, and more than a decade before he himself became president for a short while. He casts interesting light on the splintering of the MNR, which we have noted earlier.

I talked with Lidia Gueiler when she was an MNR deputy in Congress, when she was one of five women to hold that post. She was a one-time Trotskyite, who had joined the MNR in 1954. Subsequently, she was an influential member of the PRIN, established by Juan Lechín when he broke with the MNR in 1960.

Finally, Jaime Paz Zamora is president of Bolivia as this is being written. He, like the two Siles brothers, was an invitee to the inauguration of President Antonio Guzmán in 1978. It was there that I had a short conversation with him.

One final thing to note about the conversations in this section is that several of the interviewees commented more or less extensively on others with whom I have talked. These comments shed some light on the people involved which they themselves do not necessarily offer.

* * * * *
* * * * *

CONVERSATION WITH VÍCTOR PAZ ESTENSSORO IN HIS HOME IN LA PAZ, BOLIVIA, AUGUST 21, 1956

He is glad to talk with someone from the United States, because the Movimiento Nacionalista Revolucionario is very much misunderstood in the outside, and particularly in the United States. They were accused during the last war of being Nazis or pro-Nazis, and more recently they have been accused of being Communists. Of course, a great deal of this is due to the fact that there were powerful interests inside and outside of Bolivia which had an interest in painting a false picture of the Movimiento outside of the country.

He regards the MNR as a party which is more or less in the same class as the Acción Democrática of Venezuela and the Partido Aprista of Peru, taking into account differences due to the national peculiarities of the different countries. They are all national revolutionary parties.

The MNR comes out of the same climate of feeling and opinion as did the Partido Izquierda Revolucionaria (PIR) and the Partido Obrero Revolucionario (POR). In fact, there were three main streams which developed from the post-Chaco War situation, the first of which was the Falange Socialista Boliviana, a group of more or less Fascist stripe, influenced particularly by the Spanish Falange. It was founded in 1937 or 1938. A few years later there came the PIR and the MNR.

The development of all these forces was more or less as follows: The revolutionary movement for independence from Spain brought political transformation but left the previous economic situation largely intact. The only differences in the local situation after the independence movement was that the Spanish influence was no longer here. But the land remained in the hands of the large landowners, and if anything, the concentration of the land was increased.

For the first three or four decades after independence, there was a succession of military governments, coming out of the wars of independence. Then about 1880 there began a period of rule by the Conservative Party. This party represented the silver-mining elements of Potosí, and the large landholders, the feudal landholders.

This Potosí silver-mining element was purely Bolivian. During this period there was considerable modernization of the silver mines, made necessary by the abandonment of the bi-metal standard and the consequent fall in the world price of silver, which made necessary more efficient methods of production. The owners of these mines were small capitalists who for the most part lived in Potosí, where they brought the finest furniture, the finest pottery, and so on, things which one can see there to this day.

Previous to this period, there had been some capitalist development in the nitrate fields, but it was brought about by British capital, entering via Chile. With the War of the Pacific, the nitrate fields were lost in any case, along with Bolivia's outlet to the sea.

The Conservative period was one of some considerable development. It saw the extension of the railroad as far as Oruro from Antofagasta. It was a period of political stability, and presidents succeeded one another in more or less orderly fashion.

In 1899, this period of Conservative rule came to an end. In a fight over a merely formal matter--where the capital should be--the Conservative rule was brought to an end. The people of Sucre, backed by the silver-mining interests, maintained that the government should have its seat there. Those of La Paz, backed by the nascent tin-mining interests, which were already active in the northern part of the country and were closely tied to foreign, particularly British, economic interests, argued that the capital should be in La Paz. In a civil war, the forces of La Paz, and consequently of the international mining interests, gained the upper hand.

The slow growth of the tin-mining business, and even the growth of silver mining, had created a small bourgeois class. This group found political expression in the Liberal Party. The Revolution of 1899 ws a Liberal revolt against Conservative rule. However, the Liberals, who ostensibly advocated Liberal economic principles, instead of going forward with the real implementation of Liberal principles in the economic field--that is, an agrarian reform, which is a Liberal not Socialist idea--began themselves to become large landowners, using the state as a means toward this end. The most famous case was that of a president who seized the lands of a large Indian community on the edge of Lake Titicaca.

One bad aspect of this part of the Liberal rule is the fact that the Liberals won the 1899 Revolution by arousing the support of the Indians. The Liberal rebels raised an Indian army, which completely destroyed that of the Conservative government. However, once in power, the Liberals did not do anything to really meet the needs of the Indians. Once they had won the civil war for the Liberals, the Indians were sent back home.

The Liberals ruled for over twenty years, and during this period there was no change in the economic and social structure of the country. The Liberals continued to take over comunidades for their own use. However, there were some constitutional and formal changes. For instance, the country has just recently celebrated the fiftieth anniversary of the establishment of freedom of religion; civil marriage was established and other similar changes were made, but nothing changed in the fundamental structure of the nation.

During this period, the production of tin became the principal source of foreign exchange. It was in the hands of largely foreign firms.

Meanwhile, dissident elements in the Liberal ranks, and the remnants of the Conservatives, joined to form the Republican Party. This party conducted the opposition against the Liberals during the latter part of the Liberal rule. There were some very fine parliamentary debates during this period, but they all centered around purely political issues--the protection of freedom of speech, freedom of press, etc. But politics remained the monopoly of the small upper class, and social and economic issues were seldom debated.

In 1920 there was a revolution which brought the Republicans to power. Throughout the 1920s there was a period of uncertainty, with governments being overthrown by force from time to time. This period came to an end with the Chaco War.

The Chaco War came from a long-time border dispute between Paraguay and Bolivia, having its origins in the lack of certainty as to the borders of the old Spanish provinces. He does not think that it is true that the war was a fight between British oil interests backing Paraguay and American oil interests backing Bolivia. This is an oversimplified Marxist version, which he does not think faithfully reflects the real situation. This was merely a frontier dispute--and in fact, Bolivia, had no friends at all in the struggle.

There is no doubt that the war was provoked by Bolivian President

Salamanca. He was very cold and calculating in judging that Bolivia could win the war. When it was suggested that there were no roads into the Chaco, he merely replied that it would be necessary to start the Indian soldiers marching six months earlier than otherwise, so that they could get there in time.

As wars often do, this one showed up the good and bad in the country in a very stark manner. It immediately showed the uselessness of the German-trained army--trained to a rigid discipline, but without any emphasis on thinking for oneself. The "great generals" who had been developed during the period of German training failed absolutely.

There was a completely inadequate supply system. The country not only did not possess the products of heavy industry necessary in a war--munitions, canons, etc.--but it did not have such elementary things as flour and sugar, all of which had to be imported, mostly from Argentina. The then president of Argentina, General Justo, was a business partner of one of the leading political figures of Paraguay. The Argentine attitude was generally hostile toward Bolivia, and supplies were delivered late, and sometimes the border was closed entirely.

The effect of the war was to sow tremendous discontent among the soldiers who had participated in it, and a desire to right the wrongs which they saw their country suffering. The first person to take advantage of this spirit among the soldiers and ex-soldiers was Colonel David Toro. He moved not only as a means of taking advantage of widespread discontent but also in order to cover up his own miserable record during the war. He was one of those who bore most responsibility for the defeat of Bolivia. For instance, at one point there was a planned attack by the cream of the Bolivian Army, the cavalry. The whole attack was badly planned, and was foiled by the Paraguayans, who seized the only waterhole in the area and sat tight. The Bolivian troops largely died of thirst. During this whole episode, the commander of the force, Colonel Toro, was drunk, having a bacchanal with some of his fellow officers and girls specially invited for the occasion. This was one of the things he was trying to live down.

Most of the discontented ex-soldiers followed Toro, however, because he did raise the banner of a Socialist Republic. Nevertheless, he was very soon enveloped by the forces of the Rosca, and finally after eighteen months in office, he was ousted by his chief of staff, Col. Germán Busch. Busch was entirely different from Toro, was a very young man--being only thirty-three when he became president--and was one of the real heroes of the Chaco War. In the midst of defeat and general ineptitude, he had been personally courageous and brilliant as an officer.

Busch was a soldier with no experience in politics, and before very long he was hoodwinked by the Rosca, who succeeded in getting him to appoint three of their number to the cabinet, including the Minister of Finance.

This was the pre-World War II period, all nations were preparing for war, and the demand for Bolivian tin was tremendous. There were German, Japanese, and U.S. missions here seeking to buy Bolivian tin. This was a period when the country could have gotten the most possible return for its product. However, the Minister of Finance presented Busch with a proposed decree, in the preamble of which it was stated that the international situation gave Bolivia a chance to exploit to the utmost the demand for its tin, that in the interest of the country it was necessary to take the utmost advantage of the situation, and so on. However, the substantive part of the decree actually reduced the returns to the country from the sale of tin. Busch read the preamble but didn't go through the substantive part, which was written in the most obtuse legal and accounting language.

Paz Estenssoro, who was then a member of Congress from the southern part of the country, got hold of this decree and felt that there was something wrong with it. So he and another deputy went to some political friends of theirs in the Customs, and they took a sample ore lot and applied to it the tax schedule of the old system, and that of the new decree, and found very quickly that the country came out very much the loser by the new decree. The two deputies then took this to President Busch, accompanied by the Customs official who had made the calculations for them. Busch, who was a violent man, made the Customs official swear to the correctness of his calculations on the penalty of immediate shooting if they were wrong. He then called in the Minister of Finance, who had presented him the decree, and other members of the cabinet, presented them with the facts of the case, threatened to have the Minister of Finance shot, and actually had him jailed.

Paz and his friends then proposed a new law to Busch--that the tin companies be forced to sell 100 percent of the foreign exchange which they made on the sale of tin, to the Banco Central, which would then give them back the amount of foreign exchange they needed for their operations.

This occurred at the end of July. A few weeks later Busch was found dead. The official version was that he committed suicide. Another story was that he was killed by his brother-in-law. Paz Estenssoro always maintained that he had been shot by agents of the Rosca. However, since himself being president, he has come to the conclusion that Busch really committed suicide. The pressures of the office are such--and even more so then, when Busch had no political party to support him, there was not the social climate which exists at the present time, and he did not know whom to trust--and the influence of the Rosca was so all-pervading, that he thinks it probable that the Rosca got him in such a position that he felt that his only way out was suicide.

With the death of Busch, the Rosca came back to power. His chief of staff took over, and soon there was an election during which General Peñaranda, an incompetent soldier, was elected president. His was a very reactionary regime.

During this regime, the groups which had been around Toro and Busch began to take organic shape. First there was formed the PIR, headed by José Antonio Arze, though it had several predecessors, such as the Frente de Izquierda Democrática. It was a party which though not officially Communist, was nonetheless Marxist and quite doctrinaire. It was formed in 1940.

Then in 1941 the MNR was formed. It was a Nationalist Party, Socialist inclined, which attempted to be a faithful reflection of the situation of Bolivia, without any doctrinal rigidity at all. It was a Nationalist Revolutionary Party.

The party in the beginning had three members in the Chamber of Deputies who, however, had been elected individually, not as members of any party. Paz, for instance, was elected by the same constituency which he had represented during the Busch regime. Then, in the first elections of the Peñaranda regime, Hernán Siles and one other were elected as MNR members, bringing their delegation up to five.

This small parliamentary group tried to present the party's point of view on things which were occurring. However, they also used every opportunity to use debates in Congress as a means of developing and making clear the philosophy of the party and its critique of Bolivian conditions. For instance, they took advantage of debate over a strike on the railroads in Bolivia.

The railroads here were and are a perfect example of old-style imperialism. In 1904 Bolivia signed a treaty of peace with Chile, giving up all claim to the coastal area seized by Chile during the War of the Pacific, and receiving six million pounds sterling in return. The government of the time wanted to use this to extend the railroad system. However, instead of doing this itself, it made contact with some American interests, who incorporated for the purpose The Bolivian Railway Company, in Delaware naturally, with an original capitalization of $20,000. The government of Bolivia then handed over to the Bolivian Railway Company the six million pounds it had received from Chile. However, this was not enough, and a first mortgage on the line was taken by the Ferrocarril de Antofagasta a Bolivia, which had been built from Antofagasta to Oruro in the 1880s, a British company, to help pay for completing the Bolivia portion from Oruro to La Paz. The Bolivian government, which had given most of the money for the railway, got only a second mortgage. This is still the situation, and it was this situation which the MNR deputies criticized during the debate on the railway strike.

The debate on the Catavi massacre of December 1942 served to establish the contacts with the miners which have continued down to the present day. The PIR deputies had first undertaken to criticize the government on the Catavi matter. But they were cowed by a tremendous counterattack by the government spokesmen, whereupon the MNR deputies took up the case. Fortunately, they had first-hand information that the PIR and other people did not have, because the secretary general of the sindicato at Catavi, who had miraculously escaped death in the massacre and capture by the police, had made his way to La Paz, and had come to Paz's house late one night, and had given him the workers' version of what had happened at Catavi. As a result, he and other MNR members were able to blast the position of the government and defend the point of view of the workers. From that time on, the workers of the tin mines sympathized with the MNR.

The government's attitude toward the MNR grew increasingly hostile. The government began a campaign of attacking the MNR as a Nazi and Fascist Party. The restrictions on the party's activities increased.

The MNR for its part began to conspire with a group of young officers of the Army. These people were not members of the MNR, since the party did not accept active officers in its ranks, but they worked alongside of it. This was a period when elections for president were approaching, and there were various candidates in the running. So the revolutionaries on the night of the uprising went to the house of each of the pretenders to the succession, woke each of them, and told each that there was a revolution going on, that it was in support of that individual's ambitions, and when they had the person in a car, announced to him that he was a prisoner and that the revolution was something quite different.

The revolution was very well planned. It was audacious on their part to make it in the middle of World War II, which was then in full progress. The attacks on the MNR as being pro-Fascist were listened to in the

United States and elsewhere, so diplomatic recognition was held up for six months. This was what in the end ruined the revolution, since it made many of the military men afraid.

The MNR was the junior partner in the Villarroel regime. The senior partner was the group of Army officers who participated in the regime. They were members of a lodge, Radepa or Razón de Patria, which had been formed during and after the Chaco War.

It was in the Radepa that there existed the undoubted pro-Nazi influence which there was in the Villarroel regime. Some of the young officers after the Chaco War went to Italy and Germany and were much influenced by the ideas dominant in these two countries at that time. They undoubtedly had sympathy with the Axis.

However, the MNR was not pro-Nazi. Paz Estenssoro himself made a statement during this early period, when they were being attacked as Nazis, to the effect that Bolivian Nationalism, in a very backward and underdeveloped country, could not be the same thing as Nationalism in a highly developed country such as Germany.

Incidentally, during the period before the 1943 Revolution, the MNR had its periodical, La Calle, and all of the expostulations and debates of the MNR deputies in Parliament were reprinted in La Calle, and so their ideas got known all over the country.

In spite of the fact that what pre-Nazi influence there was in the Villarroel government was not on the part of the MNR but of military elements of the regime, the U.S. State Department demanded as its price for recognition of the Villarroel government that the MNR leave the government. MNR's three ministers--the party never had more than three during the Villarroel regime--withdrew and stayed out of the government until January 1945.

The Villarroel government was only half revolutionary. It did not take the kind of fundamental steps which the MNR government took in 1952 and thereafter. In fact, that was one of the Villlarroel government's defects, and one of the things which the MNR learned from the Villarroel experience was that they must make the basic changes necessary as soon as possible after coming to power.

However, a number of constructive things were done. The decree on the sale of all the tin companies' foreign exchange to the Banco Central was revived, but in a much more elastic form, so as not to be unfair to the companies. The government, and particularly the MNR, encouraged the organization of the miners, and the Federación Sindical de Trabajadores Mineros was established during this period.

Juan Lechín emerged at this time as the principal leader of the miners. He was an MNR member as early as 1942, and when the Villarroel government came to power, he was appointed sub-prefect in Oruro. The sub-prefects were paid very little, but the mining company had the habit of giving these officials a sizable contribution every month. The first "pay day" for the sub-prefect brought Lechín a large check from the company. He not only returned the money, but arrested the head of the company locally on charges of attempted bribery. This won Lechín immediate fame and set him on the road to becoming the leader of the miners.

The government also organized the First Congress of Indians. However, when the MNR suggested more drastic measures, such as nationalization of the mines and agrarian reform, the military in the government of Villarroel rejected these ideas. Nevertheless, as it was, although the measures which were taken did not give everything the workers wanted, they did serve to infuriate the landlords and the tin companies.

Villarroel himself was a very well intentioned man. However, he was the kind of person who always could see both sides of any question, and so was more often than not hesitant in action. And the fact was that he was not boss of the government; he was only the spokesman for the Radepa military group.

Meanwhile, the forces of the Rosca were very active. They worked by devious methods. For instance, they organized a demonstration during which one of the demonstrators was shot, probably by one of his own number. The oppositionists then carried his body around the city, saying that he had been killed by the government. The people of La Paz are very sentimental, or at least were then, when more important issues such as those that preoccupy the electorate now were not considered of pressing importance. As a result of the sentimentality of the people, feeling against the government rose.

The opposition to the MNR continued. The U.S. Embassy had a part in it. At that time, the new tin contract was being negotiated, and the U.S. Ambassador let it be known that an agreement would be better reached if the MNR were not in the government. Villarroel resisted this kind of pressure, but the conservative and reactionary elements continued to demand that the MNR leave the government.

Villarroel finally agreed to have the MNR members quit again. Paz told him at the time that the MNR members of the government were just the excuse and that the opposition of the Rosca would continue until the Villarroel government changed its policies. For his part, Villarroel assured the MNR leaders that they would be back in the government before long, that this was just a temporary measure.

When the MNR cabinet members withdrew, Villarroel appointed an all-military cabinet. The opposition then began to clamor about the rule of the sword, and the campaign against the government continued.

Finally, the coup against Villarroel occurred, he was overthrown and hanged. There took place scenes of murder and savagery such as Bolivia had never before seen in its admittedly bloody history.

Incidentally, it was during the first period during which the MNR was out of the Villarroel government that the massacre of leaders of the opposition took place. A number of leading politicians caught in a conspiracy were summarily shot. The MNR would certainly have opposed this had it been in the government. Of course, the fact that it was not in the government, and was not deciding government policy at the time, did not stop the opposition from casting the blame for the murders on the MNR.

With the overthrow of Villarroel there began the MNR's six long years of persecution. Paz Estenssoro himself was four months in the Paraguayan Embassy before the new government would give him a safe-conduct. Then he went to Paraguay and thence to Buenos Aires.

The relations of the MNR exiles with Perón during their six years of exile were exceedingly variable. In the beginning, Perón received them with open arms. The reason for this was that he felt certain sympathy for them, because in the Braden incident and the Blue Book, the Argentine government had been charged with the guilt of the the Revolution of December 1943; and the oligarchy of the two countries was opposed to the two groups. Not only did Filemeno Velasco, then head of the Federal Police and an old friend of Paz, and a fine man, get residence permits--which made it possible for them to work--for all of the MNR exiles in Argentina, but the secretariat to the presidency even got jobs for five of them, and promised jobs for all. However, when the second list of five was presented to the Argentines, there was no place for them. The reason for this change was that Perón in January 1947 signed an agreement with Bolivia for a customs and economic union, promising hundreds of millions of pesos investment--which he never provided--and so became sympathethic with the Hertzog government.

For the next two years, it was absolutely impossible for any of the MNR exiles to get into touch with any important Argentine official.

Then in 1949, Paz and several others led an armed raid on a Bolivian border town, from Argentine soil. As a result, he was "reexiled" to Uruguay, where he remained for almost two years. He was not treated very well there either, being forcibly relegated to a small interior town for a period of six months.

The Argentine Ambassador in La Paz reported, as a prelude to the 1950 presidential election, that Paz would come in fifth of five candidates. But when it appeared as if Paz had won, Perón did a complete about-face, inviting him to come back to Argentina from Uruguay. At the same time, he fired the Argentine Ambassador in Bolivia, and his military attaché. The Perón candidate in the 1951 election was Goçalves, who had been Bolivian Ambassador in Argentina, and had been a favorite of Perón.

During those years the MNR carried on a continual struggle. It had at one time 5,000 exiles in Argentina, and there were thousands in jails here in Bolivia. They had no press, no freedom of speech, their leaders were jailed and exiled. It presented candidates in every election, and did very well, but its leaders who were elected to public office were usually gotten rid of in one way or another, usually by being exiled.

During the period of exile, the MNR became considerably radicalized, which is generally what happens to persecuted political movements. It also changed its policy considerably with regard to the Army. Until then, the party had not accepted army officers as members of the party. However, in exile, they changed this policy. They divided the army officers into three kinds: those who were their friends; those who were their enemies; and those who were "institutionalist," loyal first of all to the Army as an institution. With the last two groups the MNR wanted nothing at all to do, but with the first group, they decided that they would admit them to the party. Most of the top military men at the present time are from this group which was admitted to the party ranks during the exile period. There were also a number of active army officers who were still in Bolivia who joined the party at that time.

However, the MNR did not have any friends in the very top circles, and they knew that the only way to overthrow the oligarchical regime was to bring about a split in the top ranks of the regime. This occurred on April 9, 1952.

Meanwhile, however, the election of 1951 was held. The MNR as usual put up candidates, although there was a considerable internal discussion in the party as to whether they should put up their own nominees or back someone who was not in the party but friendly to it. Paz maintained at the time that if the MNR felt that it was mature enough to undertake the government of the country, it should name its own people; if not, it should not back anyone. His point of view finally won out; they ran candidates and won overwhelmingly. Paz and Siles received about 70 percent of the vote. The government stopped publishing the results when it appeared that Paz was going to win. However, when the MNR took over the government, they found in the presidential palace the telegrams from various parts of the country giving the results of the elections, and these indicated that they had received some 70 percent of the vote.

Of course, to prevent the recognition of the MNR victory, the government cooked up the military coup of General Ballivián. The MNR, therefore, continued to conspire. They finally got an agreement with General Seleme, Minister of Government and head of the Carabineros-- which had some eight thosand men and armament equal to that of the Army-- for a golpe.

During the first day, the golpe seemed to be going fine. Then on the second day the government forces were reinforced and the revolt seemed to be lost. At that point, Hernán Siles advised Seleme to seek refuge in an embassy, saying that it would be better that all of the leaders not be caught. Seleme did go into an embassy. The third day the tide turned again in favor of the revolt, and Seleme came out of his embassy, but then he was told that he was no longer the top leader of the revolt and in fact had no further role to play. On the fourth day, the victory was assured. The leaders had been Hernán Siles, Juan Lechín, and several other top civilian MNR people. With General Seleme out of the way, the government was completely in the hands of the MNR.

The MNR government dissolved the Army. Subsequently, though anti-militarists, they revived the Army, but for very definite purposes. They are using the Army for constructive projects, particularly the colonization scheme in the East. This has been very successful. It has been shown that Indians from the plateau can go down to the lowlands to live without any difficulties.

It is true that there might have been danger in arming the peasants and miners as they did. If the government had betrayed the Indians and miners, they might well have come down on La Paz for vengeance, but since the MNR leaders did not propose to betray the peasants and miners, they had no fear of arming them.

He thinks that the reason why this revolution here has been able to accomplish the same general objectives as the Mexican one, but without the ten years of civil war suffered by Mexico, is that there has been a party, well organized, and knowing what it wanted to accomplish. In contrast, the program of the Mexican Revolution developed after the revolution was well under way. It is also true here that they had the example of the Mexican Revolution before them and could therefore avoid some of its pitfalls.

*   *   *   *   *

CONVERSATION WITH VÍCTOR PAZ ESTENSSORO IN BOLIVIAN CONSULATE IN NEW YORK CITY, AUGUST 5, 1958

He has just come back from Bolivia and is on the way to London to take up his duties as Ambassador to Great Britain. He will be returning to Britain by plane tomorrow.

The situation is going as well as can be expected in Bolivia. In the recent congressional elections, the Movimiento Nacionalista Revolucionario had an overwhelming victory. The opposition won only two seats in Congress, the MNR has all of the rest.

The internal situation in the party is better than it was. Of course, the various factions continue, but he thinks that feeling among them has improved. There is hope that they will be able to reorganize the cabinet, with representation in it of all of the party groups. Lechín may return to the cabinet, as Minister of Mines again, although this is by no means certain. Lechín has not as yet made up his mind about it. However, Paz Estenssoro hopes that things will work out all right.

* * * * *

CONVERSATION WITH VÍCTOR PAZ ESTENSSORO IN NEW YORK HILTON HOTEL, OCTOBER 25, 1963

One of the most important achievements of the revolutionary regime has been their work in opening up the eastern part of the country. They estimate that since the Revolution began, some 200,000 people have moved down from the altiplano to the Oriente. Now their work for helping these people to come down is much better organized than in the past, and they foresee the migration of half a million people during the next ten years.

The eastern part of the country is now producing several of the things which the country needs. They are now self-sufficient in sugar, although because of the increase in national demand, they expect that in two years the country will not be self-sufficient any more. They now have plans for a second sugar refinery which by 1966 will again make the country self-sufficient in sugar. There has also been a marked increase in the production of cotton, citrus fruits, and other tropical products.

However, all increase in output has not taken place in the eastern lowland areas. There has been considerable increase in the agricultural production of the highlands. This is noticeable, for instance, in the output of potatoes, which are perhaps the basic agricultural product of the area.

The effects of this are seen in the people themselves. For instance, in comparing the height and weight of army recruits now and before the Revolution, they find that there has been a noticeable increase in both height and weight of the recruits from the highlands. The people of the valleys are about the same as before, but they were always the people who ate best. There has been a marked increase in the weight of the recruits from the eastern area, although their height has remained much the same; they were always relatively tall for Bolivians.

He thinks that the situation in the mines has now been more or less resolved. The miners were completely convinced that the government was right in the situation which developed a few months ago. Between July and September there was a different and tense situation, with strikes in the mines. However, the workers returned to work without any conditions attached to their return. The situation was finally resolved as late as two days ago, when an attempt to organize a hunger strike of the miners was ended.

As far as the presidential election campaign is concerned, there is no real problem except that within the party. There are various people who have ambitions, and they are all out working now. He agrees that more or less the failue of the mining strikes in the July-September period ended the chances of Juan Lechín to be president.

He thinks that the likely opposition party to rise as a formidable challenge to the MNR is the Communist Party. Although in the mining situation the Communists were defeated, and their principal leaders were discharged from employment in the mines, and the former alliance of some MNR elements with the Communists has been disrupted, he does think that that party is not to be counted out. The Falange now has virtually ceased opposition, saying that it favors the Revolution, but that it could carry it out better.

As for the Auténticos of Guevara Arce, they don't have any chance of being a major opposition to the government. Most of their members have returned to the MNR, although it is virtually impossible for Guevara Arce to do so. There is too much personal bad feeling involved.

He thinks that I should come down to Bolivia again, write a sequel to my book on the Bolivian National Revolution. They have done a good deal since I wrote my book. He agrees that the Revolution is now engaged in its constructive phase, the destructive phase which was absolutely necessary, having already been achieved.

* * * * *

LETTER FROM VÍCTOR PAZ ESTENSSORO, FROM LA PAZ, OCTOBER 19, 1964

I reply to your friendly letter of the 14th. What you write me can in no way annoy me. The friends of the Revolution naturally have the right to be concerned with it, and their worries are rather something to be grateful for.

I am the one who is most pained by the internal divisions within the Party. Unfortunately, they have been inevitable. In a period of serious and responsible construction such as we have been experiencing, the collision with Lechín could not be helped due to his reluctance to act as government figure rather than as the visible head of the trade union leadership, on the one hand compromised internationally, and on the other convinced that his political survival depends on demanding from the State more than the State, honestly, can grant.

With regard to Siles, it is difficult to analyze his subjective motives, since he had no real motive to decide to support Lechín, and with Lechín, to act together with all the opposition.

The historic responsibilities of the Bolivian Revolution are, in my judgment, better served now that there doesn't exist, at least within the government, anything which impedes construction. That is exactly what we are doing, and it will be the measure of our internal success and therefore an example for Latin America.

Even so, we have never refused a truce, or even better, a good agreement. I think that it is reasonable, however, to hope that that agreement would not signify the reintroduction of anarchy in our house.

* * * * *

LETTER FROM VÍCTOR PAZ ESTENSSORO, FROM LIMA, PERU, NOVEMBER 18, 1964

First of all, I cordially thank you for the feeling of sorrow for what has happened in my country, which you express in your letter of the 8th of this month. You must feel it profoundly because you have given all your sympathy to the Bolivian National Revolution, which opened up a perspective for the people of Bolivia and was a hope for all the continent, as you say well in your letter.

The overthrow of the government of the MNR by the armed forces, which now are exercising power by the classical instrument of the Military Junta, delivers a grave blow to the cause of democracy in America. In the case of Bolivia, with one blow there has been destroyed what we have so laboriously achieved so that our people can learn to practice democracy, as the real road to political stability. And since the latter is, in turn, the fundamental requisite for economic development, the possibility for a real improvement in the levels of living which has begun to occur, has been negatively affected.

But the gravest thing is the counterrevolutionary essence of the coup, which is now unmistakable. All the reactionary groups, from the Liberal Party to the Falange, is cheering the military, while Lechín, the COB and other groups of the left, which contributed to the creation of the previous climate of the agitation, has been pushed to one side. The first measures of the Junta underscore clearly its counterrevolutionary nature. The Constitution of 1947 has been declared in effect, that is, the one adopted by the Rosca, using Bolivian terminology, after the fall of the Villarroel government. General Seleme, whose actions were a determining factor in the national victory of April 1952, has been retired, and they have announced the forthcoming dissolution of the Carabineros, who also intervened decisively in those same events. The naming of known personages of the oligarchy as advisers in the state economic organs is another clear indication that what is involved is the "restoration" of the old regime.

In all this drama, General Barrientos, moved by an uncomfortable personal ambition to occupy the presidency, is a more an instrument of reaction. Siles will pretend to appear as representative of the MNR supporting the junta, but only the opportunists will allow themselves to be misled by that pose. The MNR, as the political instrument for the redemption of the peasants, workers and the middle class, has been defeated and is being ruthlessly persecuted. The central personage of the Junta is Colonel Sanjinés Goitia, a complete reactionary who was heir to six immense landholdings which the Agrarian Reform took over. He was returned to service because he appeared to be the man with the confidence of the Americans for carrying out civic actions and programs by the armed forces.

Upon leaving Bolivia, I left a message to the peasants and workers. I'm sending a clipping of this from La Tribuna here.

It is difficult to make a firm prediction on the future course of events in Bolivia. However, even now one can point out that there are elements of contradiction even within the junta. The struggle for power between Barrientos and Ovando has not been definitively concluded. Lechín, with the miners and other groups of workers who supported our fall, are very close to a confrontation with the regime. In the countryside

(Cochabamba and La Paz) there have been bloody confrontations between peasants and people of the villages. Furthermore, once the coup took place, the MNR began to reorganize....

I think that what the friends of the Bolivian national revolution can do for the moment is a work of clarification, demonstrating the counterrevolutionary nature of what has occurred in Bolivia, so that the progressive American circles will not fall into error.

*   *   *   *   *

LETTER FROM VÍCTOR PAZ ESTENSSORO, FROM LIMA, MAY 25, 1965

In recent months I have not been able to write to you, as I would have wished. All my time has been taken up with finding means of personal livelihood and, above all, trying to reorganize the MNR on the line of intransigent opposition to the Military Junta, a very difficult task from afar and in the face of the enervating action of Siles, with the protection of Barrientos, with the purpose of splitting the party, which continues to be the only real political force in Bolivia.

In the months since my last letter, the reactionary and anti-democratic nature of the military government has been accentuated. I wrote a small pamphlet about this, with the title "Against the Restoration, For the National Revolution," giving the history of this, the role of the armed forces in the past and in the revolutionary process, the reasons for the opposition position of the MNR and giving general lines for its future action, taking into account what is its essence and the necessity of attracting again the working masses....

Subsequently there occurred even graver events. The indefinite suspension of elections shows the arbitrary and dictatorial nature of the government which, supported exclusively on the force of arms, refuses all popular consultation. The bloody repression of the workers strike intentionally provoked by the jailing and deportation of Lechín, has made clear its brutal anti-worker character. It has repeated the massacres of workers carried out by the governments of Patiño, Aramayo and Hochschild and the feudal landowners. The airplanes and modern armanent provided by the United States have been used efficiently for the murder on a large scale of miners and factory workers. Official information admits more than seventy dead and two hundred wounded, but, according to trustworthy data, in reality there were more than two hundred and four hundred, respectively.

The charges made by the government that Lechín was preparing a plot together with the Communist leader Longo, lacks all reality. Some supposed letters in code, offered as proof, have been composed with such an infantile mentality that no one believes in them.

In an attempt to justify the murders and to obtain the support of the American government, Barrientos has had recourse to accusing the strike of being Communist. That is not true. The strike began as an exclusively trade union movement of protest against the outrage suffered by Lechín. The extremists participated in it, especially in the Siglo XX mine, where they have controlled the union for more than ten years, but the great majority of the workers in the other mines and in the factories are not Communists but Movimientistas, of the party of Lechín (PRIN), and to a much smaller degree, Social Christians and even Falangistas. The paradoxical thing is that where there really were Communists, that is Siglo XX, there was not even one death. The armed forces did not go there. In contrast, where Communists did not exist, that is, the other mines and the factory area of La Paz, there were casualties by the hundreds.

The secretariat of the Communist Party has been closed, but that is a mere gesture, without effectiveness. The action of the Communists is preferably underground. The closing of their secretariat will be no obstacle for their continuing. In contrast, in additon to the killing of working-class people, there has been launched a terrible persecution of men and women of the MNR, a real man-hunt.

On the other hand, in claiming all the strikers were Communists, the Communists are being favored, making them appear as a tremendous influence and, furthermore, as taking a just position, defending social gains. From all of this painful episode, the figure who has emerged most magnified is Lechin, from a political point of view.

Finally, an argument used by Barrientos to obtain American support for these measures of violence and of blood is that it was necessary in order to bring order to the nationalized mines and that, for that reason, the presence of the armed forces was indispensable in them. In this, too, there is a paradox. The armed forces entered Milluni, which is a private mine, Kami and Viloco, which don't have more than 300 workers each, with a very low price in the present market. In contrast, in the large mines, such as Siglo XX-Catavi, Colquiri, Unificada, Quechisla-Chorolque, which determine the fate of COMIBOL, the armed forces have not appeared, and so have not achieved what is required for order in their future exploitation to exist.

What Barrientos has really sought in this series of military actions against the workers is the destruction of the trade union movement which, with all its errors, excesses, and failure to understand, was one of the important factors in the process of the National Revolution. It had to be beaten to bring about the restoration of the oligarchy to full power. The peasants, if very much more numerous, are still easily subject to confusion and don't count as an effective factor of defense of the Revolution. The great obstacle for the reactionary plans was the workers, for their greater social consciousness and greater political experience. They were the first to perceive the regressive nature of the military coup of November 4, and placed themselves against the Junta, much earlier than the political leaders.

I know what a sincere friend of the Bolivian Revolution you are. For that reason, I have expanded this letter, with the hope that my information can help you so that in the United States the vision of recent events in my country won't be distorted. We want to conserve the faith which John F. Kennedy knew how to arouse. Help us to do so.

*　　*　　*　　*　　*

LETTER FROM VÍCTOR PAZ ESTENSSORO, FROM LIMA, MAY 31, 1966

It has been a pleasure to receive your letter of last April 7. From it, I see that you maintain your interest in the political events of Bolivia, in spite of being completely absorbed with studies of Brazilian affairs. I also wanted to communicate with you. Through Guillermo Bedregal, last year, I knew that you were in Brazil, but afterward, I had no news, not knowing that you were still in that country....

Within the fluidity which Bolivian politics has always appeared to have, the electoral panorama is thus. The official candidacy of Barrientos–Siles Salinas has the support of the MPC (Movimiento Popular Cristiano), constituted of opportunists recruited from all the parties on the basis of the government's resources), the PRA of Guevara, PIR of Ricardo Anaya, and a fraction of ex-combatants of the Chaco War, plus a group of peasants, principally of Cochabamba. In addition, the PSD from which comes Luis Adolfo Siles. With the only exception of the peasants, all the other groups don't have a following and lack all political significance.

The Falange Socialista Boliviana is apparently in the opposition, with its own ticket, Gen. Bilbao Rioja and Gonzalo Romero. In reality it is acting in combination with the official ticket. For that, the government Junta has modified the Electoral Law, substituting for proportional representation of a system of a fixed minority of 20 percent. There is under way a great mechanism of fraud, which will assign the Barrientos-Siles groups the 80 percent of parliamentary seats and the 20 percent to the Falange.

This accord of the Falange with the Junta, which naturally is not made public, has dislocated Victor Andrade, who had hoped to get the representation of the minority in parliament, to which end he has broken off a small group of the MNR, at first playing the game of the military, who needed an opposition candidacy in the elections to give the appearance of democracy, but without putting in danger the officialist candidacy. The real MNR is composed of the joint forces of Siles and those who follow me, united. It continues being the largest party of Bolivia, but the Electoral Court has not legalized it and so formally it does not exist. The PRIN of Lechín, and the Christian Democratic Party (Remi di Natale) have urged electoral abstention of their people. The old parties (Liberals and Partido Unificado Republicano Socialista) as well as the various Communist and Trotskyist factions and a group of insignificant groups don't count for anything in the electoral field, although their press communiqués appear frequently. The result of all this is known in advance. Barrientos will be president, but this will have solved nothing.

On another opportunity I shall expound some ideas about the policy of the United States in Latin America. I can tell you that it is more regressive than ever. The exit of Mann from the Department of State has opened a hope. Perhaps that can take the shape of fundamental changes....

My projected return to Bolivia had to be postponed, at the request of the leadership of the party, because of absolute lack of guarantees. The government gave me a passport but simultaneously made an inferior judge issue an order of detention, and launched a wave of assaults and attacks against the people of the MNR. At a meeting to celebrate the 9th of April, we had six deaths and more than thirty wounded.

* * * * *

CONVERSATION WITH VÍCTOR PAZ ESTENSSORO IN HIS HOME IN LIMA, JUNE 30, 1966

His third presidential term was in a sense forced by the Americans. By the end of his second term, the process of economic development had really been gotten under way. They had started the Operación Triangular, which was cleaning up the situation in the mines, and between 1962 and 1964 the production of the mines had begun to rise again.

They had gotten a number of loans for other development projects, and the general economic situation of the country was improving.

The nomination for the 1964-1968 period had been promised to Juan Lechín, and he was certainly the logical candidate. However, at the time of the Cuban missile crisis in 1962, Lechín had a serious run-in with the American Ambassador, Ben Stephansky, who was a very good man and had helped them a lot. There was at that time a demonstration in front of the American Embassy, organized by the COB, and when Stephansky called Lechín about it, there were very bad words between them. So after that Stephansky began working among MNR people against the possible nomination of Lechín. At the same time, the various aid agencies-- including the Inter American Bank, the Eximbank, the International Bank, as well as, needless to say, USAID--all made it clear that if Lechín were president, the sources of aid would dry up. The military, too, came to Paz Estenssoro and indicated that they thought it would be better that Lechín not be the candidate.

It was over this issue that Lechín broke with the MNR. Paz Estenssoro thinks that if it had been up to Lechín himself, he would have been content not to have the presidency at that time, but his wife was very insistent. Indeed, she was so anxious that Lechín be president that when it became clear that he could not be, she divorced him. She is now living in New York. Also, by the time of the actual nomination, Lechín himself was very anxious to be president. It is true that generally he liked to be the power behind the throne without having the responsibility for what went on, but by this time he really wanted to be president.

Faced with this situation, it was inevitable that Paz Estenssoro would be the candidate. He didn't particularly want it because he was tired, physically tired. But the only person who had enough popularity to beat Lechín was he. Siles didn't have it and none of the lesser figures in the party did. So, Paz Estenssoro was nominated.

The break with Siles came over this same issue. Although in the beginning Siles seemed to have no objections, and attended the party's convention where the nomination was made, and showed no opposition to it, he finally came to Paz Estenssoro a few weeks before the election and told him that he should not run. Although Paz Estenssoro explained to him all the reasons for the candidacy, Siles ended the discussion by saying that if Paz Estenssoro ran, he could not support him. Paz Estenssoro doesn't know when Siles began to conspire against the government, or whether he had begun by this time. But he certainly was in the conspiracy by the time Paz Estenssoro was overthrown.

The reason for the coup against Paz Estenssoro was the personal ambition of Barrientos. He was anxious. The fact was, of course, that he would have had a good chance to get the nomination the next time, but he would not wait.

The naming of Barrientos as vice presidential candidate was the result of military pressure. They first named Federico Fortún, a civilian, but then the military came to Paz and said that they thought it would be a good thing if a military man were nominated, and he conceded this.

His great mistake was relying on General Ovando. He was not by any means unaware of the ambitions of Barrientos, but he thought that he could rely on Ovando, who had much more support in the military, to check Barrientos. In fact, he talked with Ovando on various occasions about the dangers of the ambition of Barrientos, and Ovando seemed to go along with what he said. What Paz Estenssoro didn't know was that Ovando was also in the conspiracy. When he called on Ovando to support him when Barrientos moved against him, Ovando claimed that he had lost control of the military, and there was enacted the comedy of Ovando's arrest to seem to make this apparent. But Ovando was in on the plot all along.

The plot didn't begin in November 1964. In fact, when Paz Estenssoro went to the United States late in 1963, the military had decided to strike at that time. But they had second thoughts because Paz Estenssoro's visit was very important for them in terms of getting help for arms and other things they wanted. Then they planned to strike in March, then in August. Each time they hesitated because they weren't sure of the strength of the peasant militia. It wasn't until the riots in La Paz and in the mining areas a week or so before the overthrow that they found out about the militia. Before that, the government had sent to Argentina to buy arms, and had purchased them from the Fabrica Nacional de Armas, to arm the militia. But when it came time to deliver the arms, the Argentine army, reflecting the influence of the "gorillas," refused to allow them to be delivered. As a result, the militia were armed with weapons of the Chaco War vintage, while the Army had current American arms.

As a result of this failure, Paz Estenssoro wasn't able to handle the La Paz uprising and that in the mines with only the militia; he needed the cooperation of the Army. As a result, he had to confer with Ovando, and Ovando told him what resources the Army had and Paz Estenssoro told Ovando what the militia could muster. At the same time, too, there were small guerilla bands operating, which complicated the matter still further--the Army not particularly wanting to move against them, given the fact that the military leaders were awaiting the chance to move against the government themselves. When the Army finally found out that the militia were much weaker than they had thought, they moved against the government.

The best-equipped and most dynamic militia were in the mines, under Lechin's control. The peasant militia were not as ready to move as were those in the mines. Peasant militia had been called in from nearby areas to suppress the uprising in La Paz. They were there in the last days of October, but had moved out. November 2 was the Fiesta of the Dead. It is the custom for the Indians to go to the cemeteries on that day, bring flowers, and then drink all night. So on November 3, virtually all peasants in Bolivia were drunk. When the Army insurrection began, he sent fifty trucks to nearby Indian areas, and only one came back with militia; the rest were dead drunk. He doubts if they could have won even if the fifty trucks had come back loaded with militiamen, because of the inequality of arms; after five or six thousand Indians had been killed, the Army would have won anyway.

The Carabineros were loyal to the government. However, they were not in a position to do very much. The MNR leader in Santa Cruz had

had a terrible campaign against the head of the Carabineros, over some personal political issue, which had ended in relieving the Carabinero commander of his post. With his exit, there was no one in the Carabineros who could move with the rapidity and flexibility necessay to defend the government against the Army.

One contributing factor to the downfall of the MNR was the deterioration within the party. Although Paz Estenssoro's new term had just begun, there was already campaigning for the 1968 elections within the party. Guillermo Bedregal had his group, Jordan Pando his, Fellman Valerde his, and a host of others had theirs, seeking either the presidency or the vice presidency. They were furiously fighting among themselves, weakening the party's power to resist, to unite to preserve itself.

This was due in large part to the fact that everyone felt secure and didn't believe in the possibility that the government could be overthrown. In fact, in any showdown with the opposition, which was very weak, the government could have won easily. But the downfall came from the treason of the military, and against this there was little protection. No one expected it, because the new Army, built by the Revolution, was straight MNR.

At the present time, the great bulk of the MNR is united. Those following Paz Estenssoro and those following Siles have reunited. They are boycotting the election, will vote in blank. However, Victor Andrade has been given the official title of the MNR by the electoral authorities. He apparently thought that he could be the "loyal opposition" to the present government, and that with the change in the electoral law by this government, which gives the majority 80 percent of the deputies and the largest minority the other 20 percent, he could get 20 percent. There is another group which calls itself the Movimiento Revolucionario Pazestenssorista, of MNR people. As soon as Paz heard about its organization, he sent a cable saying that he disauthorized the movement. Immediately thereupon the electoral authorities recognized the group. They consist of a number of good younger elements of the MNR, and he has urged them to return to the party.

Lechín is also boycotting the election. He was here in the last months of 1965 and January of this year, incognito. He had been in Paraguay, gone to Paris, thence to New York and thence here. He told Paz Estenssoro that he had begun to conspire against the government with Ovando in March 1964, before the election. Paz urged him to return to the MNR, but he doesn't want to. He wants to maintain his own PRIN. His party is somewhat split, a group of labor leaders having formed a movement inside it against what they consider to be the too middle class and conservative directorate of the party which Lechín had left behind in Bolivia. Lechín is now in La Paz, as is Siles, but there isn't much they can do given the present circumstances.

The Communists have a ticket headed by Iñiguez, former head of the University of Potosí. The Communists are split now into two parties, and it is the pro-Russian one which is participating in the campaign. Escobar, the labor leader, is one of the principal leaders of the pro-Chinese party. Sergio Almarás, now an ex-Communist, is in the MNR and is in La Paz.

The Trotskyites remain divided into the Guillermo Lora wing and the González Moscoso wing. Lora attended the Tri-Continental Congress in Havana early this year.

The rise of the Trotskyites in Bolivia is due to the devoted work of the Lora brothers--one of whom was killed by the Army--and others. A number of Trotskyite professional people went to work in the mines, down underground, for the purpose of party work. They are very sectarian.

The Falange was boycotting the election. However, they have apparently made a deal with the government, whereby they are going to be the minority recognized to have elected congressmen and senators. They are running General Bilbao for the presidency.

The MNR held a congress in La Paz last month. Charges were brought in the congress against Guillermo Bedregal, asserting that he had enriched himself when head of COMIBOL--Paz has no opinion on these charges--as well as against Rubén Julio, the MNR leader in Santa Cruz, and against one other top leader. These charges are now pending before the Tribunal of Honor of the party. The third person is San Román, who was head of the political police under Paz Estenssoro.

He doesn't believe the charges of brutality brought against San Román. The fact is that no one died in the prisons under Paz's two administrations. This was true even in the so-called "concentration camps", which were not in fact concentration camps. They were rehabilitation barracks in the smaller towns, where political prisoners were sent, because in La Paz they would have constituted a cause for perturbation. There were seven hundred such prisoners at the height of things. But the charges of maltreatment on a large scale in these prisons aren't true; if they had been, someone would have certainly been killed. That there was some mistreatment by lower-ranking officials is likely, but it was not the doing of San Román in any case.

He himself had experiences even in democratic Uruguay in 1949 at the time of the civil war in Bolivia. It broke out without his being notified, so he didn't have time to escape from Uruguay and go to Bolivia to participate. He was arrested while eating dinner, was kept incommunicado for forty days, and was tremendously upset because he didn't get any news about what was happening in Bolivia.

At the MNR Congress, they adopted a scheme which isn't working very well, of a "colegiado" to direct the party. Siles apparently got the idea when he was Ambassador to Uruguay. But a colegiado just doesn't work. There are certain tensions in the party, largely resulting from the current election campaign, and they cannot be resolved by a colegiado.

He is optimistic about the future. The problem will be a race between Ovando and the MNR to see who overthrows Barrientos first. Ovando will go back to be commander of the army, and certainly will fall out with the Barrientos government. It will be two years before the MNR overthrows it and goes back to power.

There are internal reasons in the MNR for it not to take any longer than that. There is a process of radicalization going on in the party, which, if the present situation endures more than two years, will mean that there is a large extremist group in the country for the first time.

He thinks that the United States government is wrong to support the present regime as it is doing. However, a friend of his came back from Washington recently, where he talked with Ben Stephansky and others who agreed that a military dictatorship was no solution for the Bolivian problem.

There will be various leaders of the MNR aside from himself to take over in the next installment of the Revolution. There is Siles, there is

Alvarez Plata, there are a number of younger people. The party will have no lack of leadership.

Edwin Moller, the ex-Trotskyite, is still a member of the PRIN. But Lechín doesn't trust him, saying that he is a perturbing element in the party. Lechín refused to see Moller's wife when she passed through here on the way to the Havana Tri-Continental Congress earlier this year.

The MNR failed when in power to get control of the students of the universities. But it is doing so now. They control the student federations in Oruro, Cochabamba, and Potosí.

The Barrientos group is very heterogeneous. It consists of the PRA of Guevara Arce, which is fundamentally of the same tendency as the MNR; of the Partido Social Democrático, a very reactionary group headed by Luís Siles, Barrientos's candidate for vice president; the PIR, headed by the avowed Marxist-Leninist Ricardo Anaya; and Barrientos's own group, known as the Christian Revolutionaries.

It is a tribute to what the MNR accomplished that Barrientos has to call on the peasants to elect him. He undoubtedly has some support from the peasants in the Cochabamba area, some of whose leaders he has bought, others who support him because he comes from Cochabamba. He has some peasants on his list of candidates for deputy and senator. The peasants outside of Cochabamba are still Movimientistas.

It is also a tribute to the MNR that the coalition backing Barrientos had to take the name of the Frente de la Revolución Boliviana.

The Military Junta regime has not made any onslaught on the agrarian reform. However, in some isolated cases it has given land back to landowners, particularly to families of military men. In other cases, the agrarian reform authorities have refused to classify land as latifundia, which obviously met all of the requirements to be labelled, and therefore to be affected by the agrarian reform.

He doesn't think that the government of President Fernando Belaúnde is making any profound structural changes in Peru. Of course, the roads which he is building into the highlands will have a tremendous social and economic effect before long, but they are not being built necessarily for that reason. There is some agrarian reform, although not on a very large scale. It has served to relieve some of the social pressure, but it doesn't represent a very profound structural change in the country, which continues to be dominated economically by the oligarchy.

He has a high regard for some of the Aprista leaders. He thinks that Ramiro Prialé is particularly capable. If he had been the candidate of the Aprista Party in 1962, he would have won, been allowed to take office, and would have been a very good president, because he is an extremely capable politician.

* * * * *

LETTER FROM VÍCTOR PAZ ESTENSSORO, FROM LIMA, AUGUST 24, 1967

With involuntary tardiness I answer your friendly letter of May 13.... As the friend that you are of the Bolivian Revolution, you have certainly been following the events which have occurred in my country, and will agree with me that the regime of Barrientos, from its origin, orientation, incompetence, and immorality has no future. All the social gains obtained in the years of the government of the MNR are systematically being annulled or rescinded by the agents of economic interests which, in reality, pull the strings of the government. Barrientos is only supported by small groups formed by persons who are benefiting from the present situation. The immense majority are against him, and he is the object of constant attacks by elements of the military.

So long as Barrientos is in power and has nothing for the popular classes except massacres and misery, one can foresee an accentuated radicalization of the masses. Therefore it is not strange that the guerrillas, in spite of being Communists, are arousing great sympathy in the people who suffer the consequences of the reactionary policy of the government.

The MNR has made considerable progress toward recuperating its great potential. A single Directorate has been formed, presided over by Senator Raúl Lema Peláez, which has the support of all the sectors, among them those of Siles and Andrade, although personally the latter continues in an ambiguous position. On the other hand, Lechín has remained with his own party, the PRIN.

I am fully convinced that the MNR will return to power, to continue the process of the national revolution. I cannot indicate with precision when this will occur, but it is evident that the accelerated deterioration of the regime is approaching.

*   *   *   *   *

CONVERSATION WITH VÍCTOR PAZ ESTENSSORO AT HIS HOME IN LIMA, JULY 21, 1968

The MNR is still split into two groups. The split really started at the time of the 1966 elections. At that time, Siles, who was in La Paz, was opposed to participating in the election, and he ordered the casting of blank votes. But a younger group formed what they called the MNR Pazestenssorista and were quite critical publicly of Siles's position, and also directed some criticisms at Paz Estenssoro himself. As a result, the government allowed the registration of the group as a political party, in spite of the fact that the government had carried out the manuever of recognizing the group of Victor Andrade as the "official" MNR. The response of the voters to the young people was very good; they got 100,000 votes, in spite of the difficulties.

This split has never really healed. It is no longer just a split between older and younger leaders, but is a struggle over who should lead the united party, if it were to be united again. One group is headed by General Monje Roja; in the other the most interesting figure is René Zavoleta. He is quite to the Left, but very intelligent and a good man.

There is a tendency now for the MNR to work together with the Falange Socialista Boliviana and the Partido Revolucionario de la Izquierda Nacionalista, of Juan Lechín. The basic reason for this is the need to put up a united civilian front against the military who control the present regime. Also, it is made more possible because there has evolved within the Falange a left wing, which is putting great pressure on the party leadership to change its traditional position. The effect of the military dictatorship is to force a general radicalization of politics. It is taking place within the MNR too.

The present situation in which President Barrientos's Minister of Government Antonio Arguedas has to flee the country because he has been shown to have sold a secret document--Ché Guevara's memoirs--to a foreign power is strange. The Minister of Government is the person in charge of security. This could only happen in this military regime. It is comic opera.

Paz Estenssoro thinks that Arguedas sold the diary of Ché to the Cubans, he didn't give it to them because of any ideological affinity with them. He had done a thorough job of rounding up everyone connected with the Guevara group. He suspects that Barrientos may have known about what Arguedas did, and wouldn't even rule out entirely the possibility that he shared in the payment which Arguedas received.

Arguedas had never really been a Movimientista. He was brought into the party by Barrientos in 1963 or thereabouts. He had been a radio operator or something of that sort, through which Barrientos had gotten to know him. Barrientos had given him a simulated rank of captain in the Air Force, although he was not really a military man. He had been a close confidante of Barrientos.

Arguedas was a bad type of person. He had directed a raid on a house where Sra. de Paz Estenssoro and some other ladies were meeting, had all of them brought out into the street in front of the house, and had them all virtually disrobed there.

He is not so sure any more that it is going to be a race between Ovando and the MNR to overthrow Barrientos, as he told me in 1966. It looks as if Ovando has decided to support Barrientos, but at the same time is preparing the ground to become his successor through elections. They are certainly planning to have Barrientos succeeded by a military man.

*   *   *   *   *

CONVERSATION WITH VÍCTOR PAZ ESTENSSORO IN HIS HOUSE IN LIMA, JULY 26, 1968

Victor Andrade's group of the MNR in Bolivia doesn't have much of a following and is not of very much importance in the situation there. Incidentally, Andrade was a member of the MNR at the time of the 1952 Revolution, having joined the party after the fall of Villarroel. He came back from being Ambassador to the United States after the fall of Villarroel. He was promptly arrested and sent to a concentration camp the regime had at Guaqui on Lake Titicaca. It was there that he joined the party.

Richard Patch is quite wrong in arguing that the MNR government was forced into making an agrarian reform. As early as the Villarroel regime, Paz and Walter Guevara Arce introduced a bill in Congress to amend the Constitution so that an agrarian reform would be possible. They were blocked by the Chief of the Military Household of Villarroel, who was a large landowner himself, and was opposed to agrarian reform. Subsequently, during the election of 1951, the party program which was worked up in Buenos Aires for that campaign called for an agrarian reform. In his first speech after getting back in 1952, he announced that the government was going to make two fundamental changes: nationalization of the mines and an agrarian reform.

The fifteen months' wait before enacting an agrarian reform law is easily explained by the fact that the Indians were completely unorganized, and unprepared for an agrarian reform, and it was necessary to organize them. There was no particular pressure from the Indians at that time to make an agrarian reform. When it was made, it was brought about from the top, not due to pressure from the peasants.

The agrarian reform and events subsequently demonstrated the error of many ideas about the Indian. For instance, it was argued that the Indians by and large didn't understand or speak Spanish. But in the first visit made to an Indian group on the altiplano after becoming president, he started making his speech in Spanish, since he doesn't know either Aymara or Quechua, with a translator breaking in after every passage. This proved inconvenient, so he told the translator to let him finish his speech in Spanish, with the translator taking notes, after which he could repeat the whole thing to the Indians. However, it was interesting to note that every reference he made in his speech to agrarian reform was applauded by the Indians, indicating that they understood very well what he ws saying. They had feigned ignorance of Spanish as a means of self-protection, of passive resistance.

He thinks that it is very possible that Antonio Arguedas, Barrientos's Minister of Government, really was working for Castro for a long while, as he now claims, and as Castro confirms. One piece of evidence in this direction is that he started his political life as a Communist. A second is that in the mining areas, the MNR mine leaders were all jailed by Arguedas for as long as two years, while the very Communist miners whom Ché Guevara mentions in his diary as ones with whom he was in contact, were only kept in jail for a couple of months. It was undoubtedly Arguedas's pressure on the judges which made them release these people on 100 pesos bail.

He thinks that this situation must be exceedingly disturbing to the United States Embassy and to the United States government.

Another piece of evidence in the whole issue of the guerrilla activity is the fact that Barrientos himself, through one of his aides, gave Régis Debray the maps of the Bolivian Air Force which they used in their guerrilla activities. Debray had come there first as a representative of a French company which allegedly wanted to undertake a colonization effort, and Debray offered to make the aide of Barrientos a partner in the project. In return for this favor, the aide got the maps from Barrientos and turned them over to Debray, supposedly so that the company could choose better just where to establish its colonies.

He thinks right now that any military coup against Barrientos would be for the better. Barrientos is evidently intending to establish a much more rigid military dictatorship, and the upshot of this is bound to be within six months or so a popular uprising, which will do great damage to the country and will cost many lives. Furthermore, if such a popular uprising succeeds, it is certain that the Army will once again be destroyed, and if it is destroyed this time, it will never be reconstituted.

Undoubtedly many of the army officers are aware of this. There is great discontent in the Army, particularly among the younger officers, who argue that the generals and colonels have enjoyed power and have gotten wealthy from it, but that they have gotten nothing.

Under these circumstances, the best thing all around would be for there to be a military coup, which would continue a military regime as a transition, but would, after a more or less short period, call real elections in which the Army-government would be neutral. In that case, the Revolution would be able to commence once again.

There is no doubt that the spirit of the Revolution has continued. Even Barrientos has to claim that he is part of the Revolution. The workers certainly look back to the MNR regime with nostalgia and are convinced that the present regime is really anti-labor. It is true that the peasants seem to support Barrientos. But like peasants all over the world, they are very pragmatic. They feel the need to be with the government, whatever it is, to assure their continued hold on the land. They have the land now, and their main objective is to hold on to it. However, if Barrientos is overthrown tomorrow, they will shift their support to the new regime. But aside from this pragmatic attitude, he is sure, from reports he has had, particularly from a Dutchman who spent a year in Bolivia studying the sindicatos campesinos, that the peasants remember that it was the MNR which gave them the land. This man saw pictures of Paz Estenssoro and Siles in peasants' homes, and they talked in a friendly way of the MNR.

The so-called "united" faction of the MNR in Bolivia includes the followers of Paz and Siles. When the group was formed, it elected Paz Estenssoro as Jefe of the party, and Siles as Sub-jefe.

There was not as much corruption during the MNR regime as people talk about. The only name which always comes to people's lips in this connection is that of Guillermo Bedregal. Francisco Alvarez Plata did not get rich in the regime. He was left a small fortune by his father, but although he talked a great deal about how much money he had during the regime, it turned out when it was all over that he didn't have very much at all. He was Ambassador to Germany when the regime fell, and he brought back a Mercedes Benz at that time. Proof of the fact that they didn't get rich in power is the fact that there is little money now to finance the MNR.

Barrientos is arresting many of the MNR people of various factions. Yesterday at 3 p.m. the senator of the Movimiento Nacionalista Revolucionario Pazestenssorista was arrested as he came out of the Senate building.

Paz is teaching here. He has a course in Problems of Latin American Integration, in Macro Planning Techniques, and others. He spends his whole day at the University, being busy the whole time with classes, meetings, theses, and the like.

He thinks that the Brazilian economist Celso Furtado has made one of the most interesting contributions to economic planning ideas in Latin America. He has been important not only in the field of theory but in practice as well. His idea that underdevelopment is not merely a necessary pre-stage to development, but may rather be a permanent condition, is of great significance.

Another Brazilian, Helio Jaguaribe, has also had some interesting ideas. For instance, he has cited Bolivia as a typical case of a country of intermediate size which has carried out basic social changes as a prerequisite for economic development. He has cited it in terms of being a model of development in the area.

*   *   *   *   *

LETTER FROM VÍCTOR PAZ ESTENSSORO, FROM LIMA, OCTOBER 19, 1968

I answer your letter of last September 21, in which you invite me to visit Rutgers University, to participate during a week in the activities of the Latin American Institute.

I have delayed my answer a little, waiting to determine with certainty that I can spare the time from my work in the National Engineering University in the periods you judge as possibly the most appropriate for the visit. Now I can say that it will be a great pleasure for me to accept your invitation. I never forget that you, with the generous book on the Bolivian Revolution, opened the way for an understanding in the international arena, with great objectivity, of the singular transforming effort of the Movimiento Nacionalista Revolucionario. Also I consider that it is today more necessary than ever to have a dialogue between the Latin Americans and North Americans, and no place would be more appropriate for its profitable realization than the university. However, I must say also that my English, if it permits me to converse, is not sufficient to give a lecture in that language. If that constitutes no major problem, I am most disposed to go.

As for the date, the most convenient for me would be the second week of April. In December it is not possible for me to leave Lima, because it is the period of examinatons and dissertations in the University.

*   *   *   *   *

CONVERSATION WITH VÍCTOR PAZ ESTENSSORO IN MY HOME IN PISCATAWAY, NEW JERSEY, APRIL 6, 1969

There is some good news from Bolivia now. Relations between Barrientos and the military high command are very strained, and Barrientos has formed a special 500-man force as a kind of Praetorian Guard. The fact is, he guesses, that Barrientos doesn't trust the military and is trying to protect himself against them.

There has been unification last December of the Paz Estenssoro and Siles factions of MNR. Victor Andrade was not included in this unification, but Paz doesn't think that he has more than twenty or thirty followers. The reunited MNR is regaining strength among working-class elements who left the party in the last year of two that the MNR was in power.

Juan Lechín is now living in Lima. He is officially in hiding, but Paz suspects that the police know where he is but don't do anything about it. Paz and Lechín have had many discussions. He asked Lechín, who bears much of the responsibility for the overthrow of the MNR regime, whether if Paz Estenssoro had been naïve to trust Ovando, Lechín didn't have much more responsibility because he actually conspired with Ovando, and asked him why he had conspired with the military. Lechín replied that his idea was that the first move would be to oust Paz Estenssoro, and then immediately take power himself. That was real naïveté.

Lechín was not a founder of the MNR. He came into it right after the Villarroel coup in 1943, and the MNR had him made sub-prefect of Catavi. At the end of the first month of Lechín in this office, the representative of Patiño Mines brought in to him a check for $300, when his government salary was perhaps $20. Lechín brought this check to La Paz, and turned it over to the government, which was the thing that first got him popularity among the miners. Then he was largely responsible for organizing the Federation of Miners.

Of course, the price of Lechín's conspiring with the military in 1964 had to be paid by the miners, and the price has been a terrible one. Lechín now admits that he erred. He continues to have considerable influence in Bolivia, particularly among the miners.

Walter Guevara Arce and his PRA party still support the Barrientos regime. Guevara Arce himself is now Permanent Representative of Bolivia at the United Nations and is in New York City. However, a number of the PRA people quit the party and went into opposition after the massacre in the mines.

Almost all of the political parties are in opposition now. There are many parties in Bolivia, and each social group virtually has its own party. There are now negotiations going on for formation of a broad alliance among the opposition groups, from the Falange to the PRIN. These will include the Falange, Christian Democrats, MNR, PRIN.

The Trotskyites of the POR had considerable influence in the first year of the COB. They were very doctrinaire, transplanting the history of the Russian Revolution mechanically to Bolivia. Then in 1954, most of the POR trade union leaders, such as Edwin Moller, and some of the other members, such as Ayala Mercado, broke with the POR and joined the MNR. However, Guillermo Lora and González Moscoso and others kept the POR going. The Trotskyites don't have any influence in Bolivia now. They are divided into two rival groups, neither of which is of much importance.

The situation in Peru is a complicated one. There is virtually universal support for the actions of General Juan Velasco's government against the International Petroleum Company, on the basis of the nationalistic reaction of the people. He would say that the government is by and large a popular one, and would be very popular were it not a military dictatorship which came to power through a coup d'état. Its origins make it less popular than it might otherwise be.

There is no deal between the Apristas and the Velasco government. Whenever the Velasco government comes out with some popular measure, the Apristas point out that they have been advocating this same thing for many years, and give the date when they first brought it up.

He agrees that it is a shame that the Apristas have never been able to take power and show what they can do. He thinks that this is due largely to El Comercio and the Miró Quesada family. He thinks that the Army's vendetta against the Apristas could have been overcome if it had not been for the continued influence of El Comercio and their fanatical opposition to the Apristas, which dates from the murder of the editor of El Comercio and his wife. The present editor of the paper is the son of those two.

The Velasco government has not enacted a new agrarian reform law. However, it has begun vigorously to apply the existing law.

The Velasco government has issued a new law reorganizing the ministries. It has set up a Transportation Ministry and has reorganized a number of the others with the idea of instituting planning.

He doesn't think that the Velasco government plans to call general elections soon. They have the perspective of staying in power five or six years "until they have reformed the country." However, there is an item in the current budget for the Electoral Power to hold municipal elections before the end of this year.

He doesn't think that the Peruvian military dictatorship can be very well compared with those of Argentina and Brazil.

Eudosio Ravines was expelled from the country. This was because on his television program he made an attack on the government. He is a strange character, very intelligent. He is cordially despised by most people, but he was regularly listened to on his television program by almost everyone.

Strange things are going on in Peru. For instance, Pedro Beltrán, with whom Ravines is still closely connected, went abroad, to the Inter American Press Association meeting, but before he left he had an interview with President Velasco.

Another interesting thing is that the Prado interests, which are very important in financial affairs, are supporting the regime. This is largely because of the new law curbing operation of foreign banks, which is favorable to the national banks.

*   *   *   *   *

TALK BY VÍCTOR PAZ ESTENSSORO AT RUTGERS UNIVERSITY IN NEW BRUNSWICK, NEW JERSEY, APRIL 7, 1969

The political history of Bolivia can be divided into several periods. The first of these is that between independence and the War of the Pacific with Chile, beginning in 1879. During this period, there were no really ideological parties, but rather organizations established by the various military leaders of the independence period, each of which organized his own party, completely personalist.

The second period was that between 1880 and 1900. This was the period of the importance of the Conservative and Liberal parties. These differed principally on the issue of the relations of Church and State, because there was very little difference between them on economic and social issues, and both were parties of the ruling oligarchy, as had been the personalist parties of the previous period.

During all of this period, the Conservatives were principally associated with the landlords, the feudal landowners, and with the traditional silver miners. During the 1880-1890 period, the silver mines were somewhat modernized, with new machinery being brought in. The Liberals were associated particularly with the artisans and new bourgeoisie which grew up in La Paz and other cities, as a result of the growth of the mining industry.

In 1889-1900 the Liberals seized power via a bloody civil war. The important element of this situation was that the Liberals called on the Indians for support, promising them various things, and mobilizing sizable elements of the Indians behind them. However, once they got to power, they forgot all about the Indians. This is in spite of the fact that it was the indicated thing for the Liberals to have carried out an agrarian reform, since such a reform which gives land to independent landowners is purely a Liberal doctrine, although such is not the case when land is given to communities or to collectives.

During the Liberal period, which was from 1900 to 1920, there were various improvements and certain progress carried out by the government. They built railroads, there was some growth of artisan industry. However, nothing fundamental was changed in the Bolivian economic and social situation.

The Liberals in power should have carried out an agrarian reform. However, they forgot all about this, and in fact used their positions of power to get hold of land and themselves become semi-feudal landowners.

The Liberals during the 1900–1920 period were associated particularly with the new tin-mining interests. The development of tin mining began in the last years of the 1890's and grew rapidly during the Liberal period in office.

In 1920 the Liberals were overthrown. The period of 1920–1930 was one of the disintegration of the Liberals. The government was in the hands of the Partido Republicano, formed by remnants of the Conservatives and dissidents from the Liberal Party. There were factions within the Partido Republicano, between supports of Bautista Saavedra and Daniel Salamanca. Saavedra was somewhat more socially minded, and Salamanca represented the more right–wing elements in the party.

Then in 1932–1935 occurred the event which really undermined the existing system. This was the Chaco War, with Paraguay. Bolivia was supposed to have a very strong army, had had a German military mission there, including among others General Kundt, who had been one of the lieutenants of General Ludendorff on the eastern front in World War I, and Ernst Roehm, who became leader of Hitler's Brown Shirts.

However, once the war began, it turned out that the highly touted military leaders were incompetent. Furthermore, those who fought in the war came to question the whole system, feeling that the country had been betrayed not only by the military leaders but by the economic and social system. He was a sergeant in the Chaco War and felt these attitudes. They were also felt by those who served as younger officers in the war, because with the collaspe of the high military leadership, the real leadership in the war fell upon the junior officers.

The first result of this situation was the installation of two successive military regimes, those of Toro and Busch. The Liberal and Republican parties had been discredited by the Chaco War and no new parties had yet developed, so that the only really organized political force in the country was the military. Hence they took the leadership.

The Toro regime carried out several important reforms. It established a Ministry of Labor for the first time, and enacted important labor laws. It also nationalized the oil industry. The Busch regime, after a period of vacillation, also enacted a number of reforms, the most important of which was a decree of July 1939 which provided that mining companies should turn over to the Central Bank all of the foreign exchange which they earned, and the Central Bank would then give the companies what they needed to pay their foreign obligations. He was a member of the commission which wrote this decree, but he was not the author of it himself.

When President Busch committed suicide in August 1939, the government went back into the hands of the conservative elements of the society. General Quintanilla took over. In October there was a demonstration of all the conservative elements in defense of the new government, and some of the young people, of whom Paz Estenssoro was one, organized a counter–demonstration, and there was a clash between the two groups. This was the first real demonstration of the new elements in the society.

Quintanilla presided over the elections in 1940. Although these were pretty much rigged, there was a certain degree of freedom in the cities, and some of the younger elements were able to elect five members of the Chamber of Deputies, as independents, not as members of the MNR, which didn't exist yet.

In January 1941 the first agreement was made to establish a new political party which became the Movimiento Nacionalista Revolucionario. However, it was not until July 1942 that the party was formally organized. Meanwhile, and thereafter, the five deputies used their positions in Congress to debate various issues and to give speeches presenting their doctrines. These speeches were reprinted generally in La Calle, a daily newspaper which they maintained. In addition, they had a weekly, entitled Busch, which was the initials for the slogan "Bolivia Unido Sin Clases Humilladas." This was largely the organ for more theoretical and ideological articles.

He would like to explain why they took the name Movimiento Nacionalista Revolucionario. They did so because it seemed to express the objectives they were trying to achieve. They called it "Movimiento" because they wanted to indicate that it was to be a very broad, multiclass organization, and they thought that in the Bolivian tradition something called "Partido" would be interpreted as indicating that it was the organ of some particular class. They called it "Nacionalista" because they felt that the major need of the country was to really form a nation, because there really wasn't a nation at that time. Not only was transportation very bad so that people felt themselves to be Cruzeños or Cochabambinos or Potosinos more than Bolivians. They also felt that the Indians should be incorporated into the nation, and that the people should have pride in the past history of their country as the basis for building its future.

They called their party "Revolucionario" for two reasons. First, they called it this because they felt that the dominant elements in the society would never permit any group which came to power to make fundamental changes in a peaceful manner. The second reason was that they felt that there was need for very fundamental changes in the social and economic and political system of Bolivia.

In the beginning, the party was founded largely by intellectuals, young professors, lawyers, and the like. It also had a following among the artisans and urban workers, and a very small number of peasants. Interestingly enough, most of the peasants who joined the party in this early period were Evangelicos. They had a civic spirit and wanted to take an active part in affairs.

In 1942 there was a massacre in one of the big mines, perpetrated by the Peñaranda government, which had been elected in 1940. This brought the MNR first into contact with the miners on a considerable scale, but it also brought them in touch with those members of the armed forces who had a social point of view. These were young officers, from major on down, who during the Chaco War had organized a lodge, known as Razón de Patria, popularly known as Radepa.

During these first years there was no attempt to bring military men into the MNR. They felt that if they could build up a civilian party of some consequence, they would be able to negotiate with sympathetic elements in the Army. This they did in 1943, and during the Villarroel regime they cooperated with the military. It was only after the overthrow of Villarroel that they began to bring military men into the party.

In December 1943, the MNR cooperated with Radepa to make a coup d'état. This put Major Gualberto Villarroel into the presidency. During his regime the real power remained in the hands of the military. The MNR established policy in a number of things, advised the military, but did not really have the power.

During the period before the 1943 coup, the government was aware that although the MNR was a small party, it was a dangerous one because it proposed basic economic and social changes. They therefore made the charge that the MNR was sympathetic to the Germans. At this time, the United States was bringing pressure on the Latin American governments to break off relations with the Germans. When the Peñaranda government finally did so, it also arrested the principal MNR leaders and put them in a detention camp. However, the people did not accept the charges against the MNR, recognizing that the charges were too fraudulent to be accepted. As a result, when the MNR leaders were released from detention and opened the lists of their party to new members, large numbers joined the party.

The Villarroel government did a number of important things. It put into effect the decree of July 1939, which required the mining companies to turn over their foreign exchange to the Central Bank. It also encouraged organization of the Miners Federation, and generally encouraged the labor movement. It called a congress of peasants, and for the first time delegates from peasants from all parts of the country met and presented their grievances and demands to the government. As a result, there were enacted various decrees, such as abolition of forced personal service of peasants to their landlords, and other things, but nothing was done to get to the root of the problem, redistribution of the land.

Paz Estenssoro was Minister of Finance of Villarroel but had resigned the day before Villarroel was overthrown. When the rebels caught President Villarroel and hanged him to a lamppost outside the presidential palace, they were also hunting for Paz Estenssoro, but he was hiding in an attic, and they did not find him.

Villarroel was overthrown in July 1946. For six years thereafter there was a conservative group in power which preserved the status quo. It was a very oppressive government and there were massacres in the mines. However, there was a certain freedom in the cities, and the MNR continued to win elections. It even won the presidential election of 1951, although the government did not allow it to take power; there was a military coup, and for eleven months a military government was in power.

During this six-year period, the Trotskyites had a considerable amount of influence among the miners. They were not as persecuted as were elements of the MNR, and so they were freer to act in the mining area. They attempted to capitalize upon this situation to build up the influence of their party.

In April 1952, the MNR carried out a revolution against the governing Military Junta. They then carried out the program which they had developed before the Revolution. During the six years the party had considerably radicalized, both as a result of the experiences of the Villarroel regime and the situation during the six years. As a result, they had come to the conclusion that the basic things they had to do were to carry out the agrarian reform and nationalize the mines.

One of the first things the MNR government did was to enact a law of universal adult suffrage even for illiterates. The effect of this was to make the peasants the single biggest political force in the country. They constituted the great majority of the population.

The MNR government also carried through the agrarian reform, dividing up the land among the peasants, and nationalized the Big Three tin-mining firms.

The party organization developed in the period before the MNR came to power had as its highest organ the National Convention, which met every two years. This elected the Jefe and Sub-jefe of the party, and its Executive Secretary and National Command. Beneath this national organization were two lines of organization. First was the territorial, which was based on the nine departmental "commands" of the party. There were in addition a few subdivisions of the country below the level of the department which were important enough, principally areas such as Catavi with a large working-class population, to have separate "special organizations" of their own, almost but not quite as important as departmental commands. Beneath the department commands were those of the provinces and localities and in the larger cities that were also subdivisions.

Alongside this territorial structure was the functional organization of the party. On a national level, there were "cells" in various labor organizations, peasant groups, professional organizations, made up of MNR members in these groups. They were necessary to bring about MNR control of these organizations. The cells were the only effective way to fight the Communists, organized on the same basis, who were trying to get control of the various parts of the labor movement.

The National Convention had representatives of both territorial and functional units of the party. Members belonged to both a territorial and a functional unit of the MNR.

He hasn't discussed the peasants. Before the Revolution of 1952, the peasants played virtually no part in national politics, although there were a few of them, as he noted, who belonged to the MNR. However, once the Revolution had occurred and the government announced its intention to carry out an agrarian reform, an effervescence broke out among the peasants, and many of them began streaming into the party.

The peasants were organized into two groups. One was units of the party. Somewhat broader organizations were the sindicatos campesinos. After the agrarian reform had begun and the peasants became owners of their own land, there might seem to have been no further need for the sindicatos, since the employers had ceased to exist. However, they continued in spite of this and became the organizations through which technical assistance was given the campesinos, and became organizations through which the peasants presented their wishes and demands to the government. They still continue to exist to this day.

The MNR suffered from several handicaps. One was common to all underdeveloped countries. He has talked with Israelis who informed him that in spite of the fact that Israel is much more developed than Bolivia, they have the same problem. This was the problem of having insufficient personnel to man both the government and the party. They just didn't have enough first rate people to do two jobs. As a result, particularly in the later part of the regime, they tended to concentrate most on the government. This was particularly true because they faced very grave problems of economic development. The upshot was that control and maintenance of the party was left in the hand of second, third, and fourth rate people.

In addition, there was the fact that during the first years of the regime the Revolution had a "mistica," but that in the later years this mistica tended to decline. This was shown in the behavior of the MNR candidates named for public posts. They sought in the internal elections in the party to get high positions on the MNR electoral lists, and if they got these, which assured their election, since the MNR won most of the posts, with the opposition getting relatively few, these candidates didn't bother to campaign because they knew they would be elected anyway. They left it up to the party.

Another weakness of the party in power was that it lacked a real opposition. It was not even important that this opposition be a loyal one. The fact was that they knew that the opposition was so weak and incompetent that members of the party tended to become complacent with the situation.

As a matter of fact, when the MNR was overthrown, it was ousted not by the opposition but rather by elements which until then had been part of the MNR. Even then, they were caught unawares and didn't realize what was happening until it had happened.

He thinks that people in Latin America tend to look not just at the process through which the government is carried on but at the things which it does. There is widespread agreement among Latin Americans concerning the reforms which should be made. The people tend to look at what a government does, and not necessarily at the kind of government which does these things. If there is a choice concerning whether the things be done by a democratic or an authoritarian regime, it is certainly preferable that they be done by a democratic one. But if there is no democratic regime to do these things, and a military one does them, people are likely to support such a military regime.

An example of this is the Perón regime in Argentina. That country was far behind in terms of social and labor legislation, and democratic regimes had done virtually nothing about this situation. When Perón came along and enacted a large amount of social and labor legislation, he rallied a good deal of popular support.

He would like to sketch the general economic situation of the Latin American countries. There had developed in the nineteenth and early twentieth centuries a modern sector of the economies of these countries, usually based on exploitation of some natural resource or some kind of plantation agriculture to provide food or raw materials. But this was a foreign-oriented segment of the economy, as was clearly shown by the development of the railroads. These were built to connect mining centers or plantation areas with the port. This was shown in Bolivia, where railroads were built from the mines to the ports of Antofagasta or Arica. It was also shown in Argentina, where all railroads tend to center on Buenos Aires and spread out to the agricultural areas of the country.

World War I, the Depression, and World War II gave substantial shocks to this economy. The upshot was that the European countries could not buy the products which Latin America had to sell and, even more importantly, could not sell those countries the manufactured goods they had been accustomed to importing. The upshot was the beginning of industrialization.

After World War II the governments became committed to industrialization and diversification of the economy. This tendency was intensified by the United Nations' setting up Economic Commissions for the various continents. In Latin America this was ECLA, the Economic Commission for Latin America, the head and ideological leader of which was Raúl Prebisch. It urged planning of the economic development of these countries.

This was topped off by the inauguration of John F. Kennedy as President of the United States and his launching of the Alliance for Progress. The Charter of Punta del Este, which launched the Alliance, called for establishment of planning in all of the Latin American countries and in fact established this as a requisite for giving what was called multilateral aid, but was in fact principally aid from the United States.

However, the Decade of Development proclaimed by the ECLA, using one of the slogans that international agencies tend to use, the 1960s has not shown results which are much better, if any better, than the decade of the 1950s when there was no serious attempt to plan development.

One of the reasons for the disillusionment which has now set in is the fact that those countries have used the import substitution process of development. They have tended to develop first the light consumer goods industries, then passing to production of intermediate products, and finally to those of heavy industry in some countries. But when they have completed this last phase, they are up against the problem of the inadequacy of the national markets.

As a result, it has now come to be recognized that they need to develop more the basic industries, and it is recognized, too, that the markets for these in the various individual Latin American countries are not sufficient. So the current rage is for the integration of the Latin American countries, but then they ask themselves the question of for whom this integration is to be, whether it is supposed to be principally for the big companies which can take advantage of it.

Another difficulty has been the inadequacy of capital. This is inherent in these countries' being underdeveloped. It has led to reliance on loans from abroad or on foreign investment. But this brings its own problems, not only in terms of the weight on the balance of payments but also upon the fact that the centers of decision making of these economies rest in other countries, not in Latin America.

He thinks that this demonstrates the need for the State to intervene more in the economy of the underdeveloped countries. He thinks that this is inherent in the dual nature of these economies. There is on the one hand a modern sector, oriented mainly to foreign markets, and a self-subsistence economy which employs the great majority of the people. But there is no likelihood that the modern economy will influence the subsistence economy to develop, because it does not have the backward and forward linkages which would stimulate the subsistence economy to change.

He thinks that it is necessary for the governments to intervene not just because the private entrepreneurs are not able to break through the dichotomy of the dual economies, but because they can prepare the way for private enterprise. He doesn't think that the dichotomy will be overcome by natural processes without government intervention.

When he talks of government intervention, he is not meaning that there should be a statist economy. Quite the contrary, he thinks that there is room for both kinds of enterprise. The Bolivian case is one example. Bolivia used to import most of its food and raw materials, its sugar, rice, and cotton, for instance, in spite of the fact that the country had vast areas which could produce these things. However, the MNR government built roads to these areas, built a sugar refinery, built rice-decasking enterprises, and after they got these well established, private entrepreneurs came in and set up other refineries and similar enterprises. Thus, government intervention established the basis for private entrepreneurship.

But there have been difficulties in the process of planning. One has been in the drawing up of plans. There has been lack of adequate statistics, and there has been the use of high-powered techniques, econometrics, to lay out plans, which have often had little real contact with the reality of the countries in which they have been made. It is easy to employ foreign experts or the experts of ECLA to draw up plans, but they may not be very reflective of the possibilities of the national economies. Sometimes, political considerations bring about establishment of unobtainable goals in these plans.

Another difficulty with the plans has been their execution. The countries have found themselves with inadequate personnel to handle the problem of dealing with thousands of people who must put the plans into execution, and of dealing with the real problems which are faced in these circumstances.

He thinks that Bolivia is a case showing the efficacy of intervention of the government in the process of economic development. Bolivia presented an extreme case of the kind of dichotomy in the economy of which he has talked. There was, on the one hand, a modern sector of the economy, the mining industry, developed for the foreign market. It had been "foreignized" in spite of the fact that most of the capital for the tin-mining firms had come from Bolivia itself. There had been invested only some $40,000 by foreign investors, but the industry had been built up largely by ploughing back its profits. During the period until 1920 this was particularly easy, since there was virtually no taxation on the industry. Even afterward, there was taxation on exports, but there was no taxation on dividends. There had been passed a law for taxation of dividends, but it was a very confused law, and during World War II, when dividends were as high as 60 percent, this law was not enforced. Subsequently, instead of modifying the law to make it applicable, it was abolished entirely.

This industry was a great drain on the economy of the country. Thus, between 1929 and 1951 some $1,200,000,000 of mineral wealth was exported by the country, but only some $400,000,000 of imports had been brought into the country. There were also some services paid for out of the exports, but on balance the industry drained vast resources from the country.

On the other hand, there was the great majority of the people working on the land. They were kept in semi-servile conditions. The Indians made up two thirds of the population, but they were virtually not part of the Bolivian nation. They were a nation apart, had no economic, social, or political influence in the society of Bolivia. Furthermore, there was no social mobility. There was not only no chance of an Indian rising into the upper classes, but there was no chance even of his rising into the middle classes. The great tin baron Simón Patiño was no exception to this; he was a mestizo, not an Indian.

When the MNR came to power, it determined to do something about this. It first nationalized the mines. This was not carried out because of any ideological reason, but because the mining interests until then had been so overpoweringly important in the economy--in terms of supplying 90 percent of the foreign exchange, employment for 50,000 people who received wages, and so on, that they were really a super-state. It was absolutely necessary to nationalize these mining enterprises because of the situation in which the country found itself, not because of any ideological considerations.

It was also necessary to take over the mines to give the government control over the resources necessary to build up the economy. This is what they did.

The MNR government also carried out the agrarian reform. This gave the Indians a real stake in the economic life of the country. It was not true that the Indians didn't want a chance to develop. They did want such a chance; they were willing to adopt new methods if these were shown to them. The Indians built hundreds of schools throughout the country, so that their children could go to school.

The MNR government also carried out development projects. For instance, they built roads to areas which had been cut off from the rest of the country, thus opening up new agricultural frontiers, where the peasants could move in a kind of homesteading program; they vastly expanded the resources of the country, and they established the basis for further development. They succeeded in time in making the country self-sufficient in terms of sugar, rice, and cotton, which they had formerly imported. Bolivia now has a quota in the United States sugar system; it exports some cattle to Brazil and Peru.

The government also established a number of other development projects. It built up the electrical resources of the country; it stimulated a little the manufacturing industries as well.

There were some things in the Bolivian picture which were not so good. For instance, he is now convinced that they spent too many resources on social development in the beginning and too little on economic development. This increased consumption and forced the importation of goods they otherwise would not have had to import.

Another mistake they made was to allow excessive inflation. There had been inflation in Bolivia ever since the Chaco War, but it certainly grew too much during the first years of the MNR regime. However, the situation has been stabilized since 1957, and the exchange value of the boliviano with the dollar has remained virtually stable since then. Of course, the dollar has declined in value in the meanwhile, but the Bolivians are not responsible for this, and they have the feeling that their situation is stable.

There was some corruption under the MNR regime. However, this was greatly exaggerated by the propaganda of interests that were hurt by the MNR reforms. The proof of this is that the MNR has been out of power for four years, and except for three or four people who definitely got rich and have a good deal of money now, most of the rest of them are poor, starting with Paz Estenssoro himself, who has to teach in a university to make his living.

The government made considerable progress in social fields as well as economic development. For instance, there were about 200,000 students in school in 1966.

He thinks that the accomplishments of the MNR regime can be summed up under a number of heads: It brought about a rapid rate of economic development, since 1958 constantly growing, and in 1963

44

getting to at least 6 percent, which, given the 2.3 percent increase in population is a good per capita increase. It brought about a more equitable distribution of property and income. It established the basis for further economic development.

* * * * *

CONVERSATION WITH VÍCTOR PAZ ESTENSSORO AT RUTGERS UNIVERSITY, NEW BRUNSWICK, NEW JERSEY, APRIL 8, 1969

He thinks that Ché Guevara made a number of mistakes. One of these was to choose Bolivia as the scene of his operations. Of course, this was the result of his being a Communist, and for Communists nothing that is done by others can possibly be a revolution, and so he argued that there had not been any revolution in Bolivia, since the Communists had not made it. But the fact was that there had been a revolution; the peasants had gotten the land and they had no immediate grievance upon which the guerrillas could grow.

The second mistake was the foreignness of the guerrilla. Guevara himself was a foreigner and his two principal lieutenants were Cubans. There is in Bolivia a strong nationalistic feeling, as there is in all of the Latin American countries, and there is resentment at the incursion of any foreign force in the country.

The third mistake was to transplant automatically an experience from Cuba into Bolivia without taking into account the differences in geography. For instance, the jungles of Bolivia are not like those of Cuba; the Bolivian jungles are hostile, full of all kinds of bugs and animals, and even to survive there, let alone conduct a guerrilla war, is a real accomplishment.

Fourth, Guevara being a kind of geopolitician and studying a map, thought that the Camiri area in which he was operating was a good place from which a guerrilla war, if successful, could expand into Argentina and Paraguay. But he forgot that for the very reason that that region was on the frontiers, ever since 1930 that had been a military area, and it was customary for the people there to consider the local colonel as the highest authority, and in fact not to know any other authority.

He thinks that if Ché hadn't quarreled with the Communist Party of Bolivia, it might have helped him a little bit, but that would not have made it possible for him to win. The Communist Party is not that important in Bolivia. Although it has some capacity for infiltrating the unions and getting some influence in them, it is not really very important.

He thinks that the fact that the United States, Brazil, and Argentina all sent help to the Bolivian government and Army at the time of the Guevara guerrilla campaign helped the Bolivian government to defeat the guerrillas quickly. But he doesn't think that in the long run the guerrillas would have won in any case. They might have undermined the regime a bit and made it more possible for other groups to overthrow them, but it would not have been possible for Guevara to overthrow the regime.

He thinks that a fifth mistake of Guevara's was to make his movement an openly Communist guerrilla effort from the beginning. This is a mistake which his friend Castro did not do, or he would not have won in Cuba. The people of Bolivia are not Communists, and are anti-

Communist, and they would not follow Guevara. If a guerrilla movement had been begun which was just against Barrientos, it would have aroused a good deal of support. However, since it was just openly Communist, it did not mobilize any appreciable backing.

An agrarian reform has both advantages and disadvantages from the point of view of revolutionaries. It tends to transform peasants from a revolutionary group into a conservative one after agrarian reform. They don't want further changes, they just want to preserve their control over the land. This is what happened in Bolivia.

He would say that now, for instance, the peasants give at least passive support to the government. The Barrientos regime has not seriously interfered with the agrarian reform, and for this reason, the peasants support it. However, they do not support Barrientos personally, but rather the power as it now is. If a new revolutionary movement should arise, and Barrientos's power seemed to be slipping, the peasants would shift their support to the new power.

One factor in the situation is that a revolution does things very rapidly. Thus, the MNR in very short order decreed the land reform, redistributed the land, granted universal suffrage, and the peasants started participating in meetings and demonstrations. However, in a cultural sense they still remained backward, and it takes much longer to overcome this backwardness. Because of this, it is still possible for politicians to manipulate the peasants.

There are various indications that Barrientos doesn't personally control the peasants. For instance, at Ucureña, a very important center of the agrarian reform--and what Richard Patch considered virtually its only important center--there were elections in the sindicato campesino a few months ago, and it was necessary for the prefect of the area to go there, with half a regiment, to impose the candidates he wanted. If this had not happened, the peasants would have elected someone else.

It is true that the peasant leaders support Barrientos. However, who are the peasant leaders? He knows, because he had a good deal to do with getting them established. When the organization of peasants began, the MNR chose people from the villages to be the first peasant leaders, who had peasant backgrounds, but were not themselves really still peasants. However, now there is developing a new breed of peasant leaders, a new generation of younger ones, who are really peasants. These people are not so easy to manipulate by the government as the older breed of leaders were.

Recently, Barrientos sought to impose a tax on the peasants, and some peasant resistance began. Barrientos argued that he had great influence among the peasants and he could convince them that the tax was right. He called a big meeting of peasants not far from La Paz, and they booed and hissed him and threw stones at him, and his guard had to shoot their rifles into the air to drive off the peasants.

Incidentally, another mistake of Ché Guevara was to follow his theory that the guerrilla group could become the focus of the revolution and could spread out from an isolated area. But the fact is that it is the cities which are decisive in Bolivian politics, and particularly the cities of La Paz and Oruro, and the center of the guerrilla activity was very far removed from these centers.

The Army in Latin American countries may sometimes become an element of revolutionary change. Usually, however, the Army in these countries tends to align itself with the conservatives, with the status quo.

Also, it has served to some degree as a channel of social mobility, through which people of the middle class can rise into the upper class.

Bolivia has had some Army regimes which have been more or less revolutionary. For instance, the Toro and Busch regimes at least moved in the direction of revolutionary change, although they didn't succeed in carrying out the fundamental changes.

He won't comment on what he thinks the MNR regime did wrong with the Army, or what should be done to assure the loyalty of the military to a revolutionary civilian regime, because he hopes to return to power arm in arm with the military. However, he doesn't think that abolition of the Army is the answer. Any state needs to have the coercive power represented by the military at its command. There has never yet been invented a regime of the kind which can get along without coercive power. It is true that courts of justice are needed, but so is coercive power.

In the Bolivian case, the Army grew principally as the result of the need for such coercive power. Once the agrarian reform began, there started to be clashes of armed peasants with the miners, conflicts among different peasant groups, clashes among elements of the MNR itself, and the need was felt for the coercive power of the armed forces.

Actually during the first MNR administration, the Army was kept small. It consisted mainly of engineering batallions and a colonization batallion, for helping to open up areas in the eastern part of the country. When Siles became president, a serious conflict broke out between Lechín and Siles, and Lechín began to mobilize the miners against Siles. As a result of this, Siles began to build up the armed forces.

The MNR leaders tended to take for granted the loyalty of the military, because they heard so many protestations of loyalty from them throughout the years. They grew careless undoubtedly. But in addition, because of the concentration in the last years on problems of economic development, they left purely political affairs, including relations with the military, in the hands of secondary or tertiary leaders.

At the present moment, both Barrientos and Ovando are running the country, although he thinks that Ovando is the more important of the two in this regard. Ovando is propping up Barrientos because he aspires to succeed him next year. However, there may be serious conflicts between them, because it appears as if Barrientos has come to enjoy running things very much,, and may try to perpetuate himself in office. In this case, he would certainly clash seriously with Ovando.

Basically Barrientos and Ovando have interests in common. But there is a group of young officers, who rank from major on down, who are growing discontented, basically for two reasons. One is that they are getting increasingly perturbed by the growing civilian hatred of the military, and they fear a popular uprising in which they would be shot down in cold blood or which would result in killing of all the military men. The second cause is that they contrast the way the military were treated under the MNR and under the present regime. During the MNR period, promotions and assignments to command were based on merit and seniority, with little consideration to politics, since all of the military were considered to be loyal. Now, in contrast, all appointments and promotions are on a purely political basis, with those who are most closely associated with particular leaders getting the best appointments. There is hope for these young military men.

The fact of the matter in Bolivia now is that there can be no hope of a revolution on a purely civilian basis. As a result of the Guevara guerrillas, the Bolivian Army was very strongly armed by the United States, Argentina, and Brazil, and in fact it was so well armed that there is little hope that a civilian uprising with the modest arms which it could mobilize could defeat the armed forces. The only hope of a revolution now is if a part of the armed forces turns against another part. This would weaken the overall strength which the Army now represents.

The miners are in a particularly bad position now. The miners' unions have been suppressed; their leaders are in jail or exile. In addition, in each important mining camp there is an Army regiment, which is there to keep the miners down and shoot them down upon occasion.

However, this does not mean that the miners are no longer an important element in national politics. They are, as demonstrated at the time of the Guevara guerrillas, when the Army did not dare withdraw any regiments from the mining camps, because they feared that the camp would revolt. The miners remain a very important element, certainly the most explosive one in the country at the present moment.

The miners have come to the conclusion that they made a mistake following their leaders into opposition to the MNR regime. They have reentered into contact with the MNR, as was shown in the 1966 election, when in spite of fraud and violence, the mining camps all went for the MNR. He doesn't think that the miners will be alienated if the MNR comes to power again in alliance with a faction of the military. The miners are politically very sophisticated, and they will realize that this alliance is a necessary tactical move.

When he says that he thinks that the MNR can only come to power with military help, this does not mean that he proposes an alliance with the military, but rather with certain of the chiefs of the military, and those who ally themselves with the MNR will in the nature of the case be taking a revolutionary position.

To return to the peasants for a moment, there are many indications that they are being integrated into the national life of the country. One is the fact that they are moving in increasing numbers down to the eastern lowlands. This means undertaking a completely different way of life. It involves their changing their kind of clothes, although for a while some of them continue to wear the heavy clothing they are accustomed to in the altiplano. It also involves learning new ways of cultivating, growing new kinds of things, etc. It also involves learning to eat new foods, and more of them, with the result that they tend to weigh five to seven kilos more than they used to.

Another indication of their integration into national life is the present tendency even on the altiplano to abandon their old garb. He suspects that within five years there won't be any campesinos left who wear their traditional clothing. For them, changing of their costume is a notification to the rest of the population that they are being integrated into the society.

He thinks that the Revolution has brought about important changes in attitudes toward the campesinos and among them. There is certainly a much greater degree of interest now, both among mestizos and whites, on the one hand, and peasants on the other, in the customs, traditions, and folklore of the Indians.

However, some attempts to reestablish old institutions haven't worked. For instance, when they wrote the agrarian reform law, the doctrinaires who were among those involved insisted on the virtues of collectivization. There was a feeling that the peasants had the tradition of the ayllu, community farming, and that they would want to revert to it. As a result, a compromise was reached, which provided that on very large estates some of the land would be divided among individual peasants, with each getting his own lot of land. The rest was kept as a collective piece, to be worked collectively. But the first thing the campesinos did was to get together and divide the collective land among themselves on an individual basis. They wanted nothing to do with collective agriculture.

There is no doubt that the aid Bolivia received from the United States was of great help to the MNR regime. It made it possible to undertake development efforts. The MNR saw the Revolution as having two parts, destruction of old institutions, with the agrarian reform and nationalization of the mines, and then building on this a more diversified economy. It was this latter part which was made possible by United States aid.

There is one important difference between the aid situation under the MNR and the present situation. The MNR was much more insistent on conditions being established on its part for the reception of aid. The Barrientos regime, on the contrary, doesn't make any demands, and he knows that the aid officials feel that they have a much easier time now, when the regime stays exactly on the rails, than was the case with the MNR regime.

There is need for setting conditions for reception of aid, particularly when aid is construed in the wider sense not only of grants and intergovernmental loans but also of foreign investment. For instance, there was an American company which wanted to open up a gold mine, and it was necessary to discuss the conditions under which it could operate, what contribution it should make to the national treasury, and so on. But conditions were also stipulated by the Bolivian government in the case of intergovernmental loans.

Sometimes there were conditions on the other side. For instance, the American government insisted that its aid be spent in the United States. As a result, for instance, they had to buy truck tires in the United States, instead of Japan, where they could have gotten them for 30 percent less. The result was that freight rates had to go up, the price of goods shipped went up, and everything went up. It was this kind of situation which was one of the things for which the common people criticized the MNR regime.

Although the MNR regime was nationalist and revolutionary, it was the government which reopened Bolivia to foreign investment in petroleum. No government before had dared to do this since the oil industry had been nationalized in 1936. But the MNR government enacted a new petroleum code which permitted foreign companies to come in, while at the same time strengthening the government's own oil company, the YPFB. But the reason why other governments before the MNR were not willing, or did not dare, to follow this was not because they were motivated by the best interests of Bolivia, but rather because the Big Three tin companies did not want the establishment in Bolivia of another large capitalist enterprise which might challenge their hegemony in the country.

The United States is giving extensive aid to the Barrientos government to stay in power. However, in the longer run it is going to do great damage to the United States, because there is developing in the minds of the people a very close association of the United States with a regime which is unpopular, corrupt, and inefficacious. The result is that there is a great deal of anti-American feeling in Bolivia today.

The Peruvian Army may be the instrument for bringing fundamental change to Peru. The problem is that the parties have proven themselves unable to do so. The one party which should have done so, the Apristas, has been kept out of power by the Army and El Comercio. Fernando Belaúnde's party, which came to power with many promises, did not carry out those promises. So that left only the Army as the means of bringing about changes which are widely recognized as being necessary.

*   *   *   *   *

TALK OF VÍCTOR PAZ ESTENSSORO AT RUTGERS UNIVERSITY IN NEWARK, NEW JERSEY, APRIL 10, 1969

When the people who were to form the MNR first ran for deputy, in 1940, the old electoral system still held good. He ran for election in his own native area, in Tarija, and he was generally considered as a local boy who had made good, so he had it easier than some. But the system was that one's supporters organized dinners for one, with lots of drinks and a great deal to eat, and one had to eat one's way through a large number of such occasions. It was quite a task.

In the altiplano, the local bosses would control an area and would surround it with police so that the opposition couldn't get in to carry on their propaganda. But the future MNR people got around this. There were in those days organ grinders who had monkeys or parrots, and people would come up to them and pull out of a little machine papers which would tell their fortunes. The future MNR arranged that when the peasants came up and pulled out their fortunes, these said, "If you want a good crop, vote for the MNR candidate."

It is hard to generalize about the attitude of youth in Latin America toward foreign investment. He would say that insofar as students are concerned, there is one group of upper-class youths who are frivolous, who don't really take much interest in public affairs, but who are generally favorable to foreign investment. There is another group which he would call responsible, who want economic development, realize that foreign investment is needed for this, but think that there should be conditions established for its entry. Then there is another group which is under Communist influence, who are strongly opposed to foreign investment. He would say that in Peru, at least, the great majority are in the second and third categories, and that the proportion between the responsible and the Communist-inclined groups is about 60-40 percent.

He would say that almost any government in Latin America realizes the need for foreign investment. Every government now is committed to economic development, and they realize that one of the great needs is capital, and that there is not enough of this in their countries, and that they must get help from the outside. However, they cannot be deaf to the feelings of their people either, and they must discuss the conditions under which foreign investment can be accepted.

The traditional kind of foreign investment was in mining, plantation agriculture, and petroleum, which were designed to serve foreign markets. There is a growing feeling that these things should be brought under national control. In the Bolivian case, for instance, his government nationalized the big mining companies, but they had to do so for a couple of reasons. One was to give the government control over the economy so that it could develop on a more broad-based basis. The second was to be able to use the country's resources. They succeeded in the first of these objectives, and the government had resources to diversify the economy; but they did not succeed in the second objective because production in the mines declined, and they were forced to resort to foreign loans in order to stimulate production of the mining industry again.

He thinks that the only areas outside mining and petroleum in which there is a tendency to expropriate foreign investments is in railroads and telephone companies. In the first case, this is often being done in conformity with the foreign investors because the railroads are no longer profitable. In the second case, the nationalized telephone companies seem to be working as well as they did in the past.

He would say that foreign investment is now most welcome in manufacturing. In more general terms, he would say that it is most welcome when it establishes enterprises which use national resources, national products, and if it produces intermediary products, or is heavy industry.

He didn't have the vice of loving power for power's sake. He had some vices. In his younger days, he certainly had a liking for women. He has never been a mandón. He hasn't liked power just to have power, but he has liked power for the things he was able to do with it. He got the same kind of thrill out of being able to establish some new part of the economy as an artist must get from his painting or the writer of a book from seeing his work in print.

For instance, there was the case of the sugar industry. There had been attempts by private investors to establish refineries in the Santa Cruz region, but these had not prospered financially and had gone bankrupt. But the Paz Estenssoro government established a sugar refinery, with credits from a French firm, which sold them the machinery on long-term credit, and they got the boliviano funds from counterpart funds from the U.S. aid program. This served to get the sugar industry started in the country, and subsequently, there were two private firms which also established sugar refineries. In his second term, he established another government sugar enterprise in the southern part of the country to serve the areas of Tarija, Potosi, and others and to ship sugar to Argentina as well. This last part was profitable, since the internal price of sugar in Argentina is very high indeed.

He was also very happy about the development of the oil industry. They built a very good system of oil pipelines. They had a big controversy with the railroad company over building an oil pipeline to La Paz because theretofore oil had been brought into the city by the railroad, and they didn't want the competition of the pipeline. The relative costs of bringing it in by pipeline and by railroad were 1 to 9.

They made a mistake in building the pipeline to Arica. It turned out that this was not the most appropriate terminal which they could have chosen.

He thinks that the other oil companies which came into Bolivia, aside from Gulf, did not succeed in finding oil because they were for the most part small companies, which didn't go at the job very seriously, didn't invest very much, and so didn't discover oil, even in areas where there might have been oil. The only serious company other than Gulf which came in was Shell, but it didn't find anything either.

There had been an agreement whereby a large area near the frontier was reserved to Brazil to look for oil, but nothing much was being done about this, and the problem was pending for a long time. However, when President Café Filho took office in Brazil, he came to Santa Cruz to dedicate the opening of the Corumbá-Santa Cruz Railway, and at that time, Paz Estenssoro reached an agreement with him to resolve the problem. It was agreed that concessions would be given to private Brazilian companies, but that they would have a time limit and if they didn't discover anything within that period, the lands would revert to Bolivia. Most of the companies which were established to get concessions were made up of people closely associated with the Brazilian government who really didn't know much about the oil industry, and the upshot was that they didn't really take the job seriously, and they did not discover any oil. As a result, the lands reverted to the Bolivian government, which passed them over to the government oil firm, YPFB. A few months later, YPFB put down a well and struck oil, which made the Brazilians ready to tear out their hair.

After the MNR government had expropriated the big mining interests, their reputation among foreign firms was zero, and they were anxious to find someone who would come in to invest in the country. Finally, a picturesque character from Texas, who had made and lost several fortunes, came and asked for a concession. He was finally given one. He was a fantastic character, who had his own airplane, which he flew directly from Houston to his oil area in Bolivia, without ever stopping at La Paz. At one point he decided that the technicians who were looking for oil on his concession didn't know their business, and he undertook to do it himself. However, because of his erratic way of behaving, he did not ever discover any oil.

Oil is a funny thing. The Gulf Company discovered a fault which they figured was perfect for oil; it suited all of the prescriptions, and they were sure that they had discovered the biggest oil field in Bolivia. They planned a ceremony to end the drilling process, to go through the last few feet which were necessary before oil would be tapped, and they invited government officials and others to the ceremony. Paz Estenssoro didn't go because there was some kind of political crisis at the time and he could not leave La Paz. When they made the last bit of drilling, they found that the well was empty; there was no oil there. What happened was that millions of years ago something occurred which made oil drain off somewhere else.

There is a story about Senator Hickenlooper's trout which was popular in Bolivia for a while. It seems that an Indian and his wife were fishing in one of their balsa boats on Lake Titicaca one day and caught a huge trout. The Indian told his wife that she should fry the fish, but she said that there was no oil available, that because of the inflation and the controls of the MNR government, there was no oil available. He said then that they would boil the fish, but she said that something else wasn't available because of the policies of the MNR government. So finally, the Indian threw the trout back into the lake, and the fish as it dove into the water shouted, "Viva el MNR!"

However, when Hickenlooper came to Bolivia, the fish decided that he owed all to the MNR and must make a sacrifice to the MNR and so he allowed himself to be caught by Hickenlooper. The senator really did catch a huge fish, which was pictured in the fishing magazines all over the world. When Paz Estenssoro visited Washington in 1963, he was taken by Hickenlooper to the senator's office, and there was the fish mounted on a beautiful mahogany board in his office. Hickenlooper was a good friend of the MNR.

Paz Estenssoro thinks that the Alliance for Progress would have been a lot more successful than it really was if Kennedy had lived, and if the Alliance had remained along the lines on which it was originally conceived. However, he is afraid that after Kennedy's death about all that was left of the Alliance was its name.

He thinks that foreign aid on balance has been very helpful to the Latin American countries. It has its drawbacks, as he has noted, but he is not one of those who argues that it is of no use to the development of the Latin American countries. It certainly has been helpful to their development.

William Atwood was at one time an important official of the State Department. His father had been a professor of geography and had written about a rain forest in Bolivia where trees grew high up on the mountains where normally only small plants grow, and had grown there because of the heavy rainfall by winds which come in from Brazil and drop their moisture on these mountains. When the Cochabamba-Santa Cruz road was opened, Atwood attended the ceremonies, and he told Paz Estenssoro that he had come particularly because he wanted to see the rain forest about which he had heard so much from his father.

There is no question that the intervention of the military is a serious problem in Latin America. If he had the answer to how to keep them from interfering in politics, he would not be in the United States today.

He doesn't think that the Peruvian government now in power has any general intention to nationalize more industries than the International Petroleum Company. However, whether it actually does so will depend in large part on whether or not the Hickenlooper Amendment, which demands quick payment to American firms expropriated by countries getting U.S. aid, is applied by the United States. If it is applied, the present government may decide that it wants to capitalize on the country's nationalistic sentiment by taking over other foreign firms. This may bring about the overthrow of the government but the leaders of it may prefer to be overthrown holding up the banner of Nationalism than to go down more easily without any banner at all.

Those who are controlling the present government in Peru are certainly not Communists, whatever may be said about them. There is an abyss in Latin America between the Army and the Communists, and this is no less true of Peru than of other countries. Furthermore, two or three years ago there was a Castroite guerrilla operation in Peru, and it was exactly the military men who now control the government who were the ones who suppressed that movement.

It is true that there is a group of civilians associated with the present Peruvian regime who are members of what is considered to be a left-wing party, the Partido Social Progresista, but it is certainly not a Communist group. It is absurd to call them Communists.

*   *   *   *   *

CONVERSATION WITH VÍCTOR PAZ ESTENSSORO AT RUTGERS UNIVERSITY, NEW BRUNSWICK, NEW JERSEY, APRIL 10, 1969

The twentieth century is the century par excellence of Nationalism. The fact is that it is the period of Nationalism, not only in Latin America, but all over the Third World, in particular.

The Revolutionary Nationalism of which the MNR is a part is in conformity with this general strength of Nationalism in the world today. It puts stress on building up the nation and incorporates in its programs social issues, as well as nationalist ones. The social part of the program is an inherent part of this kind of Nationalism.

Revolutionary Nationalism is opposed to specifically class parties. It argues that there should be an alliance of various classes, whose interests coincide. Any mass party has to have the support of popular groups such as the workers and peasants, but it also should incorporate middle-class groups, petty bourgeoisie, intellectuals. These groups all have interests in common in building up the nation, and will have such common interests for quite a long time. Although in time their interests may conflict, there will be a long period in which this is not the case.

In a country such as Bolivia, where the great mass of the population is Indian, there will be a very wide gap between the leadership and the great mass of the party. The leadership is drawn largely from the intellectuals and professional classes, whereas the great mass of the party members are drawn from the Indians. There is a very large cultural gap between the two, and the filling in of this gap is one of the major aspirations and objectives of the National Revolutionary group.

The MNR drew from various sources for the formulation of its theory. The first of these was the specific circumstances of Bolivia, its geography, its population makeup, its stage of development. Second, they drew on the ideas and experiences of other countries. Among the outside influences which were very important were the ideas and actual accomplishments of the Mexican Revolution, the early ideas of the Peruvian Apristas, and surprisingly enough the writings of Nehru and the early history of the Indian National Congress Party. A third major source of the theory of the MNR consisted of specific situations which the party had to face, and upon which it had to take decisions. All these elements served to mold the philosophy and theory of the party, which evolved considerably over the years.

He would underscore the difference between Revolutionary Nationalism of the kind he has been discussing and the Nationalism of the highly developed countries, which tends to degenerate into chauvinism and Nazism. Revolutionary Nationalism tries to build a nation, to bind it together.

Latin America is facing new situations now with which it must come to grips. One is the growth of the cities, particularly the capital cities. This growth is not similar to the development of the cities in the presently industrialized countries, which came about because of the demand of the new industries for workers. In Latin America, industrialization has not gone this far, and the growth of the cities is due to the expulsion of the peasants from the countryside, not to the demand of the cities. Fortunately, in Bolivia this movement has not been as great as in other countries because of the agrarian reform, but it is a generalized situation in the Latin American countries.

The upshot of this migration to the cities is the building up of a new class in the cities, those who occupy the squatter colonies around the cities. These people for the most part do not have fixed employment, and thus the unemployment of the countryside has been transferred to the cities. The residents of the squatter colonies have hitherto tended to support people such as the ex-dictators Odría in Peru, Rojas Pinilla in Colombia, and most recently Pérez Jiménez in the Venezuelan election of 1968.

There are other elements in the rapidly growing cities. These include bureaucrats, technocrats, administrative people, and the like.

There is necessary an ideology to deal with this situation. The National Revolutionary ideology is an answer to this need because it advocates a multiclass alliance of the kind that is necessary. These classes have common needs and interests. It is the responsibility of the National Revolutionary parties to develop programs which will stress these common interests.

He had no thought of returning to power. In effect, after his overthrow, he stepped aside for four years, hoping that there would arise a new leadership in the party. However, no such new leadership actually appeared. In an MNR meeting in La Paz a couple of months ago, Paz Estenssoro's name was put forward as the party's candidate for the 1970 elections. However, his reply when asked about this was that it was too early to talk about candidacies at this time, that this was a decision which would have to be taken by the MNR Party Congress.

General Ovando, who is expecting to be Barrientos's successor, is very fearful of the possibility of Victor Paz Estenssoro's candidacy because he knows that Paz could defeat him exactly among that portion of the population upon which the government depends in order to win next year's election, the peasantry. It may be that the peasants have forgotten about the MNR, although he doubts it, but he remains the man who gave them the land. He has been told by American students who have spent some time looking into the situation of the peasants in recent years that large numbers of them still have his picture up in their houses.

This regime is not a continuation of the MNR regime. He thinks that the situation of Barrientos as Paz's successor in the presidency after having been vice president cannot be compared with the possibility of President Nixon being succeeded by his vice president. For one thing, he doesn't think that the situation in Bolivia can be judged in terms of the United States. In the second place, he doubts very much that President Nixon's vice president would overthrow him.

Perhaps in November 1964 they could have suppressed the revolt of the military. But the fact was that the party was very badly split and dispirited. However, there was a possibility that the revolt could have been suppressed.

The dissolution of the party began with the split away of Guevara Arce. It is too bad that he could not be convinced to wait a while in his aspirations for the presidency because if he had stepped aside in 1960, he would have been the uncontested candidate of the MNR in the 1964 election. He would have been a very good president. He is very intelligent, decisive, is a very good politician, really a better one than Hernán Siles.

*   *   *   *   *

CONVERSATION WITH VÍCTOR PAZ ESTENSSORO IN MY HOME IN PISCATAWAY, NEW JERSEY, APRIL 11, 1969

There is no possibility of unity of the MNR with Juan Lechín and his followers. He wants to maintain his own party. However, the two groups are now cooperating in exile and within Bolivia very closely.

During his political career he has met a number of Latin American presidents. For instance, he met Mexican President Lázaro Cárdenas during World War II, when he went there for the Villarroel government, and Cárdenas was Minister of War for Avila Camacho. Subsequently, he met Adolfo López Mateos during his own second presidency.

Of course, he met Kennedy. In fact, he was the last chief of state whom Kennedy saw before he was shot. Paz was brought to Washington by helicopter, and after the ceremony at the White House, Kennedy rode with with him to the guest house--it wasn't Blair House then, because it was being repaired. On the way, Kennedy asked him how things were going in Bolivia. Paz answered that they were going pretty well, but would go much better if the United States wouldn't continue to sell tin from its strategic stockpile. At that point, the ice was broken between the two men, and they talked in a very friendly way. He came to regard Kennedy as a personal friend.

Among the Paraguayans, he got to know Morinigo, Joaquín González, and Stroessner.

The uncle of Celso Sánchez, a student here at Rugers who has gone around with him a good deal during his visit, was a colonel and a good friend of his. Together they had led a small invasion of a border town of Bolivia from Argentina. They were defeated and had to retire. However, the colonel remained a good friend. Unfortunately, about a year after the MNR Revolution of 1952, the colonel died of cancer; they sent him to a German sanitarium, but he couldn't be cured.

When Paz went to the Bolivian Consulate in Lima to renew his passport so that he could come here, they asked him what university he was coming to in this country. He said that he didn't think that was any concern of theirs, that he was merely coming to the United States, and that was all they had to know.

When he applied for a visa at the United States Embassy, he had no trouble at all. He went to see Peter Lord, to whom I had recommended him, and Mr. Lord put him in touch immediately with the right person in the consulate, and they issued his visa without any question.

He thinks that the military attachés of the United States, Argentina, and perhaps Brazil had a hand in the overthrow of his regime. The U.S. Air Attaché, Colonel Fox, made a statement at a party with some Bolivians a few weeks before Paz's overthrow, criticizing his regime, saying that he, Fox, knew that Paz depended a lot on help from the United States, but that what he forgot was that his friend Kennedy was no longer in power.

He is sure that the United States has two foreign policies, that of the State Department and that of the Defense Department. The Defense Department operates without any particular consultation with the State Department and does what it wants to do. Paz and the MNR regime had exceedingly good relations with the State Department, but he guesses that he cannot say the same for their relations with the Defense Department.

The Argentine military attachés were openly working with the military in Bolivia, urging them to move against the civilian government. In a way, Paz is responsible for this. He made a state trip to Argentina, when Frondizi was still in power, and took General Ovando with him and in effect introduced him to the Argentine "gorillas."

There were quite a few Peruvian Apristas in exile in Bolivia in the early 1940s. They were on very good terms with the people who founded the MNR. However, because of the old enmity between the Apristas and the Army in Peru, the Apristas were very much opposed to the idea of the MNR collaborating with some of the military to make a coup, as the MNR did in 1943 when the Villarroel regime was established. The Apristas thought that the MNR had betrayed its principles when it did this.

The present Peruvian government of General Velasco has enacted a new education law. Among other things, it reduces student participation in running the universities. Whereas before the students had one third representation, equal to that of the professors and the alumni, this percentage has been reduced in the new law to 25 percent. The law also very much strengthens the power of the rectors of the universities. However, the rectors are still elected by representatives of the faculty and students.

Former Peruvian President Fernando Belaúnde Terry was on very close terms with President Barrientos of Bolivia. Barrientos had visited Peru when both men were presidents, had given Belaúnde an abrazo and greeted him as his "master." No president of a nation should publicly proclaim the president of any other nation his master.

Paz Estenssoro himself was very much aware of this friendship of Belaúnde with Barrientos. During the first year or so that he was in Peru, he was "guarded" by policemen, outside of his house. But these police were there not so much to guard him from someone else as to keep track of what he was doing. More recently, however, these guards were removed, and at the present time he doesn't have any kind of guards at all, either to help him or to keep track of him.

He was exceedingly glad to get the invitation to come to spend a week at Rutgers. He had not left Peru since he got there in November 1964, and he was beginning to feel as if he could never get out of that country. He had traveled fairly widely in Peru itself, including a month in the North, where his Institute was making a study of regional economic development in one department. So he was very glad to get a reason to leave the country for a while. In addition, he had never really had much contact with an American university, and he has very much enjoyed the week he has spent here, talking to classes and seeing how an American university really works.

*   *   *   *   *

LETTER FROM VÍCTOR PAZ ESTENSSORO, FROM LIMA, APRIL 26, 1969

Having returned home, I wish to write you a few lines to express my thanks for all the attention which you, as well as your wife, paid me, during my visit to that University. Also, for having permitted me to have that experience, which was so interesting in all regards. The classes, the public lecture, the conversations with professors and with students were a source of real satisfaction, both for the cordiality with which I was received and for the spirit of comprehension which I encountered in all, for my interpretation of the Latin American situation and particularly the Bolivian National Revolution.

For these reasons, I think that you are right in thinking that when I began to act, won over by the atmosphere, I had no feeling of being subject to "exploitation of man by man." Now, after receiving your letter of the 17th of this month, my satisfaction is greater, knowing through your friendly words the opinion that you have about the task which I carried out.

* * * * *

CONVERSATION WITH VÍCTOR PAZ ESTENSSORO IN HIS HOME IN LIMA, JULY 10, 1971

The situation in Bolivia is very bad. The Communists, particularly the pro-Soviet ones, but also with the participation of all the other brands that are there, including the Trotskyites, are riding very high at the moment, and Juan Lechín is working with them, while President Juan José Torres is also collaborating with them and is trying to outbid them.

An example of the way Torres operates is shown by the fact that Lechín and the Communists were planning a huge May Day demonstration, the exact outcome of which Torres couldn't foresee. So at that point, on April 30, he announced expropriation of the Mathilde mine, the ironic aspect of this being that the contract giving the concession of that mine to a foreign company bore the signature of Torres, as a minister of Ovando. He argued that he had been misled, that he didn't know what it was he was signing, and so on, which is, of course, a lot of nonsense.

Another example of Torres's tactics centered on an Anti-Imperialist Week which Lechín, the Communists, and the rest organized. To head off whatever consequences this might have and to give a reason for it to be a demonstration in favor of the government instead of against it, Torres announced expulsion of the Peace Corps from Bolivia. This was pure demagoguery.

There is a complete lack of authority in the country. For instance, the Communists organized a kidnapping of two mine officials at the South American Placer silver mine and held them until the government released certain people who were being held as liaison people with Ché Guevara guerrillas. This was unnecessary, in any case, because by due process of law those people could have been released on bail, since the charges against them were of a secondary order of gravity.

Other examples of the situation are the seizure of properties by the various radical groups. They have seized the Bolivian-American Cultural Center and the Bolivian Institute of Social Research. They have walked into stores, thrown out the owners, and remained in control--in other cases, the workers of a store or other enterprise have seized it; the government has done absolutely nothing.

The economy is going rapidly downhill. In Santa Cruz, for instance, the government has decreed the merger of all the sugar enterprises--which had been built up under the MNR administration--into one large enterprise, in which the private owners are supposed to have some shares, the government some, and the workers some. But it is in a total state of confusion, as a result of which sugar production is going down.

Also in Santa Cruz, seizure of the Gulf properties has resulted in the YPFB taking over all operations--exploration, drilling, transportation, and everything else--most of which Gulf had let out to sub-contractors, so these people are without work. The upshot is that Santa Cruz is an area in virtual revolt against the government.

Much the same is true in Beni, where opposition to the government is very strong. There, the MNR government had sponsored development of a large cattle industry, with 200,000 head of cattle. Bolivia now ships cattle by air from there to Arica and to Peru. However, the grazers live in constant fear that their lands and cattle will be seized at any moment.

The regime has had a tremendous campaign against those in charge of YPFB, claiming all kinds of malfeasance and misfeasance. They finally forced those people out and put in a directorate of half government representatives, half worker representatives. That industry now is in grave danger of declining also, not so much because of the new directorate as because of the utter confusion which has been brought to it.

Even worse is the situation in the mining industry. There, the miners are demanding a completely worker-controlled directorate. In addition, there is virtually no discipline in the mines, and the upshot is that production is declining again. They are now seeking a large loan to keep COMIBOL afloat financially.

The Russians are taking the place of the Americans in Bolivia. The Soviet Embassy has seventy people in it now. There is present in Bolivia a Soviet oil mission, to help reorganize YPFB, and it is reported that there will be a similar mining mission.

The government has virtually ended all freedom of the press. They cooperativized El Diario--the only good thing the government has done, since the Carrascos, who owned it, were terrible people. But control of the paper has been turned over to the Communists. They have started a new journal, Jornada, which is far over to the Left. Radio Illimani has also been taken over by the Communists, as well as the television. The only half-way free paper still being published is Presencia of the Christian Democrats.

There are pro-Soviet Communists in the government. Also, the Vice Minister of Interior is presumed to be a member of the Ejercito de Liberación Nacional, since his brother died in Ché Guevara's column. Also, in a kidnapping, for which a ransom of $50,000 was paid, the station wagon which went to pick up the ransom was that of the Vice Minister of Interior.

There is a great flight of people from Bolivia. The Jews in particular are fleeing. Most of them are businessmen, and they are afraid that at any moment they may have their stores seized. A delegation of the Comité Israelita sought an interview with the Minister of Interior to get guarantees from the government, but he would not receive them; they were received by the Vice Minister already mentioned, who told them that they knew as well as he did the conditions in Bolivia, and the only advice he could give them was that they get together a fund to be used if any of them was kidnapped.

Juan Lechín is playing just as irresponsible a role as he did when he was with the MNR. Going back to the time of Ovando, when the government allowed reorganization of the unions, there was a congress of the Miners Federation. In that congress, the Communists, Trotskyites and others had a candidate against Lechín to head the Federation. It was the MNR delegates, forming an alliance with the PRIN of Lechín and the Christian Democrats, who saved the job for Lechín. Later, this under Torres, when the COB held its congress, there was the same alliance of MNR-PRIN-PDC which saved Lechín the post of head of the COB as well.

However, Lechín is using the situation to get as much power and as many concessions as possible, without having any responsibility for what occurs. He has gotten from the government, for instance, the concession that all workers in Bolivia, except the peasants, will have dues to the COB deducted from their wages and salaries--giving the COB a fund equivalent to $300,000 a year This makes Lechín a very powerful man in the present situation.

Previously, Lechín had gotten $100,000 from Castro. Paz Estenssoro found this out by devious ways. A group of Bolivian miners came to see Paz, asking him if he knew where Lechín was, saying that he had told them that he was going to Cuba to get money from Castro. Paz got in touch with a Peruvian friend of Lechín's, an ex-Aprista, who had been the man who helped Lechín get in and out of Bolivia, and that man informed him that Lechín should be back any time, that he had gotten a cable from him from Havana saying that he was on his way back. Paz told the miners this.

Shortly afterward, Lechín did arrive. He came to see Paz Estenssoro, and Paz asked him about his trip to Cuba. Lechín was taken aback. He denied that he had been in Cuba, said that he had been in Paris, that Simón Reyes, the Communist mine leader (who later ran against him for head of the Miners Federation), had been to Cuba, had met him in Paris, and so there was no need for Lechín to go to Cuba. But later in the conversation, Paz doesn't remember in what connection, Lechín commented that he had seen Raúl Castro but had been unable to see Fidel--indicating that he had not just been to Paris, but had been in Cuba as well.

Subsequently, Lechín came back here and got the other $50,000. However, Lechín demanded the interest on this money also. The Peruvian told him that there was no interest, that he had kept the money hidden in his house, in constant fear that it would be stolen, that he certainly would not invest it or put it in a bank because that would raise too many questions, that there was no interest, there was just $50,000 which he had given Lechín. Apparently, they had a very hot argument over the matter, and at the end were no longer friends. It was after this that the Peruvian told Paz Estenssoro the whole story.

Apparently Lechín used his second $50,000 for rebuilding the miners' organization and the COB under Ovando and Torres. But now, of course, he does not have to depend on any outside sources of money, since he has his $300,000 a year.

Lechín was the principal figure in the recent so-called "Asamblea Popular." However, that organization has proven so far to be a farce. There was great fear that it would be a kind of soviet, which would be in fact take over the government. However, although there was a great deal of talk, everything was referred to commissions for study. Lechín said that the Asamblea would carry out a popular uprising, but this was referred to a commission; he said they would organize a popular militia, but that was referred to a commission. The Asamblea Popular then adjourned for two months. It has shown all the weaknesses of the worst of bourgeois parliaments, that of Bolivia. However, it gave Lechín a chance apparently to wield power, again without responsibility.

There was representation of a variety of political elements in the Asamblea. Officially, there was representation of workers groups and political parties. Interestingly enough, and showing the strength of the MNR, the largest single bloc of representatives in the Asamblea was that of the Movimientistas. Also represented were the PRIN, the pro-Moscow Communists with the second largest group, the pro-Chinese Communists, the Partido Socialista, the MIR, the Revolutionary Christian Democrats, and the POR of Guillermo Lora. The other POR, of González Moscoso, was not represented, but will be in the next session, if there is one.

There is no question that the MNR is still by all odds the largest party in the country. It has very good organizations everywhere except in La Paz and Cochabamba, where it is particularly persecuted. It is overwhelmingly strong in Santa Cruz, Beni; very strong in Sucre, Potosí; and virtually the only party with support among the peasants, who knew very well who gave them the land and who now live in fear that the next thing which will be seized will be the land of the peasants.

The MNR is severely persecuted. Its members are frequently arrested, some of them, including one of the party's founders who is Paz Estenssoro's age but not as healthy as he, have been sent to a concentration camp in the center of the jungle which consists of two buildings--one for the prisoners and one for the guards--and where pumas come into the compound at night and people have to sleep with fires to keep the pumas away. However, persecution has not destroyed the MNR--far from it.

The Christian Democrats have split. The normal Christian Democrats still publish Presencia and are in the opposition. But there is a group of their young people who have broken away to form the Revolutionary Christian Democratic Party, who are more extreme than the Communists of various kinds. They are very active in the government, and particularly in the University.

The Partido Socialista is a new group, formed by one of those who had been sympathetic to the MNR, who was in Ovando's government. It is also an extremist group.

Then there is the MIR, formed also by ex-Movimientistas. He fears that Jordan Pando is going to join it, since his ideas have been moving in that direction.

The MNR has some internal problems. Hernán Siles had been exiled in Montevideo. He went back to Bolivia "Tupamaroized," with quite extreme ideas, and gave vent to these for a while. Then he came here in January and he and Paz and other MNR leaders had long discussions. Siles wanted them to go on record as advocating the theory of building the "new man," the kind of utopian revolutionism which is current these days. However, after a very long discussion, they worked out a decent joint statement. Siles is now in exile in Chile.

There has been a good deal of maneuvering by Bolivia's neighbors. The Brazilians, for instance, are very active in trying to push their interests in the Santa Cruz area, and he is a bit afraid of what might come out of that. The Argentines are very active in Tarija and Sucre. Their activity in Tarija is of long standing. One maneuver is their revival of a will of Belgrano, one of the leaders of Argentine independence. He left a sum of money to be used for relieving the poor in the poorer provinces of

Argentina, which included Tarija, then part of Argentina. This fund was never used, but the Argentines have suddenly "discovered" it and, among other things, are building a large school there, spending $1,000,000 on the building alone, which for Bolivia will build a veritable palace. Also, not long ago there was an outbreak of a contagious disease in Tarija, and they asked for doctors and vaccines from the Ministry of Health in La Paz, but because of the utter disorganization there, it was a week or more before doctors, nurses, and vaccine arrived. But when they got there, they found that they had nothing to do because the Argentines had sent in all that was needed the day after the outbreak started.

The Chileans are also very active. He has information that they financed the meeting of the Asamblea Popular. They are also subsidizing the newspaper Jornada, which has been carrying on a very active campaign in favor of reestablishing relations with Chile, arguing that the exit to the sea is something that can only be resolved by negotiation, and that in any case, there are now fraternal governments in the two countries, and they ought to be working together. The Chileans are undoubtedly playing a very important role in helping the present Bolivian regime.

The MNR, quite frankly, is busy conspiring. They have encountered a factor in the last year which is to their advantage. Before that, they were in danger of falling into the situation that the Apristas have in Peru, of being vetoed by the Army. However, in the light of what has happened in Bolivia during the last year, there are now many in the Army who are very much against the Communist and extremist influences in the present regime and are working with the MNR.

The present regime has an apparent popularity which in fact it does not possess. This was demonstrated during the recent Anti-Imperialist Week. The whole propaganda effort of the regime was centered on this, with programs all day on the radio and television about it, with propaganda in the government newspapers, with meetings, and so on. The whole thing was supposed to end with a huge mass meeting the last day of the week. However, this mass meeting was a total flop, with only seven hundred people turning up, and giving the lie to the government's claims of vast popular support.

The popular support it does have is declining. There are increasing shortages of things, and the inflation is very considerable. He is sure that conditions will continue to get worse.

The failure of the mass meeting of Anti-Imperialist Week had one bad effect for the MNR. They had hoped that the businessmen would help to finance their activities; many who had opposed them when they were in power were turning to them in desperation in the light of the present situation. However, with the failure of that meeting, many of these people heaved a sigh of relief, became convinced that the situation wasn't as bad as they had thought it was, and tightened up their pocketbooks.

As a result, the MNR is short of money. This has the effect that their conspiring had to move more slowly than they would like and will take a longer time to reach fruition. With a good deal more money, they could move a lot faster.

He sees three possible alternatives in the present situation. The present state of affairs cannot last very long. Something else will have to take its place.

The first alternative would be a right-wing military coup. The experience of the Barrientos regime indicates that it is possible for the military to impose a hard-fisted regime which can bring order, if nothing else. However, he thinks that this is the least likely of the alternatives.

The second alternative is that this become a frankly Communist regime, with the collaboration of the pro-Moscow, pro-Chinese Communists, Lechin, the Revolutionary Christian Democrats, the Trotskyites, and others. It might be with or without Torres at the head. He thinks that there is a good deal still which such a government could do to maintain itself in power for one or two years. For instance, it might have a so-called "urban reform" in the cities, that is, distribute among its followers houses which exist. This would keep them quiet for a year or two. It might distribute the cattle farms of the Beni. There are still things to distribute. Of course, the economic chaos would get much worse, but they could maintain themselves for a while.

The third alternative is a coup by the MNR, together with the Christian Democrats and the Falange. Of course, this is what the MNR is working toward. He thinks that the MNR would have a strong enough organization within a short time to be able to impose some kind of order again and to get ahead with the jobs which need to be done in Bolivia and which they started when they were in power before.

There is a good deal of talk about a civil war in Bolivia. If this should come to pass, it would involve the various Communist groups, the Lechinistas, the Revolutionary Christian Democrats and whatever part of the military Torres could muster, against the rest of the Army, allied with the MNR, PDC, and Falange.

During the last year and a half, Paz Estenssoro has made several trips abroad to give lectures and attend conferences on city planning. He went once to Mexico, and another time to Colombia and Venezuela.

The regime here in Peru seems to be running into considerable economic difficulties. They made a grave miscalculation with regard to fishmeal, refusing to sell below about $200 a ton, and as a result, their customers shifted to the use of soy bean substitutes for the fishmeal they had been using. There have also been problems with strikes in the mines, cutting down copper production and exports. Furthermore, they have been turned down in Paris in their bid to reschedule payments of the foreign debt.

The upshot of all of this is that there is growing conflict among the military men. This doesn't come out very much in the open as yet, although there are occasionally firings of one general or another; but there are definitely said to be rifts. He supposes that sooner or later they will get back to an elected civilian government but will run into the age-old problem of the veto on Apra's coming to power.

* * * * *

LETTER FROM VÍCTOR PAZ ESTENSSORO, FROM LA PAZ, DECEMBER 17, 1971

I have received with considerable delay, the attentive letter dated October 20 brought by our common friend Don Jaime Moscoso, and a few days later, the one you sent by Dr. Lane Vanderslice.

I really thank you for your words and rob time from my recently very busy schedule to send you these brief lines.

Incessant meetings with department leaders, trade union and miners congresses, meeting with youth groups of different classes which belong to the party, leave me really with only a few minutes to treat with my friends and my own personal matters. In this situation, I limit myself to send you three short pamphlets which will give an idea of our present situation, of the circumstances which surround our participation in power and of the present state of our relations with the Falange. You can complement this with your profound knowledge of Bolivia.

When I have a bit more time it will be a pleasure to elaborate more on these themes. Meanwhile, Bob, I ask that you receive my cordial regards and my best wishes for a Merry Christmas and a Happy New Year.

* * * * *

CONVERSATION WITH VÍCTOR PAZ ESTENSSORO IN LA PAZ, JULY 13, 1972

The coup of last August and the resulting Frente Popular Nacionalista were the results of the situation of Bolivia at that moment. There was a desperate situation in the country. Students are always radical, and that is good, because they act as a counterweight to more conservative elements in the older generations. But last year, the students were virtually dominant. President Torres was going farther and farther to the Left. He had no real control over affairs and there was virtual chaos in the country. Furthermore, there was danger of Bolivia disappearing altogether. Brazil had informally suggested a conference on the breaking up of Bolivia, to all of its neighbors.

Only Peru said no, and Allende was among those saying nothing. He got this information from the Peruvian Sub-Secretary of Foreign Relations.

The Army people first had contacts with the Falange. This was because when he was approached, Hernán Siles said that the MNR wanted to do away with the Army and substitute for it a workers' militia. So the military turned to the Falange, and before the MNR got back into the situation, negotiations were already advanced between the Army and the Falange.

There were two basic objectives of the Frente Popular Nacionalista. The first, of course, was to oust the Torres government and to save the country. The second was to bring some degree of stability to the country, without which its development would be impossible. It proved relatively easy to oust Torres, since he had little civilian support, which was in contrast to the situation the year before, when he had come to power, when a general strike was largely responsible for his becoming president. Last year, however, the workers continued to work in spite of a call for a general strike by Lechín and others. Only one military unit remained loyal to Torres, and the only civilian backing he got came from the students, who did fight.

Stability is very necessary to get economic development going again. In the seven years after the MNR was overthrown, there were nine different presidents, and no development was possible under those circumstances. Last year, the increase in national income was only 3.5 percent, whereas during its last years the MNR had 7–8 percent, and never less than 5 percent. As a result of this situation, when Torres was overthrown there was very extensive unemployment.

This regime is going on with much which was started by the MNR. By the end of the year, for instance, they will extend social security to the peasants, largely medical insurance. They have decided that petrochemicals, steel, and the metal industry generally will be in government hands. The Mathilde mine, granted in a concession by Ovando, seized by Torres with a promise of repayment, is now being negotiated. The company demands that there be both a mixed company to run it and that it be compensated. The government says that they can have one or the other but not both, they can be compensated and it will remain a government mine, or it will be a mixed enterprise and the company's contribution will be the compensation that it might otherwise have received. He'd classify this as a government of the Center-Left.

The government has all the difficulties which characterize a coalition regime. There are tugs and pulls between the partners. But generally they are able to get agreement. They look on this kind of government as one which will last for some time, perhaps three years. It should stay this long for two reasons. First, they need to concentrate on development and they can get things in this area started more quickly if there doesn't have to be long discussion in Congress. Second, the people in the government must make hard and sometimes unpopular decisions. But if a date were set for elections, these people would be thinking about their candidacies and would not be willing to make unpopular decisions as a result.

The MNR wants to change the nature of Congress. They want to have some kind of functional representation in it, and to have committees of Congress with adequate staffs to study thoroughly the problems which come before them, so that the decisions of these committees would virtually be decisive in the action of Congress.

The MNR is being reorganized. Local units have been reestablished throughout the Republic. A Congress was held early this year. The peasants are for the MNR. Thus, the party had internal elections in Cochabamba recently, and 23,000 people voted. President Banzer happened to be there, and he asked a peasant who was standing there waiting to vote what he was doing. The peasant replied that he was waiting to vote for the people who were to run his party. The president then asked him what he thought of the alliance of the MNR and the Falange, and the peasant replied that even his grandchildren would never be Falangistas. President Banzer's reaction was that the MNR was a very good party indeed.

The MNR has done well in labor. It has won in union elections in several of the big mines. Joint Communist slates of the pro-Russians and pro-Chinese won in Siglo XX and Catavi. The MNR controls the Industrial Workers Confederation, the Bank Clerks Confederation, and all of the others which have been reestablished. The COB has not been reorganized yet. Some people want the eleven MNR members and two Falangista members of the COB executive to reorganize it, but this is not the idea which won out. The COB Congress will be held when all of the sindicatos and confederations have had their elections and congresses.

One of the most notable things is the large number of new young people who have come into the MNR and into its leadership. The secretary general of the party is under thirty. These are very good people, and they are giving more vigor to the party.

He realizes that the foreign image of this government is bad. This is largely the result of the fact that the Ministry of Interior is in the hands of the military, who have done some stupid things, and the Foreign Ministry is in the hands of Mario Gutierrez of the Falange, who has no sense for this kind of thing at all.

The Army has a number of factions. The officers who entered the military academy after 1952, a few of whom have gotten to be majors or lieutenant colonels, consider themselves products of the National Revolution, but not members of the MNR. The colonels are bad Barrientistas. Banzer is the balance of the various factions which joined together because of the emergency.

The MNR has to follow a very narrow path. They don't want to look so strong that they frighten the military, or so weak that they will be moved against because of their supposed weakness. It is a difficult path to follow.

* * * * *

CONVERSATION WITH VÍCTOR PAZ ESTENSSORO IN HIS HOME IN LA PAZ, JULY 15, 1972

The historical reputations of both Presidents Germán Busch and Gualberto Villarroel are largely the result of the propaganda which the MNR has made about them. Without this, they would have gone down in history as fairly mediocre characters.

Busch is the more interesting of the two. He was the son of a German immigrant, and from him tended to get the idea that things were either black or white, and that there was no negotiating between them. His mother was an Indian woman of the selva, and the Indians there also tend to have this very simple way of looking at things. Then he was sent to the military school and in the Army got the idea, of course, that one either commanded or one obeyed; one didn't negotiate. This lesson was driven home during the Chaco War in which, of course, he participated, and where it was either a question of shooting or getting shot.

He came to the presidency at the age of thirty-one with no preparation at all for the post. His coming to power was the work of the Patiño mine interests. The Toro regime had been following policies favorable to Aramayo and Hochschild, and so the Patiño interests had conspired to get rid of Toro and in his place they put Busch. He was surrounded by ministers who were officials of the Patiño mining interests.

In those days, even after a coup, they tried to be constitutional. So a Congress was elected, which was very favorable to Busch, but in spite of that, his Patiño advisers got him to proclaim himself dictator and dissolve Congress. They felt surer of not having anything in their way this way.

However, the crisis finally came over a decree concerning the amount of foreign exchange the mining interests would have to turn over to the Banco Central. This decree considerably reduced the amount the mining companies had to pay. At that point, the young Nationalists who also had access to Busch, including Paz Estenssoro, went to see him, and pointed out the advantage which this decree gave the mining companies.

Up until that moment, Busch hadn't realized that he was being used by the Patiño interests. When he realized it, he reacted very violently and was determined to shoot the Finance Minister, who was author of this decree. There was a tragi-comic scene in which Busch was pacing up and down, saying he was going to shoot the Finance Minister; and other Ministers, also Patiño men, were trailing behind him, pleading with him not to shoot the minister.

In the end he did not shoot anyone. However, he did take drastic measures in the opposite direction from the decree mentioned. He issued a new one, which provided that the mining companies should turn over 100 percent of the foreign exchange they earned to the Banco Central. He issued other decrees nationalizing the Banco Central and the Banco Minero, and named Paz Estenssoro as president of the Banco Minero.

However, Busch continued to be surrounded by Patiño men, the only one he fired was the Minister of Finance. He found himself under terrible pressures from the Patiño interests, and being the kind of man he was, who couldn't negotiate, he didn't know how to maneuver. He escaped from the situation by committing suicide.

Villarroel was a more devious character. The MNR was in the government at the beginning of his administration, but then there arose the question of non-recognition by the United States because of the presence of the MNR in the government, which Cordell Hull and Sumner Welles tell about in their autobiographies. So Villarroel told the MNR ministers that they should resign, and that once recognition had been obtained, he would bring them back into the cabinet. They resigned, recognition came, but Villarroel did not summon them back into the government. Elections were held for a constitutional assembly and the MNR had over seventy of the hundred members of that assembly. They came to the issue of election of Villarroel as constitutional president, and at that point, the other MNR leaders told Paz Estenssoro that as Jefe of the party he had better settle the issue of entry of the MNR into the government before they voted for Villarroel as president. Paz went to see Villarroel, and the president told him that as soon as he was elected constitutional president and reorganized his cabinet, they would be in it. So they voted for him, but he still didn't bring them into the government.

However, then there occurred a right-wing revolt attempt in November 1944. As a result of this, the military shot in cold blood about twenty people, including senators and deputies of the opposition. The opposition was cowed, but so were the military themselves, very worried about the results of what they had done. So in December, Villarroel called in Paz Estenssoro and told him that the government needed the backing of the MNR, and that they should come back into the government. They finally did so in January 1945.

Colonel Banzer is another type of military man. If there had to be another military regime at this point, it is fortunate for the country that the leader of it is Banzer. He is not the typical militarote who issues orders, insists that things are going to be done just the way he wants, and that is that. On the contrary, he discusses, listens, and then reaches conclusions, is receptive to solid arguments.

He is physically a small man and has the appearance of being very calm. However, he has done several things which have shown his character and have been very good. One was the dismissal of his first Minister of Interior, who was a terror, Colonel Selich. Selich acted with an exceedingly hard hand and, very roughly, was doing the regime a lot of harm.

Paz Estenssoro had been warned about Selich before he left Lima, by the Yugoslav Ambassador there, who had been Yugoslav Ambassador in Bolivia during part of the MNR regime and who is a very good friend. The Ambassador, who incidentally has written a play about Germán Busch which did very well in Yugoslavia, told him that although he didn't know

Selich, he knew that he was the son of Montenegrins, and that they were very hard people and that Selich would probably do the MNR damage, sooner or later.

In any case, Banzer finally decided to get rid of Selich. He offered him the post of Ambassador to Paraguay. Selich refused it, so Banzer told him that the choice was the ambassadorship to Paraguay or jail. He went to Paraguay but continued his activities there, and finally Banzer dismissed him as Ambassador and retired him from the Army.

The other case in which Banzer acted very decisively concerned a group of Barrientistas in the Army. He told Paz Estenssoro that the Barrientistas were causing him all kinds of problems and that he was going to have to do something about them. The next morning, Paz Estenssoro read in the papers that a group of Barrientista officers had been arrested. What had happened was that Banzer had gotten wind of the fact that a number of them were meeting to conspire against the government in the house of one of them. So, at two o'clock in the morning he went to the house, pushed open the door, went in gun in hand, told them that he had caught them conspiring, recited some particulars about corruption and other activities of some of the individuals there present, and put them all under arrest.

He knows that the MNR is going to have to walk very carefully in order to get the military to permit them to win elections when it comes time to hold elections. The party will have to act cautiously. He doesn't think that the new young people in the leadership are going to upset this; they realize the difficulties of the situation. They will be a pressure group, on the other hand, to work against the party's moving to the Right, which is fine.

He thinks that the young officers are generally inclined to permit a victory of the MNR. There was a young major from Cochamba who was here to see him this morning. He was very friendly disposed toward the MNR, although he was clear that he didn't want to be considered a member of the party.

The opposition to the MNR's being able to go out into the countryside comes mainly from the military. They want to maintain the Pacto Militar-Campesino. This dates from the Barrientos time, when a group of corrupted old peasant leaders first signed such a pact with Barrientos, proclaiming him El Líder Campesino. They have done the same thing with each military president in turn, most lately with Colonel Banzer. However, this Pacto really has no meaning, lower-ranking peasant leaders pay no attention to it, and they are solidly with the MNR.

He realizes very well that perhaps the number one problem of the country is the incorporation of the peasants into the economy. But one must now make a differentiation among the peasantry. Those who live along the main highways, and who have comparatively rich land, are now middle class, and prosperous middle class. They have good houses, they have one or two trucks, they are living relatively well. Those living farther from the main highways live progressively worse, depending on their distance from the highways. In the more remote areas, they live much as they did before, with the difference that now they don't work for the patrón, but for themselves. Of course, this is a very great difference, but it is not enough.

Obviously much must be done for the campesinos. First all, it is necessary to build roads spanning out from the main highways, so that the peasants farther in can get their products to market. It is necessary to give them technical assistance. Also, the biggest lack now is credit, because although there are a few supervised credit loans of the Banco Agricola, these are very few compared with the need.

There is also a project to dam the Río Salguero, and to irrigate some 20,000 hectares on the altiplano. The land is good there, if it has water, for growing alfalfa. They want to develop milk cattle there. There has been constructed here in La Paz a milk plant, but now it operates on the basis of mixing imported powdered milk with water. They want instead to have it produce pasteurized milk from the cattle which will be pastured in this irrigated area.

There are two experiment stations, set up with help of the Americans, here on the altiplano. They breed breeding cattle there and hold auctions periodically. Eighty percent of those who buy these cattle are campesinos.

He is perfectly aware that there is now a second generation of peasants, the sons of the ones who originally got the land. Typical was a young man of twenty who came in to see him a few days ago. He said that he didn't remember how things were in the old days, but his father told him a lot about them, and that that was why he was a Movimientista and would remain one. But he did have things which he wanted. He expressed the now typical demands for technical help, for a neighborhood road, and for similar things. The government is going to do its utmost to meet these demands.

He also thinks that Bolivia should industrialize more than it has so far. This should be combined with a growth of La Paz. This is necessary as a counterbalance to Lima. His seven years in Lima convinced him of the dangers of that city becoming too much the center of this part of the world. He thinks that new industrial parks can be established in the altiplano just above La Paz. There are some there now, but they could be expanded. There have been some parts of the petrochemical industry which have been assigned to Bolivia, some other things. But many other kinds of industries can also be built here.

He thinks that Barrientos acted very precipitously in joining the Pacto Andino. He didn't take time or have sufficient study made to protect the interests of Bolivia in the Pacto. There will have to be some further thought about working out protection for Bolivia under the Pacto, so as not to have virtually all of Bolivia's present industries destroyed.

He agrees that Bolivia can come become an important producer of food and raw materials for the other members of the Pacto Andino, but I as an economist should know that a country will never really develop just being a producer of food and raw materials. He doesn't particularly agree with the idea that Bolivia hasn't yet reached the stage for industrialization. They need to industrialize a good deal more than they have done so far.

They are going ahead with expansion of the tin refinery at Oruro and are also going to establish an antimony refinery. The tin refinery was established by Ovando under very uneconomic conditions. A deal was made with a German firm, which was selling old iron, so to speak. It wanted to set up the refinery for a price and didn't care whether it was economic or not. It operates on the basis of charcoal, which has to be brought from Santa Cruz, and naturally it loses money. It processes a bit more than half of Bolivia's tin production.

They are now going to expand it so that it can handle all the country's output and are going to reorganize it. A gas pipeline is going to be built from the oil fields to Sucre and then to Oruro, and the tin refinery will then be reorganized on the basis of using gas, with a process which Shell has developed. This will make it economically feasible.

The Gulf issue is settled. They are paying compensation for the expropriated interests of Gulf. Ovando had entered into a very disadvantageous arrangement with a Spanish company, but that was dropped by Torres and hasn't been renewed by this government.

They have also enacted a new petroleum code. It provides that there shall be more new concessions granted. Companies will be invited to come in at their own risk, and if they find oil they will be working it on behalf of YPFB, and YPFB will get 60 percent of the gross of the oil produced. The former arrangement was 50-50 of the net profits. The companies will sell the oil abroad for YPFB, its share, that is.

There is a controversy with Peru over establishment of a basic petrochemical industry. It had first been agreed that it would be built right on the border. But then the Peruvians changed their minds and decided that they wanted to build it on the coast, and of course Bolivia had no interest in that. This controversy is in the bounds of the Pacto Andino. The problem is still unresolved.

The MNR party organization was in shambles. For seven years it had really hardly existed. One of the major things they have been doing, therefore, has been building the party organization. It has been largely rebuilt on local and regional levels and they have had a national convention.

They have brought many young people into the leadership. Of the Political Committee of twenty there are seven who are under thirty. There are very few of the old faces in the committee.

He agrees that there is a danger of the party becoming too dependent upon him as its only major leader. However, this is something which has just happened, not something which he planned. During the seven years they were out of power, all kinds of people tried to assume leadership, but none of them was able to do so. He is the only one at the present time who can give effective leadership.

A few of the old leaders remain abroad. Hernán Siles asked for permission to come back at the time of the Party Congress, got permission, but then didn't come. He is undoubtedly piqued that he was not reelected Sub-Jefe of the party. Jordan Pando also remains abroad.

Ñuflo Chávez is a special case. Actually there were two conspiracies leading up to the overthrow of Torres. One, in which Ciro Humboldt and others here were involved, was with the younger officers and Banzer; the other, in which Ñuflo Chávez and Alvarez Plata were involved, was with a general. The general finally threw in with Banzer and the young officers, who had the more viable organization, but he did so without consulting Ñuflo Chávez and Alvarez Plata. After the Revolution, Ñuflo Chávez began an awful lot of talking about what the government was and wasn't going to do, without consulting those in charge. So he was finally arrested and was released on the promise that he would go to Peru. So he left.

Many of the earlier dissidents have returned, both from Guevara Arce's Partido Revolucionario Auténtico and from the PRIN. They are discussing possible merger with the PRA of Guevara, which is small but has a few very good people in it, such as Ríos Gamarra, and also has influence in a few of the mines, and would be a worthwhile addition to the party.

The so-called MNR of Victor Andrade really didn't have anything except a few leaders. Some of those, like Monroy Block, have returned to the party. Augusto Céspedes has not done so, but he is on friendly terms with the party and has been given a little post by the government.

One of those who came back from the PRIN was Agapito Monzón, until recently Vice Minister of Economy. He is a <u>cholo</u>, a very good man, but was under severe pressure here. Since he had gone out of the MNR with the PRIN, there were those who, in spite of the fact that he is back in the MNR, insisted that he was still maintaining contacts with the PRIN, which Paz Estenssoro doesn't believe. But in any case, when the chance came for him to get a grant to go to Rutgers, Paz and others advised him to take it. He did.

There is undoubtedly repression here. This is largely due to the fact that the Ministry of Interior is in the hands of the military. They act very unreasonably sometimes. If repression is to be used, it should be used not on the basis of what one had done in the past, but on the basis of what one is doing now. The military in the Ministry of Interior have been arresting people because they belonged to the Asamblea Popular, but leave people in the streets who are conspiring today. This doesn't make sense.

The MNR, of course, had people in the Asamblea Popular, and these were arrested. At one point eighty-nine Movimientistas were in jail, and there are still fourteen in prison.

He agrees that the newspapers say very little. In this regard, <u>El Diario</u> is worse than <u>Presencia</u>. <u>El Diario</u> is a very reactionary paper, in addition. The lack of political news in the papers is not due to any previous censorship by the government, but because of self-censorship by the newspaper editors, who are afraid of sticking their foot into it. He hopes that this situation will improve before too long.

Some protests against things the government does do get into the papers. For instance, the government recently ordered an increase in electric rates--something required by the World Bank, because the electric company was earning only 7.5 percent instead of the 9 percent the Bank thought it should earn. This brought forth numerous protests from the unions and all kinds of other organizations, which did get publicity.

The Partido Demócrata Cristiano [PDC] is in opposition. Things which it has issued opposing certain government measures have been published. The fact that the PDC is in the opposition has not prevented friendly talks between it and the MNR, looking toward some kind of alliance between the two parties and the possible entrance of the PDC into the government. The main opposition to this comes from the Falange. It seems that at one time the Falange and the PDC had a Concentración Demócrata Cristiana to which both belonged, and this broke up with bad taste on both sides, and the Falange is determined, therefore, not to have anything to do with the PDC.

It is true that the government has gotten aid from Brazil and Argentina, but the help from the United States is much more substantial. Contributions of the United States to the Emergency Plan will total $40 million when the new agreement which is just about worked out has been signed. The Brazilians have so far only given a loan for importation of sugar from São Paulo. They have several longer-range and more substantial things which are being worked on. These include completing the railroad from Santa Cruz to Cochabamba, which will mean a rail connection from coast to coast. They are also working on details of roads in the northeastern part of the country and some other things. The Argentines are helping with some things, such as the gasoduct from Tarija to Sucre, and are continuing on the railroad to Santa Cruz.

There is some fear here of Brazilian imperialism. Certainly it is potentially more dangerous than American imperialism, because it is right next door, and because the Brazilians are very much in their expansive phase, just starting it in fact. However, for now at least, he is not particulary worried about this.

Getting back to the question of possibilities of agricultural development, they are very great. For instance, in Tarija, experts from Chile and Argentina have come to the conclusion that the region can produce grapes and wine which could bring in $20 million a year in foreign exchange. Also, in Tarija they are now developing the cultivation of garlic, which may bring in as much as $10 million a year, since the world demand for it is very high.

Also, of course, Bolivia has tremendous potentialities as a meat producer. They could become the principal producer of meat for the other countries of the Pacto Andino. The government is pushing development of the grazing industry, and exportation of meat, which is now being sent to Chile and Peru.

As a result of development of the East, due to the impetus given by the MNR governments, Santa Cruz has been completely changed. In 1952 it was a small provincial city of 35,000; now it has 120,000 with a number of satellite towns of 10,000 to 15,000. The complexion of the people has changed, too, of course. The old residents were largely of Spanish descent, but the increase in population is largely the result of migration from the western part of the country of cholos and Indians.

This internal migration is a very important factor in the future development of the country. There are still sizable extensions of the national territory which are virtually unpopulated. Much of the excess population of the altiplano must be encouraged to go to the East, to unoccupied areas. This is really the only answer to the problem of minifundio, which is a growing one in certain parts of the altiplano. Some of the minifundio problem, if the landholdings are not too small, can be met by improving the technology of the peasants, but some of the landholdings are too small for this to do much good.

One of the most significant things in the countryside is the presence of schools everywhere, in the remotest part of the altiplano. For the most part, these schools have been built by the peasants themselves. One of the major things the peasants are demanding is improvement of the quality of both the primary and secondary schools. In the secondary schools, they want introduction of agricultural subjects, to train their children to be better farmers, which is a good idea indeed.

One of the results of seven years of bad government has been a crisis in the sugar industry. This is a result of the governments paying no attention to what was going on in the area. As a result, there was ruthless deforestation, which has brought climatic changes in the area. The Chaco, which has dry tropical climate ran perhaps to fifty kilometers south of Santa Cruz, but now it is 50 kilometers to the north of Santa Cruz. The result has been terrible for the sugar industry. In addition, they did nothing to get the use of fertilizers and to get more productive strains of cane. The upshot is that this year the country has had to import large quantities of sugar from Brazil.

He would sum up the objectives of the MNR's participation in the Banzer government as being two: first, to bring political stability to the country so that the economic development can go on; the other is to build the party structure.

The University Law which the government has passed he thinks is basically all right. The new University Council has a good representation of Movimientistas, in spite of the Falange controlling the education ministry. Most of the rectors who have so far been appointed are independents. Insofar as professors are concerned, none has been appointed yet, but the names which have been discussed have been to a large degree Movimientistas, although the MNR doesn't broadcast the fact. This is because the Falange has virtually no one in most fields to take these jobs. They have some people in medicine and law, but in the pure sciences and engineering and so on, there are few Falangistas, so either Movimientistas or independents will inevitably get the posts. There are not to be concursos for professorship, because that would take too much time, and because it would mean the return of older conservative professors, with long records, in preference to young and more modern trained people. The basic requirement is three years' experience.

He imagines that opposition to the government will increase once the University is opened again. This is inevitable, since there will be many dissidents in the student body. However, he is not particularly worried about this.

There are many aspects to the reorganization of the party. For instance, next month they are going to open a leadership training school, which will be attended by people from all over the country. Also, parallel to the legal organization of the party, they are setting up an organization which would function in case they were forced again to go underground. This is very necessary in the present circumstances.

With regard to lack of other top leaders than Paz Estenssoro, there is the case of Guillermo Bedregal, who is excellent. However, he encounters very strong resistance both inside and outside the party. Perhaps this is because he is so intelligent. In the politics of these countries, one has to be intelligent, but one must not make it too obvious, or one engenders resistance, and he thinks that this is what happened to Bedregal. Also, the military, of course, will not forgive him his recent book, which was highly critical of the armed forces.

The reconstruction of the labor movement is going forward. He supposes that within another four or five months it will have been completely reestablished, with the COB functioning once again. There is the strange situation that the Falange, which has virtually no support in organized labor, wanted the COB reestablished immediately. Of the old executive of the COB, the majority fled into exile or have otherwise disappeared. There are left eleven Movimientistas and two Falangistas (representing the Bank Clerks Confederation). Since the Falange felt that this was the only way they would be able to get representation in the top echelons of the labor movement, they wanted these thirteen to continue to function as the executive of the COB. The Movimientistas rejected this idea, feeling that the COB should be rebuilt from the bottom, and then have a congress of the COB. This is the way things are proceeding. He is sure that the MNR will have overwhelming control of the COB once it is reconstituted.

Some of the old COB leaders are still around. These include Ireneo Pimentel, the mine union leader, who Paz Estenssoro thinks is now pro-Chinese Communist in sympathy. The mine leader who clearly was of that tendency was Escobar, who died some years ago.

The Falange controls the Ministry of Education. They have been dismissing a sizable number of teachers on all levels who they think disagree with them. They particularly did this in the beginning, although they are not doing so to the same degree now. But the Falange certainly doesn't have the people to fill these posts.

Víctor Paz Estenssoro goes to see President Banzer at Banzer's house, generally in the evenings. He very seldom goes to the presidential palace to see him. It seems more politic that way.

When Paz Estenssoro fell in 1964, his house was sacked, and most of the things in it were burned or disappeared. The only things which were saved were those his wife and a maid had taken to a nearby church for safekeeping. The place where he is now living he is renting from the Banco Hipotecario. It was formerly occupied by ex-Minister of Interior Selich, which is why it became available for him. It was terribly dirty and run down, and had to be repainted.

*   *   *   *   *

LETTER FROM VÍCTOR PAZ ESTENSSORO, BUENOS AIRES, ARGENTINA, FEBRUARY 27, 1974

I received, in La Paz, your latest letter in which, with permanent curiosity for political affairs of these countries, you asked me for information on Bolivian events. Lamentably, the weight of party activities preparing the Convention which should have taken place in January did not permit me to give you an early reply.

Soon after the New Year, things were precipitated. On January 8, I was deported to Paraguay, directly from the office of the Minister of Interior, who had invited me to converse on political matters. After more than a week in Asunción, I came to this capital, with the hope that, as a large city, it would offer greater possibilities of obtaining work. I am engaged in this, and meanwhile, I have some time to send you certain details of the Bolivian situation.

The scheme of the Frente Popular Nacionalista [FNP], about which we conversed before, had implicitly within it certain elements of contradiction. There were the emotional remains of the long struggle with the Falange, as well as substantial strategic and tactical differences on how to act politically on national problems. Also there was the latent opposition of a group of friends of President Banzer, apparently personal friends but in reality representatives of economic interests. Involved were some "middle-sized" mining entrepreneurs, who as such were not affected by the nationalization of 1952. As a result of extraordinary facilities given them by the government of Barrientos, they began to grow, something which was intensified, reaching an accelerated rate, with the exceptional rise in prices of minerals in the world market. For example, the case of tin demonstrates this clearly. In 1963 it was $0.70 a pound. Now it is $3.70.

With the unusual increase of their economic power, they came to want to exercise political power, directly without intermediaries. Thus, they sought to place their managers and lawyers in the most elevated posts in the state apparatus, to dictate measures favorable to their interests. Necessarily, that had to produce divergences with the MNR, made up of peasants, workers, and the middle class. The crisis began to become insupportable with monetary devaluation, which especially interested the mining firms as exporters; taxation, which should have been higher in accord with the higher prices; the proposal to buy the smelter of William Harvey in Liverpool, which was bankrupt, which postponed indefinitely the proposal to expand to 22,000 tons the capacity of the existing smelter in Oruro.

With the Falange and the military, our divergence was based on our opposition to massive and indiscriminate persecution, as well their preference for use of violence in the solution of social conflicts.

The development of these problems brought us, in November 1973, to the decision to retire the MNR from the cabinet, an attitude which had the support of the workers and peasants, as well as many elements of the middle class. Banzer counter-maneuvered, naming as ministers persons who, if it is true that they were inscribed in the party, had a stronger link with the new large mining enterprises and other exporting firms. He also reached out, to make them appear as favoring the continuance of collaboration with his government, to other elements involved in deals under way. In this way, the FPN was maintained, although only in a formal sense.

The dispute was to be finally resolved by the Convention. Certain that it would support separation from the government, Banzer chose forceful measures. He exiled me, and then, using as puppets those I have named, plus a group of public employees, organized a pseudo plenum which postponed the Convention and meanwhile continued participation in the government.

The present Bolivian political situation can be schematized more or less thus: On the one hand, the government maintains the FPN, but this is a pure fiction. The mass of the MNR is not with those who are part of the Frente; even more, they repudiate them. To this must be added the fact that the Falange suffered a considerable split with the exit of Carlos Valverde, who took many of the younger people. The maintenance of the government depends exclusively on the armed forces controlled by Banzer through the high command. In their ranks there are also divisions and some groups that are not in conformity with the government, but, due to the structure of the institution, they cannot express themselves.

Facing them are all of the political parties, the trade union organizations, the professionals, the Church. Among the various events which show the resistance to the latest economic measures, it is worth noting the active opposition of the peasants of Cochabamba, showing that they have acquired a clear political consciousness and don't allow themselves to be manipulated by the pseudo leaders subsidized by the government and, on the other hand, that they are now incorporated into the market economy, having left that of simple subsistence in which they formerly lived.

In personal terms, I have begun my third exile, which will be prolonged I don't know how long. As I said, I am now with the problem of looking for work. If there were any chance to give lectures or to write monographs on various aspects of the present Latin American reality, you would do me a great service in bringing them to my attention.

* * * * *

LETTER FROM VÍCTOR PAZ ESTENSSORO, FROM LIMA, MAY 17, 1975

When I was in Buenos Aires, during the first half of last year, I wrote you a long letter. Later, I was not able to do so, in spite of having this in mind various times. Meanwhile, I received some of your letters. Also, your Christmas and New Year's card. I am, therefore, in debt to you, but my failure to respond opportunely has been absolutely involuntary.

Recent times have been unfortunate for me. I was faced with pressing personal problems, submitted to unavoidable voyages, or incapacitated by illnesses. I have not been able to settle down with certain stability anywhere. My stay in Lima is not definitive. We have stayed here while the last of my daughters completed secondary school in the high school were she had begun, which will happen at the end of this year.

In the last days of December, I travelled to the United States, taking my mentioned daughter for a new checkup in the National Institute of Health of Bethesda...and on that occasion concretized an agreement for doing a work for the United Nations. I was to carry out a study on the impact of economic crisis on the urban marginal groups of the large and medium-sized countries of South America, in a period of four to five months, and visiting each one of them. In spite of the temporary assignment, the theme interested me and the remuneration was good.

When I was preparing to begin the work with a voyage to Santiago, in the first days of February ... I fell ill, suddenly, with intestinal occlusion. An emergency operation showed there was an infection. The result was a great physical decline and a slow recovery. Only recently can I say that I am well, with my health normalized. But as much time had passed before this, the contract with the United Nations, which had a rigid time schedule, was anulled. To carry it out responsibly, I had left my professorship in the National Engineering University. At the present time, I am again with the problem of obtaining work.

All of this with reference to the personal aspect. Insofar as the political situation of Bolivia is concerned, on the government's side, it is a barefaced dictatorship. As you have been able to see from the news, it has announced that it will continue until 1980 and, meanwhile, the political parties have been declared in recess, the greater part of trade union rights have been ignored, they have establish obligatory civil service, which amounts to forced labor or, in case of refusal, prison, etc., etc. The scheme, inspired and perhaps patronized by observes in other nations of the continent, was in gestation since the fall of Allende. The rebellion in Santa Cruz, which for certain reasons was not followed by moves in the other departments, gave Banzer the pretext to establish a completely military government, with dictatorial characteristics, which he planned for.

The real elements of power which sustain Banzer are the armed forces, controlled through the camarilla of the high command, who remain united and are bound by a series of interests of an economic nature. The high prices of raw materials, the new exports such as sugar, cotton, meat, petroleum, gas, wood, and the hard and soft loans contracted abroad, as well as the petroleum investments, have created an economic boom. The government has abundant resources which it distributes among its members and adherents through special expenditures and through high commissions given in the purchases which are made. Furthermore, there has been established an enormous and efficient political information service. Thanks to it, various conspiracies have been thwarted which, if they had gone forward, had great probability of success.

Another important factor which supports Banzer, is a reciprocal exchange of services, the new Rosca, formed by those who were medium-sized mining firms at the time of the nationalization of the mines and which, thanks to the favorable state of the market for metals in recent years, have increased their economic power enormously. To them are added the large agro-industrial entrepreneurs. This intimate relationship is what determines the frankly anti-worker policy of the government.

The international situation also has an important role. There is, without doubt, a Brazil-Bolivia-Chile axis with economic and financial relationships. Brazil needs petroleum and gas as well as certain nonferrous metals which it doesn't have in abundance. In addition, the exit to the Pacific, to reach the immense markets of Asia. The Chilean oligarchy is making investments in the Bolivian lowlands to develop agriculture and grazing. The renewal of relations with Chile was, in my judgment, unfavorable for Bolivia. The interruption of relations was a card in its hand because it bore witness to the existence of the problem of the country's being landlocked. Hence the interest of Chile is reestablishing relations. Having achieved this, without giving Bolivia an exit to the sea, without even promising to solve the problem, Chile has been the gainer. There is a return to the situation before the rupture, controlled by the Treaty of 1904. Banzer is playing with the problem of access to the sea, but if he doesn't achieve an acceptable solution in a reasonable time, the issue will turn against him.

This analysis would seem to demonstrate that the government's situation is completely consolidated. However, that is not the case. The armed forces are not monolithic. On the contrary, there is a fundamental division between the military men of before 1952 and those who graduated from the Military Academy after that year. Furthermore there exist ambitious leaders who want to take Banzer's place, getting power with the advantages that that implies. On the other hand, in the entrepreneurial group there are also some who think that the present rigidly anti-worker policy can be counterproductive in the long run, involving the risk of nationalizations when the present situation comes to an end, which is inevitably going to happen, sooner or later.

The party opposition has been decapitated. Also a substantial number of trade union leaders have been banished. However, there is intense clandestine activity. The bad aspect of this is that, in large degree, it is carried out by the parties of the extreme Left. They have an apparatus in place specially for this type of activity and, furthermore, receive international financing. Since de facto there has been established a union, on the ground, of all opposition parties and groups, the working masses, the great majority of which are not Communist, are being managed by leaders who are. There is the risk that as the present regime continues, the mass will end alienated from the parties to which they belonged.

The political leaders now in exile have established contacts recently. It is possible that from these contacts there will emerge the formation of a tactical alliance to confront the government, seeking to reopen, by whatever means, the institutional channels for political life and achieve the full establishment of trade union rights. To be successful, there will be necessary the installation of a transitory military government which, supported by that coalition, will convoke elections for the branches of government. When that happens there will be a division in the alliance, with the formation on the one side, if possible united, of the national revolutionaries (all of the MNR, as well as the PRA, PRIN, Christian Democrats, etc.), and on the other side those of the extreme Left.

What is in fact going to happen in the next few months and the proximate future? Political prediction is difficult, particularly in a country like Bolivia, where events are precipitated sometimes with appalling rapidity, released by something unpredictable.

Well, I think that with the many lines before this I have brought up to date the correspondence with you. I hope that, in the future, it will be regular.

*   *   *   *   *

CONVERSATION WITH VÍCTOR PAZ ESTENSSORO IN HIS HOUSE IN LIMA, JULY 17, 1975

He thinks that the situation of Bolivian President Banzer will get worse after August 6, the fourth anniversary of his coming to power. Banzer was in most difficulty a year ago June, when young officers in fact seized power, but then bargained with Banzer, who conceded all they were asking. But when it was over, he jailed a number of the leaders of the young officers. Some are out of the Army now, a few are in exile.

There are differences within the Army between the pre-1952 generations and the post-1952 ones. The latter are the product of the Revolution, and they realize it. He thinks that they may move after August 6.

Banzer is raising the issue of a seaport for Bolivia in order to raise support for his regime. However, this campaign is certain to come to naught, and it will backfire on Banzer. The issue interests Brazil, which wants an exit on the Pacific, to develop its trade with the Orient, particularly China. Chile might give a free port in Arica, but it is not going to transfer sovereignty.

Brazil is now building a road from Corumba to Santa Cruz. With this connection, there will be complete connection between the Brazilian coast and Arica.

Banzer's regime is very much under Brazilian influence. There is a reaction against this, particularly among intellectuals, but so far they can't do anything about it.

All political parties are suspended legally until 1980. The main leaders are exiled, including not only Paz but Siles, Guevara Arce, Lechín, Benjamin Miguel of the Christian Democrats, Valverde of the Falange, and others. However, the parties still exist underground. The MNR is more or less united underground, the Paz, Siles, and other factions working together. Ciro Humboldt tried to maintain a faction of the party with the government, but he was finally purged. The last underground leader of the MNR was a priest, who was jailed and then exiled to the eastern jungle. The MNR has an underground National Executive. All party groups are working together in the underground, including the MNR of Paz, the MNR de Izquierda of Siles, the PRA of Guevara Arce, the

Lechinistas, the Christian Democrats, the Valverde wing of the Falange. Mario Gutierrez of the Falange is still with the government, is Permanent Delegate to the United Nations, and so is totally discredited politically.

The Banzer government's clash with the peasants last year was very significant. The peasants have always been submissive to each successive government, largely because they had leaders who were not really peasants. The first Paz government had gotten villagers to organize and lead the peasants, and they became corrupt. So they worked with each successive regime. However, the clash with the peasants in Cochabamba last year indicated that there is now a new younger leadership, not willing to work any longer with the government. Also the clash was significant because the issue over which it occurred was a rise in the prices of bread, butter, and other products, which indicates that the peasants are now in the market.

It is not only the Cochabamba peasants who are in the market. There have been remarkable changes around Lake Titicaca and in the Yungas. The peasants bargain in the markets with the lambs which they bring in on their bicycles, with the lamb slung around their necks. They buy considerable amounts of goods. They are also willing to sell their sheep and wool now, so that sheep are no longer just a social status symbol.

He thinks that the next government won't be a civilian one. He doesn't believe in the possibility of a popular insurrection. So the next regime will be a military one, with a different orientation, that of paving the way toward a return to a real constitutional regime.

Banzer's government, of course, started out as that. The problem was the elections which were scheduled. They were planning to constitutionalize the regime with elections, in which he would be the candidate supported by the MNR and the Falange. They had worked out an Uruguayan kind of electoral system, with lemas and sub-lemas. The lema would be the Frente Popular Nacionalista, the sub-lemas the MNR and Falange. The military, however, wanted a single ticket for all posts, which the MNR refused. The peasants told Paz that if he and the MNR had a joint ticket with the Falange for posts beneath the presidency, they would not vote. Paz was called to a meeting with the military command, to try to get him to agree to a joint ticket with the Falange, but he refused.

Banzer then met with military leaders in Cochabamba to discuss the election. Most high officers agreed that although the cities were against the government, Banzer could win with the peasant vote. However, one young officer said that that wasn't true, which caused consternation in the meeting. So they adjourned for a few weeks to make secret sounding among the peasants. These confirmed what the young officer had said, so the elections were canceled.

Banzer is a clever politician. He knows how to maneuver, he is ruthless, and he is opportunistic.

Barrientos has been very much discredited. They had tried to build up a Barrientos mystique, and Banzer pictured himself as the successor of Barrientos. However, the disclosure that Barrientos had taken a bribe from Gulf created a situation in which no one wanted to claim any relationship with him. However, there are a number of Barrientistas in the government and in ambassadorial positions. For instance, Sanjines, former Ambassador to Washington, now Ambassador to Peru, is one.

Bolivia is part of a three-cornered armament race with Peru and Chile.

Banzer says he is arming to maintain Bolivian neutrality in case of war between Peru and Chile. However, this is silly, since either of those countries could walk over Bolivia in no time. These expenditures are a waste; they are buying "old iron."

The real danger in Bolivia is something like what has been occurring in Portugal, although, of course, no two situations are exactly the same. The Communists are the only ones with a really solid underground organization. The other parties were organized mainly out in the open; their real leaders were well known and most of them have been deported. The Communists, in contrast, had real leaders who were not known. All are very active now. The pro-Moscow party has funds from the Soviet Union; the pro-Peking one receives money from China, the far Left receives money from the ERP in Argentina, from its ransoms and robberies. There was a small pro-Peking guerrilla movement in the northern part of Santa Cruz.

It is these far Left parties which are now assuming leadership of the unions. Other union leaders are too obvious, or have been deported or jailed.

Banzer has invented what he calls compulsory civil service. If you are named to a city council or to a position in a ministry, or to lead a union, you have to serve or go to jail. As a result, the trade unions have been taken over by the government, with "coordinators" being appointed. Some workers have refused to serve and have gone to jail. Those who have accepted are discredited.

A few days ago the government picked up the Executive Committee of the clandestine Central Obrera Bolivana. Almost all the members were Communists, except for three peasant leaders, who were MNR. But this shows that the Communists have assumed the leadership, and other parties have to accept this.

There is a danger, therefore, that when the present military regime is overthrown, the only organized force will be the Communist parties. Their leaders won't appear to be politicians, but will come out as leaders of the labor and peasant movements. The longer the present situation goes on, the more likely the emergence of the Communists in this way will be.

The Communists won't have one of their own members as leader and candidate for president, but rather someone apparently not associated with them. For instance, it might be Hernán Siles, who is now on the extreme Left, which is ironic because he was on the far Right of the MNR. Last November, Siles was in La Paz and joined, under protest, a united front with all parties from the Falange to the Communist Party. But then he was deported to Chile, where he renewed his contacts with the far Left, and now he is talking the language of the far Left again.

It is true that the far Left is very much divided. For instance, Guillermo Lora was thrown out of the Lora POR as an entregista, a pro-imperialist. He is now in Oxford. His three-volume history of the Bolivian labor movement has been published in English, in England.

The government here in Peru is moving to the Right. The influence of the prime minister, General Morales Bermúdez, is growing. He is a real prime minister. President Velasco is sick, leaving much up to Morales Bermúdez. One day Velasco may decide to retire, or Morales Bermúdez, having all of the effective power in his hands, will make Velasco retire. Perhaps it is not quite correct to say that the government is moving to the Right, but that it is purging the Communists who had infiltrated the regime.

The agrarian reform here is real. It certainly is so on the coast, in the sugar plantations, which are called cooperatives but are really government firms. These are working very well.

The students here are largely dominated by the pro-Peking Communists. This is certainly true in the Engineering University, where he was formerly teaching, and where many of the professors are also on the far Left.

*   *   *   *   *

LETTER FROM VÍCTOR PAZ ESTENSSORO, FROM LIMA, NOVEMBER 5, 1975

I have not had news from you since your stay here last July, when, in conformity with your permanent search for information, it was a pleasure for me to converse about the political situation of various South American nations and especially Bolivia. I suppose that now you are involved in your academic labors, without abandoning work on a new book about the changing reality of these countries.

With the objective of writing a work on the economic policy of the Bolivian National Revolution, I have sought a grant from the Woodrow Wilson International Center for Scholars in Washington. To fulfill one of the requirements in the application form, I took the liberty of mentioning you as one who could pass judgment on my capacity to carry out the project. I did so because of the knowledge you have of the material, because of the publication of your book on the Bolivian Revolution, and your keeping track subsequently of political developments, keeping up constantly with the current information. Also a factor --I must confess-- was the hope for benevolence in your judgment, because of your personal knowledge. In advance, then, my thanks for what you say with respect to this.

A considerable amount has been produced about the Bolivian Revolution, since your book, which continues to be the basic reference work. However, so far, nothing has been written, more or less fully and systematically, with a vision from inside the process. That is what I propose to do, making use of knowledge of the intentions, subjective aspects, and other materials resulting from my having been one of the principal actors. The structure of the outline for the work which I sent with my application is tentative and in no way should be considered as rigid. I adopted it provisionally to cover all aspects which the work should include. The definitive form I shall give, if they give me the grant, taking into account the totality of the material which I succeeded in gathering.

Given your continuing interest in the things of Bolivia, I think that it would not be superfluous, by means of this letter, to give you some news. In spite of the tranquility which exists, with an apparent consolidation of the regime in its present form, several important events are expected in the near future. The government recently has been playing with the question of the exit to the sea, as one of its principal cards to distract public attention and, insofar as possible, rally it to its support. Among the various steps, acts and gestures, the most remarkable has been the interview of Banzer and Pinochet in Charaña to reestablish relations.

The justification that is given is that this will soon happen. But now it turns out that the conversations between the Foreign Ministries have reached a deadlock, without the possibility of a favorable agreement immediately. In the face of this virtual failure, Banzer will have to confront the reaction of the military groups, which accepted with great reticence the 180 degree change in international position implied by the new and apparently close friendship with Chile. Its possible result is a new turn toward rupture of relations. On the other hand, with the fall in prices of minerals, cotton, and sugar, the economic boom has ended. The treasury and the exporters, which had been accustomed to a high level of income, are in difficulty. Now there is discussion of a new monetary devaluation and other measure to deal with the crisis. It is said that to adopt them, some civilians will be brought into the cabinet. If these predictions become a reality, there will have been demonstrated once more the extraordinary fluidity of politics in Bolivia. The situation is so singular that the characteristics of the government model adopted a year ago, in spite of its international support, has not lasted in its basic form.

* * * * *

LETTER FROM VÍCTOR PAZ ESTENSSORO, FROM WASHINGTON, D.C., JULY 18, 1977

I refer to your letter of the 12th of this month. My receipt of it was very welcome to thus renew our correspondence, and also for your interesting comments on my coloquium at the Woodrow Wilson Center.

During my stay at the Center, I wrote a very extensive text in Spanish. With economic policies as its central theme, I wanted to make as comprehensive a presentation as possible of the process of the Bolivian National Revolution, insisting above all on those aspects in which knowledge from inside was important. Lamentably, time did not permit me to finish it. I allowed myself to be seduced by some new perspectives which I discovered while doing the research. I shall attempt to finish the work when I have a little time. I must revise it in general and develop some parts that are in rough draft, to complete the total structure of the work.

The paper I sent you was written in compliance with one of the regulations of the Center, for cases in which the principal work is done in another language. Furthermore, when I was there I found that almost all of the fellows didn't have the least idea of Bolivian events, being interested in other fields of research and also because of general lack of attention to Latin America which has been prevalent in recent years. So I had the idea of putting aside the contents and sequence of the Spanish text, to write a document which was a kind of primer on the Bolivian Revolution. Therefore, I necessarily had to be a bit superficial, but with a wide scope insofar as subjects touched upon, so as to give a complete vision of what had happened, and of the determining factors in it.

With regard to the specific point about the Alliance for Progress mentioned by you, it is evident that one can say that there was excessive simplification in phraseology. It is the result of a desire to summarize and my difficulty in handling English. It is true that years before the appearance of Castro on the Latin American scene, many of the ideas had been put forward which were systematized, coordinated, and complemented and constituted the core of the Alliance. The requirement to organize a regional bank, made in the Economic Conference of 1957, in Buenos Aires; the proposals of President Kubitschek in 1958, concretized in Operation Panamerica, can be cited, among others. However, the attitude of the United States was not favorable to accepting Latin American initiatives until the urgency of neutralizing the impact of the Cuban Revolution was made clear, particularly in the social field.

From last February to June I was at UCLA as a Visiting Professor. I gave a course on the contemporary history of South America. More specifically, it dealt with the period between 1920 and 1975. The idea of limiting it only to South America, and the period of about half a century, was my personal decision. Within those limits I could provide an original presentation because of the experiences I had to a greater or less degree with South American affairs in those years. I have been an actor in some of these events, I had personal relationships with many of the other protagonists and I was a conscious witness to the events, and had special interest in politics and economics. Additionally, I could point out that the 1920-1975 period has exceptional importance because it was then, to a large degree, that the present reality of that part of the continent took shape.

The period mentioned was divided to deal with it methodically, in the following sub-periods: (1) Liquidation of the effects of World War I and the false prosperity of the 1920s; (2) the world depression of the 30's and its consequences; (3) World War II; (4) readjustment to new conditions: 1945–1960; (5) countervailing currents: 1960–1975; (6) the present period and prospects of the future. In each of these periods, the approach was to first take South America as a whole, and then particularization by country. Previously, in view of exogenous factors, as a point of reference, mention was made at appropriate points in the chronology to significant events on a world scale and/or in the United States, which had a decisive influence on the region, particularly insofar as the economy is concerned.

The course, which was for graduate students in history, economics, social sciences and political science, aroused great interest. There were thirty regular students who continued to the end. There were in addition a good number of people who audited it. It was given in Spanish so as not to reduce its quality because of my imperfect knowledge of English.

In addition to the course, in Los Angeles, I edited the text of an oral history project which years before had been recorded by Professor James Wilkie. Also, we had with Professor Bruce Herrick of Economics a small seminar on the experiences with planning in development in South America.

Certainly next January I shall return to UCLA. Meanwhile, since I continue exiled and the economic conditions in Peru are terrible, I am looking for the possibility of teaching a course more or less like the UCLA one, or some other type of work, in one of the universities in the East, for the semester beginning in September.

Well, I think that I have brought you up to date on my stay in the United States. Now I shall tell you something of what I know about Bolivian politics. That is not much, since I have been concentrating on work of a different sort.

The information on the situation is absolutely contradictory, both in what concerns the economy and politics. On the one hand, there is an extremely optimistic vision, based on the boom in construction, the high level of employment, the confidence of the credit sources, insofar as the economy is concerned. Order, stability, and the total control of the situation by the government, insofar as politics is concerned. Therefore, things in the immediate future will develop according to the lines laid down by the government.

At the other extreme, the critics point out that the level of external debt has surpassed the capacity of the national economy, that the fiscal deficit is growing and a new monetary devaluation is pending; that there is high concentration of income in a very small circle, while the great majority of the populace has suffered a real decline in its level of living; that administrative corruption, especially on a high level, has reached, for its magnitude and openness, a level not known before in Bolivian life. Insofar as the political situation is concerned, beneath apparent tranquility, there are conspiratorial movements both of the military graduated since 1952, and of elements of the regime closely associated with them, who seek a relatively suave transition to protect their own personal profits.

It is difficult to say which of these presentations is correct, and even more, to make a prediction. Bolivia has always been an unpredictable country insofar as its politics is concerned, because of the number of imponderables there are in it. What I can reasonably say is that if the attitude of the American government toward human rights is to a certain degree implemented, that may give rise to an electoral opening, although it will be more or less manipulated. Bolivia, for many characteristics and circumstances, is the weakest link in the chain of military dictatorships of the continent.

*   *   *   *   *
*   *   *   *   *

CONVERSATION WITH HERNÁN SILES IN HIS VICE PRESIDENTIAL OFFICE IN LA PAZ, JULY 31, 1954

They are carrying out here a fundamental revolution, which they hope will have lessons for other countries in a similar situation. However, they are faced with tremendous difficulties. The country is heterogeneous in geography, with very different temperatures and resources in the different parts of the country. With the mountains, it is harder to build roads and other types of transportation than it is in most parts of the world. Then, too, there is great heterogeneity in population, with at least two very distinct racial groups here. All of these things present great problems to the Revolution.

The most fundamental part of the Revolution is the agrarian reform. They are giving land to all of the Indians and are breaking the chains of servitude under which this great majority of the people lived. They are incorporating the Indians into the life of the country. All of this involves some two million people. They hope that it will not only bring freedom for these people, but that it will also bring greater political stability for the country as a whole.

He was the leader of the Revolution in April 1952. The military leader of the revolt took refuge in an embassy. However, the decision to continue fighting after this occurred was taken not only by Siles, but by all of the civilian leaders of the uprising.

The question of La Razón is a complicated one. First of all, in the face of the movement to give freedom to the two million people who were virtually slaves here, the problem of La Razón is of minor importance. In the second place, La Razón was the spokesman for those who had kept the Indians in slavery, and it was always on the side of those who were shooting down the workers and peasants. As a result, the mass of the people had a tremendous hatred for La Razón. As in 1943, at the time of the Villarroel Revolution, the people attacked the building of La Razón, and he, as representative of his party, went down there and convinced the people to let the paper alone. Now, if the government were to allow La Razón to open again--and they did take that decision once--the only way it would be able to publish would be if there were a cordon of troops around it who, sooner or later, would have to fire on the people. He does not see why they should shoot down their own people in order to defend their principal enemy. This enemy, if given complete freedom, would again begin to plot against the regime.

There will probably be elections next year for Congress, and the following year for the presidency. As the constitution now stands, the president cannot be reelected. However, constitutions can be changed, and he thinks it would be a good idea to change this one. Four years is not enough really to carry out a program, particularly when a good part of the time must be spent in putting down attempts at rebellion.

As to the constitutionality of this regime, it has more claim than any other to be constitutional. In 1951, the MNR won the election, but the government counted only the earlier ballots. When these showed that the MNR had won, there was a coup d'état and an end was put to the counting of the ballots. This regime now has more claim to be constitutional than any other because it has incorporated into the civic life of the nation the majority of the people, who back it.

The Communists have said that Siles heads the right wing of the MNR. In the same way, the Falange has said that there is a Communist element in the MNR. This is an attempt to divide the government and the party. There is no doubt that there are personal ambitions in politics; that is only human. However, the party now is united in its desire to carry out its basic program: to put the nation's resources in the hands of the nation, to end servitude and give the Indians the land they work, and to diversify the country's economy, so that it will not depend solely on the export of minerals. These are the things they are carrying out. After them, the party may well break up on other issues; this is very possible. But so long as they are carrying out these parts of its program, they remain united.

Siles himself has done and proposed things which might classify him as left-wing. In the Agrarian Reform Commission, for instance, he urged that each Indian be given a piece of land and a gun to defend it with. At the present time, he is head of the Planning Commission, which is drawing up a long-range plan for four to six years. This might seem to be patterned after Russia, but it is not so; it is only a logical thing for a country such as this to do to develop its resources. On the other hand, Siles is not a Marxist and makes no bones about it. He is just a Christian, which perhaps might make him a conservative, at least in some people's eyes.

*   *   *   *   *

TALK BY HERNÁN SILES AT SOLIDARITY MEETING FOR PARTIDO REVOLUCIONARIO DOMINICANO IN SANTO DOMINGO, DOMINICAN REPUBLIC, AUGUST 15, 1978

He wants to thank Partido Revolucionario Dominicano and the Socialist International for their solidarity with Bolivia at the time of recent attempts to maintain the dictatorship there. A quarter of a century ago the workers of the cities, mines, and countryside, in the Movimiento Nacionalista Revolucionario, institutionalized pluralistic democracy in Bolivia comparable to the Mexican Revolution.

Later, this revolutionary effort in Bolivia, a landlocked and backward country in which there was intervention by Washington and Brasilia, resulted in the return of dictatorship, corruption, and persecutions. But the seeds of the 1952 Revolution, in spite of the force used against it, found renewal of the anti-imperialist anti-feudal struggle through the coalition of opposition forces, the Unión Democrática y Popular [UDP]. This mobilization included the workers of the countryside and mines, and the youth. It resulted in an electoral triumph earlier this year, which was not admitted by the military and the entrepreneurial group controlling the country. But the Unión Democrática y Popular continues in its struggle. They are willing to undergo any sacrifice to restore the rights of the people, the rights of all the people of Latin America.

In this struggle which is being renewed, he is sure that the dictatorship will have to call new elections. It will try again to engage in misinformation and fraud, and those struggling against the dictatorship will need the solidarity of the Socialist International and of its parties, and of sister countries in Latin America, Europe, Africa, and Asia. In this connection, he wants particularly to recognize the help that the Bolivian struggle has gotten from the people and government of Venezuela-- support both for the political struggle and for Bolivia's right to an exit to the sea.

He promises in the name of the Unión Democrática y Popular its solidarity with the Dominican PRD. This solidarity is being offered from all over America, because the Dominican problem is a problem of all America.

*   *   *   *   *

CONVERSATION WITH HERNÁN SILES IN HOTEL SHERATON, SANTO DOMINGO, DOMINICAN REPUBLIC, AUGUST 15, 1978

In 1971 the MNR group led by Víctor Paz Estenssoro betrayed the party principles and allied itself with the Falange and the reactionary wing of the Army under Banzer. So it had to share responsibility for the repression of the workers, students, and others, and for the massacre of peasants in Cochabamba.

When this year's election approached, Paz Estenssoro approached Siles for an electoral arrangement on the presidential and vice presidential nominations. But Siles had already joined the Unión Democrática y Popular, consisting of the MNR of the Left, the MIR, a part of the Partido Socialista, the pro-Moscow Communist Party, and a peasant political group. He couldn't dissociate from the Unión Democrática y Popular, so negotiations with Estenssoro fell through.

The UDP is in effect the reconstruction of the multiclass alliance which was the MNR in 1952. Its purpose is to continue and to expand the Revolution which was started in 1952.

The Partido Comunista de Bolivia [PCB] is the pro-Moscow wing of the Communist Party. It is very much opposed to Maoist wing, which wants to use violence to seize power. It supports his party's position to trying to get power through peaceful means, and it says that it is free of international control.

The UDP really won a strong majority in the recent election. It won 72 percent in the Department of La Paz, and also won in Chuquisaca (Sucre) and Potosí. Víctor Paz won in Tarija, Pando, and Santa Cruz. The Christian Democrats, led by General Bernal, won in Cochabamba and Oruro. Thus, General Pereda didn't win in a single department, although the government officially claimed that he won the election.

The Banzer government carried out the most outrageous fraud. Even observers the government itself had brought in testified to this fraud. In one voting precinct, for instance, the Movimiento Democratico Popular [MDP] got 242 of the 300 votes and the rest were spread among the other candidates. But the government reported that Pereda had gotten 242 votes and the rest were spread among the other candidates. This kind of thing was repeated by the thousands throughout Bolivia. Each voting precinct has 300 voters.

He thinks that the hunger strike he launched soon after the election brought down Banzer. This was good, because it meant that there was an obvious split within the military.

He thinks that the only alternative for the government is to call new elections. All of the opposition political parties are calling for this, all but Paz Estenssoro demanding new elections within six months. Paz says that they should be held within a year.

If new elections are held, as he expects, this time they will be relatively without fraud, because the government won't be able to repeat what happened this year. In that case, the MDP will have an even stronger vote than it had this time, and the result will be in fact a renewal of the Revolution of 1952.

As a result of the situation, he is now moderately optimistic.

*   *   *   *   *
*   *   *   *   *

CONVERSATION WITH RENÉ BARRIENTOS IN MUNICIPAL BUILDING, LA PAZ, APRIL, 9, 1952

The old military forces of Bolivia were destroyed in the April 1952 Revolution. He and a small group of others began immediately the work of rebuilding the armed forces after the April Revolution. By 1953 the work was well advanced and then the decision to reestablish the armed forces was officially made.

The Air Force was before a part of the Army. It was separated in 1957 and is now entirely independent.

*   *   *   *   *

TALK BY RENÉ BARRIENTOS IN SPECIAL MEETING OF MNR POLITICAL COMMITTEE, IN LA PAZ, CELEBRATING TENTH ANNIVERSARY OF BOLIVIAN NATIONAL REVOLUTION, APRIL 10, 1962

Before April 9, 1952, Bolivia was dominated by the minero-feudal group. It made and unmade governments, and the armed forces were only the instrument of this group. However, the great mass of the people, the Indians, were virtually slaves of the landowners. They had no voice in the government, with only about 200,000 literates being entitled to vote. Those military men who broke with the ruling oligarchy, such as Germán Busch and Gualberto Villarroel, were quickly done away with.

Since 1952 there has been a complete change in the social structure of Bolivia. The land has been taken from the Rosca and has been given to the peasants. The Indians have been given the right to vote. Education has been taken to them. At the same time, the armed forces have been rebuilt, with their roots in the people. They are very strong, but they are now playing their key role in carrying out the basic transformation through which Bolivia is now passing.

* * * * *
* * * * *

CONVERSATION WITH LUÍS ADOLFO SILES AT MY HOME IN NEW BRUNSWICK, NEW JERSEY, DECEMBER 30, 1955

The Siles family is very much divided politically. Hernán is vice president; another brother is a leader of the Falange Socialista Boliviana and is in exile in Chile, teaching at the Catholic University in Valparaíso; and Luís is a Social Catholic, affiliated with a new Christian Democratic Party in Bolivia.

He does not sympathize too much with the present government. He thinks that the agrarian reform is a very good thing, but there are other aspects of the regime which are very bad. In particular, he thinks that they have gone entirely too far in their suppression of the opposition, and they have shown an exceptional lack of administrative ability.

It is true that every government in Bolivia has mistreated its opponents, and to a certain degree this is necessary, given the situation there, in order to maintain stability. However, the Movimiento has gone entirely too far. There is a whole series of concentration camps in which things are done of which he has not even read about in Jan Valtin and other books which have come out about the situation in Europe since World War II. One of his closest friends was brutally mistreated for many months in one of these concentration camps and was made to beat his fellow party members in one of them. He has subsequently been released.

As to administrative ability, it is also true that with a few exceptions-- his father being one, when he was president--Bolivia has not produced statesmen who were good administrators. But this situation is exaggerated in the present regime. For instance, the Corporación Minera, which took over the Big Three mining companies and is the biggest mining enterprise in the world, is so badly administered that it is losing between five and six billion bolivianos a month--which is more money than was issued from the time of independence until the Movimiento came to power.

He does not think very much of Paz Estenssoro. He is a cold, calculating man. And he has permitted things to take place which Siles has described. He does not think that he is at all indispensable.

Siles's brother Hernán is now going to be the candidate for president. Hernán sincerely does not want to run for the job. He has just returned home, and he told Luís that he was going to urge Paz to run again. However, Paz wants him to run, and in spite of the somewhat cool relations between Hernán Siles and Lechín, the latter is also backing Hernán Siles for the post.

Luís Siles does not understand why the government has been so violent against its opponents. It does not have to be because the opposition is very badly split and disorganized. He suspects that it is due partly to the fact that the Movimientistas themselves were badly treated for six years and they are taking revenge, but it is very bad in any case.

The old parties are very much on the rocks. The only one which can give a certain amount of effective opposition to the regime is the Falange. It is an extremely right-wing organization and is not so good.

There is a dangerous situation in Bolivia today. The overwhelming majority of the people are Indians. They are ignorant and are not subject to the city or its pressures--growing and building and making of the products they use. Furthermore, the influence of the white group is much less than before, since they have been badly discredited by past regimes. The middle class is small and disorganized. Now they are going to have elections in which even the illiterates can vote, and they don't know just how to control this mass of Indians. The Movimientistas themselves are upset by the situation.

The agrarian reform is going along pretty well. It has taken place with much less violence and bloodshed than the agrarian reforms of Mexico and China. It has not been as serious from the point of view of displacing a group which really contributed something to the economy and the nation as did these other two, since the Bolivian landlord was largely an absentee, drawing his income from the land, but in no way directing the agricultural process himself.

Bolivians know virtually nothing about the United States. They know about Wall Street and Hollywood, and that is about all. They have the impression that the United States is interested in efficiency and the increase in the productivity of labor but has no interest in human relations. He has been here just about a month, studying labor relations in this country. Although most of his contacts so far have been with "Wall Street," he is coming more and more to the conclusion that this Bolivian view of the United States is not true.

*   *   *   *   *

CONVERSATION WITH LUÍS ADOLFO SILES IN HOTEL SUCRE PALACE, LA PAZ, AUGUST 23, 1956

The elections have shown a change in the situation here. After the Revolution, the opposition was disbanded and demoralized, and virtually all public opinion was with the MNR. The only alternative to the MNR seemed to be the Communists. Now there is another alternative, the Falange Socialista Boliviana. The State Department, which is a factor to consider in the Bolivian situation, must take this into account, and perhaps will change its policy of backing the MNR.

The elections showed that about 130,000 of the 150,000 people who were able to vote before 1952 have voted for the Falange. The middle class has completely abandoned the MNR.

He doesn't think that the united front of the miners, workers, and peasants, which has been the backbone of the MNR, will last much longer. Now a revolt attempt could still bring the peasants down upon La Paz, but he is not sure how much this would be true within another year.

There are undoubtedly elements which are still plotting against the government, among the old landlords, the Army, and the mining interests. But he does not think that the Falange is doing this. It has become much more democratic and has taken the road of legality and reconciliation. It now has the possibility of getting to power legally. The FSB has evolved a great deal since 1952.

His Partido Social Democrático [PSD] has two elements, one following a Marxism a la Laski, the other Social Christian, to which Siles belongs. A number of young people who became disillusioned in the possibility of converting the PSD into a Social Christian Party have launched the Partido Social Cristiano. It is very small. Meanwhile, the PSD has had the cream of the professional classes in its ranks. There is now some possibility of merging with the FSB, and conversations to this end have been under way for some time. The FSB has become much more democratic, although in the beginning it was frankly totalitarian, being more or less in the line of the Spanish Falange.

The persecution of the opposition by the Paz Estenssoro government was the worst in Bolivian history. The kind of things which went on in Europe during World War II were done here under Paz. However, the situation has improved in recent months. There was an amnesty a few months before the election, although many of the exiles are afraid to come back. There are now two elements in the government. His brother's group favors amnesty and reconciliation, the other faction wants drastic measures against the opposition.

The positive side of the MNR Revolution is that it has aroused the consciousness of the Indian peasants. But that could have been done without arousing class and race hatred in the way it has been aroused under the MNR regime.

*   *   *   *   *

CONVERSATION WITH LUÍS ADOLFO SILES, IN NATIONAL PALACE OF SANTO DOMINGO, DOMINICAN REPUBLIC, AUGUST 16, 1978

He was out of politics quite a while after the late 1950s. He was devoting his time to university teaching, and he built up quite a following among students and young professional people.

He was chosen by René Barrientos as his vice presidential candidate because although Barrientos was strong in the countryside, he was weak in the cities, particularly among the intellectuals. In that sense, they made a good ticket.

He had problems with Barrientos almost from the beginning of their term. These were mainly over human rights problems. Barrientos would jail people, and Siles would try to get them out. Also, he opposed a number of laws restricting human rights which Barrientos had passed.

Most people are now agreed that Barrientos was killed in an accident.

When Ovando became so oppressive afterward, people thought that he had had Barrientos murdered. But most people don't think so now. Even Barrientos's family thinks that his death was accidental.

Barrientos couldn't stay still. He couldn't see a movie through. He was abnormally active. Also, he didn't like administrative duties. So he took off to all parts of the country. He particularly liked to spend time with the peasants. He spoke Quechua, and he would appear in an isolated Indian village, eating with the peasants. This had a great psychological impact, although he didn't really do very much materially for them. Barrientos undoubtedly had charisma.

Siles proposed to Barrientos that he, Siles, do the administrative work of the presidency and that Barrientos do the political side of the job. But Barrientos rejected the idea. He tended to centralize everything in his own hands.

Siles knew that he would be overthrown by General Ovando. Right after the death of Barrientos, Ovando came to see him, and Siles told Ovando that he needed Ovando's support because he had no base in the Army and had problems with Congress. Ovando laid down twelve conditions, which would have made Siles a veritable puppet. This took place in Cochabamba, and he told Ovando that he would reply when he got back to La Paz. There was also an attempt to kill him while he was in Cochabamba. He did not agree to Ovando's conditions, and thereafter he had a number of other crises with Ovando before Ovando finally overthrew him.

He has become active in the Unión Democrática y Popular, headed by Hernán Siles. He was elected senator from La Paz on its ticket. But of course, he never took office, since the election results were cancelled.

He is optimistic about the situation in Bolivia. He thinks that the military regime has been weakened by three things in 1978. First, it was weakened by the hunger strike early in the year, which was started by three women, but which Luis Adolfo Siles organized. This hunger strike forced the election. The second setback for the military was the result of the election itself and the third setback was the fact that General Pereda seized power, which severely split the military.

Pereda has virtually no civilian support. He has had difficulty in getting members in his cabinet.

It will be hard for Luis Adolfo Siles ever to be president again. He has no party; he also lacks any base in the military.

* * * * *
* * * * *

CONVERSATION WITH WALTER GUEVARA ARCE IN HIS OFFICE IN LA PAZ, JULY 23, 1968

The whole cause of the downfall of the Movimiento Nacionalista Revolucionario was the personalism of Víctor Paz Estenssoro. He confused the Revolution with himself. Where Luis XIV said I Am the State, Víctor Paz said I Am the Revolution. He followed a policy of divide and rule within the party.

The situation which existed reminds him of Dante's Inferno, and the circles of Hell. In the center was Víctor Paz Estenssoro. In the first circle around him was a group of gangsters, like General San Román, the police chief. In the next circle were the demagogues like Juan Lechín. Finally, in the third circle, on the outside, were good people of the party.

The MNR government passed through various phases. Its real accomplishments, insofar as the Revolution was concerned, were in the first four years, the first term of Victor Paz. He could do nothing because of the economic situation which he faced, so it was also a period of marking time.

If it had not been for Victor Paz, the Bolivian Revolution could have followed the Mexican model. The revolutionary party could have stayed in power almost indefinitely. With different administrations, each would have had its own emphasis. But Victor Paz wouldn't allow this.

The errors of the Revolution were many. Basically, they never went beyond the first step of the Revolution. There was need after the first Paz Estenssoro administration for administrative changes and economic changes.

For instance, there was one absurdity in the agrarian reform. The law provided that every title deed granted by the government had to be signed by the president. This not only meant an absurd centralization of the process, but also meant that it was physically impossible to grant titles with sufficient rapidity. It would have taken scores of years, signing two title deeds a minute for the president to have signed all that should have been issued. There should have been a more decentralized process, whereby deeds could be issued by agrarian reform officials in the departmental capitals. Only those questions over which there was dispute should have come to La Paz, and in the last instance, to the president. But this part of the law was put in because Victor Paz wanted to be able to say to the peasants that he had given them their land.

There was also need for moves to bring the peasants into the market. Like peasants all over the world, they are essentially very conservative. They must be shown that efficiency and new methods and practices are worthwhile. For instance, an Indian is used to letting part of his land lie fallow for seven years, and he won't change, other things being equal, because he has always done it that way, his father did, his grandfather did, and so on. But the government should have had people who would go out, get his permission to experiment with fertilizer on the part which the Indian thought should lay fallow, and when they saw the results, the peasants would have been convinced.

There were other grave errors of the Revolution. These included the concentration camps which were maintained, the sending of people into exile. Victor Paz followed the carrot and stick policy, offering people the alternative of some job or other and loyalty to him, or persecution. Most, quite naturally, took the job.

But Paz Estenssoro was ruthless with the opposition, particularly in his second period. For instance, at Caliza, where the Partido Revolucionario Auténtico of Guevara Arce won in 1960, Paz sent in troops who burned down the houses of the peasants and blew up their wells. In another rural area, fields were burned, some of the peasants were killed and others were wounded, and their houses were burned down.

These are not things which Guevara Arce is saying for the first time in 1968. He said them in 1960, when he broke with the MNR. He saw what was happening and warned against it even before he broke with the party.

The agrarian reform wasn't forced on the government. He knows, because he was a member of the first Paz Estenssoro government and participated in its decisions. The MNR came to power in 1952 with the full intention to have an agrarian reform. Where there was seizure of land by the peasants, this was because it was encouraged and stimulated by the government.

By 1964, the civilian political forces had been completely atomized by Paz Estenssoro. The only force left was the Army. When Paz, under United States pressure to do something about the situation in the mines, ordered in the Army to the mining areas, the military refused to take this drastic step for the benefit of Paz Estenssoro, which was quite natural. They overthrew him, and they did this for their own benefit.

The Army is now the only effective political party in the country. It is acting like a political party which wants to continue in office, with General Ovando, or with someone else. All efforts to convince them of the danger to the Army itself of such a policy have failed. The situation has become such that every high officer in the Army is head of his own "party."

The forces of the Revolution are still the great majority of the people. They ought to be reorganized to carry on the process which was started in 1952. However, they cannot be reorganized on the basis of what is left of the MNR. Rather, all of the MNR factions, as well as the PRIN, the PRA, and other groups which support the basic program of the Revolution, should be brought together in a new grouping which can make a fresh start.

However, under present conditions, even if such a move were possible, there is no assurance that it would be successful. It couldn't win an election because the Army would use the system established by Victor Paz Estenssoro to "win" any election for its own candidate. The only hope would be if the Army would agree to retire to the barracks and preside over an honest election, which would certainly be won by a regrouping of the revolutionary forces. In such an election, the forces of the Revolution would face the Falange and other elements of the old regime, and the result would be certain, a victory for the revolutionary forces.

However, this doesn't seem very likely under the present circumstances. There are other possibilities. One of these is a further military coup in alliance with the Falange. If this were to take place, it would launch a reign of terror such as the country has never seen before.

He collaborated with the military regime because he felt that it was necessary to reestablish some kind of political stability. Out of chaos nothing constructive could come. It was also necessary to convince the Army of the need for it to get out of the government. However, all efforts in this direction have failed so far.

*   *   *   *   *
*   *   *   *   *

CONVERSATION WITH LIDIA GUEILER, IN THE CHAMBER OF DEPUTIES IN LA PAZ, AUGUST 20, 1956

There is one woman deputy and there are four women substitute deputies in Congress now. All are members of the MNR. The opposition had one woman candidate, but she was defeated.

Women participate with men in the MNR party organization. They are going to form a separate group within the MNR, so that they can better handle specifically women's problems, however.

The opposition is following a purely obstructive course in Congress. They are not voting on anything. Belmonte, who was elected to the Congress by the Falange, is staying in Argentina, not because he has to but because he wants to. He has been invited by Congress to come back and take his seat. So far, only three of the five Falangista deputies have taken their seats in Congress.

* * * * *
* * * * *

CONVERSATION WITH JAIME PAZ ZAMORA IN HOTEL SHERATON, SANTO DOMINGO, DOMINICAN REPUBLIC, AUGUST 15, 1978

The Movimiento de Izquierda Revolucionaria, his party, has no connection with the MIR in Chile. They are very different parties. The Bolivian MIR was formed in 1971 by a breakaway of youth from the Partido Demócrata Cristiano.

The MIR is now in the Unión Democrática y Popular, headed by Hernán Siles, and supported him in the recent election. With the MNR of the Left of Siles,the MIR constitutes the ideological axis of the Unión Democrática y Popular. They want to renew the Revolution of 1952. They are developing a program for the next phase of the Revolution, and in doing so they have referred a lot to my book on the Revolution of 1952.

He is a nephew of Víctor Paz Estenssoro.

* * * * *
* * * * *

Peru

INTRODUCTION

This section deals with only one Peruvian president, Fernando Belaúnde Terry. He was first elected president in 1963 and served until he was overthrown by the Army on October 3, 1968. Then, at the end of a twelve-year military regime, he was rather surprisingly reelected in 1980 and served out his full constitutional period in office.

I met Belaúnde in three different periods. I first talked with him in 1956, soon after his first candidacy for president, which he lost. My second encounter with him was in the middle of the 1962 campaign in which he was once again the nominee of his party, Acción Popular, for president. Finally, I had several conversations with Belaúnde early in 1969, when he was in exile in the United States, a few months after he was overthrown.

In these conversations, President Belaúnde sketches in some detail the circumstances of his becoming a politician, his various efforts to become president, and his actions when he was chief executive the first time. However, some further elaboration of the background of his career is in order.

During the 1920s, Peru had been governed by a dictator, President Augusto Leguía. His regime was overthrown in 1930 by a military coup led by Lt. Col. Luís M. Sánchez Cerro. A year later, Sánchez Cerro was elected president, officially defeating Víctor Raúl Haya de la Torre, the leader of the Aprista Party (Partido Aprista Peruano).

Haya de la Torre was undoubtedly the most important single Peruvian politician in the twentieth century.

Starting his political career as a student leader at the time of World War I, he had been driven into exile by Leguía in 1923. In the next seven years, with young intellectuals in exile he organized the American Popular Revolutionary Alliance (Alianza Popular Revolucionaria Americana--Apra). The Apra also had a base within the country, largely among students, young intellectuals, and the organized labor movement.

The Apristas always argued that the election of 1931 was stolen from them by the government, which favored Sánchez Cerro. President Belaúnde discusses this issue at one point. Although that question will never be resolved satisfactorily, what is certain is that for the next half century or more the Partido Aprista Peruano, the name Apra took after 1930, remained the country's largest and most durable political party.

However, during most of this time, it suffered from the fact that the Army had a veto on Apra's ever coming to power. This arose as the result of an insurrection led by the Apristas in the northern city of Trujillo in 1932, which the Army suppressed, but at the cost of very considerable bloodshed on both sides.

A candidate backed by the Apristas probably won the presidential election of 1936, but instead of recognizing that victory, the military extended the term of the then president, Marshal Oscar Benavides. In 1939 Benavides presided over an election in which the Apristas were not allowed to participate, which placed a rich banker, Manuel Prado, in the presidency.

At the end of Prado's term in 1945, the Aprista Party was legalized for the first time in thirteen years under the name People's Party. It organized a coalition with various independents, including friends of Oscar Benavides, the Frente Democrático. Although the Apristas were allowed to run for Congress on the Frente Democrático ticket, they were not allowed to run one of their own as candidate for president. Their nominee, therefore, was a distinguished jurist (with very little political experience), José Bustamante y Rivero. It was in this election that Fernando Belaúnde first ran for office, on the urging of Bustamante and as a candidate of the Frente Democrático.

Bustamante's three years in office were turbulent. Although the Apristas served in his government part of the time, they showed an impatience which was fatal for the Bustamante regime. For all practical purposes, there were two presidents--Bustamante in the presidential palace and Víctor Raúl de la Torre in the Apristas' headquarters, the Casa del Pueblo. Finally, after a frustrated naval mutiny in Callao early in October 1948, in which some Apristas had taken part, the Aprista Party was outlawed by Bustamante. A few weeks later, Bustamante was overthrown by a military coup led by his Minister of War, General Manuel Odría.

Odría remained in the presidency until 1956. In that year, he called elections, in which the two principal candidates were ex-President Manuel Prado and Fernando Belaúnde Terry. At that point, whether because they thought that he could not be elected, or because, as Belaúnde asserts, they thought that he would not be allowed by Odría to take office if elected, the Apristas did not support Belaúnde, although he had once been their ally. Rather, they made a deal with their old enemy Manuel Prado to support him, in return for which he would, upon taking office, once again legalize the Aprista Party. The engineer of this deal was the party's underground leader Ramiro Prialé, who is mentioned by Belaúnde. Prado won.

When Prado's term was about to expire, new elections were held in 1962. There were three principal candidates: Haya de la Torre, Fernando Belaúnde, and ex-President Manuel Odría. No one got the necessary one third of the total vote, and so negotiations were necessary, since Congress would have to decide the contest. The Aprista leadership made a deal with Odría to throw their votes in Congress to him, apparently in the hope of at least attenuating the military veto on their party. One prominent leader of Apra told me a few years later that the military coup which followed this agreement was a blessing in disguise for the Partido Aprista, which, if the deal had been consummated, would have split wide open because of internal opposition within the party to the arrangement with Odría.

A year after the 1962 coup, new elections were held. This time the same three candidates ran, but Belaúnde was the clear winner. But although he won the presidency, he did not win control of Congress, where the Apristas had the largest group and, in collaboration with Odría's supporters, organized a majority bloc.

Belaúnde elaborates at some length in my conversations with him on the things which he did in his first presidency. He also discusses the circumstances in which he was overthrown on October 3, 1948, attributing this to the continuing veto of the military on the Partido Aprista coming to power, as seemed likely to happen in elections scheduled for early 1969.

Unfortunately, I did not see Fernando Belaúnde again after his first visit to Rutgers in 1969. I did not have a chance to talk with him about the experiences of his second administration. It was during that period that the catastrophic crisis through which Peru is still passing, *the combination of uncontrollable drug trade and Pol Pot sort of Maoist insurrection of the so-called "Shining Path" Communists began.*

One thing that Belaúnde refers to requires some explanation. Right after Belaúnde was overthrown, the new military regime seized the property of the International Petroleum Corporation (IPC), an Esso affiliate. They claimed that chicanery had been involved in a concession agreement which Belaúnde's government had signed with the IPC, and that one page of that agreement had mysteriously disappeared. Belaúnde gives his version of what had taken place.

* * * * *

* * * * *

CONVERSATION WITH FERNANDO BELAÚNDE TERRY IN PARTIDO ACCIÓN POPULAR HEADQUARTERS IN LIMA, PERU, SEPTEMBER 3, 1956

Belaúnde was brought up largely abroad because his father was in exile for a long time. He went to high school and college in the United States. He was thus out of the country during the battles of Apra in the early 1930s, which established Apra as the country's major party. He returned in 1936 and dedicated himself largely to his profession as an architect and could do nothing but have sympathy with Apra, which was the only popular political movement in the country at that time.

In 1945, he was part of the Frente Democrático, an independent group allied with Apra. This alliance was not like that of Apra with Prado at the present time. It was not an alliance of a democratic group with the oligarchy, but an alliance of democrats with democrats.

He was a deputy in the 1945-1948 period. He generally worked with Apra, although he disagreed with them on a number of issues. For instance, when General Odría was Minister of Interior of Bustamante, Belaúnde offered a motion of censure of Odría, which Apra opposed and defeated. He thinks that he was right on this issue.

As deputy, Belaúnde introduced a number of important laws. One of these created the Corporación Nacional de Vivienda and provided for so-called <u>centros</u> <u>vecinales</u>. Another provided for a school building program. There were one or two others. He had the support of Apra for these measures. They needed him, and he needed their votes for this projects.

When Apra fell, Belaúnde and two other people, both lawyers, at the risk of their own freedom went to the Supreme Court with a writ to get the relegalization of the Aprista Party. They failed in this endeavor.

Hence, Belaúnde's appearance on the political scene has not been sudden. Furthermore, he had a good deal of support in the University, and the workers knew of his work in public housing and other fields. He is not exactly a newcomer to politics.

He wanted no quarrel with the Apristas in this last campaign. He announced his presidential candidacy at the urging of a number of young people in the University. Soon afterward, Ramiro Prialé issued an order that the Apristas were not to back him, and so Belaúnde had to reply in an energetic manner. The Apristas no doubt feared that he would capture some of their people. Apra continued to attack him throughout the campaign.

He doesn't know how many votes he received. He does know the minimum number, which was what the government credited him with—460,000. Probably Prado received the 500,000 with which he was credited—having perhaps 250,000 votes of his own, plus another 300,000 from the Apristas. But he does not know what he himself received and can't honestly say whether he really won or not. In any case, although he was recognized as getting 35 percent of the vote, he received only 10 percent of the Congress.

Belaúnde is now forming a political party, Acción Popular. He is doing so not because he is politically ambitious, because he is not. He has gotten to the top of his profession, as Dean of the Architecture Faculty. However, Belaúnde cannot let down those who backed him in the campaign, and they want to go on with the struggle.

Acción Popular is presenting a number of concrete projects to Congress. One of these is for the establishment of a kind of community development program—whereby the government will help local communities to help themselves. He got this idea during his campaign tours throughout the country and only later read about similar programs in India and elsewhere. They are also presenting projects for improvement of the workmen's compensation law and other items.

His party will try to meet the needs of the Peruvian reality. He does not consider himself capable of giving a new philosophy for underdeveloped countries. He is a Socialist in his general tendency. His party advocates an agrarian reform on the basis of converting Indian communities into cooperatives. They are also for decentralization of government. They are for an extensive housing program. These are things which the country specifically needs.

Many of the criticisms of him are unjustified. For instance, it is said that he is a big employer of labor, that he does contracting. This is not the case. He is merely an architect who himself works for contractors. The charge was made during the campaign that he was a tool of Pedro Beltrán, but this is disproved because Beltrán is now backing the Prado government. The claim was made that he was allied with Admiral Saldrías, Odría's minister, because Saldrías was his uncle. This is false; Saldrías is a relative of his wife and backed Odría's candidate Lavalle. The charge is made that his movement is personalist, but this isn't true, as is shown by the fact that he is not even president of Acción Popular.

The charge is made that he works with the Communists. This is not true. He is a democrat, as people who know him in the United States know. In the South of Peru, for sure, he had the support of a kind of indigenous Communism which exists in Cuzco and Puno. But this indigenous Communism has nothing to do with the Soviet Union, is a sentimental attachment to the Inca tradition, and is nationalistic. Perhaps one or two of his candidates elected in that area were of this nationalist Communist sort, but he in any case did not dictate local candidates, leaving their selection up to his local supporters.

*   *   *   *   *

CONVERSATION WITH FERNANDO BELAÚNDE TERRY IN HIS HOUSE IN LIMA, PERU, APRIL 6, 1962

The campaign is going very well. He had a meeting tonight in one of the barrios of Lima where 20,000 people were in attendance. He had another such meeting last night. He has been touring the country ever since 1956, when he was last candidate for the presidency, and has been in all but four of the one hundred twenty-five provinces of Peru. He will visit these four in the next few weeks.

He doesn't think that there will be any interference from the Army in the results of the election. The Army will let anyone who wins the election take power. They have reiterated this position over and over again.

He thinks that the election campaign now lies between Apra and Acción Popular. Odría doesn't have much popular support. He has a little in Lima on the basis of spending a great deal of money, but he has no such support in the provinces.

Acción Popular thinks that Apra is subordinate now to the big bankers, the big industrialists, and oligarchy. Such a party as Apra now is cannot make the kind of a revolution which Peru needs.

Acción Popular has a program. Basic is a plan for road building, not just for transport purposes but also to aid the process of colonization. They are particularly backing the construction of a road on the edge of the jungle, to be part of a larger South American road, linking the Orinoco, Amazon, and Río de la Plata areas. The party is also for the agrarian reform.

* * * * *

CONVERSATION WITH FERNANDO BELAÚNDE TERRY IN PRINCETON, NEW JERSEY, JANUARY 26, 1969

He began his political career in 1945, when he became a candidate for the Chamber of Deputies from Lima. There were nine candidates named on a list backed by the Apristas and by José Bustamante y Rivero. He ran on the suggestion of Bustamante, and he knows that Haya de la Torre had someone else he would have preferred to run for that post. However, Belaúnde ran and was elected.

He has often wondered why the Apristas did not back him in 1956, because he certainly had always been closer to them than Prado had been. He supposes that one of the reasons why the Apristas backed Prado was that he had a great deal of money and some of this was made available to them for their campaign once they had decided to back him.

He thinks that often the role of the "oligarchy," meaning the large landholders in the altiplano, in Peruvian affairs is overstated, particularly abroad. The situation of the oligarchy is certainly changing. For one thing, under his administration, a land reform was launched which resulted in granting some 60,000 land titles to peasants. Most of these were titles to the bits of land they had been allowed by the landlords to use for their own purposes, and these present a new problem, that of minifundio, since they they are really too small to be economical. The titles which have been given are provisional, not definitive, but they serve to give the peasants the feeling that the land is theirs. Definitive titles will be given later, when the process of breaking up the estates is completed.

When he became president, he called in the Director of Indian Affairs, and asked him to present Belaúnde with a detailed survey of the situation of the Indian communities. The man came in first with some global statistics, which were not very useful. Then Belaúnde asked him for extensive details on each community. When he got this material, he had it run through an IBM computer, and as a result, they now have a very good catalogue of all the communities and the characteristics of all of them.

The Indian communities are more important than they are usually considered to be. Only about less than 2 percent of the land of the altiplano is cultivated and about 17 percent is in pasture. In each case, but particularly in the pasture land, the communities still have about half the land.

His government felt that the communities were good organizations upon which to base modernization. If they have confidence, the community leaders are willing to bring advancement in cultivating techniques and other things. This was the basis of the Community Development Program which Belaúnde's government had, trying to help the community leaders modernize their communities, to get better cultivation methods, build running water facilities, schools, etc. The government got a $20 million loan from the Inter American Bank for this and matched it with another equivalent $20 million. The program was far advanced when he left the presidency.

However, he thinks that in addition to these measures, there is a great need to open up new lands. This was the purpose of the Transversal Highway in the Amazon area, which was started in his regime. The highway, with its connections with the altiplano, was a means of opening up whole new areas which are virtually unsettled. He thinks that it is of immense importance for the future development of the country.

He thinks that his solution of the oil problem was a correct one. There were in fact two agreements, and it is from this fact that there arose the false charge that there was a hidden part of the agreement signed between the Peruvian government and the International Petroleum Corporation. The first was a direct agreement on the concessions between the government and the company; the other was an agreement between the Empresa Nacional de Petroleo with the IPC, by which a sizable amount of the government oil firm's output would be refined in the IPC refinery, which was not working at capacity with the oil produced by the IPC. This was an agreement between two companies, and the government did not enter into it directly.

He thinks that his overthrow was more a blow at the Apristas than a blow at him. His term was almost over in any case, and he was going to preside over elections in June. The fact that in municipal elections and some bye-elections for the Chamber the government had been defeated but had done nothing to cancel the results of the election, indicating to everyone that Belaúnde would preside over honest elections for his successor. In this situation, the Apristas stood a pretty good chance of winning. He doubts that they would have gotten much more than the necessary 33 percent, but they might have gotten that. There was also a chance that Luis Bedoya, the mayor of Lima, who is a very good and capable man with considerable popularity, might have won. In any case, the prospect of a possible victory by the Apristas was what touched off the overthrow of Belaúnde.

Edgardo Seoane, his former vice president, is a very ambitious man. An issue between them first arose at the time of the last Punta del Este Conference, which Belaúnde attended. At that time, he had doubts about whether he should turn over the government to Seoane for the interim, doubts based on constitutional grounds, since he would be exercising his presidential functions when he was in Punta del Este. He approached the Apristas on this, and they told him that they didn't want to have Seoane as acting president, but that if he felt he wanted to make Seoane such, he should merely notify Congress that he was doing so, not submit the issue to Congress for decision, because in that case, the Apristas would be forced to oppose it.

That was what Belaúnde did. He was away only a few days, but in that period Seoane apparently got to like being president. There were even rumors which Belaúnde received that Seoane had tried in this period to foment a plot to oust him, but the military men would not go along. Thereafter, the pro-Communist elements in Acción Popular began to try to get the party nomination for president for Seoane. This Seoane began to do, becoming extremely critical of the government, even on television. Of course, there is a tradition that the government candidate does not win elections in Peru, and perhaps he felt that he had to separate himself in the public's eyes from the administration.

In any case, Seoane's criticisms had a false ring to them. They were very leftist and he is sure that Seoane didn't believe most of what he said, since before that time he had the reputation for being one of he most right wing elements in the party.

As a result of these activities of Seoane, it became necessary to reorganize the party, which Belaúnde was doing just before he was overthrown. Since Belaúnde's ouster, Seoane has claimed that he has assumed leadership of the party, but the fact is that he has broken away from it with a small group of followers and has set up his own organization. The great majority of the party has not followed him.

The military accused the Belaúnde government of corruption. They particularly charged that Sando Mariátegui, who was his Minister of Finance for two years, had been corrupt. They jailed him, but after thorough investigation, were forced to release him unconditionally.

There is no question that the Apristas gave him a good deal of trouble during his administration, particularly in Congress. He talked with them a number of times and tried to get them to see that when one had a certain amount of power but not all of it, a party should try to do the most possible to make a record for themselves. However, the Apristas didn't do this; they tended to want to postpone everything until they had control of the government. This was the root of his difficulties with them.

General Juan Velasco, who now is president, is a very ambitious man. In the last cabinet shuffle before he was overthrown, Belaúnde consulted with the military to see whom he should appoint as Minister of War, Velasco or the head of the Army Engineers, a very capable man. They were unanimous in suggesting that he appoint the head of the Engineers, which he did. But not wanting to push Velasco aside, he left him as Chief of the Combined General Staffs, and it was from that post that he moved to overthrow Belaúnde.

Velasco is a man of ambition but without ideas. Belaúnde expects that he will be ousted soon, perhaps in the next week. His post may be taken by General Benavides, who is a very intelligent man, with more ideas and capacity than Velasco has.

At the time of the 1962 election, the charge of fraud in the balloting was raised by the military ministers in Prado's own cabinet. When this happened, it was clear to Belaúnde that the election results were not going to be honored. That is why he went to Arequippa and demanded new elections, because he saw that new elections were the only way out of the situation. The Army was determined not to allow the Apristas to make a deal which would return Odría to the presidency. They did make such a deal, quite publicly, just before the 1962 coup.

He thinks that the break between Odría and the Apristas last July was due in large part to the fact that Odría really had little popular support. It was a move against a plot, in which Odría was involved, to overthrow the government.

*   *   *   *   *

CONVERSATION WITH FERNANDO BELAÚNDE TERRY AT RUTGERS UNIVERSITY IN NEW BRUNSWICK, NEW JERSEY, JANUARY 27, 1969

While he was president, he tried to pay the military the honors which were their due. But during this time, he acted differently from his predecessors in not paying much attention to the police. It is traditional that the Director de Gobierno, the head of the police, spend a good deal of his time with the president. But Belaúnde didn't spend more than half an hour with him each week. In addition, he wanted to do away with the presidential secret police, but the military leaders told him that he should keep that group in existence, and so he did.

He knew more or less well the members of the present Military Junta. He was responsible for promoting most of them to general and had treated them all quite well.

The coup against him was pulled by a small part of the Army. The Navy was strongly against it, and the Air Force was also. Likewise, a sizable part of the Army was against it, but the coup was pulled very rapidly and without knowledge of much of the military.

He thinks that the Latin American countries, including Peru, need strong armed forces. Thus, he would defend acquisition of some French jets last year as necessary to keep the armed forces modern. In case of a war in which the Latin American countries were not involved, those countries would have to be in a situation to defend themselves from any eventuality. If the United States would become involved, it would certainly want those countries to take care of themselves; in addition, in case of a war involving the United States, the Latin American countries would also become involved, hopefully on the democratic side, and it would be necessary for them to be able to defend themselves from attacks by the enemy.

He generally favored use of the military in civic action programs. The Navy was involved in a shipbuilding program in Callao, which turned out two sizable ships a year on the average. Also, in the Amazon region, the Navy used its ships to carry out a number of civic action programs. Likewise, the Air Force was very good in civic action programs, establishing regular air connections with parts of the Amazon area where the commercial airlines did not go because there was not enough business.

He had been very busy the day before the night that he was overthrown. He had spent a good deal of time that day dealing with people in charge of a big irrigation project which represents a large investment. He went to bed very tired. About 2. A.M. he was awakened by the sound of tanks outside of the palace. He called the commander of the palace guard to ask what was happening, but that man professed not to know. He then called his military aide, who also didn't know, he said. The fact was that although the palace guards were supposed to defend him in such a situation, they did not actually do so.

The only thing he could do was to resist physically, but he didn't have anything to resist with, except his fists. He was taken to the airport and was going to be placed on a plane. The pilot was an American, and as Belaúnde approached the plane, surrounded by military men, he called up to the pilot and told him to record in his log that he was being put on board against his will and that his being taken would be kidnapping. This upset the pilot for a while, but he finally took off. Belaúnde didn't know where he was going. But he was landed in Buenos Aires some hours later. When he got off the plane, he was met by Argentine government officials, and they asked if he wanted to be regarded as a political refugee. He answered that he did not, that if he had come of his own accord he might want such treatment, but that if they wanted to place him back on the plane and return him to Peru, he would be perfectly willing to go. They didn't want to do so.

A few days later, he bought a ticket to Miami on a Braniff plane that stopped at Lima on the way. His passport was in order and the American Consul gave him a visa. The plane moved out, but before they had taken off, the pilot announced that because of certain "mechanical difficulties," they had to return. When they got back, the police and Braniff officials came aboard and told him that the Peruvian government knew that he was on the plane, and that if he continued, the plane would not be able to land in Lima. They said they could give him passage on a Panama plane which went directly and ended up in New York. When he got here, he got a call from Harvard, offering him his present job.

He is working in Harvard as head of a project to study the problem of integration of South America. They are not only going to study the problems of economic integration, such as working out the difficulties of currencies which vary a great deal in their stability, but also cultural problems such as the fact that history is portrayed very differently in the various countries, and there is a great deal of illiteracy in the various countries.

They want to try to work out ideas for establishment of new institutions which can coordinate the development of various sub-regions, such as the Andean area, the Río de la Plata area, the Amazon region, and possibly coordinate all these areas sometime in the future. They expect that it will take a year or so to make this study and come up with ideas which can be seriously presented to the governments for future action. They think that such proposals coming from a really international university such as Harvard, where there are quite a few Latin American professors and students, will be taken seriously.

The Andean Pact was an attempt to get such a regional program started. It was worked out last year among Chile, Bolivia, Peru, Ecuador, Colombia, and Venezuela, and the Peruvian government, Congress included, had ratified the treaty. It was hoped that the Andean Pact could help to plan the development of the whole Andean region, and that it could be useful in getting capital abroad for this development. They felt that an organization such as this would be able to raise money better in the world capital markets than any one of the governments could do, both in terms of interest rates and longevity of bonds. He thinks that the project is well enough started so that the present Peruvian regime won't be able to stop it.

There is also need for something like an international group to raise money for housing. There has been a proposal for a Latin American Housing Bank, for providing low-cost mortgages on an international basis. So far, this idea hasn't been adopted, but he thinks that it would be a move in the right direction.

When he was president, he urged the Inter American Bank (BID) to issue a new kind of bonds for the purpose of absorbing some of the funds which tend to escape from Latin America, the so-called "refugee currency." He suggested that the BID issue bonds to be bought in the respective Latin American countries, with the bonds being labelled according to the country from which they were bought, but to be payable in dollars and by the Bank in that country. This would be a way of attracting funds which would otherwise be put in numbered Swiss bank accounts or in the United States, and using them for development of the various Latin American countries. But the Bank turned down this idea, he is certain because of pressure from certain interests, although he has not been able to identify the interests which would be opposed to the idea.

One idea he had in Peru itself, and which he had enacted, was for issuance of all stock in Peru not to the bearer any more, but to the individuals to whom it belonged. This was a good way of preventing tax evasion. However, the military regime has just recently announced that they were going to suspend this law for two years. Of course, this is because of interests which have brought their power to bear on the new "revolutionary" government.

He was never anti-Aprista. He was in the United States as a student at the University of Texas during the earliest years of the Aprista Party in the 1930s. At that time, it was a Marxist Party, although subsequently Haya de la Torre made a clever 180 degree turn against Marxism. The party reached its high point of influence right at the end of World War II when having been persecuted by various governments. It pictured itself as a democratic party, something about which Belaúnde had certain reservations, since earlier their form of organization had had certain Fascist overtones.

When Belaúnde returned from studying in the United States, he was neither for nor against Apra. However, he did favor reestablishment of the legal rights of Apra. As a result, he joined the Frente Democrático coalition in 1945 and ran for Congress on the suggestion of José Bustamante. However, the Apristas made life very difficult for the Bustamante regime, being very arrogant toward the president and his followers. In October 1948 there was an attempted naval mutiny which failed, and subsequently the Odría regime, another dictatorship, was established. During that regime, Belaúnde favored legalization of Apra and was never particularly against the Apristas.

In the 1956 presidential election, he was a candidate. He forced the Odría government to register him, by a struggle in the streets, even though Odría didn't want to do so. He also thinks that he actually won the election, but that he was counted out by fraud. He almost won in any case, and he is sure that if he had gotten a solid majority, Odría would have had no alternative but to recognize his victory and let him take power. Therefore, he does not believe the Aprista excuse for their support of Prado on the grounds that Odría would not have allowed Belaúnde to take power, and that therefore the Apristas didn't support him, since they wanted a regime to come to power which would legalize them.

The support which Apra gave to Prado in 1956 went very far to discredit them. As a result, his own position very considerably improved. When he was elected in 1963, the Apristas joined forces with their worst enemy, General Odría, having a majority in Congress in this way. They caused him a great deal of trouble, frequently censuring members of his cabinet, so that in about five years he had more than eighty ministers. He thinks that the perspective of Apra was to get Belaúnde overthrown during his first six months, but they failed because Belaúnde began his own program immediately and won popularity with it.

A year and a half ago, the Apristas provoked a considerable government financial crisis. They had generally followed the policy of hampering his budget. They generally vastly overestimated the government's income by from 25 percent to 50 percent. A 2 or 3 percent error is understandable, but not such a big one as the Apristas regularly made. They were purposely trying to hamstring his government because after overestimating the income, they would appropriate a long list of public works, and of course, the government would not be able to carry all of them out, since the income of the government would not be as great as the budget provided for.

In 1967 he called in the Apristas, told them that the government faced a serious fiscal crisis, and that if they did not vote for taxes, the government would have a large deficit and would have to undertake a devaluation. However, Haya, the supposed great revolutionary, then launched the slogan "No new taxes." The upshot was a devaluation.

It was with the devaluation that the crisis of the regime really began. By the middle of 1968, the government was faced with a new crisis. He again asked the Apristas to vote for new taxes, and when they refused to assume this responsibility, he asked them at least to authorize the government to enact new taxes. They agreed to this, allowing the government to enact a financial program by decree, as a result of which some two hundred different decrees were passed revising the tax system. Also, strong restrictions were put on imports. The upshot is that the military government is now faced with a fine budget situation, and with a good balance of trade situation.

However, the actions of his government in the middle of last year were too late. They probably contributed to the overthrow of the government. What the Apristas didn't understand was that they could not blindly oppose the government as they did and still support it institutionally, so that it could hold elections, as they wanted it to do.

The Aprista Party is a vertical party. It has a single leader and it does anything that its leader wants it to do. This is the explanation for why Haya de la Torre has been the party's only candidate for president during the thirty-seven years in which it has been in existence.

He is not sure that it is correct that Haya was ever elected president. Certainly in the election of 1931 he was not elected. Sánchez Cerro was popular, partly because of his race, since he was very definitely a cholo. They did support candidates who were elected, but it is not clear that Haya ever was.

He doubts very much that he will be called back to the presidency, no matter what happens. His term is almost ready to expire in any case. However, he does think that if Velasco is removed from the presidency, as he suspects he might be within the next week, that the new regime will call elections. He will be willing to go back to Peru at any time. The people at Harvard realize this.

In 1959 he was jailed by the Prado regime. This was when his party was going to hold a convention in Arequippa. He was arrested on the way down there and was taken to the Frontón prison, on an island off Callao. With the aid of a friend, he escaped, just by dashing off into the water when he was being walked from one part of the prison to the other. The man to whose boat he swam, who had arranged to pick him up, first argued with him, telling him that he should not try to escape, but finally picked Belaúnde up when he cried out that he would drown if he wasn't taken aboard pretty soon. The government finally dropped charges against him, since he had really not done anything. However, he had been picked up before this and actually spent twelve days in Frontón, in which he had a chance to talk at great length with the hardened criminals who make up most of the population of that jail. Most of them were responsible for sex crimes against minors.

On one occasion, he fought a duel. This was when he was badly insulted by a member of Congress, between the 1956 and 1962 elections. Belaúnde chose weapons and they used sabres. They met at the airport at the cock's crow, and it was a bloody but not very serious duel. He cannot say just who won. However, it was a very interesting experience, and it has been useful in the sense that since then he has never been publicly insulted again in the same way.

Acción Popular has been reorganized. They held a party convention early in January and elected a new secretary general. Edgardo Seoane led his own group and had his own convention, but he represents only a small group.

He has never been really against the Apristas, as he has said. At the present moment, he is working with them, as is his party, in a united front to get the government to call new elections. He thinks that it is necessary that all the civilian parties work together against the military regime.

Various important figures visited Peru when he was president. These included the Italian President Giuseppe Saragat, de Gaulle, and others. He found de Gaulle a very friendly character, not at all the way he is pictured in the press. They got along quite well.

The Apristas during his regime rated Congress very highly. They referred to it as "the first power," which certainly was debatable. However, Congress undoubtedly had a very important role during that period. It was highlighted in the middle of last year when the Inter Parliamentary Union held its conference in Lima. The Apristas apparently thought that this would strengthen the prestige of the Peruvian Parliament, but it apparently did not do so, since the coup took place only a few weeks later.

Because of the hampering of his regime by Congress, military men on various occasions came to him and told him that when he was ready to dissolve Congress, they would be willing to do so. However, he always rejected this idea, saying that it was not the right thing to do, and that

Congress had the right to function, and it would be against the democratic regime to try to dissolve them.

* * * * *

CONVERSATION WITH FERNANDO BELAÚNDE TERRY AT RUTGERS UNIVERSITY, NEW BRUNSWICK, NEW JERSEY, JANUARY 28, 1969

He thinks that there are few countries where the people have faced such a geographical challenge as in Peru. Perhaps in the Himalayas, in the Congo, and in the Sahara there are similar challenges, but Peru has all three--along the coast it has a desert which has been compared with that of the Sahara; in the mountains it has a region perhaps comparable to the Himalayas; in the Amazon Basin it has a region comparable to the ex-Belgian Congo.

If modern Peru is going to find a way to meet these challenges, it is good for it to know something of its own history, and this history has much to tell. In the time of the Incas, there was a civilization which was based on agrarian social justice, which had as its basic purpose the provision of a means of living for its people. It was a civilization which produced a surplus of agricultural production, which was kept in storehouses which dotted the whole Inca empire, and the ruins of which are still extant in many areas.

That society did seek to tame the deserts. It extended great irrigation systems both in the North and South, which had been started by the pre-Inca civilizations and expanded by the Incas. Without modern engineering, without money, without modern knowledge, they were able to build these, and they built them so well that even today in many regions it is just necessary to clear out and connect the channels for water which they had built many hundreds of years ago.

So one of the basic purposes of Belaúnde's regime was to meet this challenge of nature. His regime spent much attention and finance on expanding the irrigation systems of the North and South. They got some financial help for this from and international lending agencies, but those agencies scanned these projects very carefully. This has been an expensive way of expanding the cultivable land area, since in many cases it has been necessary to bring water from the eastern to the western side of the Andes.

However, this was not all they attempted to do. They found in looking back into history that the Incas had very laboriously terraced the narrow mountain valleys, a work which has been compared to the pyramids. However, it differed from the pyramids in that unlike them, the terraces were a monument to the living, not to the dead.

He sought some other way to expand the cultivable area for the people living in the altiplano. This has been to open up the eastern slopes of the Andes, and this they have been doing with the Marginal Highway, on the eastern slopes, alongside the forests. He is proud to say that one of his fist acts as president was to meet with the Ministers of Public Works of Ecuador, Colombia, and Bolivia and sign with them an agreement for building this road. It is now well advanced; some four hundred kilometers had been finished by the time that he left the presidency.

Another great feature of the Inca civilization had been the system of mutual aid, the "minca," which is translated into Spanish as acción popular. This was a system whereby the people themselves built the great roads which linked together the Inca Empire, larger than the Roman Empire, extending from the southern Colombia, through all Ecuador, all Peru, all Bolivia, to parts of Argentina and Chile. It was the way, too, that they built other things which were for use of the community.

This tradition has survived. In the communities and villages today, the people make the church, they build the school, they construct the neighborhood roads. So his government wanted to build upon this tradition. When he formed his party, he called it Acción Popular, seeking to associate it with this traditional philosophy of mutual aid.

They have sought to modernize this ancient institution, to provide it with the implements, the trained engineers and technicians that were needed. They have thus combined the old system dating from the Inca period, which worked without money, with the new system which uses money, the system first introduced by the Spaniards after the Conquest, because the engineers have to be paid salaries, the implements and machines have to be bought with money.

He thinks that in this way the program of mutual aid of his government was typically Peruvian. It was a mixture of the heritage of the Inca civilization and that of the Spaniards. It is like the architecture of Cuzco, planned by Spaniards but executed by the Indians, who gave it their own touch. It is like the poetry of the country, and about the country, such as Neruda's poem on Macchu Picchu, written as one of the great poems of the Spanish language, but catching the spirit of the great Indian town. It is like the poet César Vallejo, or going further back, like Garcilasso de la Vega, the son of an Indian princess and a Spanish Conquistador, who wrote about his mother's people, but in the language of his father.

The road on the eastern slope of the Andes has been successful in its objective. There have been many new colonies established along it, and branching out from it. He thinks that the development of a vertical takeoff airplane, such as Rutgers is working on, could be of immense use in this program of colonization of the East, since it could establish villages and concentrations of people ahead of the road and give good reason for the road to be built to those places.

Of course, the unique things about his administration are these of which he has spoken. But they also had a big program for industrialization. They concentrated particularly on provision of hydroelectric power, and by July the country will have twice as much installed kilowatt capacity as they had in 1963. It was only 800,000 kilowatts then; now it is about 1,400,000 kilowatts and will be considerably larger when several other projects are completed.

They also modified the industries law to make it more attractive to investors, giving ten-year tax exemptions in a number of places. They encouraged development of a car assembly industry, which uses a certain percentage of Peruvian made components. They also continued a program of chemical development which had been started before he came into office, extending protection to new parts of the industry as it is constructed. They have started a large petrochemical complex, which is being undertaken by the W.R. Grace Company.

They also worked on establishment of industrial parks, a large one in Arequippa, and smaller ones in Trujillo and one other city. In these, the government puts in the overhead requirements, such as electricity, water, sewerage, and the like, and the industrialists have to provide the factories. This is working out very well.

They tried to encourage industrial development on the eastern side of the Andes. In one town, they established a small industrial complex on the basis of lumber and pulp, since the area has very good raw materials for this.

All of this he would call a nationalist program. As he sees Nationalism, it is a policy of looking into the country's own history, its resources and people, and trying to develop the nation in conformity with these characteristics. This has not been the policy of all politicians. Many have found inspiration in Karl Marx, who never said anything about Peru; others have found inspiration in Christian Democracy because it was successful in Germany and Italy, but he doesn't think that is any reason why it should be successful in Peru. He has, rather, tried to find the policy and program of his party within Peru itself.

Not all Peruvians, particularly the present military group in power, interpret Nationalism as he does. They tend to interpret it as getting rid of foreign investors. However, he thinks that is a very narrow and self-defeating vision of Nationalism.

He never had any crises with the military. They never pressured him. He only had one problem with them, on October 3. He thinks that the coup at that time had much more to do with his successor than with his own regime. It was also the result of the ambitions of some of those involved.

One thing he was trying to do during his administration was to restore the country's credit. He thinks that he succeeded in doing this, and during the latter part of his regime he could have borrowed money from any of the New York banks, $40 million if necessary. Of course, he didn't want to do that because the interest rate from the private banks was high and the terms were short.

Although he was overthrown by a military coup, and there is a military regime in power in Peru today, he does not think that the United States should react to such a situation by cutting off its aid. He thinks that United States aid should be given to the people of Latin America, and they would be the ones to suffer if aid were cut off.

There's been a great deal of talk about "forty families" running Peru. This was written some time in the nineteenth century by an American writer on Peru. This myth has been kept alive, and even the same number, forty, is used to describe the situation. But it has changed a good deal, and if one really wrote correctly about the situation now, one would have to talk about five thousand families. Furthermore, there is a new middle class in Peru now, which didn't exist until relatively few years ago.

In fact, one of the things his government tried to do was to strengthen the middle class. This was particularly true with regard to housing. It was general before that the middle class either lived among people culturally their inferiors, or with people culturally on a par with them, but financially way beyond them. As a result, the Belaúnde government constructed a great deal of housing, some 100,000 units, particularly for this middle-class element.

He doesn't think that birth control is particularly desirous in Peru now. The rate of population increase is 3.1 percent a year, and he thinks that perhaps it is higher than that. In time, the rate might fall to about 3 percent a year. But he would be inclined to say what Peru needs now is a counter-pill rather than the pill.

He thinks that this is the "hour of the tropics." There have been three major changes made which make a difference in the tropics. One of these is the medical revolution which has resulted in virtual elimination of malaria and reduction of yellow fever to the point where it is no menace. He and others like him who have a good deal to do with the tropics always have yellow fever shots. The second thing is invention of dehydration, which developed during World War II and makes it possible to transport much larger amounts of products from the tropical areas in small bulk. A third thing is the development of transportation, particularly of aviation, which makes it possible to connect areas which had virtually no contact with the outside world before.

He has been much impressed with the United States students whom he has met here, at Harvard and at Cornell. However, he sees a difference between them and the United States students he knew when he was a student here himself thirty-five years ago. This is that the students now give the impression that they are "unemployed pioneers." The pioneer tradition is very strong in the United States, and the students are looking for a way in which they can be pioneers now. He thinks this is one of the reasons why economic development of Latin America should be something undertaken on an international basis. He thinks that American students could find a good outlet for their search for a frontier in helping out in the economic development of Latin America.

In this connection, he has seen many Peace Corps volunteers in Peru. He has visited them in community development projects, road building, and in other things in which they have been involved. He found them to be very dedicated young people, who were making a real contribution to the development of his country.

He thinks that the building of Brasilia was a very fine idea. President Kubitschek has been very much criticized for it, but he thinks that it was very important for its role in opening up the interior of Brazil, for turning its face inward from the Atlantic coast to the great interior. He thinks that it was also very important for the international prestige which it gave to Brazil, for the fact that it put Brazil on the map and raised the country's prestige a great deal. For both these reasons, he would defend Brasilia. It is said that it stimulated the country's inflation, and there may be some truth in this, but he thinks that it was well worth anything that it cost.

He thinks that there is a difference between General Juan Carlos Ongania's seizure of power in Argentina and that of General Velasco. Ongania had retired from the Army some time before he came to power and was not in a position of authority. However, Velasco held a position which was of the confidence of the President, which he betrayed with his coup. He has known Ongania for some time. Of course, Belaúnde must admit that Ongania has not announced any date for new elections. He thinks it is bad enough that the military should overthrow a constitutional regime, but it is worse when they do not even announce any date for new elections, to lead to reestablishment of a democratic and constitutional regime.

He is not particularly enthusiastic about the Christian Democrats in Latin America. In the case of Chile, the party was not really very large, but because of peculiar circumstances it was thrust into a leading place in the country's politics. One factor was the fact that it had a very outstanding leader in Eduardo Frei, who was much better than his party. In the case of Venezuela, the Copei only won because of the split in Acción Democrática.

In Peru, the Christian Democrats are not very important. They were supposed to be allied with him, but they really were not much help to him. He would make an exception of Luis Bedoya, now mayor of Lima, who is a very good man indeed. He was in Belaúnde's first cabinet, and did a very good job. Then when Belaúnde asked him to run for mayor of Lima, which was quite risky under the circumstances, he willingly did so. He is a man of considerable popularity, and Belaúnde thinks he is a very good political leader.

Héctor Cornejo Chávez is rather different. He is a good speaker, but he is very dogmatic. He broke with Bedoya because he was jealous of him. He tried to expel Bedoya from the Christian Democratic Party, and it was then that Bedoya broke away and formed his own party. He is still mayor of Lima--the military have not dared to remove him--and he will remain mayor until January of next year.

He is a nephew of Victor Andrés Belaúnde, the historian, who was a brother of his father, and to whom he was quite close. Their family without any question belongs to the traditional Peruvian elite, but Belaúnde has never had an elitist role in politics and has always followed a policy of popular politics. His family has roots in Arequippa, although he himself was born in Lima and lived most of his life there. He had a solid base of political support in Arequippa, but also had strength in Cuzco and in the jungle.

*   *   *   *   *
*   *   *   *   *

Ecuador

INTRODUCTION

Ecuador's traditional parties were the Conservatives and Liberals. The former represented particularly the rural aristocracy of the highlands and were strong supporters of the Catholic Church. The Liberals were stronger in the coastal area centering on Guayaquil, were anti-clerical and more generally represented the nascent middle class and artisan workers.

By the 1930s, the traditional parties had begun to disintegrate. This was particularly the case with the Liberals. Both a Socialist and a Communist Party appeared in that decade, which was marked by frequent military coups.

During the 1930s there also emerged the amazing career of José María Velasco Ibarra, who during the next four decades served five times as President of the Republic (1933-1935; 1944-1947; 1952-1956; 1960-1961; 1968-1972). Velasco Ibarra was overthrown four different times, serving out his full term only in the 1952-1956 period.

Unfortunately, I never had a chance to talk with Velasco Ibarra. However, three of his periods in office are relevant to the conversations which follow. One is his 1944-1947 dictatorship, when in elections following his overthrow Galo Plaza was elected president, beginning a thirteen-year period in which constitutionally elected presidents succeeded one another peacefully.

The second Velasco Ibarra period which is dealt with in what follows is the one in which he served out his full term, 1952-1956. President Galo Plaza makes reference to that period in one of his conversations with me.

The third Velasco Ibarra period which is obliquely referred to in these interviews is that of 1960-1961. In the latter year, he was ousted from office and was succeeded by his vice president, Carlos Julio Arosemena. President Galo Plaza refers to Arosemena's difficulties in his third conversation with me. Arosemena was overthrown by the military a year after our talk.

The military coup of 1972, which ousted Velasco Ibarra for the last time, brought to power a reformist military regime, patterned after that of General Juan Velasco in neighboring Peru and led by General Guillermo Rodríguez Lara. However, with the ouster of Rodríguez Lara, the military junta which took charge began the process of return to an elected constitutional government, although the junta imposed severe restrictions on that process, as is indicated by the talk by President Osvaldo Hurtado which is recorded here. The election of 1978 and the runoff presidential election and accompanying congressional poll of the following year began a period of elected governments which still continues as this is being written. President Hurtado and Borja served during this constitutional democratic phase.

President Galo Plaza belonged to the rural landed elite of the highlands of Ecuador. However, by family tradition, he was associated with the Liberal Party, and he was elected president in 1948 as a Liberal, although it is not clear that he actually belonged to the Liberal Party. His father, General Leónidas Plaza had been president twice, as a Liberal, during the early years of the twentieth century, and was Minister to the United States when Galo Plaza was born.

Galo Plaza was educated in the United States and attended three different universities there. After completing his education he was for a while in the diplomatic corps. He entered politics in 1936 when he was elected mayor of Quito, the national capital. Subsequently, he served as Minister of Defense and Ambassador to Washington. He was elected president in 1948 after the fall Of Velasco Ibarra's second dictatorship.

Galo Plaza remained active in politics, as well as taking care of his family's estates, but never ran for president again. Between 1968 and 1975, he was Secretary General of the Organization of American States [OAS].

The aristocratic background of Galo Plaza is reflected in what he had to say to me. It reflects a spirit of "noblesse oblige" rather than of any fundamental belief in reform, even less in revolution.

There are three parts of what follows dealing with Galo Plaza. The first is a talk he gave at the Conference on

Responsible Freedom in the Americas run by Columbia University as part of the celebration of its bicentenary in 1954. The second is a conversation at the Overseas Press Club in New York City the following year. Third is a conversation I had with him in Salvador, Brazil, in 1962, when we both were attending a conference in that city.

The background and career of President Osvaldo Hurtado was quite different from that of Galo Plaza. He started his political career in the Christian Democratic Party, which merged in 1978 with a "progressive" element of the Conservative Party to form Popular Democracy and Christian Democratic Union.

Hurtado's party coalesced in the 1978 election with Concentration of Popular Forces (CFP), with Jaime Roldós Aguilera of the CFP as the presidential nominee and Osvaldo Hurtado as candidate for vice president. The 1978 election was inconclusive, but in the runoff election of April 1979, the Roldós-Hurtado ticket won overwhelmingly. Hurtado succeeded to the presidency early in 1981 when President Roldós was killed in an airplane accident.

What I have recorded here is a talk which Osvaldo Hurtado gave to a meeting of the Latin American Studies Association in Albuquerque, New Mexico, in April 1985. In that talk, Hurtado expounded considerably on what he had done in his presidency, and his general political outlook.

Our third Ecuadorean president, Rodrigo Borja, began his political career as a member of a fraction of the traditional Liberals, the Radical Party. However, in 1968 he broke with that party and formed his own, the Democratic Left (ID), which in addition to its Liberal adherents absorbed much of the remnant of the Socialist Party. His party was an equivalent of Acción Democrática in Venezuela, Apra in Peru, and the MNR of Bolivia and, like them, joined the Socialist International. After two attempts to be elected president, Rodrigo Borja (and ID) succeeded on the third candidacy, in 1988. He served out his full term but was succeeded by a more conservative candidate in the 1992 election.

One prediction of Rodrigo Borja is worthy of note. He said that he expected that once Jaime Roldós became president, he would quickly fall out with Asad Bucarám, the head of his party, the Concentration of Popular Forces. This proved to be the case. Bucarám, who became the head of the Chamber of Deputies, did everything possible to frustrate President Roldós and his administrative program, leading to a serious split in the CPF, with the Roldós faction joining forces in Congress with Rodrigo Borja's Izquierda Democrática.

There are two items in the entry on President Borja.

116

One is a conservation I had with him in Santo Domingo, Dominican Republic, when we were both invitees at the inauguration of President Antonio Guzmán, of the Dominican Revolutionary Party, (PRD), the Dominican counterpart of the ID, in August 1978. The second is a short talk, which he gave on the day following our conversation, to the meeting of Solidarity with the new PRD government organized by the Socialist International.

*　*　*　*　*
*　*　*　*　*

TALK BY GALO PLAZA AT COLUMBIA UNIVERSITY CONFERENCE ON RESPONSIBLE FREEDOM IN THE AMERICAS, IN NEW YORK CITY, OCTOBER 25, 1954

There are six to seven million Indians in Bolivia, Peru, and Ecuador, who have for four centuries been under the domination of the Spaniards and their successors. They have lived in almost sub-human conditions, and some people feel that they are a total loss.

Galo Plaza has been trying to prove that the Indians can be redeemed and to show that they are already the basic economic element in those countries. The Indians should be absorbed into modern civilization. But he is also trying to make the Indians proud of their ancestors, to revive their arts and crafts. The Indian is intelligent, mechanical, mathematical. Plaza is trying to introduce better methods to the Indians for their own arts and crafts.

One of the problems of education is that of language. This was shown by the case of Quechua, which is a relatively complex language. When the Incas conquered Ecuador, six years before the coming of the Spaniards, the language of the local Indians was a very poor one. Although it had not been conquered by Quechua by the time the Spaniards arrived, it did succumb to Quechua with the passing of several more generations.

Galo Plaza has been running a rural school for a year and a half, where they have been trying to teach the Indians to improve their arts and crafts, while at the same time giving them a basic education. This school is keyed to the needs of the Indians themselves. They have proved within a year and a half that with sympathetic help the Indians can improve their own situation. They have improved their crafts, at which the women particularly are working, and what they produce is now sold by one of the principal stores in Quito.

He has also been involved in the American School in Quito. In 1940, they were worried by the influence of the German School, which in addition to giving a good education to many of the students of Quito was also inculcating Nazi propaganda. So they decided to launch an American School. Teaching there is in both English and Spanish. They go through both primary and secondary school. They have both Ecuadorean and United States teachers. There are several hundred students in the school, and it has been a very successful experiment in international education.

He feels that the system of Latin American primary and secondary schools puts too much emphasis on philosophy and theory. Philosophy is more appropriate to the university than to primary and secondary schools.

The Ministry of Education has detailed control of education throughout the country. He thinks that the educational system would be much better if the national government had less to say, if control were in the hands of local governments, and even private organizations. The American School in Quito got special recognition from the government as an experimental school, and so is not so much under the control of the Ministry.

* * * * *

CONVERSATION WITH GALO PLAZA AT OVERSEAS PRESS CLUB IN NEW YORK CITY, OCTOBER 11, 1955

He thinks that democracy is safe in Ecuador now. Velasco Ibarra will not be overthrown, the democrats of Ecuador won't allow it. Velasco was always overthrown by Velasco in the past, but this time the democratic elements in the country won't allow it.

The Ecuadorean parties are out of date. They are fighting over issues which are out of date. This is true of both the Liberals and the Conservatives. The Socialists are really pro-Communist. Some of the leaders know well enough where they are going, but most of the rank-and-filers do not, and they are not pro-Communist.

The 1956 election campaign is already under way. Several pre-candidates have announced themselves in the Conservative Party. But the other parties do not as yet have any candidates. He will not be a candidate. He is against "indispensable" men, and if he were to run, inevitably he would be pictured as "indispensable." He is not.

The labor movement in Ecuador is confused. The revolt against its pro-Communist orientation last year has subsided. The Communist influence is great in the labor movement not only in Ecuador but throughout Latin America.

Ecuador has made progress in recent years. Average income has risen from $40 a year to $150. He does not know how much real income has gone up, but he knows that it has risen substantially. Exports have quintupled.

He is conducting an experiment in his valley, on land owned by his mother, which has been in the family since 1595. He already had the confidence of the Indians, to whom he was the "patron," and anything he suggested must be all right. They have brought in a corps of educators, nurses, and others. Already there is a marked effect, although the experiment is only two and a half years old. The Indians now bring their kids in to be innoculated. When it was suggested that they take them to the nearby town of Ibarra to be given tuberculosis tests at a government clinic, they did so voluntarily. They want their children to go to school, and there has been built a six-year primary school in the neighborhood.

The problem of agrarian reform in Ecuador is comparatively easy. There is plenty of good land, the best in the country, available at the foot of the Andes, on the Coast. The altitude of Ecuador is not as high as that of Bolivia, so it is not quite so hard to get the Indians to move down to this new land. They do so when their little plots get so much divided that they can no longer get even a meager living out of them.

Many times the impression of the United States citizen must be that the cause of democracy is lost in Latin America. Admittedly, it is sometimes discouraging. There are still old-style "paternalistic" dictatorships; there is frequent military intervention. Sometimes one reaches the point of fearing for the very existence of democratic institutions. This is the case in Colombia, where the country was basically democratic, yet has fallen under a dictatorship, which raises fears for democracy in other countries.

However, we should realize that the people of Latin America are genuinely democratic. They have always fought for democracy. There has always been a group which has kept its spark alive. Venezuela is an outstanding example. Generations of Venezuelans never voted for candidates for office. The country lived under a dictatorship which was convinced that the underground parties didn't have a chance--so the dictatorship made the mistake of allowing an election and was defeated. There had always remained a tremendous democratic conviction, a democratic tradition in the people. This is one reason for optimism in Latin America.

Is there a need for an Inter American Society of Educators? Yes, there definitely is. There are many differences of opinion between the educators of the two areas. The major differences stem from the different historical backgrounds of the two areas. The difference in the value systems and ways of life of the people of the two regions have created differences in the educational system.

The semi-feudal Spanish system was transplanted to America, with Catholicism as the only religion. In the English colonies there was freedom and religious tolerance, with government by charters, which paved the way for democratic state and national governments. In Latin America, colonial despotism bred military dictatorships in the newly freed republics. The North benefited from the Reformation and the Industrial Revolution. In Latin America, the environment bred aristocratic education under the Church. In the North, education was influenced by German science; in the South, the French cultural model was followed, with culture for culture's sake being the objective.

Although there are growing cross-currents between the two regions now, with more emphasis on practical training in Latin America, and more emphasis on cultural training in the United states, the differences still exist. He would like to quote Irma Salas, the Chilean educator, who has given the best summary of the differences. She says that in the United States education is democratic, in Latin America it is aristocratic; U.S. education is a community enterprise, in Latin America it is an enterprise of the State alone. In Latin America, there is uniformity, in the U.S. there is diversity in education. The Latin American liceo gives a general education, the U.S. high school stresses usefulness. The administration of schools in the U.S. is unified, with elementary, secondary, and in some cases even university education being under the same authorities; in Latin America it is separated, with entirely different administrations of the three levels of education.

The advocates of the Latin American educational system say that United States education is pragmatic, utilitarian, and lacking in spiritual values. North Americans say that Latin American education is purely cultural and impractical. In certain parts of Latin America it is argued that the Latin American kind of life doesn't go well with pragmatism. All of this indicates that there is need for exchange of ideas.

Elementary education should be universal. That it should be so is written into the constitutions of all the Latin American countries. But this is not always carried out. The countries have limited resources. Public education is submitted to all kinds of limitations. What has actually been accomplished is a tribute to all of those involved in education in Latin America.

Private schools, particularly those of the Catholic Church, have helped with primary education. But in general not enough is being done and there are still many children who don't go to school at all.

The quality of Latin American education needs improvement. New European methods are making some headway, but traditional methods still predominate--copying from the blackboard, little opportunity to develop individual capacities or learn about the community in which the children live. The relationships between the student and the teacher are still very formal. Individual needs of the student are not paid heed to.

As a result of all this, adult illiteracy is a major problem. Without a minimum of knowledge, how can a citizen be a participant in democracy? The Latin American countries have intensive programs of adult education, but illiteracy is still a menace. The future of the countries is at stake. Governments are increasing their budgets, adopting new methods, and the school is becoming increasingly a living part of the community.

He thinks that the immediate problem is to get enough schools for everyone. For the time being, quality will have to be sacrificed to quantity. Later, they can pay attention to improving the system, once it is really universal.

Secondary education is the weakest link in the Latin American school system. Its roots are in the past, when it was completely in the hand of the Church and was avowedly only for a minority. After independence, the French concept of an intellectual elite was prevalent. The object of the secondary schools under this system was to train only the best minds. In general, educational emphasis was on classical subjects, and the school was for the purpose of training one to enter the university.

Rapid economic development and a certain degree of industrialization is slowly bringing a new set of cultural values to Latin America. National leaders are realizing the necessity of bringing education to all, so as to qualify the people for life in a democracy.

Education should stimulate vocations for those not going to the university. It should change personality. Nowhere else is the struggle between classical ideas and modern ones more notable than in the secondary schools. The programs of study are continually being revised. The pull of tradition in some cases is still too great. The best example of what can and should be done is the renovation of the secondary education system in Chile several years ago. He hopes that the hopes aroused by this experiment will be fulfilled. The objective is to broaden the cultural base, to prepare for democratic life, to prepare for vocations.

There are a dozen universities in Latin America older than Harvard. The University of Santo Domingo was established one hundred years before Harvard. The university reflected the times--its teaching was academic abstract. There were a few universities which were exceptions, where mathematics and the natural sciences were introduced. All universities during colonial times were under Church control.

With the birth of the republics, the universities were nationalized, and the Church lost its hold on higher education. In this present century, the universities have been adapting themselves to the times, adding schools of engineering, architecture, agriculture. The universities now find that their limited resources are their main problem. Part-time professorships still predominate. But the influence of the universities is greatly felt in the economic, social, and political life of the Latin American countries.

The things which he has said about Latin American education could no doubt be matched by criticisms of the United States educational system, and would be equally interesting. There is great need for greater contacts among Inter American educators. Of course, there are many United States agencies active in this field--Point Four, university to university relationships, the work of U.S. religious agencies which are giving valuable service. Foundations in the U.S. have helped, as have business firms. The UN and its specialized agencies, and the OAS, have also done some things in the field.

Significant changes are needed in the North and the South if we are to enjoy growing prosperity in democracy. There is a new interest in the humanities in the U.S., and the growth of interest in "practical" subjects in Latin America. However, progress is slow because there are deep-rooted traditions involved. Sometimes there are conflicts, too, with national sensitivities. Public agencies are not the most adequate vehicles for handling problems where national sentiment is a consideration. A voluntary agency without government ties, such as an Inter American Association of Educators, would be an ideal device for progress in education in both parts of the hemisphere.

*   *   *   *   *

CONVERSATION WITH GALO PLAZA IN HOTEL DE LA BAHIA, SALVADOR, BRAZIL, AUGUST 5, 1962

The situation in Ecuador is better now, more stable. The Frente Democrático has just recently won a majority in Congressional elections. They can also count on the Concentración de Fuerzas Populares and on some dissident Conservatives. He thinks that the defeat of the Conservatives in the last election was sufficient to deprive them of much chance of organizing a coup against President Arosemena, which ex-President Ponce Enríquez was trying to do. In fact, the Conservatives have begun to turn on Ponce Enríquez and to blame him for their defeat.

He thinks that the need now in Ecuador is stability, to get the constitutional system firmly entrenched again. It will certainly be necessary to make serious changes in the economy, including an agrarian reform. However, the agrarian reform will have to be done in an organized way, and in such a manner as not to undermine the production of the country's agriculture.

He is very much opposed to the idea of an Inter American Military Academy, and an Inter American General Staff. The only effect of that would be to institutionalize the "logia" of Latin American military men who are ambitious to take over the rule of their various countries, and to give them the feeling that they have the support of the United States military men, and even the United States government, in that objective.

*　　*　　*　　*　　*
*　　*　　*　　*　　*

TALK BY OSVALDO HURTADO AT MEETING OF LATIN AMERICAN STUDIES ASSOCIATION, IN ALBUQUERQUE, NEW MEXICO, APRIL 19, 1985

He would note the autonomy of the Ecuadorean state because of the development of the petroleum industry. Most of its income was taken by the State, first in the form of taxes, then by the government's own firm. This is a basic change from the 150-year tradition in which the oligarchy of exporters determined public policy.

Employers are always critical of the trade unions and opposed the trade unions' policy of intervening in politics. But the employers have become political under the recent military and democratic regimes, and they participated very openly in the 1984 election.

He doesn't think that the Chamber of Commerce was less in opposition to his regime than the Chamber of Industry, as has been argued here. Under his government, he had to take measures to deal with the balance of payments, restricting imports, and the Chamber of Commerce reacted strongly against that. The more radical opposition of the industrialists was due more to personalities than to particular interests, especially in the case of the leader in Guayaquil.

He doesn't agree that his policy of reduction of expenditures and of austerity favored particularly the private sector. If the State runs most investment, the private sector wants the State to spend those funds and so won't favor reduction of them. One must look at each sector to see to what degree these policies favored private sectors. The austerity program basically had to do with government expenditures and revenues.

Also, the law by which the government took over the dollar debts of the private sector was important. But it is was necessary to reach agreement with the international banking authorities. Without this, there would have been bankruptcy of important firms and an economic crisis. Private firms, of course, had to pay in sucres, and to pay interest and an insurance premium to cover the risk of foreign exchange. The present government has given up the insurance charge.

In his government, there were people associated with the private sector. That was his decision. If he had to have an austerity policy, it was better to have it carried out by independents and not by party people. The independents were associated with business.

He thinks that the success of his government was that he had some knowledge of economics and could discriminate among ideas which were offered to him.

The oil development sector was not dependent on the State expenditure. The Development Bank was established just before President Roldós took over. The reason for it was to keep a large part of government expenditures out of the budget. That was a bank for public investment and for projects of the government. It took those expenditures out of politics. This explains the great advances in infrastructure under the democratic government.

There was a difference between the Roldós government and his. There were differences in government expenditures and revenues. His emphasis was on segregation of government expenditures in petroleum, electricity, the Development Bank. This was a lesser evil, given the instability of

Ecuadorean politics. There was a government deficit equivalent to about 7 percent of the GDP under Roldós, and it was virtually eliminated under him.

The present government of President Febres Cordero is following Neo-Liberal policies. It is going to reduce protection of Ecuadorean industry on the grounds that it should be able to compete or should not exist. Perhaps some modification of protection was needed, but basically it was still necessary. This will create a crisis for industry, in long-term investment.

Foreign exchange and monetary policies after 1980 were protectionist, but they did not have that intention. The policies were designed to deal with the crisis of the moment. In any case, one must look at the social and political aspects of protection.

Since 1972, Ecuador has had the most spectacular economic development in its history. It is based on exports. Petroleum exports shot up from $400 million to $2 billion a year. This permitted the government to carry on a program of construction of ports, roads, water supplies, education. As a consequence, Ecuador is now a substantially different country from what it was in 1972. No other Latin American country has changed so much in so short a time. It has moved to become a middle-developed country from a very underdeveloped one.

The second result has been the strengthening of the role of the State. The foreign sector of the economy is not as vulnerable as it was before when it was in the hands of the oligarchy and vulnerable to changing economic forces. Now, 90 percent of the oil is in the hands of the State, and oil is more solid than the agricultural products exported before.

Also, the public enterprise and national government's financial institutions helped local governments. Now the State has relative independence from the economic powers that be.

Petroleum has also stimulated national integration. It has generated physical integration through making it possible to build roads in all parts of the country, bring electricity in rural areas, foment rural education and general rural development. It has also promoted acculturation, mestizaje, a mixture of social classes. It has stimulated very much the growth of the middle class. It has helped to create a real proletariat in industry. Generally, the formation of real nationhood has been given a strong impulse.

Although the economy has greatly advanced, the politics have lagged behind. This is natural, because political change must be qualitative. It was political development which was defeated in the last presidential election.

To the degree that political development has lagged, there has been a lack of representativity of politics. This has been marked by the unscrupulousness of the Right. There is still a multiparty system, but the nature of the parties has changed.

According to present rules, 5 percent of the total vote is the requisite to have a legal party.

The petroleum boom provoked a regrouping of the Right and consolidation of the entrepreneurial groups. Before, the Liberal Party and the Conservative Party were irreconcilable, particularly on religious issues. There were several Right parties in the 1968 election, but only one in 1984, and the Chambers of Commerce and Industry participated openly in the campaign. About three fourths of the highest officials of the present government are businessmen. The unity of the Right began during his government and was consolidated in the 1984 election.

His government wasn't anti-business. It couldn't be. But it is true that business didn't have access to the government every time it wanted it, wasn't consulted on all policies, and the government took steps the business community did not like. That was in a country in which business leaders were accustomed to dining regularly with the President of the Republic, etc. But he felt that the President should not be associated with any one group.

Why was there the political consolidation of business? It was because of the economic crisis, which reinforced the businessmen's determination to have the government in their own hands. They saw danger for that in an ideological government. Also, since oil is the core of the economy, and it is in the hands of the State, the businessmen felt that they had to control the State.

It is said that the role of Right business elements is a menace to the democratic system. He disagrees. At the time of the referendum vote on the Constitution, they failed to get much support for the blank vote they advocated. They also weren't successful in getting a coup started after the first round of elections of President Roldós. Under Hurtado, the Right violently opposed him. He doesn't think that by itself the Right can bring down the democratic regime. It will need a number of interest groups, including parties, to have a coup. This depends on what role the president plays. The president's role will determine the role of the military, the conduct of the economy, and the position of the parties.

But it is true that the Right is not committed to democracy. In power since last year, the Right has been acting undemocratically, violating the wording of the constitution, even resorting to some violence.

He thinks that no legal arrangement by itself can determine the nature of a regime. The present Law of Parties has been in effect for five years, for instance. His government adhered to the Constitution and the law in spite of a grave economic crisis.

Latin American culture is favorable to conflict. His government was criticized for its seeking compromise. There is a tendency toward conflict in Roman law, with its tendency of "liquidate" opponents instead of conciliating various interests.

Local political leaders were the key to the success of populist parties in Ecuador. But their clientele won't follow the local caiques in voting for someone if that person is not charismatic. In 1984, the barrios voted for Febres Cordero, who made an exceedingly populist campaign.

There are reasons for the relatively low vote in the marginal barrios in the big cities. One is that the people there in many cases have to go to vote in their home areas rather than in the cities.

He thinks that President Carter's human rights policy was of key importance. In fact, it largely made possible the holding of elections in Ecuador for a democratic regime. However, in connection with the economic crisis of the early 1980s, the United States government said that the problem was much more simple than it really was. Under President Reagan there has been no action against democracy in Ecuador. On the contrary, the Reagan government has expressed support for democracy, although it has taken no concrete steps in that direction.

Velasco Ibarra had little direct contact with people. He had an aristocratic bearing. But he had a nationwide group of local leaders who worked for him. Also, he had a myth, particularly in Guayaquil, as being

El Hombre, and the local leaders could not regularly have mobilized support for Velasco Ibarra without this myth of El Hombre.

* * * * *
* * * * *

CONVERSATION WITH RODRIGO BORJA IN SANTO DOMINGO, DOMINICAN REPUBLIC, AUGUST 14, 1978

Izquierda Democrática did quite well in the recent election. This was its first time at the polls. It got the second largest vote of any single party, being surpassed only by Concentración de Fuerzas Populares (CFP). The CFP got the largest vote, and even though it was supported by other parties, even if one calculated that only half its vote was from the followers of the CFP, these votes would still be more than ID got. Izquierda Democrática got about 12 percent of the total vote, at least that is how much the government credited it with. It did pretty well in the municipal council elections which were held at the same time as the presidential one.

The traditional elements controlled the electoral process. The polls all showed Sixto Duran, the Conservative candidate, and Raúl Clemente Huerta, the Liberal, getting almost all of the votes. The same was shown in the "sidewalk interviews" that they had on television and radio. But the fact was that the ID did very well, and particularly in Quito, where most of the sidewalk interviews took place.

The ID has some influence in the labor movement. The Confederación de Trabajadores del Ecuador, of course, is traditionally controlled by the Communists. However, the ID has some considerable influence in the Confederación Ecuatoriana de Organizaciones Sindicales Libres (CEOSL). The leader of the CEOSL, José Chávez, originally was friendly to the ID but ended up supporting Huerta, the Liberal candidate, although many of his colleagues backed ID.

Borja was originally a member of the Radical Liberal Party, a left-wing Liberal. But he became disgusted with the Liberals and felt that there was need for a new ideological Democratic Left party. He joined with a number of other Liberals and some Socialists, to form Izquierda Democrática. The Socialist Party is virtually dead now.

It is interesting that the personalist parties all did badly in the recent election. This was true of the Velazquistas, as well as of Arosemena's party, and of the Poncistas, who continue even though Ponce has died. ID is not a personalist party.

Asad Bucarám, chief of the CFP, is interested only in power. He has no particular ideas and no ideology. Borja thinks that Roldós, who came in first in the presidential election, on the CFP ticket, will try to make the CFP more of an ideological party, and he is likely to clash with Bucarám in trying to do so. He thinks that there will be a clash between the two men within three months of Roldós's taking office.

He thinks that the second round in the presidential election, made necessary by the fact that no candidate got a clear majority, will probably be held at the beginning of October. It will perhaps be a year before Congress is elected. There will thus be a virtual constitutional dictatorship for a year. This is not so bad because it will make it possible to pass by decree a number of things which would not be possible otherwise, if there were a Congress in operation. But the congressional election will be the next big electoral test for the various parties, and he thinks that the top party people of all the parties will be candidates in that election. The ID will support Roldós in the second-round presidential election, since he is nearest to them in ideological terms.

The new constitution calls for universal adult suffrage of all from eighteen years of age and up. There is no literacy qualification. However, this doesn't apply to the presidential election, where there are roughly 1.3 million voters.

Agrarian reform is very difficult. On the one hand, the Indians are still very much out of the mainstream of national affairs. Many don't even know what country they are in. It is very difficult, therefore, to talk politics with them. The ID controls a few small peasant federations, but the largest of these has only 15,000 members nationally, which is virtually nothing. Also, they don't want to have a situation in which, because of agrarian reform, there is a drastic fall in agricultural production. Agrarian reform is not the simple thing which the Communists claim that it is.

*   *   *   *   *

TALK BY RODRIGO BORJA AT SOLIDARITY MEETING WITH PARTIDO REVOLUCIONARIO DOMINICANO ORGANIZED BY SOCIALIST INTERNATIONAL IN SANTO DOMINGO, DOMINICAN REPUBLIC, AUGUST 15, 1978

The Izquierda Democrática of Ecuador is convinced that the triumph of the people and the PRD in the Dominican Republic is a constructive example for all of Latin America, particularly for those countries which are under dictatorships. The behavior of the Dominican people will teach the other people of Latin America that governments should come from elections, not from bayonets. In the name of the young Partido Izquierda Democrática, he says that they are convinced that democracy is not just electoralism, but that elections are absolutely necessary. He wants to pay homage to the PRD, the people of the Dominican Republic, and to assure them that they have the full solidarity of Izquierda Democrática. He hopes that the PRD in power will construct social democracy here. Democracy is not just institutions, but a way of behaving, which allows the people to participate in decisions, as well as in the output of society. He hopes that the PRD will build a new society in which people can share equitably in the results of economic activity.

*   *   *   *   *
*   *   *   *   *

Colombia

INTRODUCTION

Two traditional parties, the Conservatives and the Liberals, have dominated Colombian formal politics since the middle of the nineteenth century. From 1886 until 1930, the Conservatives ruled, but in that year a split in the Conservative ranks brought the Liberals to power, with the election of Enrique Olaya Herrera. Then, in 1934 the Liberals won again with the candidacy of Alfonso López Pumarejo, who launched a series of important reforms. These included encouragement of the organized labor movement, tax reforms, and strong State support for economic development.

However, although the Conservatives under the leadership of the reactionary Laureano Gómez largely refused to participate in elections between 1934 and 1946, the reform program of Alfonso López Pumarejo aroused considerable opposition within the Liberal ranks. As a consequence, the "moderate" Liberal Eduardo Santos, publisher of the country's most important newspaper, *El Tiempo*, was elected in 1938, and he restrained the Liberals' reforming zeal.

Alfonso López Pumarejo was reelected in 1942. However, faced with economic problems generated by World War II, considerable corruption within the regime, and growing disillusionment on the part of organized workers and other popular elements, López resigned early in 1945, and his place was taken by Alberto Lleras Camargo, his vice president.

At the end of Lleras Camargo's term in 1946, the Conservatives returned to the hustings. As a consequence of a split in the Liberal Party between the "official" candidate and the dissident Liberal candidacy of Jorge Eliécer Gaitán, the Conservative nominee, Mariano Ospina Pérez, won the election. Shortly afterward, Gaitán gained control of the Liberal Party and carried on a very vigorous opposition to the Ospina Pérez government. For their part, the Conservatives exploited their control of the national government to carry out widespread purges of Liberals in the various departments and municipalities.

In April 1948, Jorge Eliécer Gaitán was assassinated, giving rise to a popular insurrection in the capital city, which was usually called the "Bogatazo," in which mobs attacked and burned many buildings associated with the Conservatives, including the edifice of *El Siglo*, the newspaper of Laureano Gómez. President Ospina Pérez refused to resign in the face of this insurrection, but the Bogotazo launched what came to be known as "La Violencia," an extended period of virtual civil war between the Liberals and Conservatives in various parts of the country.

In 1950, with the Liberals boycotting the election, the Conservative leader Laureano Gómez was elected president. Under him, La Violencia was intensified, and he proclaimed his intention of mounting a fascist-like "corporative state" in Colombia. However, in 1953, Gómez was ousted by a military coup, headed by General Gustavo Rojas Pinilla, which had the support of the Liberals and moderate Conservatives.

Rojas Pinilla soon alienated his supporters in both the Liberal and Conservative parties. He moved toward establishing a regime more or less patterned after that of Juan Pérón in Argentina, seeking to mobilize the urban workers and peasants against the "oligarchy" which he said (correctly) dominated the two traditional parties.

Among his other attacks on the "oligarchy" was his closing of Eduardo Santos's newspaper *El Tiempo* and the exile of ex-President Santos. This action aroused widespread denunciation on the part of the press in both Latin America and the United States, since *El Tiempo* was widely viewed as one of the most important newspapers of the hemisphere.

Finally, in 1956, Alberto Lleras Camargo, then the titular head of the Liberal Party, went to Spain, where Laureano Gómez, still the principal Conservative leader, was then living in exile. These two men worked out a compromise agreement between the two traditional parties, whereby they would share power for a considerable period of time, once Rojas Pinilla was overthrown. This became known as the National Front, and after the ouster of Rojas Pinilla by a military coup in 1957, it was incorporated in an amendment to the Colombian constitution.

The National Front continued in full force from 1958 until 1974, with Liberal and Conservative presidents alternating in office. The first contested election for the presidency after the National Front was won by Alfonso López Michelson, the son of former President Alfonso López Pumarejo. López Michelson had been a strong opponent of the National Front, and for some years had headed his own party, the Liberal Revolutionary Movement (MRL). But by the early 1970s the MRL had been reincorporated within the Liberal Party, and López Michelson emerged in 1974 as that party's victorious candidate.

In the pages that follow, we shall deal with Presidents Eduardo Santos, Alberto Lleras Camargo, and Alfonso Michelson. The first entry for President Santos is a talk he gave at the Bicentenary Conference at Columbia University in October 1954. The second is a talk by Santos at a Conference on Freedom of the Press in the Americas at an Overseas Press Club in October 1955, in New York City, where Santos was then in exile. The third entry for Santos is a conversation with him in New York in 1960, when Alberto Lleras Camargo, the first president under the National Front, was still in office.

Three references by Santos require some explanation. First, in his reference to "one of the greatest of the Latin American countries" in which "the dictator was indiscreet enough to have elections," Santos is referring to Venezuela, where General Marcos Pérez Jiménez had engaged in that "indiscretion," in 1952, lost the elections but stayed in power anyway.

Second, Santos comments on a forthcoming meeting of the Inter American Association for Democracy and Freedom (IADF). This was an organization established at a conference in Havana, Cuba, in 1950, which linked democratic leaders of many different political persuasions in Latin America (one of whom was Eduardo Santos), with liberal political leaders, academics, and others in the United States. With the advent to power of the administration of President Rómulo Betancourt in Venezuela, he invited the holding of the IADF's second conference in that country. It did in fact meet in Caracas and Maracay, Venezuela, in May 1960.

Finally, President Santos comments on the United States' giving "arms to the Latin American dictators, medals for the Latin American dictators." Here he is referring to the fact that President Dwight Eisenhower had recently given medals to General Manuel Odría and General Marcos Pérez, the dictators of Peru and Venezuela, respectively.

The conversation with Alberto Lleras Camargo took place in his house in Bogota, in September 1956, after he had *reached the National Front agreement with Laureano Gómez, but when General Rojas Pinilla was still in power. He elaborates on the nature of the Rojas Pinilla dictatorship and on his negotiations with Laureano Gómez.*

Finally, the entry for Alfonso López Michelson is a talk he gave at the Center for Latin American Affairs in New York City, in January 1974, when he was the Liberal candidate for president. He was in New York soliciting votes from Colombians who were residents in that city but had the right to cast absentee ballots. He elaborates on the National Front, his opposition to it, and the situation that existed when the National Front was approaching its end.

*   *   *   *   *

*   *   *   *   *

EDUARDO SANTOS, SPEAKING TO COLUMBIA UNIVERSITY CONFERENCE ON RESPONSIBLE FREEDOM IN THE AMERICAS, NEW YORK CITY, OCTOBER 26, 1954

He is an enemy of Nationalism in the bad sense of the term. He opposes those who talk about forming a "national" culture. Culture is one and indivisible. We are all the children of European culture, which is still very much alive. One of the governments of Colombia said that it wanted to stimulate "Colombian" culture, but such a thing does not exist. Colombian culture is a reflection, and a pale one at that, of universal Western culture.

The problem of liberty in America is a problem of the present. Many Latin Americans agree with the Spanish writer José Antonio that they love their country because they do not like it. All of America needs liberty. They don't need the four freedoms, they need one, freedom in general. They need to be freed from fear, which has a paralyzing effect in some parts of Latin America. They need full democracy, which lives up to the Charter of Human Rights.

It is not true that Latin America is not "ready for liberty." Its history shows that they have had liberty. They have failed to keep their liberty many times, but so have other people. They have also had their successes. The Comuneros of Spain were defending the liberty of their fueros, and they did so without having to learn about it from books, they did it naturally. He himself has had many democratic experiences which give him hope for democracy and liberty in his continent.

There are many splendid cases of defense of liberty in Latin America. Galo Plaza aided an opposition publication, while he was president, so that it would not disappear, so that there would be a healthy opposition. Another Latin American president refused a move made by his partisans in the Senate to have the attorney general take action against an opposition paper which was bitterly attacking the president. The six presidents at this conference have known how to govern democratically; they have not known how to govern by state of siege.

Latin America, to be sure, is passing through a hard time. Democracy is in peril there. But this is in large part a result of the universal confusion which plagues not only Latin America but the whole world.

Everything will fail without liberty. Big buildings, roads, and other masterpieces of material construction are no good without human freedom. If the University is at the service of the dictators, what good is it? It is better not to learn than to learn only what the dictatorship has to teach.

One of the dangers to liberty in the continent is the banner of "Anti-Communism." The worst elements in the hemisphere use this banner. The best democrats, the worst enemies of Communism in the continent, are attacked by these people as "Communists." This attitude finds an echo in the United States. Latin American Liberals are suspected here because they are said to be a "vanguard of Communism." The Liberals are against the anti-libertarian aspects of Communism. They don't care what kind of an economic system there is, if the essential human freedoms are maintained. If the first thing that "anti-Communism" does is to destroy liberty, it means nothing.

The best way to foment Communism in Latin America is through dictatorship. This is shown in the case of Spain. It is shown in the case of Italy, where those who were Fascists found it easy to become Communists. In Latin America, if the dictatorships pose as "anti-Communist" they will fertilize the soil of Communism. It is correct to be anti-Communist, but one can only be so with the banner of liberty.

He is much impressed by the hypocrisy of international politics. The Pan American Union, for instance, is based on the doctrine of democracy and human rights. In spite of this, it is a living demonstration of this hypocrisy, and the Pan American Union is not democratic in fact.

He and others have dreamed of what kind of an America could come into existence--an America peaceful, free, democratic, united. Why doesn't the United States aid the achievement of this dream? Why is the United States arming Latin America? Only the personal interests of the dictators and the militarists are served by these arms. They do no good to the countries which receive them. They have brought a dominant militarism to Latin America.

The armies of Latin America can never be useful in defending these countries from outside attack. These armies are insignificant internationally; they are terrible locally. He remembers, when he was president of Colombia, telling Summer Welles that the United States should not arm the Latin American countries, that to do so was to give them morphine and to make them addicted to it. He also told the same thing to Roosevelt.

The Chapultepec Conference set up a collective security system which made the arming of the Latin American countries unnecessary. The worst crime in Latin America, therefore, is the arming of these countries. The United States is compromising the future of the whole of Latin America with its armaments program. This growth of militarism is intimately related to the future of liberty in Latin America. The worst danger in that region is from violence, from intolerance. Intolerance is not so bad if it is weak and unarmed, but an armed intolerance destroys liberty. He wants to see America united and disarmed.

He believes sincerely in U.S. economic aid to Latin America. And he does not think that it is charity. Such aid is merely the extension of a principle which is very well recognized within the United States, this is the principle of the income tax. Of course, the United States can isolate itself in its wealth. Or it can aid the poor of the hemisphere, in its own self-interest. Since the Latin Americans share the bad consequences of the fluctuations of the U.S. economy, during depressions and other crises, they should, he feels, participate in its prosperity as well.

One world is not possible with the absolute richness of the United States and the grave poverty of Latin America. The Marshall Plan was not charity, but rather intelligence. Just so, the Latin Americans hope that the United States will apply the principle of the Marshall Plan to Latin America in this same intelligent way.

In Latin America, there are strong elements working for liberty. They ask that the United States recognize the Liberals of Latin America for what they are. They are the real enemies of Communism, not the dictators. Liberty needs courage. He asks the Latin Americans not to lose this courage, the courage to say that they love liberty.

*   *   *   *   *

TALK BY EDUARDO SANTOS AT CONFERENCE ON FREEDOM OF THE PRESS IN THE AMERICAS AT OVERSEAS PRESS CLUB IN NEW YORK CITY, OCTOBER 11, 1955

For forty-five years he has been interested in Inter American relations. As a journalist--which he has always remained--as President of the Republic, Minister of Foreign Affairs, delegate to the League of Nations, vice president of UNRRA, and as head of his party, this has always been one of his main preoccupations.

It is this belief that it is the people who count, not the governments. The great importance of such meetings as this is that they rectify the idea that relations between the Americas should only be between governments, and not between peoples. If they become only between governments, Inter American affairs are doomed.

The most dangerous supporters of Communism in Latin America are certain U.S. businessmen. As good Marxists, they follow only their own economic self-interest.

In one of the greatest of the Latin American countries, the government of the dictator was indiscreet enough to have elections. The opposition won by a vote of four to one. So the government cancelled the election, put in its own puppet congress. Such things as this are much more dangerous than any other economic problem could be to the cause of better Inter American relations.

The most sad aspect of the problem is that the truth about Latin America is completely distorted. Many Latin Americans are living under dictatorships because they are faced with thousands of machine guns, not because they wish to be. The people are capable of democracy. They have practiced it. Citizenship is a reality in Latin America. Although the dictatorial regimes may appear to be tolerated by the people, this is a caricature of the facts. His own country, Colombia, is basically a democracy; they know how to practice democracy. What exists now in Colombia is not really Colombian.

The Latin American countries are small. They suffer. They have great resentment when they see that larger countries apparently ignore the situation in Latin America and deal only with those people who are in control. For example, the U.S. government cannot recover in a long time the loss it has suffered as a result of its attitude toward Péron in the

133

period before he fell.

He has great gratitude to the U.S. press for its position on Colombian affairs. When the government of Colombia complains that the attitude of the U.S. press is "interference" by a foreigner, he denies it. Colombia asks for such "interference."

One must understand what intervention really is. It is arms to the Latin American dictators, medals for the Latin American dictators. This may be looked at as "merely diplomatic," but such aid to the dictators is tremendously resented by the people of Latin America. If the U.S. feels that it has to maintain formally friendly relations with all governments in the hemisphere, it at least does not need to back the dictatorships morally and otherwise.

He knows about intervention. He supported Republican Spain even after its fall. When the Germans invaded Belgium, he, as President of Colombia, protested. There are times when a word of support is a great help to democracy. Why are such words no longer forthcoming as they were in the times of Franklin D. Roosevelt?

The Pan American Union is not only an alliance of governments and people. It has a body of treaties which make it a union of democracies. Isn't domination of an American country by a dictatorship a violation of international treaties?

Latin Americans see with joy private organizations such as this one which fight for real friendship between Latin America and the United States. Such organizations fight against the greatest danger in Latin America, that the masses may go Left because of the failure of democracy. This failure is the greatest ally of the Communists. The frustrated democrats of Latin America are tending to turn to Communism because they get no help elsewhere.

The U.S. should not be so concerned about exports, but rather with liberty. The most important export of Latin America is its political exiles. The Latin Americans want not only progress but rights, liberty, elections.

He believes that the only kind of press freedom is full press freedom. He believes we must allow the totalitarian press to appear even at the risk which is involved in this.

There are three kinds of censorship. The first is censorship of political news, and with that one can still say many things, in other parts of the paper. The second type is total censorship. Even with that kind of control, one can say quite a bit--it is a constant game with the censors to see what one can say without the censor's realizing it. The worst kind of censorship is "self-censorship," where the government does not put any censors in the paper, but "leaves it up to the editors." Although the first kind of censorship, and the second kind, can be fought, the third kind cannot be fought. Under it, there is total fear.

In Colombia they are awaiting the appearance of an Army paper. It is going to try to drive all others out of existence by underselling them. It may well be able to do this, since it can charge a ridiculously low price because it will have unlimited government subsidy.

El Espectador, the other big Liberal paper in Bogotá, is a very good paper. It has always supported the Liberal Party. One need fear nothing about its giving in to the attacks of the government.

World War II began when he was president of Colombia. He immediately offered to work for the protection of the Panama Canal and notified President Roosevelt that he had nothing to fear from the Colombian quarter. Colombia did carry out this policy, and there was no attempt at all from the Colombian territory upon the Canal; the Colombians policed the situation well. They did this because Colombian public opinion was on the side of the United States and supported the position represented by Franklin D. Roosevelt. Colombian aid was effective because public opinion was unanimous. Roosevelt's words were an evangel for the Colombians. When popular opinion is favorable to the United States, one need have no fear about U.S.-Colombian cooperation.

*　　*　　*　　*　　*

CONVERSATION WITH EDUARDO SANTOS IN NEW YORK CITY, JANUARY 18, 1960

Things are going fine in Colombia now. The democratic regime has been able to solidify itself. There is fighting within the Conservative Party, but it is not such as to destroy the unity of the two parties as provided for in the present regime.

One thing which is a bit disconcerting at the present moment is the fact that congressional elections are to be held shortly. Although each party is to have half of the elected members, the relative strength of groups within the various parties is important, and the popular vote is also important as showing the relative standing of the two parties.

He has always thought that it was silly to have congressional elections every two years. When he was president, he urged that the Constitution be amended to call for four-year terms of office for the deputies, arguing that the first year of each term of Congress is spent paying off debts of the past election, the second year in laying the groundwork for the next election. However, his recommendations on this score were never heeded.

He thinks it is better not to hold the continental meeting of the Inter American Association for Democracy and Freedom now. The Castro issue has confused things too much. The conference couldn't take a position against Castro because such a motion would be repudiated throughout the hemisphere. On the other hand, to endorse his regime now would be wrong in view of the grave suspicions which are aroused in the minds of all good democrats by the Castro regime.

*　　*　　*　　*　　*
*　　*　　*　　*　　*

CONVERSATION WITH ALBERTO LLERAS CAMARGO IN HIS HOME IN BOGOTA, COLOMBIA, SEPTEMBER 12, 1956

Lleras Camargo's job now is to line up all factions of the Liberals and Conservatives behind the pact which he signed with Laureano Gómez. This is particularly hard in the Conservative Party, where there are several factions which hate one another. It is hard to get them to accept something signed by Gómez. However, he thinks that all are generally in opposition to the present regime and desire a return to democratic civilian government. Alzate Avendaño told him that he backs the idea of a coalition, and that he regards himself as an exile in his post as Ambassador to Spain. In the Liberal ranks it is not true, as the government papers claim, that Alfonso López Pumarejo doesn't support the Lleras-Gómez agreement. He called López from New York City, on his way home from Spain, and read the agreement to him over the phone, and López said that he backed it.

This is not only an agreement for the period of the dictatorship. They foresee a regime of coalition for a couple of presidential terms after the fall of Rojas Pinilla. It won't be like 1949, because the parties won't be competing for positions in the election, while ostensibly cooperating in a coalition. It won't be important to have a neutral as president, if the president agrees with the coalition idea. In any case, it is hard to find a neutral in Colombia.

The party organizations were destroyed by the dictatorship. The parties used to have committees in every town and village, and the parties gave direction to the party organizations through leading party newspapers, El Tiempo and El Espectador in the Liberal case. This has all been destroyed by persecution and arrest and even killing of local Liberal leaders, and by the censoring of the press.

The top Liberal and Conservative leaders have not been jailed or tortured. The only exiles are Gómez and his family, and perhaps Eduardo Santos. However, the top party leaders are persecuted in a number of ways. He, for instance, wasn't allowed to found a paper, he is shadowed by the police, his mail is censored; he is not free to write or speak. He and others can't travel and visit party leaders on a local level because of the danger to those whom he might visit. The government hasn't persecuted leaders more violently because of its fear of international public opinion.

Rojas Pinilla has taken the turn which he has because of his liking for power, and wanting to continue in office, and because he is getting very wealthy. He is almost crazy in his desire to get rich.

SENDAS, the organization set up by the regime, hasn't aroused much popular support because it has done little effective work. It is largely a propaganda organization. In Cali, for instance, there was rivalry between SENDAS and private charity organizations such as the Red Cross and the Church organizations. SENDAS tried to take over the private relief activities. It aroused tremendous hatred among the people of Cali.

The success of Lleras and others is shown by the fact that the regime is now weak. A year ago, it was very strong, but now it is weak. People know of his and others' campaigns against the government, and what they say. Everything that happens in Bogotá becomes known throughout the country within a week or two.

*   *   *   *   *
*   *   *   *   *

CONVERSATION BY ALFONSO LÓPEZ MICHELSON AT CENTER FOR LATIN AMERICAN AFFAIRS IN NEW YORK CITY, JANUARY 8, 1974

The National Front is coming to an end in Colombia. He has long been one of the principal critics of the National Front, in spite of the fact that the media abroad have given it the reputation for being one of the most interesting democratic experiments.

In some senses, the National Front was his father's idea. His father, during the period of the military dictatorship of General Rojas Pinilla, put forward the idea of the two major parties, Conservatives and Liberals, naming the same candidate for president to demonstrate to the military that it was not true that without a military dictatorship the two parties would return to violent confrontation. This idea was taken up, and the Liberals finally backed a Conservative as presidential candidate.

Then there were further negotiations, the National Front was formed, and the dictatorship was overthrown. The National Front's original agreement provided that there should be parity in apportionment of all cabinet posts and all governorships of departments, which are appointive offices in Colombia. But since the two parties didn't trust one another, since there had been party agreements which had been broken in the past, this agreement was put in the form of a constitutional amendment, which provided that there should be such parity for a period of twelve years, or three presidential terms.

However, further difficulties appeared in selecting the candidate of the Conservatives, whom the Liberals had agreed to support. As a result, there were new negotiations, and a further constitutional amendment was passed by Congress, since it had already been elected. This provided for the Liberals and Conservatives alternating in the presidency for four terms, with the first incumbent to be a Liberal. He supported the first agreement and amendment, but not the second one.

Anyway, the four terms are now up, and that part of the National Front agreement has now run its course. This time there is freedom for any citizen to run and be elected as president. However, the National Front arrangement is not yet completely dead because it will not be until after the 1978 election that the parity arrangement for ministers and governors will expire.

This continuation of parity of the National Front is not well understood abroad. Thus he has met many questions as to whether he intended to follow the kind of course which Allende followed in Chile, nationalizing all foreign enterprises, and doing other such things. His answer to that has to be that even if he had the desire to do that, he would not be constitutionally able to do so because the coalition arrangement still holds.

Of course, this arrangement is unfair to those who are not Liberals or Conservatives. There is a third candidate in the election, Sra. de Moreno, and if her party, ANAPO, should win, she would not constitutionally be able to have a single member of it in the cabinet or a governorship.

If he is asked why he runs under this restriction, his answer is that what he will be able to do if elected will depend upon the kind of majority the Liberals are able to get in Congress. If they can get a substantial majority there, they will be in a position to carry out the program on which he is elected.

He thinks that the first priority for the new government has to be controlling inflation. If the rise in cost of living goes on at the rate it now has, nothing else will be possible, and the stability of the democratic regime will definitely be in danger. So the first thing he will try to do will be to deal with inflation. For the last two or three years he has been urging adoption of an incomes policy, which would restrict the increase in prices, and would only allow wage increases where they are clearly justified. He does not think they can go on any longer with the situation in which unions are in a position to get whatever wage increase they have force enough to get and the employers are equally free to increase their prices.

He is not opposed to a policy of population control and planning. However, he thinks that there is a misunderstanding of this issue, a belief that it is a kind of panacea for the problems of development. He thinks that it is naive merely to take the GNP and divide it by the number of people in the country. One basic aspect of the problem is the very unequal division of wealth and income in a country like Colombia, and one of the risks of a population control program is that it will intensify this inequality because it is well known that upper - and middle-class families tend more readily to adopt family planning, and poorer families tend to do so less readily, a situation which would quickly result in greater inequality of income and wealth. However, he is in favor of adoption of some kind of population control program, and whatever reservations he has arise from economic considerations, not religious ones.

The Colombian Institute of Agrarian Reform [INCORA] and the agrarian reform program in Colombia are highly controversial. It is pointed out that during the last decade, INCORA has given land to only 30,000 families, whereas in his five-year term President Caldera of Venezuela has given out land to 40,000 families. However, it is also pointed out that INCORA has spent between seven and eight billion pesos in this decade, and there is great complaint that it is wasting money. But this is not a true appreciation of the situation. Most of the expenditures of INCORA have not been made on division of land, but on building infrastructure, such as neighborhood roads to help the peasants get products to market; on technical assistance; providing public utilities; and in loans to the peasants.

The fact is that the new crops which are spreading in Colombia, including cotton, rice, and wheat, are increasingly technological. Particularly with the Green Revolution, which is spreading in Colombia, they require that the farmer be a technician. Hence, the kind of expenditures which INCORA has made are justified. Furthermore, the time when the problems of the peasants could be solved merely by giving them land and allowing them to cultivate it as they were habitually accustomed to doing, is now past. Agrarian reform has to incorporate technological factors.

Furthermore, Colombia by and large does not have really large estates. It is true that in the eastern part of the country there are cattle ranches of as many as 30,000 to 40,000 hectares. However, these are far removed from the centers of rural population, and they are the exception. In the savannah of Bogotá, for instance, he doubts that there is any holding which is larger than 500 hectares. And in the coffee-growing areas, there is the problem that the holdings are generally of four or five hectares, too small. In fact, Colombia's rural problem is generally more one of too small holdings rather than of too large ones.

He thinks that the Andean Group is being very successful. He thinks that it may well prove to be a model for the economic integration of all of Latin America. However, the matter goes beyond that. Intra-Latin American trade is growing very generally. For instance, whereas a few years ago Colombia had virtually no trade with other Latin American countries, now 20 percent of its total trade is with Latin America, principally with the Andean Group, but also with other Latin American countries. Whereas a few years ago, there was no place to sell the country's cattle, there is now very great demand, particularly elsewhere in Latin America. The fact is that the development of the Andean Group has taken place at a time in which the general demand for the kinds of products which the Latin Americans have to sell has been rising.

If the United States faces problems in dealing on the one hand with the individual countries of the Andean group and on the other with the Andean Group as a whole, that is a situation which it must also have with the European Common Market, where it certainly cannot deal, for instance, with France without taking into account the Common Market. He suggests that when the United States has figured out how to deal with such a problem with regard to the industrialized countries, it then apply this understanding to the Andean Group.

In general, he thinks that the United States ought to keep its hands out of the internal affairs of Colombia. Those are internal affairs, and they are not the business of the United States. He thinks that the term for this now is "low profile," which he would take to be another name for non-intervention.

However, he thinks that there is another aspect of the relations between the United States and Latin America which needs revision. He thinks that there is too much of a tendency for the United States to look upon Latin America as being made up more or less of countries which are pretty much alike. However, in this the United States is very much mistaken. Certainly the United States in its dealing with Europe doesn't deal with France, Germany, or Britain as if they were all "Europe," making no distinctions in its attitudes and behavior toward them.

He is not urging that the United States ignore something like the Andean Group. He is not essentially talking about economic matters at all, but more generally with the relations, political, cultural, and so on, of this country with the Latin American nations. Those must come to be handled on an individual country-by-country basis, with full recognition of the differences among the countries, with regard to the traditions of the individual countries.

For instance, this comes up with regard to discussion which he has with United States government and business officials when they ask concerning the future of foreign investments in Colombia. They always bring up the specter of Chile. But the fact is that Colombia is different from Chile. There is a long tradition in Colombia of guaranteeing the rights of foreign firms in the administrative behavior of the government as well as in the Colombian courts. There is a long tradition of non-discrimination between foreign firms and individuals and Colombian firms and individuals. He sees no reason why the North Americans concerned with these questions shouldn't look at the traditions of Colombia and treat Colombia within the context of its own traditions, not those of some other nation.

He is very skeptical of the talk of a "new dialogue" between Latin America and the United States, which Secretary of State Henry Kissinger has reportedly put forward. He fears that too often the same old policies are merely put under a new name.

As to whether there is a "special relationship" between United States and Latin America, he wants to be very frank. It is true that until recently there was a sentimental feeling in Latin America about the United States and the Latin American countries being in the same hemisphere and therefore having certain things peculiarly in common.

However, since pragmatists and "practical men" came to be in charge of United States foreign policy, the Latin Americans have been frankly told by these men that nothing of military importance, of cultural importance, and in terms of importance of raw materials exists in the Southern Hemisphere. They have been told that there is a line, he thinks it is called the Tropic of Cancer, which runs through the United States,

Japan, Vladivostock, Moscow, and Europe, and that it is there that things of importance in the world are taking place and will take place. The Latin Americans are all below that line, so they are told, and therefore are of little importance in world considerations.

However, he would comment, things change quickly. Certainly, ten years ago these same men would not have said that the Arab countries were of any importance.

* * * * *
* * * * *

Venezuela

INTRODUCTION

This section deals with all but one of the democratic presidents of Venezuela between 1945 and the early 1990s and contains as well a short entry on Lt. Col. Carlos Delgado Chalbaud, the military man who seized power in October 1948. The one democratic chief executive of Venezuela who is obviously not dealt with in these pages is Rómulo Betancourt. This is because the first book in this series, <u>Venezuela's Voice for Democracy</u>, dealt exclusively with him.

The period covered by this book really began with the revolution of October 1945, when what had until then been the principal opposition party, Acción Democrática (AD), and a group of younger military men seized power. This revolution marked the definitive end of the rule of Venezuela by the "Tyrant of the Andes," Juan Vicente Gómez (who died in bed in December 1935), and his associates and heirs.

Of equal importance with these political and socio-economic changes was the establishment of a new relationship between the Venezuelan government and the foreign-owned oil industry which provided most of the country's foreign exchange. The "50-50 principle" was established for the first time in any country, which provided that half of the profits the oil firms generated in Venezuela should stay in Venezuela either as taxes or as investments agreed upon between the government and the petroleum companies.

Between October 1945 and February 1948, there was in power a Revolutionary Junta, headed by Rómulo Betancourt.

This was a seven-man body consisting of five civilians, four of whom were members of Acción Democrática, and one of the two military men was Lt. Col. Carlos Delgado Chalbaud. Then, as the result of elections, in which Rómulo Gallegos of Acción Democrática and Rafael Caldera of Copei were the two principal candidates, Gallegos was victorious and became president in February 1948.

President Gallegos was overthrown by a military coup late in November 1948. The leader of this coup was Colonel Marcos Pérez Jiménez. Although he had not been one of the plotters to overthrow Gallegos, Colonel Delgado Chalbaud emerged as the head of the Military Junta established on Gallegos's ouster. He held that post until he was assassinated in 1950.

After the death of Delgado Chalbaud, power was clearly in the hands of Pérez Jiménez. In October 1952, he made the mistake of having elections for a new Constitutional Assembly. Acción Democrática and the Communists, who had been outlawed, were banned from participating in those elections, and under these circumstances AD threw its support to the Unión Republicana Democrática [URD], headed by Jóvito Villalba, which clearly won. However, Pérez Jiménez, rather than recognizing the results, seized formal power and proceeded to "recount" the votes to give his supporters control of the new Constitutional Assembly. It ended up electing him as "constitutional president." Although the Copei Party was offered some seats in the Constitutional Assembly, it refused to accept them, and remained from then on the principal legal opposition party in Venezuela.

Pérez Jiménez continued to rule until January 23, 1958, when he was overthrown in a military coup, led by Admiral Wolfgang Larrazábal. It called elections in November of that year, in which Rómulo Betancourt of AD, Rafael Caldera of Copei, and Admiral Larrazábal with the backing of the Unión Republicana Democrática and the Communists were the candidates. Betancourt was the victor.

Shortly before the election, Betancourt, Caldera, and Larrazábal signed what came to be known as the Pact of Punto Fijo (named after Rafael Caldera's house, where it was signed). This pledged the two losers in the forthcoming poll to recognize the victory of the winner, and that for an indefinite period Acción Democrática, Copei, and the URD would participate in a coalition government.

Rómulo Betancourt remained in power his full five-year term and established what came to be known as the "Venedemocracia." The Copei stayed in his government throughout that period; the URD withdrew after a few years and joined the opposition.

During Betancourt's term, two splits took place in his party, Acción Democrática, which are relevant to the conversations which follow. The first happened in 1960, when much of the party's youth group, which in the underground had been much influenced by the Communists (who did not suffer the degree of persecution by the Pérez Jiménez regime that AD received) and were entranced by the Castro Revolution in Cuba, broke away to form the Movement of the Revolutionary Left (MIR). They quickly proclaimed themselves Marxists-Leninists and soon launched guerrilla warfare, which the Communist Party joined. How to deal with this guerrilla conflict, and subsequently how to reintegrate the Communist Party and the MIR into the democratic system, is touched on in conversations with several of the Venezuelan presidents.

The second AD split formed what popularly came to be known as the ARS, named after an advertising agency which had the slogan "Let us do your thinking for you." The ARS split, led by Raúl Ramos Giménez, was fundamentally a division over the 1963 presidential nomination, rather than over ideological issues.

The AD's candidate in 1963 was Raúl Leoni. He had been a member of the Junta Revolucionaria and Minister of Labor between 1945 and 1948, and had gone into exile after Gallegos's overthrow, and under Betancourt had been President of Congress for some time. He won with a very narrow plurality in an election in which his principal opponents were Rafael Caldera, Admiral Larrazábal, who had organized his own party, the Frente Democrático Popular, Jóvito Villalba of the URD, and the businessman and novelist Arturo Uslar Pietri.

During Leoni's period in office, the most serious split occurred in Acción Democrática, once again over the party's presidential candidacy, in 1968. There were two leading "pre-candidates," Gonzalo Barrios and Luis Beltrán Prieto, both of whom had been among the party's founders. Prieto was favored by the party's secretary general, Jesús Paz Galarraga, but when it appeared as if Prieto was not going to get the nomination, he and Paz Galarraga led a split in the AD and set up the Electoral Movement of the People (MEP). At a crucial point in this quarrel, Rómulo Betancourt, then living in Switzerland, sent a strong letter attacking Paz Galarraga and endorsing Gonzalo Barrios, a letter which is referred to below in several conversations.

Another significant political split took place in the late 1960s, that in the Communist Party. Following the Warsaw Pact invasion of Czechoslovakia in 1968, Tedoro

Petkoff, one of the party's younger leaders and a one-time participant in guerrilla activities against the Betancourt and Leoni governments, wrote a book devastatingly critical of the invasion, and of the Venezuelan Communist Party's utter dependence on the Soviet Union. When steps were taken to discipline him, he led a split in the Communist Party, which took virtually all of its younger members, as well as quite a few old timers, to form the Movimiento A Socialismo (MAS). The MAS is referred to in conversations with several of the presidents.

As a result of the MEP split in AD, Rafael Caldera of the Copei won the 1968 election, on his fourth try, although AD got a plurality in Congress. A disturbing element in that election was a resurgence of support for the fallen dictator General Marcos Pérez Jiménez. This is discussed by both President Caldera and President Carlos Andrés Pérez below. Pérez Jiménez was elected senator from Caracas, but the Supreme Court denied him his seat on the grounds that he had not been in Venezuela when he ran, as was required by the electoral law. Subsequently, an amendment to the constitution was adopted, which disqualified from holding public office anyone who had been convicted of crimes in connection with exercising any public post, as Pérez Jiménez had been. That effectively ended Pérez Jiménez's boomlet, although his supporters continued during the 1969-1974 period to have an appreciable representation in Congress.

As the 1973 election approached, Rómulo Betancourt was able to run again in conformity with the constitutional provision that a president had to be out of office for two presidential terms before he could again be a candidate for that office. However, he decided not to run and threw his support to Carlos Andrés Pérez, who was the easy victor.

Pérez presided over Venezuela during the period of the "first oil crisis" of the 1970s, which for Venezuela was a bonanza. President Pérez expounds on what he did with the great increase in oil revenues in his first term, in one of my conversations with him.

In spite of the economic euphoria of the 1970s Acción Democrática was defeated at the end of the administration of Carlos Andrés Pérez, and Luis Herrera Campins of Copei was elected. He is the democratic leader in this volume with whom I have had the smallest contact.

Power again changed hands with the victory of Acción Democrática in 1983 and the election of the AD nominee, Jaime Lusinchi. Finally, in 1988 for the first time in a quarter of a century the nominee of the incumbent party was successful, with the reelection of President Carlos Andrés Pérez.

However, the second administration of Carlos Andrés Pérez was disastrous. A few weeks after Pérez took office, there was a massive uprising of the people of the slums of Caracas, which was only put down with many deaths and other casualties. Then in 1992 there were two serious attempted military insurrections, the first such events in almost thirty years.

Finally, in 1993 official charges of corruption were brought against President Carlos Andrés Pérez. The Supreme Court asked the Congress, as prescribed in the Constitution, for permission to have Pérez formally brought to trial. When Congress unanimously granted this permission, the President could no longer carry out his oficial duties, and Congress had to elect someone to take over in June 1993, in effect to serve until the end of Pérez's constitutional term.

Meanwhile, the 1993 presidential election campaign had begun. Although Acción Democrática and Copei named their candidates, a third major nominee was put forward by a relatively new party, Causa Radical. But the most notable candidate was ex-President Rafael Caldera, who broke with the party he had founded, Copei, in order to maintain his independent candidacy, which was backed by the Movimiento a Socialismo, and several smaller parties, as well as dissidents from Acción Democrática.

The first president dealt with below is Rómulo Gallegos. In addition to being a somewhat amateurish politician, he was his country's most famous novelist. In my conversations with him, he talked both about politics and about his career as a writer. My first encounter with him, in 1947, was in Caracas, where he was president of Acción Democrática; my subsequent conversations with him were when he was in exile after his overthrow.

Rómulo Gallegos is followed by Lt. Col. Carlos Delgado Chalbaud, who in 1947, when I talked with him, was a member of the Revolutionary Junta and Minister of Defense. Although our conversation was very limited, he certainly gave no indication of any disenchantment with the revolutionary regime of which he was a part.

My first contact with Raúl Leoni was also in 1947, when he, too, was a member of the Revolutionary Junta and was Minister of Labor. Subsequently, I saw him when he was in exile in Bolivia and various times after his return to Venezuela following the overthrow of the Pérez Jiménez dictatorship. I talked with him before he was president, while he held that office, and subsequent to his leaving it.

Several things in the conversations with Leoni need some explanation. First, in one of the early conversations,

146

Leoni refers to the "Machamiques." These were a faction of
the Communists who had broken away from the main Communist
Party in the 1940s. They were also known as the "Black
Communists," because they used the color black in the
peculiar Venezuelan electoral system whereby the ballot of
each party had a particular color. Since the main
Communist Party used red, the Machamiques had to be
satisfied with black. (Acción Democrática was white, and
Copei was green.)

In our discussion when Raúl Leoni was president, he
mentions problems he was having with the petroleum
companies. These were finally settled with the payment of
substantial extraordinary taxes by the oil firms.

President Leoni also refers to the U.S. invasion of the
Dominican Republic in 1965 as does President Caldera. This
invasion came about following an uprising against a de
facto government which had seized power with the overthrow
of the democratically elected regime of President Juan
Bosch a year and a half before. After the U.S. invasion,
President Lyndon Johnson sought (successfully) to convert
the occupation force into one of the Organization of
American States. Leoni explains his reasons for not going
along with that move under the circumstances demanded by
Johnson. President Caldera also comments on the Dominican
invasion.

Raúl Leoni's visceral dislike of the Copei Party is
evident in several of my conversations with him. This was
a major factor in blocking the naming of a coalition
candidate for president in 1963, between Acción Democrática
and Copei, who had collaborated throughout the
administration of Rómulo Betancourt. Leoni was not
Betancourt's nominee for the AD presidential candidacy, and
undoubtedly Leoni's strong aversion to Copei was one factor
in Betancourt's thinking at the time.

It may also be noted that in my conversations with Leoni
while he was president, he disliked very much having his
administration compared to that of Rómulo Betancourt.
Although the two men remained good friends until Leoni's
death, Leoni indicated in these discussions a certain
jealousy of his friend.

Finally, Raúl Leoni discusses the issue of Venezuela's
boundary with what was then still British Guiana. After a
long controversy over the boundary issue in the nineteenth
century, it was presumably settled by an arbitration
commission (on which Venezuela had no direct
representation) in 1899. However, President Betancourt had
formally reopened the issue in 1962, when it appeared as if
British Guiana was soon to become independent--which it did
in 1966. Raúl Leoni expounds on this problem at

considerable length and with much passion.

One of my oldest friends in Venezuela has been President Rafael Caldera. I met him first in 1947, when he was the leader of the opposition in the constitutional assembly. This encounter was followed in February 1949 by a letter from him dealing with Copei's attitude toward the military coup which had overthrown President Gallegos.

During the Pérez Jiménez dictatorship, I talked with Caldera three times, on short visits to Caracas when I was travelling for the American Federation of Labor. When he was for a short while in exile in New York City, I had one short talk with him over the telephone. All of my other conversations with him were during the Venedemocracia, when he was leader of Copei during the Betancourt and Leoni regimes, when he was President of the Republic, and subsequently.

My last conversation with Caldera was in August 1993, when he was once again running for president. His comments in that meeting shed considerable light on the state of Venezuela which provoked the sixth presidential campaign of the seventy-seven year old Rafael Caldera.

I also have had some interesting correspondence with Rafael Caldera. Two letters early in 1979 should perhaps be particularly noted. In the first, he was apparently unhappy about my lack of enthusiasm for the victory of the Copei candidate, Luis Herrera Campins, but in the second one he indicates that my attitude is not reason for disrupting our friendship.

Several things should be noted about these conversations with Rafael Caldera. In the first place, at one point he refers to the OAS Conference held in Caracas in 1954 during the Pérez Jiménez dictatorship. Both the legal and underground opposition had tried to get the United States to bring pressure on the dictatorship to free its numerous political prisoners before that meeting. However, President Eisenhower and Secretary of State John Foster Dulles had little interest in bringing such pressure. Dulles in particular was interested mainly in using the OAS meeting to get a condemnation of the Communist-influenced regime then in power in Guatemala. Once that was achieved, Dulles returned home, without discussing what most interested the Latin American delegates, that is, U.S. aid to Latin American economic development. Costa Rica boycotted the Conference.

Caldera also makes reference to the "Betancourt Doctrine." This was the policy of President Betancourt to refuse diplomatic recognition to Latin American regimes which seized power by force. Caldera reversed that policy.

Both Rafael Caldera and Luis Herrera Campins mention the

revolt attempt led by General Jesús María Castro León in May 1960. This was the first of four revolts by elements of the Venezuelan military during the administration of President Betancourt—that of Castro León and one other by right-wing elements and two by Leftists (centered, interestingly enough, in the Marine Corps). As Caldera and Herrera Campins both note, supporters of Copei were important in putting down the Castro León attempt.

Caldera also takes note of a mission on which President Nixon sent Nelson Rockefeller, seeking to mend relations with Latin America. President Caldera had refused to have Rockefeller include Caracas on his itinerary, and in my conversation with him explains why.

The conversations with Caldera in 1978 and 1979 deal rather extensively with Rómulo Betancourt. This was because I was at the time working on my biography of Betancourt.

Finally, a curious incident is referred to in one of my conversations with Caldera while he was president. Apparently after my trips to Venezuela in 1952, 1953, and 1954, my name had been put on the Pérez Jiménez regime's list of foreigners who were not to be admitted to the country. Subsequent to the overthrow of Pérez Jiménez, my name continued to be on a such a list at the Maiquitía airport, and telephone calls to friends in Caracas had been necessary to gain me admittance to the country. I brought this fact to President Caldera's attention, and (as he says to me he will) he got my name removed.

My contacts with Carlos Andrés Pérez extend back to 1952. At that time he, who had been President Betancourt's secretary during the Junta Revolucionaria days, was Betancourt's secretary in exile. In the early 1950s I met him in San José, Costa Rica, where he and Betancourt were both living, and had extensive correspondence with him over various issues.

Two things are particularly prominent in this correspondence. One was that of the problem of Acción Democrática exiles in the island of Trinidad, off the Venezuelan coast, then a British colony. For reasons which Pérez explains, the governor of the territory made life very difficult for AD leaders who had been exiled there. At one point, through my friend D.H. Daines, then head of the British Labour Party in the County of London, I succeeded in getting a Labor M.P. to ask a question about this issue in the House of Commons. That and other pressures Pérez talks about finally brought an end to the mistreatment of Venezuelan exiles in Trinidad.

The second issue which is dealt with extensively in the early letters of Carlos Andrés Pérez is the case of Alberto

Carnevali. He had been secretary general of AD at the time of Gallegos' overthrow. After being exiled to New York following Gallegos' overthrow, he returned to Venezuela to lead the AD underground there. He had finally been captured, escaped jail once, and then been recaptured. When Carlos Andrés Pérez writes about him, he was mortally ill in Pérez Jiménez's prison. He ultimately died there. I had gotten to know Carnevali quite well when he was in New York, studying at Columbia University. So Pérez and Betancourt were particularly anxious for me to do what I could bring publicity to his plight.

One other reference in these letters should be noted. This is Pérez's mentioning of Pedro Estrada, who was head of Seguridad Nacional, the dictatorship's secret police which had the reputation of being one of the most brutal such institutions in the Americas. Caldera also mentions the Seguridad Nacional and its spying on him.

A few other things should be noted about my conversations with Carlos Andrés Pérez. One is that in my conversations with him in the years immediately preceding his candidacy for the presidency in 1973, he was secretary general of Acción Democrática, a post which undoubtedly helped him prepare the ground for running for president.

In connection with that election, Carlos Andrés Pérez at one point predicts that the real contest in 1973 will be between the candidate of Acción Democrática and the ex-dictator Pérez Jiménez. However, as we have noted, by 1973 the possibility of Pérez Jiménez running for office had been eliminated. The real polarization in 1973 was between Acción Democrática and Copei. That essentially bi-partisan system was to persist through the elections of 1978, 1983, and 1988. Although a number of smaller parties continued to exist, only Acción Democrática and Copei had a chance to win the presidency and gain a majority in Congress during that period.

In my conversation with him in 1969, Carlos Andrés Pérez mentions that friends of Rómulo Betancourt were buying a house for him in Caracas, but he wasn't sure that Betancourt would accept it. Betancourt did accept it and lived in it with his second wife, Renée, until his death. After her death, it became the headquarters of the Rómulo Betancourt Foundation.

Finally, in some of his conversations and in one letter, Carlos Andrés Pérez mentions the "Nueva Fuerza" (New Force) which was formed in preparation for the 1973 election. This started out as an alliance among the Unión Republicana Democrática, the Communist Party, and the MEP, the party formed by those who broke away from Acción Democrática in 1967–1968. It was inspired by the Popular Unity coalition *which had won the presidency of Chile for Salvador Allende in 1970. However, the Nueva Fuerza split asunder over who should be its nominee for president. When the MEP and Communists joined forces to support Jesús Paz Galarraga of MEP, the URD broke away and named its traditional leader Jóvito Villalba as that party's nominee. (Jaime Lusinchi also refers several times to the New Force.)*

My contacts with President Luis Herrera Campins, the Copei leader who won the 1978 election, were confined to one conversation in 1960. At that time, he was one of the younger generation of Copei leaders, who had been in exile during most of the Pérez Jiménez dictatorship, and when I talked with him he was a rising star in his party.

I knew Jaime Lusinchi over a period of years, when he was international secretary of Acción Democrática and then leader of that group's bloc in Congress. Frankly, I was quite surprised when he emerged as his party's nominee for president in 1983, since I had never really regarded him as "presidenciable." He had a reputation for a certain lack of seriousness, both within AD and generally in the Venezuelan political community. All of my conversations with him were before he became chief executive.

Unfortunately, the Lusinchi administration had the reputation of having been marked by extensive corruption. Charges were brought against ex-President Lusinchi himself, and as President Carlos Andrés Pérez indicates in my last conversation with him, those charges had not been cleared up more than three years after Lusinchi left office.

My last conversations were with Ramón Velázquez, who in mid-1993 was chosen to serve out the remainder of the term of Carlos Andrés Pérez. I had first met him in 1954, during the Pérez Jiménez dictatorship, when I saw him as an informal representative of the underground Acción Democrática at that time. My second talk with him was when he was secretary general of the presidency under Rómulo Betancourt, a position roughly equivalent to prime minister. Finally I saw him in 1978, when I was collecting material for my biography of Rómulo Betancourt, which explains why our conversation dealt principally with Betancourt.

*   *   *   *   *
*   *   *   *   *

CONVERSATION WITH RÓMULO GALLEGOS IN ACCIÓN DEMOCRÁTICA HEADQUARTERS, CARACAS, JULY 31, 1947

As to the question as to whether Acción Democrática is a Socialist party, he would prefer that this question be asked of the party's trade union leaders, who have a particular point of view in this regard. It is true that generally they think more in socialist terms than do the party's intellectuals. Acción Democrática is a party which is adapted to the surroundings in which it operates. It is a democratic party which wishes to introduce socialist measures when the time is ripe, but not to hurry the matter in a doctrinaire fashion. The similarities which this party has with the Apra in Peru are not intentional, but rather the result of similar conditions breeding a similar kind of reaction. There is no conscious copying of the activities or ideas of the Apristas.

Gallegos was Minister of Education of President López Contrearas in 1936. However, this was a period when López was trying to stage a kind of comedy and include everyone in his administration. Gallegos only remained in López's ministry for three months. Thereafter, López cracked down and it was in fact impossible legally to organize political parties during the regime of López, in spite of the fact that he is now posing as a defender of democracy. At that time, Gallegos did not have any very defined political ideas and devoted most of his energies to his literary activities, and little to politics. However, although he didn't belong to the Partido Democrático Nacional, the predecessor of Acción Democrática, he had friendly relations with its leaders. As a result, in 1941, when López had the stage all rigged for the election of General Medina by Congress, the PDN put up Gallegos as a symbolic candidate, primarily in a move to force the government to grant legal status to what soon after became Acción Democrática. This move was a success, and with the legalization of the party, Gallegos became its first, and so far only, president.

The Copei is the most reactionary party of the opposition. The URD is led by Jóvito Villalba, whose ideological tendencies are similar to those of Acción Democrática, but who for personal reasons is not in AD and fights it ferociously. However, Copei is definitely a party of the Right. As to the elements of the Medina and López regimes, they are pretty well scattered, although there is a high proportion of them in the URD. There are a number in Copei and a considerable number in the Communist Party, since the CP was an ardent supporter of Medina. There are even a few who have entered Acción Democrática.

The Communists' worst enemies are the Socialist parties, and this explains the ferocity with which the Communists here attack Acción Democrática. The Socialist parties are fighting the Communists in their stronghold, the working-class masses, and have somewhat the same kind of appeal and therefore are the Communists' worst enemies.

It is true that this is the first government which is composed of elements which were anti-Gómez. In contrast, the government of López was the direct heir of the Gómez regime and that of Medina was the heir of the López regime. Hence,the grandfather of the Medina regime was that of Gómez. In contrast, this present government is composed of those who had always fought Gómez and had fought his successors as well.

* * * * *

CONVERSATION WITH RÓMULO GALLEGOS IN MORELIA, MEXICO, SEPTEMBER 2, 1953

He is writing a novel about the Mexican agrarian reform but now wants to go to the United States and Canada to get away from the scene of his novel, to survey it from afar, before he sits down finally to put it into shape. That is his way of working. His last published novel, which was about Cuba, he finished in New York City. He went there after some time in Cuba, and the grippe confined him to his room. It was snowing outside, and he was able to sit there and think of Cuba where they never have snow.

He doesn't think that he'll ever go back to Venezuela. This regime is going to last a long time. It is not a personal regime, but a dictatorship of the Army. That is why it will last a long time. His government was overthrown because it was trying to establish civilian control of the Venezuelan government, and this meant ousting the Army from the privileges which it has had since independence. He announced in his inauguration address that the Army must return to its barracks. The Army did not like that.

The Army has traditionally ruled Venezuela and would not agree that this control be taken away. To prevent this, they overthrew his government. They would not agree now that this control be abolished, and for this reason, he thinks the dictatorship will last a long time. Anyway, Gallegos does not expect to live long enough to return. And he is out of politics pretty much now.

*   *   *   *   *

CONVERSATION WITH RÓMULO GALLEGOS IN NEW YORK CITY, APRIL 14, 1955

When he writes a novel, he makes a general outline of his story and then lets the characters themselves develop the story. Sometimes they develop it in a direction that surprises him, and sometimes in one which does not please him. He writes by inspiration, and when nothing more comes, he puts it aside for a while and then comes back to it when he feels he has something more to put down. After he has written it the first time, he has to do it all over again because the characters have developed the story in ways which he doesn't like, and he has to set them to work again.

He has published nine novels so far. He has a few others which have not been published. Several compendiums of his novels have been published, but one Complete Works of Rómulo Gallegos published in Cuba didn't have in it his Cuban novel.

His novel on the Mexican agrarian reform is not yet completed. Although he had thought to bring into it something about the wetbacks and was coming to the southwestern United States to get material for this, he has now decided to leave that material out of the novel. It is at best peripheral to the story and isn't needed.

*   *   *   *   *
*   *   *   *   *

CONVERSATION WITH LT. COLONEL CARLOS DELGADO CHALBAUD IN MINISTRY OF DEFENSE, CARACAS, AUGUST 2, 1947

This is too short to be taken for an interview of any kind, and he doesn't like to give interviews in this hurried fashion. It is merely a reception, at the request of the president's secretary, Dr. Nass.

Delgado Chalbaud was, it is true, exiled by Juan Vicente Gómez, but he holds no rancor for this, since he is a Venezuelan. Furthermore, one shouldn't act out of rancor, but out of reason in any case.

The Revolution of October 18 was a movement of all the people to institute a democratic government. There had never been real elections before, and this Revolution was meant to obtain them. The act of Revolution was, if you like, an alliance of the Army with the political party Acción Democrática. However, the armed forces are an institution which is outside of the political field, and the position of the Army at the present time is not that of an ally of any political party. Rather, the Army is fulfilling its constitutional duty of defending the government, one of the reasons for which it exists. But one cannot properly talk of a political alliance of the Army with anyone. The Army is an institution outside the political ring.

*   *   *   *   *
*   *   *   *   *

CONVERSATION WITH RAÚL LEONI AT ACCIÓN DEMOCRÁTICA HEADQUARTERS, CARACAS, JULY 28, 1947

There has always been a fight between the Communists and what is now Acción Democrática in the labor movement. The Communists were the first to organize unions in the oil fields, although in the first spurt after the death of Juan Vicente Gómez, the ORVE, as the Acción Democrática was then called, rallied considerable support. However, the Left all combined into one party in the underground, and as a result, when the Communists left that group soon after it was formed, they walked off with all the trade union support. The PDN, as it was then called, was left with but five members in Caracas, with Rómulo Betancourt as secretary general, with four other secretaries and no members. However, that small nucleus worked hard and before long, they got control of one of the petroleum unions, and from then on the AD began to grow in the labor movement. However, until the year 1942, one can say that the majority of the labor unions of the country were controlled by the Communists.

The labor movement has gained immensely since the October Revolution. Leoni estimates that there were in October 1945 a bit more than two hundred trade unions recognized by the government, and that now there are over nine hundred. The number of union members has increased from about twenty thousand to some one hundred twenty-five thousand. Now one can say about 60 percent of the workers are organized. This increase in unions has been most marked in the countryside, where some three hundred to three hundred fifty unions have organized since October 1945. These unions were severely fought by previous governments, which were afraid that if the peasants got organized, they'd begin asking for land--which is just what has happened.

The worker has gained a good deal as the result of the Revolution, so far as the real standard of living goes. For instance, in 1945, a peon got as a basic wage about five bolivares a day, which has now been increased to about eight bolivares a day, an increase of some 76.6 percent. On the other hand, the cost of living has gone up from one hundred to about one hundred forty on the index. Of course, the worker also gets paid for Sundays, which means a 16.6 percent increase--accounting for the difference between the 60 percent in wages and the 76 percent in total income. Another instance: A bricklayer gets from forty to fifty bolivares a day now, where he got twenty before.

The fact that the worker is much better off is shown by the large increases in consumption of meat, butter, milk, and other articles of food. The country now imports considerably more meat than in 1945, but there is still a shortage. One can go to working-class areas now and find people queuing up for meat and milk, things which they never thought of eating before; before they didn't have the money to do so.

The claim the Copei leaders make that the government has spent a lot of money and has nothing to show for it is absurd. The money is not invested in flashy things, no, but it is certainly invested where it is doing good. For instance, the system of school lunchrooms which the government is establishing is like nothing else in America. Also, the series of popular restaurants, where meals are sold at one bolivar that cost two, also are a useful addition to the country. Then there is the housing program of the government. Forty million bolivares has been spent on housing, and so far there have been built some four thousand houses, most of them individual one-family homes. One thousand of these have been built in Maracaibo, and most of the rest have been built in provincial towns, in complete contrast to the working of the Medina and López governments, which concentrated everything in Caracas, where foreigners could see it and comment on it. There have been some houses built here in Caracas, too.

There are other things. For instance, in Leoni's ministry, the program of Cultura Obrera, started by Medina, has been expanded--although not as much as Leoni would have liked--by the present government and they are now organizing a Workers University, with an initial appropriation of one hundred fifty thousand bolivares. This university will be governed by five workers and one representative of the Ministry of Labor and one of the Ministry of Education. It will have courses in history, geography, economics, and law of Venezuela, and it will have as its principal objective the training of trade union leaders, so that they can handle their job more intelligently.

Of course, one big change in the labor field which came in with this government was the change in the Ministry itself. Before October there had been no real Ministry of Labor. There was a Ministry of Labor and Communications, but the only labor angle to it was the Dirección General del Trabajo, which was lost in a large number of other directorates, and most of the time and energy of the Ministry was devoted to communications problems and little to labor. Now labor has a ministry all its own, and much more is being done.

The claim of the Communists, particularly the Machamiques, that the Labor Ministry has favored Acción Democrática unions and hindered those of the Communists is false. There has been only one in which a union application for recognition has been held up, and it was finally granted. There has generally been no stalling in connection with recognizing Communist unions. All unions which meet the necessary requirements have been legalized. There has been no preference given any union by the Ministry, although, of course, the Ministry knows who is in the labor movement and keeps track of what the various groups are doing.

Right now the Communists are involved in a campaign to try to embarrass the government. They are calling wildcat strikes, particularly in the oil industry, with the purpose of forcing the government to take strong measures and thus arouse the opposition of the workers to the government. This is a maneuver, of course. In some cases, there have been union leaders arrested in these illegal strikes--the Labor Law says the leaders responsible for illegal strikes shall be jailed for fifteen days, or rather can be so jailed, and if the leaders aren't known, that the officials of the unions can be so jailed. So some have been jailed in connection with the outlaw strikes. However, there has been no discrimination. There have been cases where AD union leaders were also jailed. Of course, they understood the situation, and still remain AD. They know that these maneuvers of the Communists are just maneuvers, but if they'd refuse to go out on strike when the unions do, they'd be labelled saboteurs, traitors, etc., and they don't want that.

One of the things money has been spent on--which can't be seen, particularly--is on keeping down the price of butter. Butter still sells for three bolivares a kilo, although the price has increased from $400 a ton to $1400 since 1945, and the government is paying the difference.

The Copei is a reactionary party, and its alleged Social Catholicism is only a camouflage and demagogy.

The Revolution of October was first planned by the military men. They were disgusted with the terrific corruption and lack of civic consciousness of the Medina regime. They were also irked by the fact that the old Gomecista generals were sitting on top of the military heap and effectively preventing advance of younger officers. The young officers started planning their coup, but they went to Acción Democrática some six months before the coup and proposed that AD take part in it. They'd never have made the coup if they had not had a popular political party to cooperate with them. They didn't want to set up a military dictatorship, in fact wanted to break the succession of military dictatorships under which Venezuela has suffered almost from its independence. Therefore, they looked for a political party which could cooperate with them. They decided that Acción Democrática was the only party with popular following, a progressive program, and not subject to foreign orders, which could cooperate. AD was receptive, and the revolution was planned by the two groups.

They established a Junta Revolucionaria de Gobierno in place of a provisional president for various reasons. First, it was something new, and they thought it would attract attention and might help to rally support. Second, this was a reaction to very personalist government which had preceded October 18, and so they decided it would be a break in this tradition of personalism if instead of having one provisional president there were seven. Finally, they thought that the people would feel that there was less chance of a dictatorship with seven than with one man in the president's chair. So they set up the Junta. They've maintained it ever since.

The Junta functions thus: It meets every week or more often if necessary and takes decisions on the vital things which a president would have to decide--appointment of important officials, making political decisions, etc. However, in the minor day-to-day things, the president of the Junta and the respective ministers deal with the problems. There has been more or less complete harmony within the Junta. They have had two military men in the Junta to ensure support of the Army, and this has been quite effective.

*   *   *   *   *

CONVERSATION WITH RAÚL LEONI AT HIS HOUSE IN LA PAZ, BOLIVIA, AUGUST 21, 1956

In Venezuela, the AD was the one to impose the 50-50 formula. The companies generally accepted it, with Creole setting the pace, Shell following, and the smaller companies more resistant. Under Gómez, the companies began to be forced to change. The oil camps became pretty good, but were surrounded by slums. The AD government wanted to do away with those campamientos. The first experiment with this was carried out in one of the oil regions of the East, where regular towns were set up instead of campamientos. The present government has just followed the policy set by the AD government, in this respect, with the iron mining companies. U.S. Steel has a good policy in Venezuela, Bethlehem has a bad one.

The present government has not demanded the 50-50 policy from the oil companies, and of course the companies are happy.

He was in Colombia for a number of years as an exile. That country is now reaping the result of the fact that the social structure of the country is very rigid. When he first got to Colombia he talked with Sanin, the Liberal leader, who told him that Venezuela was better prepared for democracy than was Colombia, because the castes had never been destroyed in Colombia as happened in Venezuela in the Federal War of the 1850s. Colombia never had such a war. Both parties were controlled by people with aristocratic names, but there was no real party organization. There was a National Committee and nothing else. So the parties were unable to resist the attacks of General Rojas Pinilla.

He is working on editing a Labor Code for Bolivia. There are a large number of labor laws on the books which have never been brought together in a code. If the country wants to attract foreign capital, it must have a body of laws, so new industries know what will be expected of them. They don't know now what they must do under these laws. Furthermore, the laws are not enforced. Each Minister of Labor does as he wishes, does or doesn't enforce the law, as he sees fit. The Labor Code must be ratified by Congress.

The cost of living here is terribly high. He doesn't see how the Bolivian workers can live. Some goods have tripled in price since he has been here. Indian peddlers know about the increase in the value of the dollar, and when asked why they have increased their prices, they cite the increase in the value of the dollar.

The government has made a contract with Gulf Corporation to develop the oil here. The government claims that it has signed a contract on a 50-50 percent basis. Leoni doesn't think that this is so. There is no provision for balancing accounts after each year's operations. There is a 16.6 percent royalty, and this won't provide the 50 percent. This is like the 1942 system in Venezuela, which AD opposed and revised in 1945-1946.

There is a lack of organization in the government here. A deputy has just introduced a new labor law without consulting the committee drawing up the Labor Code, and without consulting President Hernán Siles. This would freeze a number of workers on a job at any given time, which would make it virtually impossible for a company ever to reduce its staff. This was o.k. as an emergency measure, but not for a permanent law.

The Labor Code is finished, but he lacks the secretarial help necessary to get it typed rapidly. The government's salaries are so poor that they can't get good secretaries. It will be the end of September before he can get it typed.

* * * * *

CONVERSATION WITH RAÚL LEONI AT THE HOME OF RÓMULO BETANCOURT, IN CARACAS, AUGUST 16, 1959

The experiment with coalition government is going all right so far. All of those in the government are determined that it will work. This is something new, not only for Venezuela but for Latin America as a whole, and they all realize that it must not fail.

The Unión Republicana Democrática is a bit of a problem. There is undoubtedly a split in that party. Jóvito Villalba does not really control it. The ministers and other members of the government from the party are all loyal in the attempt to make the coalition work. However, there are others, such as Luis Miqulena, who was a Black Communist before, who are acting more the way the Black Communists did than like a democratic party, and so sometimes he comes out with some strange things. The Copei are more serious and more loyal, and they are working very well with the government.

The Senate over which he presides, operates on the basis of committees or commissions. There were thirteen, but they have now been reduced to nine. The first discussion of a bill in the Chamber is on the basis of a report by the commission to which it was assigned; the second is on the bill as changed in the first reading; the third is to accept or reject it. They hope in the constitutional changes which are to be made to reduce the readings to two or even to one, or perhaps have a system of declaring certain bills to be "of national urgency," in which case there would only be one reading, on the basis of the report of the commission which has studied the bill. This would hasten the process of getting bills passed, which is now rather long and cumbersome.

* * * * *

CONVERSATION WITH RAÚL LEONI AT ACCIÓN DEMOCRÁTICA HEADQUARTERS IN CARACAS, JULY 31, 1962

The government is solid now. The repressive measures of the government against the Left insurrectionary attempts have succeeded in demoralizing the Communist and the MIR to a great extent. One of the things which this government has shown is that it is possible to have a regime which is democratic and carries out social reforms, but which also can govern with a strong hand. This, Betancourt has done.

Acción Democrática has not yet discussed presidential candidates. There are, it is true, three who are being discussed--Leoni, Gonzalo Barrios, and Juan Pablo Pérez Alfonso. Whichever one it will be, the others will support him. There is absolutely no danger of a further split in the party as a result of selection of a presidential candidate.

The ARS split didn't damage the party in its rank and file, any more than that of the MIR did. The leadership ranks are a different thing. The ARS is largely a party of parliamentarians, who use their strength in Congress to blackmail the government. He doesn't think that it will be possible for the ARSistas to come back into the AD. The leadership might be willing to have this occur, but the rank and file would not accept it. Certainly, it couldn't occur unless and until the ARSistas recognize that this is the genuine AD.

The economic situation is definitely better than it was last year. This is due to a very considerable degree to the 200 million-bolivar fund for private construction which was established last year, with the help of the oil companies, which bought government bonds. This has stimulated private construction a good deal, and the stimulation of construction has stimulated the industries which depend upon construction.

There is still some unemployment. Frankly, he doesn't think that there are the 200,000 unemployed in Caracas that some people talk about, or even the 175,000 whom others mention, but there is unemployment.

Much of this unemployment in Caracas was fomented, some for economic reasons, some for political. People cleared land on the hills, then brought in other people to occupy it, getting the people who moved in to pay them something for the shacks which they constructed with these "entrepreneurs'" help. Also, some political groups fostered this, bringing in people they thought would be their supporters.

The elections are going to be honest, there is no doubt of that. They will be presided over by the Concejo Supremo Electoral, named by Congress, in which no party can have a majority. There are representatives there of AD, ARS (one of those originally named by AD), MIR (one originally named by AD), Copei, URD, and the Communist Party. There are similar concejos on state and departmental levels. The Concejo Supremo Electoral will have to decide which of the ADs is entitled to the white color and the name and symbols of the party. Stacked as it is by anti-government people, the Consejo may well decide to award them to ARS. But the AD will fight this in the courts.

However, the ARS won't gain many votes by this, even if they get the name and colors. If they get 100,000 votes under any circumstances, they should consider themselves lucky. The peasants will vote for the pipe of Rómulo Betancourt, whether it has the color white or the the color black. It won't matter.

*　　*　　*　　*　　*

CONVERSATION WITH RAÚL LEONI AT HIS HOUSE IN CARACAS, MARCH 10, 1964

The secret of Acción Democrática's success in the 1963 election was its extensive organization. The party has local organizations all over the country, in the smallest and most remote hamlet. The other parties are not as well organized; they may have one or two people in distant localities, but they don't have the network of organization that AD possesses. Acción Democrática received 957,000 recorded votes; but of the 150,000 votes which were declared null and void, the majority in all likelihood were cast by peasants who were intending to vote for AD.

He never doubted that Acción Democrática would win, by a large or small majority. Even if all the other parties had united against it, AD would have won, particularly if there had been a more or less clear Right-versus-Left alignment, with the AD standing on the Left.

The AD had certain disadvantages. It had undergone two splits during the last five years. Those tended to deprive it of many second-rank leaders, particularly in the provinces, who couldn't take the masses with them, but who nevertheless were not working for Acción Democrática this time, and whose absence made a difference.

The problem of the lineup in the new Congress is still vague. It depends more on Acción Democrática than upon him. The AD parliamentary group is still negotiating with the other parties. He hopes that there will evolve a broad front, including, of course, the Copei, but also the URD, Uslar Pietri's party, and that of Larrazábal. He would include all but the ARS.

He thinks that the campaign of violence is in recess rather than being completely solved. There are undoubtedly splits in the Communist Party and the MIR over whether or not the violence campaign should be renewed or whether these parties should return to the constitutional road.

He as president will not have the constitutional power to issue any general amnesty to those involved in the terrorist attempts. That will have to be taken up by Congress. He could send a proposed bill to Congress on the matter, but he will not do so. The parties which have certain commitments with the inhabilitated parties, such as URD, Uslar's party and that of Larrazábal, may present a bill for such a general amnesty. However, such a measure will not pass because both AD and Copei are opposed to it, and they constitute a strong majority in Congress. On the other hand, he has the right to issue individual pardons, and he may see his way to doing so, particularly if it stimulated controversy within the inhabilitated parties on the violence issue.

Whether the inhabilitated parties will participate in the democratic process or not is up to them, not to the government. If, after a year and a half or so there is no significant violence, the government will find the means of letting them participate again, but if there is not such a hiatus in the violence, it will have no incentive to do so.

The United States could be more sensitive to the feelings of the Latin Americans. In the Panama case, for example, if the United States had taken the lead in negotiating, the whole crisis could have been avoided. There is need for less red tape in aid to the Latin American countries. There is need for more consistent policy with regard to the problem of coups d' état in the Latin American countries.

He does not expect that there will be any major changes in his government, as compared with that of Betancourt. He and Betancourt have different styles, because they are different men. But they belong to the same party and believe in the same program. He will look at certain programs of the government and will try to correct their faults.

The important thing about the Acción Democrática government is that it is the first government in the country's history which has paid attention to the interior of the country. All others have concentrated on the capital. His administration will also be a government of the interior.

*   *   *   *   *

CONVERSATION WITH RAÚL LEONI IN THE PRESIDENTIAL RESIDENCE IN CARACAS, JULY 26, 1965

The situation in Venezuela is basically good. However, he is faced with a number of serious problems. One of these is financial. It is not that the government finances are not in good shape, but that in spite of the government's large revenues there is still not enough money to carry out all of the social and economic development programs which they would like to undertake.

Another serious problem is the coalition government. AD is in the government together with the URD and the Frente Nacional Democrático [FDN] of Uslar Pietri. It is not that the three parties don't work pretty well together, but the fact that everything which comes up is a potential government crisis. If someone quits a job, it may cause a crisis; if Leoni wants to propose some measure to Congress, it may cause a crisis among the parties. It would be very much simpler if he had an AD majority in Congress, because then the party could decide what measures to push, he would send them to Congress, and that would be that; there would be a majority to pass them. But with a coalition, it is infinitely more difficult.

Then, of course, there is the problem of the extremists and their guerrilla activities. There were four foci of guerrilla activities in the West, in Portugesa, Trujillo, Falcon, and Lara. Now there is only the one in Lara which is still active. This is not to say that he will be able to stamp out guerrilla activity completely. This is a big country with vast distances and many mountains. He wouldn't promise within three days or three months or a year to end guerrilla activity completely. But he can say that they have succeeded in preventing the guerrilla activity from establishing any firm base, and "tierra libre," as they would call it, from which they can operate and which they dominate. He suspects that the guerrilla activity will die of its own weight, when the extremists become discouraged from lack of results.

In the East, there are some"floating guerrillas" active. These are small groups which decide to raid a plantation, do so, then post their Armed Forces of National Liberation [FALN] signs. But common criminals could do this kind of thing, and it cannot be entirely prevented, and more than any kind of common crime can be completely eliminated, here or anywhere else.

He doesn't put much stock in the idea that the Communists and the MIR are really seriously divided into soft and hard factions. When he was still president of Congress, he once talked with Jesús Faria about this, when Faria was denying that the Communist leaders controlled the terrorist and guerrilla activities. He told Faria that this would mean that they had ceased to be Communists, that the stock in trade of the Communists was strong discipline, and that either they controlled the guerrillas or the guerrillas controlled the party leaders. On the other hand, there is no doubt that the split between Russia and China has had its reflection among the Communists here.

The military situation is good. He can say truthfully that he has not lost a single night's sleep since becoming president from worrying about a possible coup. Of course, this is not to say that the government is not being vigilant about the possibility of a coup and keeping aware of all of those who conspire. When there are meetings between military men and civilians with conspiracy in mind, these are always reported to the government.

However, there are people here who are professional conspirators. These include both civilians and military men. Among the latter, the worst are the retired officers who still maintain certain friendly relations and contacts among officers in active service. Among the civilians, he will say confidentially that there is one faction of Copei which is doing some conspiring, a so-called "Nasserite" group. He has told some of these people that for them to conspire is to say that they have lost confidence in themselves. When the reply is made that AD must have lost confidence in itself to have carried out the 18th of October coup, he notes that the circumstances were completely different. First, the AD didn't start the conspiracy of the 18th of October. In the second place, there did not exist then universal suffrage and the secret ballot. Rather, the presidency and other officials were chosen by the little camarilla in power.

Of course, the guerrilla activities are a strain on the Army. This army was not constituted for this kind of activity, but rather for barracks routine. They find it very difficult to go out and find guerrillas and deal with them. Also, the whole thing is costly, since new equipment and other things must be bought.

The government is having some considerable success in carrying out its political program. For instance, the agrarian reform is going ahead quite satisfactorily. At the time of his speech in Congress in March he said that there were then some 77,000 families settled on the land; he thinks that there are perhaps close to 100,000 by now. He has promised to settle 150,000 families by the time he goes out of office, which will mean a total in two AD terms of 200,000, which will mean that the worst of the agrarian reform problem will have been solved. The reform will be more or less completed in the more populated areas where the pressure for the reform is greatest.

They have been consolidating the agrarian reform. This means providing the peasant settlements with adequate roads, drainage, equipment, and other things which were not provided right at the beginning. As a result, there have been a number of cases in which peasants have returned to settlements that they had abandoned.

He admits that marketing is one of the major problems of the agrarian reform. With the very marked increased in production--resulting from better methods and the cultivation of more land by the people in the agrarian reform settlements--there are difficulties in getting adequate marketing facilities. This year they are about doubling capacity, which should be of considerable help--building 60,000 metric tons' worth of capacity. In addition, the Peasants Federation is arranging for establishment of some peasant markets in the cities, the first of which will open in Caracas very soon. This will eliminate the profits of the middlemen.

They have been getting some markets for their agricultural products abroad. For instance, they have been selling a certain number of tomatoes in the United States.

As for petroleum policy, they are finding their way. The situation is that since the increase in the income tax on the oil companies in 1958, the companies have been reticent about expanding their activities here. In addition, the policy of Rómulo Betancourt of not giving new concessions has increased their reticence. Finally, there is a question pending concerning taxes which are due. All of this has meant that the companies have been trying to pressure the government, figuring that if they don't expand their activities on their existing concessions, they will be able to get the government to open up new concessions.

The government has been trying to work out the contract for service system. However, this is not something for which one can give a blueprint in detail because each contract must be different, in the nature of the case. So he has refused to define the contracts system. So far it has not functioned too well. The idea of getting companies other than those which are here now to come in hasn't worked out very well either.

All of this doesn't mean that there is bad feeling between the government and the companies. Leoni has continued to tell the companies that their present concessions are secure, and more than that, the government is anxious to have them expand operations as much as possible. He and others in the government are realists. They know that the companies have the know-how, the markets, and the transport, and Venezuela has the oil. There must be cooperation between them. He has told them that the problem is not only for them to exploit their concessions while they have them, but also figure out how to continue this cooperation after the concessions have expired.

One of the problems he has had has been the United States' action in Santo Domingo. The extremists have not been able to use it as a banner against the government here because he has taken a firm and decided position on the issue. He has not been anti-Yankee; indeed, his government is friendly with the United States. He feels that it is very important for all of these countries and for peaceful coexistence in the world as a whole, that the United States prestige and moral position be as high as possible. Anything that lowers U.S. prestige and moral position hurts Venezuela.

It was with this attitude that he approached the Dominican problem. He had a feeling before it occurred that there was going to be U.S. armed intervention there. That intervention was wrong. Once it occurred, he was interested in getting the United States out of the situation it had created, by some kind of face-saving device. However, he did not want to justify the United States' action, which was wrong.

Thus, in the Council of the Organization of American States his Ambassador proposed a motion which would have authorized establishment of the OAS peace force there as well as an OAS mediation committee, but which would not have been couched in language which justified United States intervention. He thinks that even Mexico would have voted for the Venezuelan resolution, although it would not have been willing to send troops, as he would have been. Nevertheless, the United States rejected the Venezuelan motion out of hand. They would not agree to using it as a basis and then modify it--he would have been willing to accept reasonable modifications. As a result of this, Venezuela had to vote against the United States motion, which finally passed.

When he calls for revision of the OAS, he means he thinks the political organizations of the OAS must be strengthened so as to take rapid decisions. He thinks also that it is most important that the economic and social organs be strengthened and that there be greater economic cooperation, which in the last analysis has to mean more help from the United States to economic and social development in Latin America.

He thinks that the principle of non-intervention is one which no Latin American country can repudiate. He even thinks that this is of special importance for a government such as this, which for years has urged multilateral action in defense of democracy in the hemisphere, not in a military sense, but rather the use of diplomatic, political, and economic pressure against offending governments.

He thinks that AD stands a good chance of winning the next election. If the economic situation stays as good as it now is, if he can continue to carry out the programs which he has under way, and particularly the housing effort which he has scheduled, if the guerrilla activity can be kept at a minimum, he thinks that there isn't much doubt that the party can win, and with a greater majority than last time. If there is a straight fight between Rafael Caldera and an AD candidate, the AD will win two to one.

One reason for this will be that the people of Venezuela are fundamentally liberal and anti-clerical. The Copei is basically a conservative party, backed by the Church. Although its leaders talk a Christian Social language, and sometimes border on the demagogic in their attacks on the government, they are still essentially a conservative party.

One of the things they attack the government for is alleged failure to do anything about the guerrillas. But this is nonsense. He is the only one who has really done something about the guerrillas; he has done a good deal more than Rómulo did.

There are no real factions in AD now. There are supporters of the various possible candidates for the presidency, but these are not organized as was the ARS in the party, with a party within a party. The predenciables are many and include Gonzalo Barrios, Eligio Anzola, Carlos Andrés Pérez, Jesús Paz Galarraga, Luis Dubuc, and others. However, it is premature to try to say who is likely to be the candidate. Indeed, any candidate who starts out too early is bound to be defeated.

This fact was indicated in the last election campaign. Early in the Betancourt administration, the only obvious candidate for the AD nomination was Raúl Ramos Giménez, and he ended up entirely outside of the party by the time election time rolled around.

As for Leoni himself, he never sought the AD nomination. He told those of his friends who were urging that he run that he would do so if the party wanted him to, but that he would do nothing to seek the nomination, and this is indeed what happened. He never really did work for it; he was chosen by the party rather than consciously wanting to be the candidate.

He has been criticized as a candidate on the grounds that he was not an orator. It is true that he had not had much experience in addressing mass meetings, but he has had his way of appealing to the masses in public meetings. He accompanied Betancourt in his campaign in 1958, which was really his first big experience on the stump. So he can testify to the fact that he himself had as big, if not bigger, meetings than Rómulo in most parts of the country, and that they were at least as enthusiastic as Rómulo's meetings had been in 1958.

It is true that he had to force himself to do this kind of oratory. But he did do so, and he addressed some 500 meetings in a few months of the campaign. Of course, he had to repeat himself many times, but he tried to give as much variety as possible to his talks. When he is making a policy speech, he likes to read it because he wants to say what he has thought out about the subject, knowing that no matter how experienced in speaking one is ,one is sometimes likely to put one's foot in it if he speaks extemporaneously.

He has a mortal fear of television. He didn't use it much in the campaign, although both Caldera and Uslar did. They both have had a lot of experience, Uslar having had a regular program throughout the Pérez Jiménez period.

He thinks that the 970,000 votes which AD was counted as getting in the 1963 election was not their true vote. They received more than

200,000 more than this, about the same as Rómulo's 1,250,000 in 1958. But many of the AD votes were not counted. This was possible because the Electoral Board on the national as well as local level was dominated by the parties opposed to AD. Each party--AD, Copei, URD, ARS, Uslar's--had a representative on the Junta, and they were all out to cut down AD's vote, so that the party was faced with a situation of five against one. The other parties knew that if AD got one million votes, it would have a majority in the Senate, and if it got 1,200,000, it would also have a majority in the House. As a result, they were all anxious to see that the AD vote was kept below 1 million and they succeeded finally in keeping it below that. Leoni has proofs available on this question and someday will write about it. Of course, he cannot say anything publicly about it now, since he is President of the Republic, and it would not be appropriate.

The Copei will never become a mass party because of its clerical connections and innate conservatism. The AD is really the only mass party, with the Communists and URD also having some pretensions to being one. But the Copei certainly is not.

He agrees that AD has not adapted itself sufficiently to the changes which it has brought about in Venezuela. In 1963, as president of the party, he made the point that AD had to do more to attract the new middle class of technicians than it had done up to that point. He thinks that the party is becoming aware of this. It has been holding a series of conferences of AD technicians in various parts of the country to lay the ground-work for making the party more attractive to this group of people. He agrees that this is essential for the future of the party.

He thinks that if he can succeed in turning the government over to his constitutionally elected successor, that Venezuela will be saved. That will mean that the country has had ten years of stable government, and the tradition will by that time have been established that governments are changed by the ballot box and not by coup d'état. He thinks that his chances of being able to pass the government on to an elected successor are quite good and that the future of Venezuela is basically a good one, therefore.

* * * * *

CONVERSATION WITH RAÚL LEONI OVER THE PHONE IN CARACAS, MAY 29, 1968

He is sorry that he will not be able to receive me. If he had gotten word earlier of my being in town, he would certainly have done so, but today he is preparing the speeches which he is going to make during a trip in the eastern part of the country, which he is going to start on tomorrow, particularly a major speech which he has to give in Maturín.

The economic and political situation of the country is very good. He thinks that Acción Democrática has a good chance to win a third victory in the election in December of this year.

* * * * *

CONVERSATION WITH RAÚL LEONI IN HIS OFFICE IN CARACAS, JULY 2, 1969

For ten years, Rómulo and he worked to establish firm foundations for a constitutional democratic regime. He would have felt surer of their success if the third term, that is, the next five years, had been under the leadership of the Acción Democrática. But at this point, he would not like to predict with any certainty what is going to happen.

The Copei government is out to discredit everything which Acción Democrática did. He doesn't think that this is the way that a democratic regime should behave about its predecessor. Certainly, it does not occur where the bases of democratic government are firmly rooted, as in the United States, where the advent of an administration of a different party from the outgoing one may bring a different style, even different programs, but where the new government does not try to discredit the acts of its predecessor.

One of the things the Copei government is doing is to discharge large numbers of government employees who were there under the AD administration. This goes not only for top officials with some responsibility but for humble workers as well. He doesn't think that that is right.

By the time he left office, the guerrillas had been reduced to exceedingly small proportions, of no real significance. He fears that the "pacification" policy, so-called, of Caldera, has served to raise the prestige of the guerrillas, to make them appear much more important than they really are. He fears, too, that it may have rekindled the romantic view of the guerrillas in the minds of young people, and that the upshot of this is likely to be resurgence of guerrilla activity, not only in the countryside but in the cities, with bombings, robberies, murders and all the rest of it. He hopes that he is wrong, but this is what he fears.

He is now in political retirement. This will last until the end of December. He is going to go abroad after another few weeks, and after that he will return to more or less active political affairs.

He is not serving actively in the Senate, although as ex-president he is a lifetime senator. He thinks that this institution of lifetime senatorships for ex-presidents was intended more as an honor for the retiring chief executive than for a real addition to the Senate. In any case, he has no desire to go to plenary sessions of the Senate and hear himself denounced by the Communists and others. He will be glad to serve in committees of the senate, if his knowledge and experience can be of use there, but he has no intention of being a regular attender at plenary sessions. In any case, Betancourt has never really served a day in the Senate, and until he does, Leoni doesn't think that he should. Perhaps the day will come when there are enough ex-presidents in the Senate that they can act as mediators and be of some use as a group, but for now he doesn't want to participate.

He thinks that Acción Democrática has recovered pretty well from the latest split. Its organization is in good shape, and the party is united and solid. The cause of that split was purely and simply the legitimate ambitions of Luis Beltrán Prieto to be President of the Republic. Prieto was never Leoni's candidate for the presidency because he feared that he would be like Rómulo Gallegos, a good candidate but a bad president. He favored Gonzalo Barrios from the beginning, although as president he did not take any active part in the party's choice.

Since the election, Prieto has engaged in violent attacks on Acción Democrática. He has said that he is happy to have contributed to the defeat of the party, and that he has come to the conclusion that he was never really a member of AD. This is silly coming from one of the party's founders, but he has said it. Leoni doesn't read these attacks any more; there is no point to it.

There is certainly no truth to the allegation of Prieto's followers that there were racial issues involved in the split. There is certainly no racialism in Acción Democrática or in Venezuela as a whole. This is one of the two countries in the world where there really are no racial problems, where there is evolving a new race which is a mixture of white, the Negro, and the Indian. The other is Brazil.

The real facts are that Jesús Paz Galarraga and his group were looking around for someone to support for president who would assure them continued control of the party machinery. They first approached Gonzalo Barrios, and when he turned them down, they turned to Luis Beltrán Prieto. He succumbed to their blandishments, and everything followed from that.

One of the problems with Prieto is that he is easily influenced by those close to him. This is particularly true of members of his family, who were the ones who originally put the idea in his head that he might become president and continued to press the idea until he gave in.

During Leoni's administration there was a new program of the Corporación Venezolana de Fomento, labelled "democratization of capital." The idea was to sell small denominations of stock and try to interest the mass of the workers and lower middle class people to buy these. This would serve several purposes. First of all, it would prevent the concentration of ownership of the country's industries in the hands of a small group. In the second place, it would prevent, or mitigate, one aspect of foreign investment in the country, which the Marxist comrades in particular like to talk about, the fact that in the case of direct investments, unlike loans, the country must go on indefinitely paying for not only patents which are used but dividends to the foreign stockholders. Democratization of capital would make it possible for expansion of firms to take place within Venezuela, getting the resources from the small investors.

There has been a change in the nature of corporations here in the last twenty-five or thirty years. They used to be a means of making the directors of the corporations wealthy. He remembers the instance of the Central Venezuela, one of the first sugar mills established here, which came to his attention when he was Minister of Labor in the 1945-1948 government. That Central had permanent labor troubles, and so he sent one of his assistants there, to Zulia, to find out what the matter was. He came back and reported that the labor conditions were virtually feudal in the Central, which was controlled by a single family. As a result of Leoni's intervention, the management was forced to sign its first collective bargaining agreement. This brought the matter to the attention of the small stockholders in the firm, who came to him and said that although they owned something like 40 to 45 percent of the stock, they had never gotten dividends since 1918. These had all gone in high salaries to management or to firms doing business with the Central which were owned by the majority stockholders of the firm. As a result, the government decided to offer to buy the stock of these small stockholders, which it did, giving it in one move about 45 percent stock interest. The idea was to go on and get a controlling interest, but with the coup of November 1948, this idea was abandoned.

The Venezuelan government is quite serious about the issue of the Guyana frontier. The fact is that the British over a long period of time had been encroaching on the Venezuelan frontier, and Spain had never recognized these encroachments legally. Venezuela during the nineteenth century didn't recognize them either, maintained its claim to the areas involved, but during most of the period Venezuela was involved in civil wars and other upheavals, or had dictatorial governments which were not really concerned with the matter. The British took advantage of a civil war in 1899 to press their claim to a very large area, including most of the Venezuelan Guyana of today. It is only an accident that Leoni wasn't born a British subject, because he was born within the area that the British were claiming.

Finally, the American government pressured the Venezuelans into accepting a decision of arbitration. This was the only arbitration on record where one of the parties was not represented. The British were represented, but the Venezuelans were not, the United States serving as Venezuela's representative. The American serving in this capacity was ex-President Benjamin Harrison. He signed an agreement ceding to the British much of the area involved, and the Venezuelans contented themselves with merely lodging a protest. But they never conceded the case. It was logical, therefore, that once the country had a really elected democratic government that the issue would be revived. This is what Betancourt did, and Leoni strongly supported him because he had always argued that the Venezuelans should try to redress this grievance of seventy years.

He maintained the issue on the peaceful and democratic and discussion level. He could have sent in troops and taken the area, the world is full of small wars, and this would just have been one more. However, he didn't want to do this and kept the issue on a pacific plane. He offered some compromise to the Guyanese, for instance, that the area be governed jointly by the two countries, and that they both contribute to developing it. However, the Guyanese would not discuss the idea, in spite of the fact that they themselves agreed in writing to the treaty which sets these boundaries, and the arbitral award should be revised.

He doesn't think that the fact that Guyana is now independent has any influence on the matter one way or the other. For one thing, the area in dispute is not any more occupied by them than by the Venezuelans, since no one lives there at all. Second, "those Negritos" led by Forbes Burnham, who is as crooked as they come and runs the worst government in South America, have no real basis to stand on. It is really a joke to talk of Guyana, Trinidad, Barbados, and Jamaica as independent. They are not really independent in spite of the fact that they have Ambassadors. They are more dependencies than Puerto Rico is. This is not decolonization, it is a step toward decolonization, but not the real thing. Such small states are ridiculous; this is an age for large states, even of empires, and such small independent states are jokes.

Of course, Venezuela couldn't do anything to the Lion while it was strong and had teeth. But now that the Lion is old, weak, and has no teeth any more, Venezuela is in a position to act. At the moment, the Eagle of the United States is strong; in fact there are only two really strong countries in the world, the United States and the Soviet Union, and no one knows which will knock out the other. In any case, it is a law of mankind that nations rise in strength and then fall in strength. When the United States really begins to fall, there won't be one Cuba in the hemisphere, there will be many Cubas.

Venezuela will prevent the entry of Guyana into the Organization of American States. It encouraged Trinidad to join, and introduced her, as it supported the entry of Barbados and Jamaica, but it will never permit Guyana to get in so long as this boundary question hangs fire without resolution. It could go on until the end of the century because in 1970 the mixed commission runs out, and the matter goes to the United Nations secretary general.

They are not fearful of Cheddi Jajan's coming to power in Guyana as a result of Venezuelan pressure on the Burnham government. They're not afraid of that little country in Communist hands. It would be different if it were Brazil, but not Guyana. In any case, he is sure that Brazil would be the United States' policeman if Guyana really went Communist.

He says what he does about Burnham, in spite of the fact that the Venezuelans gave him money and helped him get to power.

* * * * *

CONVERSATION WITH RAÚL LEONI IN HIS OFFICE IN CARACAS, JUNE 8, 1971

Acción Democrática is doing fine. It has largely recovered from the MEP split, and various MEPistas have come back to AD. The party hasn't yet opened its doors very wide for MEPistas to return, in the sense that there are some who want to come back and immediately occupy positions of importance in the party, but the party is not willing to allow this, as yet any way. He thinks that MEP has basically lost its chance, which doesn't mean that it is going to disappear, but does mean that its chance to rival the AD is past. Within MEP there is a Paz Galarraga group, but many who just prefered the candidacy of Prieto, who will return to AD.

AD is again the largest force in the trade union movement. They have been winning back a number of unions which they lost with the MEP split. The AD controls the federations of construction workers, transport workers, health workers, peasants, and a number of other important ones. MEP still controls much of the labor movement in Zulia, and the petroleum workers and some others.

He thinks that it is too bad that the presidential election campaign for 1973 has started so early. Election campaigns always have a depressing economic effect because potential investors wait to see what will happen, and this is already beginning to occur.

The AD will hold its regular convention in January, as the statutes require. It will be this convention which will decide when the party will name its candidate, but he hopes that it will not make the nomination itself. He thinks that it would be better to wait, although if all of the other parties have named theirs or are about to, AD will be forced to do so also. He thinks that it is better to have a longer time for discussion within the party, since the fortunes of pre-candidates rise and fall, and it is better to let things settle a bit before the party chooses its nominee.

He doesn't think that AD will split over its candidate this time. They have learned their lesson, he thinks. They learned it the hard way this last time, by losing the election as a result of the split. There are various people being talked about as candidates, including Rómulo Betancourt,

Gonzalo Barrios, Carlos Andrés Pérez, Leandro Mora, and José Siso Matínez. He thinks that the party would be united behind any of these, although there might be a bit of a struggle over just which one it would be. However, we shall have to wait and see whether he is correct.

Although he is a lifetime senator, he has not participated in the Senate. If he were to participate, he would be called upon from time to time to defend acts of his regime, and since the lifetime senatorship is supposed to be an honor for ex-presidents, he doesn't see the point of having to do this. However, next year he may decide to participate, not necessarily in full sessions of the Senate, but in committee work.

The MEP is now trying to put together a Nueva Fuerza. They have an alliance with the URD and the Communist Party. He thinks that they will find it very hard to choose a candidate because there are too many aspirants in those parties. However, if they do succeed in naming a candidate, then they will be a force to reckon with. They're not likely to win, but they will be an important element in the next election.

There is no question that there is a good deal of sentiment for Pérez Jiménez. This is because there is a good deal of general discontent in the general public because there are many just grievances which people have. They think mistakenly that one way to express this discontent is to vote for Pérez Jiménez. Many have forgotten what kind of a regime he had, or seem to have forgotten. It would be a morally degrading thing for him to run for president. Leoni doubts very much that he will come back to contest an election. He is a coward, and he undoubtedly fears that an attempt would be made on his life were he to return.

An interesting thing has happened among the Pérez Jiménez people. In the 1968 election, they were willing to put anyone on their ticket, and they elected a number of people. However, there is a move by Llovera Páez and others close to Pérez Jiménez to push these people aside and take control of the movement themselves. There might be a struggle.

The case of Pérez Jiménez is not like that of Perón. At least Perón engaged in a good deal of social demagoguery when he was president, and won support then which lasted. Pérez Jiménez was nothing like that; he destroyed the workers' organization, tortured and killed and robbed, and that was that.

Pérez Jiménez is rather tight fisted with his money, and is not likely to spend very much on a campaign. However, there are various others who got rich during the regime, like Llovera Páez, for example, who are likely to be willing to spend a certain amount of money.

The Pérez Jimenistas were the first force in Caracas in the last election. However, Acción Democrática recuperated very well here and was the second force to the Pérez Jimenistas. As a political party, the AD is the leading party in Caracas at the present moment. They have been gaining strength since the election as a result of the errors of the government of Copei; many who were anti-AD before now see that its government was much better than that of Copei.

There is a good deal of confusion now. There has been a certain deterioration in the political sphere, the trade union sphere, the economic sphere, in everything, even including the military sphere. He doesn't think that this deterioration is sufficient to constitute a real danger to the government and the democratic system, but it would have been better if it had not occurred at all.

The AD was pictured when in power as very sectarian. However, the real sectarians have proved to be the Copeyanos in power. They have insisted on having a uni-party government, in spite of the fact that they are a minority. He thinks that in this country it is always good to have a coalition because this tends to cut down the influence of the perpetual sowers of conspiracies. If people are completely out of government, have no chance for jobs, influence, and so on, they tend to listen to the conspirators. He thinks that even if AD should win the next election, with complete control of Congress, they ought to seek to establish a coalition.

There is loose in Latin America, including Venezuela, a strong feeling of Nationalism. This has taken the place of the old kind of anti-Imperialism, anti-Yankeeism of the Communists, and is much more virulent than their kind of propaganda was. It infects all political groups, even Acción Democrática. He has advised his comrades in the party that they cannot afford to be left behind in this, although they should try to keep it within as much control as possible. This finds expression in such things as the bill on return of property of the oil companies which is now being discussed in Congress. The issue there is that the oil concessions will revert to the state in 1983 and 1984, but the companies say that this reversion does not apply to the equipment and so on which they have here, and that they are perfectly free to take out this equipment between now and then, and to some degree they have been doing so. However, this law will provide that the reversion involves all of their investment here, and that they don't have the right between now and 1983 to take out this equipment.

There has finally been enacted the system of service contracts. This is a new way of exploiting the country's oil, in which the international companies are partners of the Compañia Venezolana de Petroleo. So far, five lots have been given out in the Maracaibo area, to Creole, Shell, Texaco, Occidental, and one other company.

The Communists have succeeded in infiltrating both the MEP and Copei. There were elements of MEP who even when they were in AD were anxious to cooperate with the Communists. Thus at the time of the MIR split in 1960, both Salóm Mesa and José González Navarro were at first involved with MIR, and only the strong urging of Leoni and Betancourt prevented them from going out with MIR, at that time. But beyond these elements, there has been real Communist infiltration in the lower ranks of MEP.

The same is true of Copei. The leadership of Copei is very anxious to live down their past of pro-Falangismo, corporativism, and to do this, they will be willing to go to almost any lengths to appear to be Left. Furthermore, fundamentally, they are totalitarians, as are all Catholic and Christian parties, here and elsewhere.

He is going to leave the country for the first time since he was president. He is going to pick up a son whom he sent to California for a year to learn English, and then go to Europe for a while.

* * * * *
* * * * *

CONVERSATION WITH RAFAEL CALDERA IN CAPITOL BUILDING, CARACAS, JULY 28, 1947

The Copei is a new party and its general trend it is similar to the MRP of France and the Christian Democrats of De Gasperi in Italy, or the party of Dolfuss in Austria before World War II. It is socialist, but it is moderate and not materialist. It stems rather from the humanitarianism than from the strictly economic side of Socialism, and the large majority of the leaders and members are definitely Catholic. However, the party doesn't have any particular support from the Church, although one of the Copei deputies is a priest. The party is socialist in the sense of putting the interests of the collectivity above those of the individual.

Caldera and his friends were in contact with Acción Democrática before the Revolution, knew in a general way that it was coming, and Caldera at the end of October 1945 was made attorney general, a position which he held during the first six months of the revolutionary government. However, later he had a falling out politically with AD and quit the government. The Copei was actually organized in February or March 1946, when freedom of political activity was restored after the Revolution.

This party certainly has nothing to do with the López Contreras and Medina factions and condemns them completely as reactionaries, and he thinks that the restoration of either would be a step backward in the history of the country. Copei thinks that the country should look forward and not backward. They are against Conservatism. They are for democracy, and have nothing to do with the recent military attempts against the government, believing that the military men should stay in their barracks and not meddle in politics. The party is Centrist, rather than Rightist, and they don't like to be labelled Rightist.

The basis of support of the party is different in different parts of the country. In Táchira, where 70 percent of the electorate voted for Copei, the support is mainly from workers and peasants. They are founding a labor movement there under the wing of Copei and so far have a Sindicato de Construcción and some Ligas de Campesinos already organized. However, in the cities, and here in Caracas particularly, the support of the party comes from the middle class, and there are even some rich people among them. Of course, there are rich people in all of the parties, not omitting the Communists, who have Miguel Otero Silva, who is one of the richest people in Venezuela. However, the basis of Copei is popular, and they realize that the politics of the country from now on is to be found in the masses, and so Copei is devoting its attention to campaigns among the masses.

Copei criticizes this government on many points. First of all, it is spending money in a form which is disastrous and getting no results therefore. At least the Medina government had some things to show for the millions of bolivares it wasted--it had the El Silencio housing project and school buildings, for instance. This government has spent much more than any previous government and has practically nothing to show for it in concrete reforms. In the second place, the government is completely without a plan. In the budget just passed, which is the biggest in the history of the country, there is an entire lack of plan as to how the money appropriated is to be spent. Thus, in their vast immigration program, the government isn't bothered with how to take care of the immigrants once they get here, is just dumping them on the country.

On the other hand, the government is seriously infringing liberty. For instance, there is a drive to make the State all powerful--as in the case of education, where the famous Decree 321 would put the State completely in control of the education system, and in the new constitution provides

172

that the State alone will train teachers. On the other hand, freedom of
religion is not a reality, since the government uses the age-old privilege of
naming bishops and other officials of the Church as an instrument of its
political policies. Furthermore, although the elections on election day
were clean, the year before the election the government had been busy
buying votes by creating all kinds of useless jobs, by giving land to
peasants, etc., all of which assured them a majority.

Furthermore, there is a large measure of corruption in the
government. The top leaders are certainly idealists--Rómulo Betancourt
himself isn't capable of stealing a bolivar, nor is Raúl Leoni, but that
doesn't go with people further down in the regime. There are many
Acción Democratistas who think that because they are in the government
they have the right to everything, and they are busy putting this theory
into practice. This is, of course, is eating into the party organization itself
and will prejudice the government.

The positive side of the regime, however, is that it threw out all the old
elements which were corrupted by the Gómez regime and its successors,
and has replaced them with youths. The government is exceedingly
young, and so is the opposition. Caldera is thirty-three and hardly any of
the other Copei leaders are much older. This positive break with the past
is a good thing and should be recognized as such. But these youths have
been incompetent in the government.

Copei is growing. It is the principal party of the opposition, and it is
gaining support and members very fast. It is the logical successor to
Acción Democrática. In fact, Copei hopes that the AD regime will
continue some time longer to give Copei a chance to develop its leadership
and its principles so that it can take over power as a mature group. It is
going to have a candidate in the coming election for president, and it
hopes that it will at least double the vote it got in the 1946 election. In
fact, at that time, if the AD and Copei had both been running as parties
of the opposition, Copei would have gotten as much support as the AD.
It was the advantage of being in the government which balanced the
elections toward the AD.

*   *   *   *   *

LETTER FROM RAFAEL CALDERA, FEBRUARY 2, 1949

The lack of reply indicates to me that surely you did not receive my
note in reply to the questionnaire you left with me on July 2, 1948. The
circumstances of the country, indeed, were not of the happiest, and this
explains what occurred last November. My country is now in a definitive
situation; and the civilian forces, like Copei, work and act to make the
military coup only the point of departure for an institutional
reorganization of the country in conformity with democratic principles.
Are you still interested in Venezuela? Have you published anything about
our country? Perhaps American public opinion is not sufficiently
informed concerning our specific problems and for that reason I thought
that perhaps you, now more than before, would have an interest in
obtaining more information.

If this is the case, I am happy to offer you, insofar as possible, my
modest collaboration.

*   *   *   *   *

CONVERSATION WITH RAFAEL CALDERA IN HIS OFFICE IN CARACAS, JULY 22, 1952

Right after the coup d'état, Copei issued a statement that it had had nothing to do with the preparation or execution of that coup. At the same time, it said it would cooperate in every move to restore constitutional government. Members of the party sit in the Supreme Electoral Tribunal, and in the early days one Copyano held the job of governor of Táchira--to which the party really is entitled, since it has always been in a majority in that state, even under Acción Democrática-- for two years. The man did a creditable job. Now Copei is quite frankly in the opposition, however.

So long as Carlos Delgado Chalbaud was alive, the tendency of the government seemed to be to return things as quickly as possible to constitutional normalcy. He was a different kind of man from Pérez Jiménez, and when things got to the crisis stage, he would call in opposition leaders and try to straighten things out to their satisfaction. However, Pérez Jiménez is a horse of a different color, and things are infinitely worse now. Political leaders are being jailed, as was he for about two days over the weekend before last. These constant arrests are designed to terrorize everyone into supporting the government, or at least remaining mum. So far, they have not succeeded, however.

Difficulties are made worse by the establishment of a political party by the government and by the government's apparent attempt to make the current state of things permanent. The new political party, the Independent Electoral Front [FEI] is recruited from people who have never been in politics before; from those who are with every government, not matter what kind it is; and those who are forced into it, such as government employees. In this connection, for instance, recently one of the leading figures in Acción Democrática was arrested, and he was found to have on his person a membership card in the FEI.

The government will do all in its power to keep Copei from winning the coming election. It will have to fight very hard to avoid it. At the moment, the Copei is represented by two of the fifteen members of the National Election Board. There are two representing the URD and one the Socialist Party of Venezuela, the rest being so-called independents, who are government people. In most states, the Copei has one out of five or one out of seven members of the State Electoral Board. However, in the State of Táchira, which is the principal center of Copei strength, but which is also the birthplace of Pérez Jiménez, for which reason the government is particularly anxious to carry it, the Copei does not have a single member on the State Electoral Board.

If the Copei wins, it will certainly work for the return of full constitutionality, with the return to legality of Acción Democrática. He thinks that Acción Democrática and Copei are destined to be the two major parties of the country, the first representing more or less the Socialist point of view, the Copei representing the Christian Social doctrine. Other parties are small, and although like the URD they may have very outstanding men among their members, they are nevertheless destined to remain small.

Caldera will also favor legalization of the Communist Party, not because he thinks it has any moral or judicial right to be recognized by the law, because it would deprive all other parties of legality were it to win, but because it is more convenient to have Communists out where you can see them than to have them illegal.

The URD has followed more or less the same tactics, vis-à-vis the government that Copei has, although at first it was perhaps a little more in the government's corner because of its previous violent opposition to Acción Democrática. However, now it is as firmly in the opposition as is Copei.

Copei's first trade union was recognized only ten days before the fall of Acción Democrática. It was a petroleum union which still exists. Copei would have preferred to have had the unions apolitical, but the fact was that the Copei people just were not given a chance in the Marxist unions, and for this reason the Copei had to go out and organize unions of its own. Their unions are not now officially persecuted, but they encounter endless procrastination in the Ministry of Labor when they go there with their problems, as well as when they originally go to the Ministry to get legal recognition.

* * * * *

CONVERSATION WITH RAFAEL CALDERA IN HIS OFFICE, IN CARACAS, JUNE 2, 1953

The Copei is still in the opposition and is still fighting hard. It is not participating in the current Congress, although the government allotted it several seats, because the government merely hand-picked the members of the group. The Constituent Assembly, which was itself hand-picked by the government, selected those who would sit in the Congress. In fact, in one afternoon's sitting all members of Congress, the state legislatures, and city councils of the Republic were picked at the same time.

The Unión Republicana Democrática won the election last November for several reasons. First of all, it won because Acción Democrática seems to have supported it. In the second place, it seems likely that it had support from certain elements within the government itself, including Germán Suárez Flamerich, who was then one of the members of the ruling Military Junta. Suárez Flamerich is now out of the country on a long vacation. The URD may have had support as well from Colonel Llovera Páez, who was another member of the Military Junta. He went away for a while after the election but is back here now and is demanding the Ministry of War. He was offered this post after Pérez Jiménez's coup d'état last December 2, but he turned it down then. Upon his return, however, he demanded it, but Pérez Jiménez then refused, saying that conditions had changed and that offer was no longer open.

Alberto Carnevali had had the service of army doctors who operated on him. They were good doctors. However, they were not enough, and the government would not allow him to be moved to a hospital, and so he died of cancer. His wife went to the United States three months before he died.

The University remains largely closed because there has been no agreement reached between the students and faculty, on the one hand, and the government, on the other, on the conditions for its opening again. Caldera's young law clerk, an active leader of the Copei youth group, was in jail for some four months, having just recently been released. He was a leader of the student group in the University.

The Copei is still very active in the trade union movement, and the sindicatos under its influence recently held a convention which was very well attended and was quite enthusiastic. Of course, the government is doing all it can to hinder the trade union activities of Copei.

* * * * *

CONVERSATION WITH RAFAEL CALDERA IN HIS OFFICE IN CARACAS, JUNE 25, 1954

Conditions are very bad. The Copei is the only legal party, but it cannot carry on any open activities. The government party, the FEI, was dissolved after the 1952 election. There is talk of founding a new one, but it is so far just talk.

There have been moves to form phony Copei parties in several states. The Copei national leadership got wind of these attempts and so published a repudiation of them and of those who were claiming to be Copeyanos without really being such. As a result, the whole National Executive was jailed for eight days, held incommunicado without any beds to sleep on. They were finally released, due to the commotion that was being kicked up outside, about which they had known nothing.

The election results of 1952 were due to various causes. For one thing, four days before the election, Acción Democrática passed word to its people to vote for URD. Those who just wanted to vote against the government sought the most extreme party to vote for, and the URD more fitted that description. There were elements in the government itself which supported the URD, including the then secretary of the Junta Militar, Miguel Moreno, and probably Suárez Flamerich. Finally, the murder of the AD underground leader Leonardo Ruíz Pineda in plain daylight in the street was violently resented by the people, many of whom voted for URD for that reason.

The government is completely unpopular. The government has put up pictures of Pérez Jiménez in all of the buses, but they are frequently torn down. The same thing happens in buildings where they appear.

There is an apparent prosperity here, but it is all on top. There is considerable unemployment, although no one knows how much, since the government does not keep statistics on the matter. The government has done little to help the productive capacity of the country. It has spent all its money on gigantic projects here in Caracas.

The labor movement is in a bad way. The Cofetrov, of Copei, is still going, against great odds. The Acción Democrática has a small group. The URD has nothing left in the labor movement. The Communists still have Rodolfo Quintero's federation, although he himself has been jailed.

The attitude of the U.S. toward Venezuela is deplorable. He would like to have had contact with the Ambassador, but apparently the Ambassador is afraid of offending Pérez Jiménez by having contacts with the opposition. What he has to fear from Pérez Jiménez, Caldera can't see. Caldera has various friends in the Embassy, but during the Tenth Inter American Conference here, they were all "sick." Dulles and other members of the delegation were strictly isolated. Dulles saw no one, apparently. Caldera would have liked to talk to him, but it was not possible. The U.S. is losing friends by this apparent lack of concern for the interests of democracy in Latin America.

The people here who knew about it applauded Costa Rica's attitude toward the Conference. However, not very many people knew about it, and Costa Rica's statement on it was not published here. Uruguay behaved pretty well here.

Caldera thinks that the convention on territorial refuge adopted here is very dangerous. It provides for the host country to supervise and restrict activities of exiles.

Acción Democrática is still in existence. However, it is badly disorganized after the series of murders of its leaders. They have had many spies in their ranks, as well as turncoats, and they are especially suspicious of anyone now, afraid of new betrayals.

He would like to receive material from the AFL and CIO.

* * * * *

CONVERSATION WITH RAFAEL CALDERA OVER THE TELEPHONE IN NEW YORK CITY, JANUARY 31, 1958

Things seem to be going well in Venezuela now. Quiet and stability have returned, work has resumed. The new government seems to be behaving itself. He thinks that for the present there is no further danger of establishment of a military dictatorship. Whether such a danger will recur in the future will depend on how the political parties behave. They now all want to maintain a friendly atmosphere, and he hopes that it continues this way.

He is leaving in ten minutes to take the car for the airport to return to Venezuela.

* * * * *

CONVERSATION WITH RAFAEL CALDERA IN HIS OFFICE IN CARACAS, MARCH 27, 1958

The situation is certainly much better now than the last time I was here, in 1954. There is full freedom for the political parties. It is not yet clear when the election will be held, but the Copei prefers that the provisional government be as short as possible. The Copei and URD have both come out for a single candidate among the parties. The AD is waiting until their National Convention before they make a pronouncement on the subject. It is true that the parties will have to learn to oppose one another loyally, but in the present provisional situation, it is better not to have the violence of an all-out campaign. The top leaders would undoubtedly behave civilly to one another, but they cannot be sure that the lower-echelon leaders would.

He doesn't see any reason why the single candidate couldn't be one of the party leaders. Each would be surer of what would happen under the presidency of one of the rival party leaders than he would under the presidency of an unknown, without party affiliation or record.

It is not clear which party is strongest. Betancourt says the AD support is what won for URD in 1952; Jóvito Villalba thinks that this was not the case. Copei feels that it lost many votes in 1952 among those who wanted to give the strongest possible indication of opposition to Pérez Jiménez, and so voted for URD, which was more to the Left. There were others who might have voted for Copei but still feared a deal between Copei and the dictatorship. He thinks that after what has happened in the last five years, these people will no longer have any such fear.

The present Junta de Gobierno is not political, in the sense of having any party representation in it. Eugenio Mendoza, one of the civilian members, was a member of Medina's cabinet for one year, but he is the only one with any political past. It is a democratic government. President Larrazábal is almost too democratic; anything the parties propose, he agrees to. His apparent weakness as a Navy man may be his strength.

The Junta Patriótica was an alliance of four parties. Its members were drawn mainly from student ranks because most of the older leaders were in exile. He, for instance, chose one of their student leaders to be the Copei representative. The AD and Communists did the same, and Fabricio Ojeda, the URD representative, was a youth leader. The Junta Patriótica has now been expanded to seventeen members instead of four, with two from each party and the rest independents. They say that they will continue until the elections. But their position and exact reason for staying in existence is not clear. It is not likely that it will be the nucleus of a new party, since it is a coalition of the existing parties.

There has been one new political group formed, Integración Republicana. It has been established by a group of very important professional and business people who don't belong to any of the other parties, but although they say that they do not intend to become a political party, but want to remain a movement, he thinks it is inevitable that they will become a party. The principal leader is Elías Toro. There are rumors that Mariano Picón Salas is going to form a party too, but that seems unlikely now since he is going to be Ambassador to Peru. In December last, Picón Galas headed a list who signed a manifesto against the government.

The Church played a big role in the overthrow of Pérez Jiménez. The hierarchy felt it its duty for the archbishop to issue the May 1 pastoral letter. The letter was social and not political, but that was just as bad as if it had been political insofar as the government was concerned. The government took reprisals, and the Church opposition grew more intense. Priests were arrested, churches were invaded by the police, and so there was open war between the Church and the government.

The Communists are in the Junta Patriótica. However, the other party leaders have agreed to work together without the Communists. There were some protests about this from the Communists, but they have generally accepted this, realizing that they are in a peculiar position.

Trade union unity is being tried. The unions are being reconstituted all over the country. There will undoubtedly be a fight over the issue of international affiliation. The Acción Democrática people are strongly in favor of having the new central labor organization join the Organización Regional Interamericana de Trabajadores [ORIT] and the International Confederation of Free Trade Unions, except for a small group of Adecos influenced by the Communists. The Communists are now for neutrality, for the Venezuelan labor movement to stay out of any international group, which is somewhat peculiar in the light of the supposed Internationalism of the Communists.

*   *   *   *   *

TALK BY RAFAEL CALDERA TO JUVENTUD REVOLUCIONARIA COPEYANA IN CARACAS, MARCH 27, 1958

First, he wants to compliment the youth on the role which they played in the struggle against the Pérez Jiménez dictatorship, the events of January 23, and the country's politics since that time. The Copei Party and the nation both need their continued activity, not only because of their eagerness and willingness to work and sacrifice but also because of the purity of their motives. This purity of motive serves to remind the oldsters of their duties from time to time.

He thinks that political activity by the youth is very necessary. However, he would also like to urge that the youth, and particularly those of the Juventud Revolucionaria Copeyana, not abandon their studies and their efforts to improve themselves, intellectually and otherwise. Such improvement is fundamental to the future of the country.

*   *   *   *   *

CONVERSATION WITH RAFAEL CALDERA IN CARACAS, FEBRUARY 14, 1959

Copei did not do too well in the recent election. Everyone thought that Caldera had no chance to win the presidential election and felt that the fight was between Rómulo Betancourt and the Admiral Larrazábal. Hence, there was a channeling of votes into the AD and URD. But the Copei is in good shape in spite of this defeat.

All pipes are sold out in Caracas. Betancourt smokes one, so everyone is adopting the habit.

*   *   *   *   *

CONVERSATION WITH RAFAEL CALDERA IN CHAMBER OF DEPUTIES, CARACAS, AUGUST 17, 1959

Things are being stabilized here. There is firm unity among the parties. Of course, there is always some danger of an attempted coup, but such an attempt is unlikely to be successful in the face of the unity of the people. Betancourt says that there is no danger of a coup, and Caldera thinks that there really is none. The URD people are working loyally with AD and Copei on the top level, although there are some difficulties with URD in the states.

Copei is doing o.k. Their vote fell relatively in last year's election, but he thinks that they are regaining ground. The party is gaining prestige because the people of Copei in public office are making very good records. Recently, the governor of the Federal District, Francisco Carrillo Batalla, told him that when he, the governor, began visiting hillside slums in Caracas, he had the impression that there was no Copei support there at all. Now, he says, he does definitely see evidence of such support.

The Communists gained much ground and penetrated widely last year. However, he has the impression that the tide has turned, and this year they are beginning to be isolated. Congress refused to pick a Communist as a member of its delegation to the Inter Parliamentary Union meeting in Warsaw, both to give the Communists here a lesson and because they feared that the Communists would go there and try to give the impression that they really ruled Venezuela. The elimination of them from the delegation will give the Poles the hint that the Communists are not of so much consequence here.

There are those who are impatient and want the government to do everything at once. However, this is not possible. The government is trying to plan its work carefully. Pérez Jiménez left virtually no plans for further public works, and what he did leave were for sumptuous kinds of things which are of no use now. It is therefore necessary to draw up plans in detail before a public works program of a large size can be gotten under way.

The projects Pérez Jiménez built were big and showy, such as one or two huge dams--one of which leaks. What the country really needs is a large number of relatively small irrigation projects to serve different and scattered parts of the country.

The completion of the iron and steel plant is being held up by a controversy over the terms of the contract under which Pérez Jiménez had it started. Negotiations are now in progress to revise it. There was much fraud involved. The company says that once the contract is settled, they can have the plant operating within a year and a half.

Pérez Jiménez built things without any plan. For instance, at the steel plant they finished huge office and residence buildings and a special swimming beach years before the plant itself was to be ready. The same thing was done at the petrochemical plant. The only exception was at the Caroní hydroelectric project, which was supervised by a major who was the only honest man in the Pérez Jiménez administration. The houses there are modest but adequate to the needs of the project, and the project itself had first priority.

* * * * *

CONVERSATION WITH RAFAEL CALDERA IN MARACAY, VENEZUELA, APRIL 25, 1960

He thinks that the recent revolt attempt by General Jesús María Castro León has stabilized the situation through its failure. It was feared for a long time, and the fact that it failed will mean that they won't try again for quite some time. Castro León will get five or ten years in prison, which will take him out of circulation for a long enough time to make him harmless.

Copei is doing all right. The peasant who captured Castro León was a Copeyano. So was the local mayor to whom he first took the general. Two Copeyano deputies, one of them Valmore Acevedo, led the peasants in the fight against Castro León. It is particularly good that the revolt failed in a solidly Copeyano state.

* * * * *

CONVERSATION WITH RAFAEL CALDERA IN THE CAPITOL, CARACAS, SEPTEMBER 14, 1961

He hopes that I have discovered that the allegations about Copei's being a conservative party dedicated to defending entrenched interests are wrong. He would not deny that in 1945-1948 period conservative elements tended to support Copei as the least of the possible evils. Nor would Betancourt deny that in the 1945-1948 period AD was very sectarian and hard in its attacks on Copei, which was then the principal opposition party, which it did to the accompaniment of charges that Copei was reactionary.

In fact, Copei is a party which has a definite Social Christian philosophy, and it is not scared by such things as the agrarian reform, the strengthening of the labor movement, the forcing of those who have higher incomes to pay higher taxes, and so on. Quite to the contrary, Copei supports these ideas and is in favor of a democratic revolution in this country, where it is long overdue.

In writing about Venezuela, I should keep in mind the Federal War. It was a terrible struggle in which many people were killed; it destroyed the more or less efficient civil service which had existed until that time and did other kinds of damage. However, its positive aspect was that it did away once and for all with the entrenched aristocracy and introduced a kind of social democracy which is unique in Latin America.

The Federal War is also to a considerable degree responsible for the racial situation in this country. He thinks that Venezuela is the only country in Latin America which has a thorough racial mixture. Virtually everyone in the country is of mixed blood. There were about 50,000 whites from Spain, about 150,000 native whites, about 200,000 Indians, about 100,000 people of pure African descent, and about 500,000 mixed bloods. The struggle for independence intensified this situation, doing away in one way or another with many of the pure whites. The succeeding civil wars had the same effect and this culminated in the Federal War, which was a real social war, won by the representatives of the lower classes.

The Federal War also did away once and for all with the privileges of the descendants of the Conquistadores. Of course, all of the civil wars tended to have somewhat the same effect, with the victors redistributing the property formerly belonging to the losers. But the Federal War was the one in which this tendency to dispossess the hereditary aristocracy was most marked. It is notable that the Conservative Party was defeated in that war, and so thoroughly so that no party since then has dared to call itself Conservative. Cipriano Castro, for instance, another barbudo dictator in these parts some fifty or more years ago, called his party Partido Liberal Restaurador.

He thinks that the 1963-1964 period will present the next major crisis to the democratic regime. Almost everyone is an agreement that Betancourt will not be overthrown and that the regime is secure until the end of his term. But the election period is going to be difficult. It is too early to say who the candidates will be. He thinks that it is advisable for the two democratic parties to support the same candidate. However, speeches by Raúl Ramos Giménez and Jesús Paz Galarraga yesterday, on the twentieth anniversary of AD, both indicated that AD would have its candidate. It would be very difficult, admittedly, to get AD to support Copei, and there are resistances in Copei to backing an Adeco. Much will depend on the circumstances at the time the election is held.

He thinks that there is some merit in the idea that Copei would render worthwhile service if it would leave the government during the next administration and demonstrate how one conducts a loyal and democratic opposition. However, there is at least one serious argument against that. It is that if Copei were to leave the government, particularly now, the Communists might well attempt to make overtures to AD, or to a part of it.

Betancourt and the top leadership of AD are strongly anti-Communist, but there are some in the party, like César Rondón Lovera, who feel uncomfortable about the conflict with the Communists and who want their party to be more Left than the Communists. There might be some danger in this. However, the anti-Communism of AD in general is attested to by a conversation he had with Betancourt, in which Betancourt noted that he was the leader of AD, that he made strong anti-Communist speeches, and that he would certainly not be able to do so if he didn't think that his people would follow him in this.

He doubts that the new Movimiento Republicano Progresista will amount to very much. It might attract a few of the votes which went to Copei last time as the lesser evil. It might attract a larger number of votes from URD. But the group in whose name it particularly speaks is very small numerically in this country. The property-owning middle-class and managerial class is very small indeed.

It is not possible for any Venezuelan to muckrake Simón Bolívar. He thinks that this semi-deification of Bolívar goes back to the situation of Venezuela during most of the nineteenth century and the early part of the current one. Boíívar was like a stroke of lightening which shone throughout the hemisphere, was a hemispheric figure, and after him, Venezuela slipped back into a backwash of history, preoccupied with its civil wars and its dictators. Bolívar, therefore, symbolized what Venezuela might have been or what it still might be. He doubts that any feeling of bad conscience plays a part in this.

* * * * *

CONVERSATION WITH RAFAEL CALDERA IN HIS OFFICE IN CARACAS, AUGUST 1, 1962

He was supposed to go to the same congress on world tensions in Brazil that I'm going to attend. However, he is not sure whether he will be able to do so or not because he has a great deal of work to do, and the dialogue among the four democratic parties will be starting again, and so he should be here for that. He doesn't know whether his absence from those sessions would be understood here.

The position of the government is more stable than it was a couple months ago. However, the overthrow of President Prado in Peru by the Army is alarming for everyone here because of its being a possible precedent here. He recognizes that the Army here is different, is more aware of the danger of the Communists than was the Peruvian Army, and that Betancourt has handled the Army well, devoting a great deal of time to them. But the Peruvian events are still cause for concern.

Worst of all is the fact that there seems to be very little resistance in Peru. It is something like the situation here in November 1948, when a general strike against the military coup failed. Also, he doesn't put too much faith in the fact that the Army there hasn't yet outlawed Apra. Here in 1948, the military men allowed the AD paper El País to come out for two weeks after their coup and didn't outlaw AD for three months.

He thinks that the dialogue among the four democratic parties can be fruitful. Its first fruit has been the formation of the Comisión Delegada of Congress. This is important because it means that the organizations of the democratic state continue to function and that is good. He hopes that the conversations can bring about enough spirit of understanding that the climate will be propitious for the elections. Concretely, though, only a limited number of things can be achieved by these conversations, perhaps the passage of some essential legislation.

He thinks that the opposition parties will participate in the elections. However, if they become convinced that they are going to lose, it might well be that they would try to sabotage them in some manner or other. It is true in the Latin American countries and particularly in Venezuela, that the last year of an administration is its most dangerous year. This was true for Medina and Pérez Jiménez, both of whom fell shortly before the end of their terms.

Copei hasn't adopted a position yet on a candidate. There is much sentiment for some kind of unity candidate with AD. Whether Copei would support a candidate of AD cannot be said for sure now. There would have to be discussion between the parties and consultation of the membership. There would be some resistance certainly among the members.

*　　*　　*　　*　　*

CONVERSATION WITH RAFAEL CALDERA IN HOTEL CARLYLE, NEW YORK CITY, JANUARY 17, 1964

He thinks that the successful fulfillment of the election in Venezuela has been a severe blow for the extreme Leftists there. There has been a considerable diminution of their terrorist activities. There are also reports that in jail the Communist leaders have been fighting a great deal among themselves concerning the question of terrorism. Jesús Faria is reputedly the leader of the more moderate elements, and Eduardo Machado the leader of the extremists. Gustavo Machado is also rated as being with the more moderate element, in spite of the position of his brother. Caldera doesn't know whether this will result in a split of the party.

He did not run for deputy this time as he did in 1958. This was because he wanted to make it clear that he was a serious candidate for president. He knew that Leoni was not running for senator or deputy, and that Jóvito Villalba was not doing so. Hence, he thought that it was a good idea that he not run for anything except the presidency either.

He thinks that it is very good that Pompeyo Márquez, the Communist leader, has been finally caught by the police. He was reputed not only to be a leader of the extreme Leftist terrorists but to be the intellectual author of the whole terrorism campaign.

He thinks that the Alliance for Progress has not as yet caught the imagination of the masses of the people of Latin America. He recognizes that in part this is due to the failure of the political leaders of Latin American democratic parties to sell the Alliance. However, it is also due to the fact that the United States has tended to deal with it too much as a bi-lateral program between it and each of the individual Latin American countries involved. It is necessary that there be action on both sides to make the Alliance really popular.

*　　*　　*　　*　　*

CONVERSATION WITH RAFAEL CALDERA IN HIS OFFICE IN CARACAS, JULY 28, 1965

He and other Venezuelan leaders are considerably preoccupied by the United States intervention in Santo Domingo. They think it reflects a hardness of line and a failure to understand the situation in Latin

America which doesn't bode well for the future. They don't like to see the United States put in his kind of a position, because it does damage to the democratic cause all throughout the hemisphere.

He is also worried about the Vietnam situation. It makes the United States seem like the heir to the colonialism of the European nations, a colonialism which is past. When President Kennedy was here, Caldera had a considerable conversation with him, along these same lines. Kennedy reacted rather strongly, in the sense that he appeared also to be worried about the impact of the Vietnam situation on world opinion. However, he argued that the United States would not get out and abandon these people to the control of a tyrannical party which represented only a small minority of the population. Caldera agrees that it would be disastrous for the United States just to withdraw, but he thinks that it would be wise for the United States to negotiate if possible. He agrees that it looks as if the Johnson administration has been trying to do this via the Russians, but that route doesn't seem to have been productive of any particular results. The Russians have installed missiles in North Vietnam which have shot down American planes.

The guerrillas here are a danger; there is no doubt about that. He thinks that the facts given in Norman Gall's article on the subject in the New Leader are fairly accurate. The guerrillas are very active; they hit here and run, hit there and run. In one part of Lara, near the border of Guárico, they have a kind of base where they exercise a kind of control, although cars can pass through the area, the government has its police posts and so on. The Communists have what they call "militia" there, composed of local peasants who have been given some military training, then have been sent home to be used as reserves some time in the future.

There is a split in both the MIR and the Communist Party on the issue of the armed action. For practical purposes, there are now two MIR's, that of Domingo Alberto Rangel, who is against the military action, and that of Simón Sáez Merida, who supports it. The Sáez Merida faction certainly dominates the MIR at the University. The Communist leaders such as Gustavo Machado and Jesús Faria are said to be against the violence, but they haven't any influence in stopping it. At the last plenum of the party, the leaders of the guerrilla groups were brought in to participate in the discussions, and they dominated them.

The Copei is working very hard, with an eye to winning the next election. The general public opinion atmosphere is very favorable to the party, and there is a widespread conviction that Copei will win in 1968. However, Caldera himself is not quite so sure. It depends on many things.

In the meanwhile, they are conducting a responsible and democratic opposition to the government. This is very important because were they not in the opposition, it would consist only of the extremists on the one hand, and dissident military men on the other, and this would be very dangerous. So Copei is playing a constructive role from the opposition.

He thinks that the impact of the visit of Chilean President Eduardo Frei here last Friday was very good. He thinks that it is very important that an alliance be formed between the populist government here and the Christian Democratic one in Chile, somewhat along the lines of the alliance which existed here in Venezuela during the Betancourt regime. This can be an element of considerable progress for Latin America as a whole. It was with malice aforethought that Frei stopped off only here and in Peru on the way back. Frei was worried by the fact that he had to stop in Argentina and Brazil on his way to Europe.

Caldera is an optimist by nature, but he is a bit preoccupied by the general situation in Latin America. For instance, in Mexico, he fears that there is a wide gulf between the people and the government which may result someday soon in an explosion. He wouldn't like to see this, but he rather fears it. He is also worried by the situation in Bolivia where Paz Estenssoro made a grave mistake in having the constitution changed and having himself reelected. He remembers talking with Betancourt about that at the time it was announced that they were going to change the Constitution to permit reelection, and Rómulo thought that Paz had no way out but to get reelected, or Juan Lechín would have become president. He is also very dubious about the situation in Brazil. He gathers that the United States supports President Castelo Branco very strongly, but he has serious doubts about whether Castelo Branco will be able to resolve the country's problems.

*   *   *   *   *

CONVERSATION WITH RAFAEL CALDERA IN HIS OFFICE IN CARACAS, MAY 29, 1968

He thinks that he has a good chance of being the next president. The contest now seems to be between him and Gonzalo Barrios of Acción Democrática. Until a few weeks ago, it seemed to be between him and Luis Beltrán Prieto, candidate of the Electoral Movement of the People, the dissident AD group, but Prieto seems to be losing ground.

If he becomes president, he will try to make the government more efficient. He will try to eliminate the corruption which has crept in in recent years, particularly through URD's participation in the government. He will try to make various parts of the government, such as Congress, the ministries, and autonomous agencies work better. He may have the same problem with Congress as Betancourt and Leoni have had, of having minority support there. However, he will try to work out a coalition, either in Congress or in the government itself, which will give the government a majority in Congress. He will also try to keep Congress busy on projects presented by the administration, instead of sort of leaving it to its own devices as Leoni has done. For instance, he will present bills for some of the fundamental laws called for by the 1961 Constitution, such as the Law of the Ministries, which have never been presented by the AD governments. He will also try to make the reform and development programs started by AD more efficient--things such as the agrarian reform--and give them more dynamism. He will continue most of the programs which AD has started, but will try to give all of them a new impulse and spirit.

The main difficulty of Copei in this campaign is lack of sufficient money. Although the party is accused of being the party of the rich by its opponents, the party is not rich, and its campaign activities are very much limited by lack of financial resources.

The Copei will perhaps have the backing of the Frente Nacional Democrático [FND] of Uslar Pietri. There is a strong element in the FND which wants to back Copei. URD will probably go with Prieto. Larrazábal will go on his own, because it is only his prestige which can get his party some seats in Congress, which is what they really want.

He is a bit preoccupied by what is happening in Chile, with the Christian Democratic regime there. He gets many conflicting reports. He would appreciate my writing him after I have been there perhaps a month, and giving him my impressions of how it is going.

He thinks that the Army won't give any trouble in the election no matter who is elected. AD has placed a number of people in high commands who are sympathetic to them and who may fear being replaced if the opposition wins, but he doesn't think that they will do anything to interfere with the election results. He thinks that the great majority of officers, for conviction or convenience, are institutionalists and and will honor the election results. There is some opposition to him in the Army, but he also has friends there. Prieto also has friends, although there would be more opposition to him in the armed forces than to Caldera, but Caldera doesn't think that the opposition would be strong enough to provoke a coup.

There have been some internal problems in Copei. However, this is nothing new, and it is exaggerated by the party's opponents. The party had to expel some of its people in 1947, 1948, and 1958, but these acts did not break the basic unity of the party. There is now some restlessness in the youth movement of the party, but this is natural in a democratic party. Furthermore, Caldera has not followed the example of Betancourt, who in 1958 postponed the problem of internal dissension in the party until after AD had won the election. He, at the risk of losing the presidency, has dealt with the problem in Copei immediately. He doesn't think that there will be any split. Copei is the only party which hasn't had a major split, and other parties cannot understand this and tend to see splits in Copei where they do not exist.

The interesting thing is that Copei is the only party which still has the full delegation which was elected to Congress in 1963. In fact, it has a few more now than were elected in 1963 because some have come over to it from other parties. All of the others including AD, URD, FND, FDP, have had at least some members split away since the last election. Only in Copei has this not happened. It attests to the party's internal unity.

* * * * *

LETTER FROM RAFAEL CALDERA, SEPTEMBER 12, 1968

I have to give you sincere thanks for the extensive, analytical, and well reasoned report which you sent me on the Chilean situation. I have read it very carefully and have found in it many valuable observations. I must recognize that with it you have responded to my request with great kindness.

Insofar as Venezuela is concerned, I read in a Milwaukee newspaper an article of yours. I think I can tell you that the situation each day becomes more clearly in my favor, in spite of the enthusiasm, and great propaganda effort carried out by Acción Democrática. I think that you have always believed in a Copeyano triumph, but later; I assure you that this year is going to be "the year of change."

I have asked Eduardo Fernández, a young political science graduate and a member of the National Directorate of Copei, who is working for me as secretary in the electoral campaign to send you some material and ample news.

With a cordial greeting I am happy to reiterate my appreciation and personal friendship.

*   *   *   *   *

LETTER FROM RAFAEL CALDERA, FEBRUARY 13, 1969

I received your letter of December 19, which includes one of the 10th, which undoubtedly was lost with the airplane which crashed. I very much thank you for your congratulations on my election to the presidency of Venezuela.

It has been the culmination of a long effort and although the responsibilities which befall me are very delicate, I have great optimism because of the admirable behavior of the people and the cooperation which I hope to obtain from all Venezuelans of good will.

I thank you also for your generous comments on me personally.

With cordial greetings I reiterate my sentiments of consideration and friendship.

*   *   *   *   *

CONVERSATION WITH RAFAEL CALDERA IN PRESIDENTIAL PALACE IN CARACAS, JULY 3, 1969

His government is having the problems of transition from one regime to another. In some ways it is easier when there is an illegal seizure, because then one brushes out all of the old. But when one comes in constitutionally, one must abide with holdovers from the previous regime, adapt oneself to certain circumstances, and move slowly and cautiously.

He has the added problem that he does not have a majority in Congress. Acción Democrática is the strongest party there, but no one has a majority, and Congress is very much split up because of the proportional representation law, with many small groups.

He doesn't think that a coalition government is possible or advisable at the present time. The only coalition which would give the government a comfortable majority in Congress would be that of Copei and AD, but that would arouse a good deal of resistance in both AD and Copei. The Adecos would fiind it strange being a minority party in a coalition when they had previously been the majority. In the ranks of Copei, where the emphasis has been on change, it would seem very strange to have in the administration elements which made up the previous government. He doesn't think, in conclusion, that such a coalition is possible or desirable. That there may evolve after a while an agreement on particular pieces of legislation is very possible, but nothing much more than this.

Any other coalition would have to include virtually all of the other parties in Congress. This would be very hard to put together, and it would be very unpalatable to have to deal with the Pérezjimenistas, for example.

Of course, AD and other groups feel very uncomfortable being out of power. AD has chosen to go on the offensive largely because the government has been cautious. If the government had gone over to the offensive, AD would have had to be on the defensive.

The immediate issue is that of a request for permission to borrow money to pay about 2 billion bolivares in debts left by the AD government. The fact is that our Adeco friends spent a large amount of money during the election year, and continued to spend it in the three months that Caldera was President-elect. Some of it was quite legitimate, expenditures which had not been foreseen but had to be undertaken, other things which cost somewhat more than was foreseen, and so on. Naturally, AD is taking the position that Copei is trying to float a number of its own projects under the guise of paying off debt acquired during the AD regime. That is the natural play of politics, and is to be expected.

He has not presented any general program to Congress. His first real chance for that is when he presents next year's budget in October. Until then, he will largely be engaged in taking care of immediate needs and doing things that have to be done right now.

He has sought to make some changes from the policies of the AD government. He thinks that the policy of pacification, to try to end once and for all the guerrilla activity, is a change which is very hopeful and which he trusts will bring positive results. He has renewed diplomatic relations with Hungary and Czechoslovakia. There are conversations with the Soviet Union, but Venezuela wants to put certain conditions on recognition, chiefly a limitation on the size of their embassy here, so that it doesn't become something which they don't want it to be. The Russians want an unlimited delegation, arguing that the Peruvians, who recently recognized them, put no strings at all on their recognition, in their hurry to get on with it. Caldera has also reestablished relations with Argentina, Peru, and Panama, and thus has ended the Betancourt Doctrine. Although he respects Betancourt's reasons and objectives for his policy, Caldera does not think it is convenient for Venezuela at the present time.

In terms of internal policy, he wants to launch a sizable program for the barrios of Caracas and other cities. They have five experimental projects now going here in Caracas, where the government gives help to the residents to pave their own streets and convert their houses into respectable dwellings. Perhaps there will be a chance to involve university youth in some of these activities, although now they are all wrapped up in politics. In Chile there have been some programs under Frei to involve university students in programs of this sort, and they seem to have worked out pretty well; perhaps they can do something along these lines here.

The politician in the opposition who is most pained is Jóvito Villalba. He has had two major political opponents in his life, Rómulo Betancourt and Rafael Caldera. Betancourt was of his own generation, and Caldera came along some years later but still challenged Jóvito's position when he did appear on the scene. For Jóvito, it was very painful that Rómulo Betancourt should become president; it was more painful when he became president the second time, but when Rafael Caldera becomes president it is unsupportable for Villalba.

One of the other changes in policy which Caldera has made has been the rehabilitation of the Communist Party. This is really a part of the pacification effort, to bring them fully back into participation in the democratic process.

It is natural that AD and other elements of the opposition should say that the present situation is disquieting, that the government is bungling things. But Caldera is not particularly perturbed. He thinks that these are the natural problems which are faced by a new regime.

In terms of foreign policy, Caldera wants to follow an independent one. He wants to maintain friendly relations with the United States but at the same time to make decisions on the basis of what is right for Venezuela. In this connection, there is the problem of the Rockefeller

Mission. Caldera did not see any reason, for the pure matter of form, for having Rockefeller come here. It would have been necessary to run the risk of having stores and factories burned, to have to take repressive measures which would be very counterproductive in terms of the situation here. So in a very friendly fashion, he informed the United States government that he didn't think that there would be any benefit served either for the United States or Venezuela to have Rockefeller come at that price. It was not a matter of the personal safety of Rockefeller, they had taken all necessary measures here to assure that--but it was just the unnecessary disturbances which would have been caused by the visit. For him to take the decision not to have Rockefeller come was something virtually unheard of in the present state of Inter American relations. It was an example of his seeking an independent policy.

He has followed the policy of having a weekly talk and press conference on Thursday evenings. Actually it is recorded every week at noon on Thursday, and the television stations run it some time during during the evening on prime time. They have done so voluntarily, although it would have been possible to order them to carry it as a chain, all at the same time. However, he didn't think that this would be a very good idea; it would arouse resistance on the part of the viewers, who would feel that they were being forced to listen to Caldera. This weekly press conference has the added advantage that he got agreement from the reporters not to ask him questions except in this period. The period each week is an hour because after the half hour which is filmed, he continues to talk with the reporters for another half hour. He has done this for fourteen weeks, ever since he took office, although he was told by some of his friends that it would be too difficult a thing to do every week.

He thinks that there is merit in the idea that I wrote him about, that Venezuela sponsor a program of encouraging art, literature, and music throughout the hemisphere, to compete with Cuba's Casa de las Americas. He has asked that this be looked into.

He doesn't understand why my name should still be on the list of people not to be admitted to Venezuela, which is kept at Maiquetía and dates in my case from Pérez Jiménez's time in 1954. He thinks they'll have to abolish the list, but in any case, he'll see that my name is removed from it.

* * * * *

TALK BY RAFAEL CALDERA TO THE PRESS IN PRESIDENTIAL PALACE, CARACAS, JUNE 10, 1971

For the hundred fiftieth anniversary of the Battle of Carabobo, which is this year, aside from the economic and social projects which the government is going to complete, it is also going to inaugurate a number of monuments. These are modest and have not cost the government very much, but he thinks that it is a fitting demonstration of patriotism to inaugurate these monuments this year. One will be the long overdue monument to José Antonio Páez in the Pantheon. The speech at the dedication of that monument will be given by Cardinal Quintero, Archbishop of Caracas. Another monument to Páez will be placed in Valencia, at the beginning of the superhighway going to the battlefield of Corabobo, and will be dedicated the day that the superhighway is opened. The speech there will be given by the president of the Sociedad

Bolivariana of Venezuela. There will also be dedicated the Monument to the Venezuelan Soldier, which is particularly sponsored by the Venezuelan Army and is a fit monument in its honor. Also, a Diorama will be opened at the battlefield of Carabobo, which will give those who visit there a ten-minute show to give them the feeling of what actually happened there. In the Palacio Académico, a bust will be raised to the historian Eduardo Blanco, who was an aide to Páez and got from his lips much of the material which went into his histories. Here in Caracas, too, there will be dedicated a monument to the Battle of Boyacá, which assured the independence of Nueva Granada, and which will mark the traditional unity between Venezuela and Colombia; and the speech at that dedication will be given by the Venezuelan Ambassador to Colombia, who has been working hard and long in a friendly and fraternal fashion to present the point of view of the people and the government to the neighboring country.

Last week he sent to the Senate, as is the custom every six months, the names of officers to be promoted from lieutenant colonel to colonel and to the equivalent rank in the Navy. The decisions concerning these promotions were taken only after profound study. The decisions were very difficult because the number of eligible candidates far exceeds the number of posts which are open. The situation at that level is different from that in lower ranks, where promotion is almost regarded as automatic after a certain time and after certain requisites have been fulfilled. But because of the pyramidal structure of the armed forces, established in the law and regulations of the military itself, promotion above the rank of lieutenant colonel is much more difficult, and a much more thorough screening has to be done. The process has been carried on with great seriousness, and the decisions have been made on a professional basis. There is need for other kinds of incentives and rewards for officers who do not get such promotions, and this problem is being studied. He has also proposed to Congress the promotion of Martín García Villasamil, the Minister of Defense, from brigadier to major general, and a similar promotion for a ranking admiral. He thinks that particularly since there has been considerable talk about the armed forces, he owes it to the people of Venezuela to inform them on these matters.

Much has been written recently about the powers of the president and Congress. For the first time, perhaps, the people have come to realize the extent of the constitutional powers of Congress, particularly in approving financial matters. This is so in spite of this being a presidential form of government. The problem is to maintain harmony between the president and the Congress. Before, it was often the case that negotiations took place among leaders of various parties making up a governing coalition. But given the special circumstances which now prevail, such discussions are taking place out in the open. His government has given more respect to Congress than any previous one, and this is not a disaster. For instance, in the United States, the president is often faced with a situation in which Congress is controlled by the party of the opposition. This is different from the situation here, where, although the party of the government is in the minority in Congress, there is no single opposition party which has a majority. Rather, each party makes up its own mind about each issue as it arises.

There is also the interesting fact that all of the parties represented in Congress have participated in the government at one time or another, in some way or the other, and thus know what governmental responsibility is. This is not only true of the present government party, Copei, but also of Acción Democrática, the Movimiento Electoral del Pueblo, the Unión Republicana Democrática, the Frente Democrático del Pueblo, the Frente Nacional Democrática, and the National Civic Crusade [CCN]. They know that they must fortify the interests of the State,or they will ruin their own chances to carry out their objectives.

In addition, the president has ample means in the constitution to maintain his powers, and Caldera intends to use those powers to the fullest. They include the right to name his ministers, to propose bills to Congress, to command the armed forces, and to approve or disapprove of laws passed by Congress.

The College of Industrial Experts and Technicians has recently submitted to him a question concerning the future of technical schools. The Ministry of Education certainly has no intention of abolishing the technical schools. They just want there to be pre-University schools as well as technical schools. He wants by this announcement to stimulate a dialogue between the College and the Ministry of Education. It is a fundamental principle of this government that there be a dialogue on all problems.

The position of the Venezuelan government with regard to oil is one of eternal vigilance. A constant dialogue on the subject is maintained with the United States government through the Venezuelan Ambassador in Washington. He does not think that the president of the United States, in his proposals for an energy pool with Canada, is abandoning his agreement which affects Venezuela. The hemispheric source of oil for the United States is more important now for the U.S. than it is even for Venezuela. This is particularly the case since disloyal competition in oil prices has been eliminated by the agreements of OPEC. He reiterates that the United States has great interest in maintaining hemispheric sources of oil, in view of the rising consumption in the United States and in the world in general, and particular interest in the Venezuelan source, which has proved reliable, not only in normal periods but in those of crisis.

He thinks that a law on the reversion of oil concessions is necessary. Venezuela's interest is that such a law be just and within the country's legal framework, that it not violate the established rights of anyone. However, he would point out that the most important law concerning the petroleum industry now before Congress is that on the nationalization of natural gas, and that Congress has thought it necessary to give this bill long study and has not acted finally on it. It also saw fit to spend a great deal of time on the law on service contracts.

The characteristics of Venezuela's problem with Guyana are not at all the same as those of its problem with Colombia over territorial limits in the Gulf of Venezuela. The conversations in Rome with the Colombian government are going ahead, and the government is keeping the many party groups in Congress amply informed on the progress of these talks.

The resources of the State are administered through its various institutions. He thinks that the Policia Judicial has shown itself very efficient in capturing participants in a recent bank robbery and recovering the money. He has asked for more money for the Policia Judicial, and he is sure that Congress will provide such money.

Foreign Ministers travel a lot today. He has been informed that the Italian Foreign Minister, Aldo Moro, who hated to travel in a plane, is travelling a good part of the time these days and spends almost as much time abroad as he does in Italy. Therefore, he doesn't think that it is strange that Venezuela's Foreign Minister Calvani is travelling a good deal.

Insofar as rumors about a considerable amount of money being wasted by the Instituto Venezolano de Petroquímica, this is being investigated by the Controller General of the Republic, the official most qualified to do so. The government will certainly follow what he finds with interest. Caldera thinks, however, that it is perhaps best at this point not to concentrate on what bad things the Instituto may have done in the past, but rather on the job of making it fully qualified to carry out its tasks in the future.

He won't say anything about when the Minister of Defense will retire, even though his Army retirement comes at the end of this year, after thirty years of service. One of the attributes of the president is to appoint his ministers, and in this he is not bound by retirement ages or any other such consideration.

* * * * *

CONVERSATION WITH RAFAEL CALDERA IN PRESIDENTIAL PALACE, CARACAS, MAY 29, 1972

It is hard to say what is the most important thing which his administration has done during its three and a half years in office. They have done so many things. But among these are the broadening of Venezuela's international relations; the pacification program, which in spite of all its difficulties he thinks has been successful; the reorganization of the public administration to give it more rational form, and which will bear its fruits in the years to come. Then there has been the general atmosphere which has been created, that democracy does work, that it doesn't persecute anyone, that it is a better kind of regime to have.

The resurgence of Pérez Jiménez is strange, in view of his tyranny, his robbery, and the fact that the first time he ran into any really serious difficulty, on the 23rd of January, he ran away. But people forget these things, and there are always people who have grievances against the incumbent regime, and they tend now to gravitate toward him. There are also people who don't understand the apparent turbulence and conflict of democratic politics and who think that a dictatorship can put an end to all of this.

However, he doesn't think that Pérez Jiménez is a real menace. He is certainly none at all insofar as the possibilities of a coup are concerned, since he has no support in the armed forces. Insofar as votes are concerned, he also doubts very much that Pérez Jiménez can get to the presidency through the ballot box.

The electoral campaign has started early, perhaps too early. The reason for this is that various people in the Copei had announced their candidacy, starting with Luis Herrera Campins, and the Copei leaders thought that it was better to have one candidate in the street than three or four. So they held their convention early and named Lorenzo Fernández.

Lorenzo Fernández is the candidate of Caldera's party. But he kept aloof from the process of the party's choosing, and all sides recognize that he did not interfere, and say so.

He cannot say who is going to win. He cannot predict. He has to remain very cautious. However, it is clear that there will be many candidates. There are practically speaking three now. Lorenzo Fernández is there for the Copei, José Vicente Rangel for the MAS, and practically Pérez Jiménez's candidacy is launched. His candidacy is an amorphous kind of thing, supported by many small groups, which divide and subdivide. Caldera expects that Rómulo Betancourt will be the AD candidate, although that is not entirely clear as yet. And it looks as if Jóvito Villalba will be the candidate of the Nueva Fuerza. Caldera agrees that Jóvito is a strange "new force."

For the first time under his government, the Venezuelan government sets the official oil prices, regardless of what the companies actually receive. The oil companies have been very unhappy about that, bringing all kinds of pressure, reducing Venezuelan production from 3,600,000 barrels to 3,000,000, an 18 percent reduction, on the argument that the winter in the United States was warm, that costs of production in the Middle East are lower, and so on. The production has now begun to recover. He is quite aware of the fact that the oil companies play games with the countries in which they operate.

The Peruvians have just given service contracts for exploitation of oil there, and 90 percent of their production will be on that basis, but the terms are the old 50-50 percent basis. This contrasts with the terms of concessions here, which are about 80-20 percent, and of service contracts here, which are nearly 90-10 percent, in favor of the government. The Venezuelan Minister of Mines and Petroleum is returning tomorrow from a visit to Argentina, Chile, Bolivia, and Peru, to explain the conditions under which oil is being exploited here and urge these countries not to make special deals with the oil companies.

The agrarian reform goes on. However, after a while something like this almost gets routinized. There has been an interesting study of the results of the agrarian reform here, which indicates that about 25 percent of those who got land abandoned it, and giving reasons why they have done so.

In spite of rumors in the streets, he had no problem with the armed forces when he relieved García Villasmil of his post as Minister of Defense. He was making a number of changes in his cabinet and decided that among them would be a change in that ministry. He called the leaders of the armed forces together and told them about it, and they had no objections at all. He knows that García Villasmil is making some strange statements to the press, but the facts concerning the matter are as Caldera has said.

*   *   *   *   *

CONVERSATION WITH RAFAEL CALDERA IN PRESIDENTIAL PALACE, CARACAS, JUNE 25, 1973

He thinks that in its four years his regime has accomplished a number of important things. For one, there has been a fundamental change in petroleum policy. Venezuela now sets the reference prices of oil; they have settled the conditions for the reversion of the oil concessions; they have declared natural gas to be a national monopoly.

During these years there has been a complete reform of public administration. There has been a thorough series of job studies, classifications have been established; a real civil service has been established. This is the kind of reform, of course, which is not felt immediately, which will take years to become generally appreciated.

There has been progress in terms of development. Expansion of the Guyana region has been pushed energetically. This year, for instance, over a billion bolivares has been invested in installing the facilities to make steel plate in the steel mill. Among other things, this will provide raw material for the auto industry.

The regionalization of the country has been definitely established. There are now eight regions, each with its own development corporation. These regional corporations have some resources of their own, but most of their funds come from the federal government. Before, the states each developed their own programs, and there was no attempt to coordinate those of neighboring states. Now there is such coordination through the development corporations.

In terms of education, during these four years they have doubled the number of universities and secondary schools. The budget for education has also been doubled.

In social terms, they have raised wages periodically, at the same time keeping inflation more or less in check; it is the lowest inflation in America. The teachers now get double what they did when he came in; the civil servants have gotten wage increases amounting to double what they had received in the previous twelve years.

There has also been a great political change. When he came into office, he felt that the moment had arrived for an attempt at reconciliation. Not only has he legalized the Communist Party but also relegalized the parties to the Left of the Communists, that is, the MAS and the MIR, which has just recently been given legal recognition. The MIR split with a small group which calls itself the MIR Bandera Roja, still trying to carry on a campaign of violence, but the main group under Sáez Merida and others have returned fully to legal political activities.

The fact is that this policy has worked. Virtually all of the guerrilla groups have quit their activities, the small ones still active being of no real importance, although they occasionally cause some trouble. No one whom he pardoned has gone back to violence; he has had the security forces keep a particularly close check on them, since he does not think that a policy of reconciliation should mean that one foolishly lets down one's guard. One or two of the people whom Leoni pardoned have been caught again in violent activities; but this was to be expected, that there would be some who relapsed; it has just been his luck that none whom he let free has done so.

He thinks that the abolition of conscription in the United States is an interesting experiment. The Roman Empire also did without it. He admits that like me, he doesn't particularly like that comparison.

He would prefer not to express an opinion on how the election in December will go. The polls seem to indicate that the Copei candidate, Lorenzo Fernández, is slightly ahead, but the polls are not always correct. He thinks that Fernández will win, but he cannot be sure. In any case, the only real contenders are Copei and Acción Democrática. He is sure that these two parties together will get a higher percent of the votes than they did in 1968. He expects that it will be as high as 70 percent. That will be good for Venezuelan democracy.

*   *   *   *   *

CONVERSATION WITH RAFAEL CALDERA AT HIS HOME IN CARACAS, JULY 29, 1974

It is perhaps small consolation, but Copei actually did quite well in last year's election. Lorenzo Fernández received 1.5 million votes, to the 1.1 million which he himself had received five years before. If the party people had just heard that they had received that vote without hearing other aspects of the election, they would have thought that they had won. It is also small consolation, but Copei has done better in each election in which it has participated than in the previous one.

One thing that occurred was the collapse of the small parties. They were reduced to very small dimensions. Another was that there were thirteen presidential candidates, and all but one of them was an opposition nominee. When it began to appear that only AD's candidate really had a chance to win, there tended to be a mass movement in the direction of Carlos Andrés Pérez.

Another factor was undoubtedly the inflation. Although his government had been able to hold the increase in prices down to one of the lowest in Latin America, it was inevitable that there should be some inflation. He thinks that in the case of price increases in some products there may have been some conscious efforts to raise them. For instance, one day the press announced that sugar was in short supply, as a result of which housewives who had been accustomed to buying two pounds bought twenty. This then became a self-fulfilling prophecy.

Insofar as the collapse of the small parties is concerned, although it may sound self-serving, he thinks that it was due in considerable part to the perfect freedom which his government gave them to function. As a result, they began quarreling bitterly among themselves, and splitting. If the government had persecuted them, they would have tended to stick together, forgetting their differences.

There were some peculiar cases. Miguel Burelli Rivas, who had the support of three parties in the previous election, ran without the support of any of them, backed only by a small group around one fellow who has been very successful over the years in finding ways to get himself elected to the Chamber of Deputies. Of course, Burelli, who had gotten 900,000 votes last time, got very few this time. Another case was Pedro Tinoco, who apparently had great hopes, but got in fact a very small vote.

Insofar as MEP was concerned, it first participated in an attempt to repeat here the Popular Unity of Chile, with the Nueva Fuerza, composed of the MEP, URD, and the Communist Party. They had a method of choosing a candidate which gave the Communist Party the casting vote between Jóvito Villalba of URD and Jesús Paz Galarraga of MEP. Although there were some Communists who favored Jóvito--who thought that he was sure to be the candidate because of his greater prestige--the majority sentiment in the Communist Party was that they should support Paz Galarraga, who had taken a much more Socialist position than Jóvito, who has often changed his position. So Paz Galarraga got the nomination, and although Jóvito said he would accept that, and went off to Europe, his people had second thoughts, rejected Paz Galarraga's nomination, and named Jóvito to run as URD candidate. When this happened, it was clear that Paz Galarraga had absolutely no chance to win, so the great proportion of the MEPistas returned to their original AD loyalties and voted for Carlos Andrés. The alliance of MEP with the Communists may have alienated some of the MEPistas, but it wasn't as important as the growing feeling that Paz Galarraga couldn't win.

The MAS did better. It never felt that it could win the election, but rather used it to establish itself as a real party, and in this it succeeded. Since Carlos Andrés came in, the MAS has been offering very moderate opposition to the AD government. In fact, in a meeting of young people with President Echeverría of Mexico, who just left today, the MAS representative said that MAS supported the government in most of its positions.

Carlos Andrés made a very strong beginning in his administration, taking a number of dramatic steps which won him very wide support. Some surveys showed his support going up from 48 percent he got in the election to 70 percent, and some people even mentioned it as being as high as 85 percent. But in the last month his popularity has fallen to 44 percent again. This is largely due to the severe price increases, which are much more rapid than under Copei. But these ups and downs are to be expected.

The Copei is offering opposition to the government. It is responsible, constitutional opposition, but opposition. On the AD side, there has been a tendency to defame Copei. There were undoubtedly some cases of corruption, and in these cases, Copei would not be opposed to the people being brought to justice, but they don't like accusations being made and then hanging in the air, with nothing being done to clarify whether or not they are justified.

On the other hand, personal relations of Caldera and other Copei leaders with Carlos Andrés remain cordial. He was asked by Carlos Andrés to head the Venezuelan delegation which went to London to participate in a ceremony giving a statue of Bolívar by Venezuela, Colombia, Ecuador, Peru, and Bolivia, and he agreed with pleasure to do so. The Foreign Minister accompanied him. The presence of Caldera in this capacity was commented upon very favorably by the British press. Also, today, for instance, there was a funeral of an old leader of Copei, and Carlos Andrés was there. This kind of cordiality continues.

He has been quite busy since leaving the presidency, getting his house in order, reorganizing his personal papers, and meeting with friends and others who come to see him. He spends at least a couple of hours a day speaking to such people, and this is fine and necessary. However, he hopes soon to get down to doing some writing. He is committed to a chapter for a book on Bolívar to be written by one historian and one statesman or politician from each of the six Bolivarian countries. This appeals to him. He is also committed to doing a paper for a Bolivarian conference on the significance of Bolívar for contemporary Latin America. He also wants to revise his book on labor law and to write a book on Venezuelan sociology, which he promised to do when he published many years ago a very small study on the same subject.

He heard Betancourt tell a group of young Christian Democrats of Latin America here some years ago that he had first had serious doubts raised in his mind about Communism and the Soviet Union by reading Trotsky. He was asked if he had ever been a Communist, and he replied that he had not been a member but had worked very closely with them during the years that he was in Costa Rica. But in reading Trotsky, he had begun to have doubts about their sectarianism and their lack of concern for national problems.

He thinks that trends in Chile are a tragedy. The policies of the Allende government created a polarization which could not continue for long. As a result, a large part of the population of Chile accepted the coup almost as a liberation, on the basis of the general belief that the Chilean Army was the most democratic-minded one in Latin America. However, he has the impression now that the popularity of the Junta is declining rapidly because of its increasingly harsh attitude and its complete inability to deal with the problem of inflation.

The Chilean Democratic leader Tomás Reyes was here a few weeks ago and told them about what is going on. He said that the Christian Democrats are in increasingly strong opposition to the Junta government. In January there was a very sharp exchange of letters between the party president, Patricio Aylwin, and the Minister of Interior.

When he saw Allende, during his trip around South America in 1972, Allende was still optimistic. He boasted to Caldera that he had military men, Communists, and Socialists all in his cabinet. Caldera thinks that Allende made a serious mistake when he brought the military men into his cabinet because this so much as said that when there is a serious situation, the military men will resolve it. Caldera urged Allende to have a frank talk with Eduardo Frei, since the two were personal friends, and it was very important that they come to a common understanding. Allende more or less brushed aside the idea, saying that he would do so after the congressional elections. But by then it was too late.

He is amazed by the revelations concerning President Nixon. He doesn't understand how he could do the things which he has apparently done. He is also surprised that people appear to have forgotten the case of Vice President Agnew. He agrees, however, that the events are demonstrating the strength of the United States constitutional system to handle even this sort of crisis.

He knows of the criticism of his administration for having been too exclusively Copei. But it is a kind of theoretical criticism. In order to have had a cabinet which would have had a majority in Congress, either he would have had to have brought together MEP, URD, FDN, FNP, and the Cruzada Cívica or he would have had to have a coalition with Acción Democrática. It is certain that AD had no interest in entering the government as a junior partner. And to have tried the other alternative would have meant to have had a small duplicate of he Congress in his cabinet, and this would have brought nothing but headaches. So he had little alternative but to govern only with Copei. Carlos Andrés, incidentally, has more party members in his cabinet than Caldera did.

Copei supports the idea of reversion of petroleum and the declaration of petrolem to be a reserve of the State. During the first week of the present Congress, when he was still president, there were two bills presented on the issue in Congress, one by Copei, the other by MEP. However, Carlos Andrés appointed a sixty-man commission to study the question, which suspended any action on these bills.

A heavy rain always causes the collapse of some of the shanties in Caracas. His government started a modest program to help the shanty dwellers rebuild their homes in a more sturdy and permanent fashion, when the Banco Obrero set up a fund for this purpose. However, they were faced with lack of sufficient funds to take care of this.

One of the charges some ADers are making against the Copei government is that some of the state governors spent money they didn't have. However, there is nothing corrupt about this, since governors who were short at the time would authorize projects on the basis of knowledge that they were going to get more funds later. In any case, whatever debts they left, whatever debts Venezuela has at all, whether internal or external, could be paid for with a small part of this year's oil income.

He has wondered if the events in Portugal, particularly if the Spinola government succeeds in establishing a really democratic regime and in bringing about decolonization, will have any effect on the younger officers of the Brazilian Army. After all, it is the younger officers of the Portuguese Army who are responsible for what is happening there now.

The average Venezuelan, and even the average Venezuelan politician, doesn't give much thought to Brazil. This is because the vital center of Brazil is in the South, and there is a great deal of vacant territory between there and Venezuela. However, some of the political leaders do worry a bit about of flexing muscles in which Brazil seems to be engaged.

*　*　*　*　*

CONVERSATION WITH RAFAEL CALDERA IN HIS OFFICE IN CARACAS, JANUARY 2, 1978

He is too young to be of the generation of 1928. He was just twelve when the events of that year took place. He was a student leader after the death of Juan Vicente Gómez and was not associated with Betancourt or those around him. On the contrary, he was of a decidedly opposed ideological tendency to that of Betancourt.

He first met Betancourt in 1941 or 1942. He appeared with him at a meeting in which all the opposition participated, calling for a law to declare membership in Congress incompatible with holding executive offices. It was quite customary for members of Congress to have sinecures in the public administration. Jóvito Villalba also spoke at this meeting, although he was not exactly in opposition to the Medina government.

At that time, Caldera headed a small political group called Acción Nacional. However, it broke up in 1945, before the golpe of October 18, because some of its members wanted to support the presidential candidacy of López Contreras, which Caldera and others decidedly did not want to do. Also, it was moving too slowly toward organization of a real political party, and they decided to end their efforts until a better opportunity presented itself.

A week after October 18, he was offered by Betancourt the post of Procurador General. The post then combined that of attorney General and Fiscalía General, but it was not a cabinet-rank position. Rómulo told him that he wanted someone who was not a member of AD to have the post, which was supposed to keep track of the honesty of the public administration.

Caldera held that post for six months. During the period, he was supposed to be the one who organized the prosecution of the misdeeds of the people of the previous administration. He had a discrepancy with the AD people over that. He held that only cases of robbing funds should be prosecuted, while the AD people insisted that people should be tried for "mis-spending" money. That is a very difficult thing to agree on, whether money has been misspent or not, and particularly so in a revolutionary atmosphere such as then existed. Luis Beltrán Prieto told him subsequently that when they went into the room to write the decree on that subject, they left their law books outside.

He broke definitively with the Junta Revolucionaria government after six months, over the issue of a political meeting which he addressed in

Táchira which was attacked by people of AD. Leonardo Ruíz Pineda, who was then governor of Táchira, did nothing about that incident, didn't try to find out who had attacked the meeting, and to punish them.

Copei was founded in January 1946. It was at first a committee to organize political independents. Hence the initials Copei. But when they finally established it formally as a party, the initials stuck, so it became the Partido Copei. A few years later they took the name Social Cristiano. That was the period of the apogee of the Christian Democratic parties in Europe, and so they adopted the name. He guesses that they didn't use Christian Democratic because they wanted to emphasize the social aspects of their ideas.

Copei had rough going under the first AD government. For instance, they held a big meeting in the Nuevo Circo in Caracas. Before it, throwaways circulated threatening that AD would break up the meeting. Caldera sought the help of Gonzalo Barrios, the governor of the Federal District, and Mario Vargas, the Minister of Interior, to have police guard the outside of the building, since Copei had its own squads who they thought could handle the situation inside the Nuevo Circo. But they got no police protection, they were attacked by AD toughs and three people were killed in the fighting. No one was ever prosecuted for this.

Copei was the largest opposition party. In the Constituent Assembly elections, it got 100,000 votes to URD's 50,000. In the presidential election, Caldera got 280,000 to 50,000 for Gustavo Machado, the Communist, and 800,000 for Rómulo Gallegos. He was only thirty-one when he ran. He had been only twenty-nine when he became Procurador General, and if it had been a constitutional regime, he could not have served, since one had to be thirty.

He thinks that Rómulo Gallegos could have prevented the coup against him. Such a coup would not have been successful if Betancourt had been president. Gallegos was not willing to maneuver to prevent it. For instance, he was urged to go to the Ministry of Defense and confront the military men who were plotting, but he refused, saying that he could not since he had not gone to any other ministry. One of the demands of the military was that Betancourt leave the country, and Rómulo was willing to do so. But Gallegos refused this absolutely. The fact was that Gallegos was not a politician.

There is a report that before the 1947 election campaign, Carlos Delgado Chalbaud asked for a private conversation with Betancourt, and they met in a country retreat the president had in those days. It is said that Delgado Chalbaud warned Betancourt against having Gallegos become president, warning that he couldn't handle the military and would be overthrown. The story goes that Delgado Chalbaud urged Rómulo to abrogate the pledge of the members of the Junta Revolucionaria that none of them would run for president, and that Betancourt should run himself. Betancourt replied that he could not do this for two reasons, because the pledge not to run was sacred, and because AD had a commitment to Gallegos that it could not break.

The coup was in the morning of November 24. That evening he was called from the Ministry of Defense and was told that the president of the Junta Militar wanted to talk with him. When he asked who the president was, and was told that it was Delgado Chalbaud, Caldera expressed surprise that Delgado Chalbaud wasn't in jail. Delgado asked him to come to the Ministry of Defense, and after first objecting, Caldera agreed. A military car was sent to pick him up because there was a curfew. When Delgado Chalbaud greeted him, he said that this was a very bad situation, that he couldn't prevent the coup, and so he had joined it to keep it from being worse. Delgado Chalbaud may have been telling the truth. But Betancourt never forgave Delgado Chalbaud for participating in the coup. Mario Vargas was among those who were there with Delgado Chalbaud that night, and he also signed the document declaring Gallegos deposed. Betancourt apparently forgave him.

After the coup, Copei put out a document saying that this was a lamentable end to a very bad situation. They said that they wouldn't pass judgment on the new regime until they saw how it worked out. They added that if it paved the way for new elections held in a democratic fashion, it would be all right, but that if it did not have this result, it would have to answer to history.

Copei cooperated to some degree with the new regime at first. They asked for and received the governorship of Mérida, where they had a strong majority. However, the person who was named betrayed Copei, going over to Pérez Jiménez. By a year after the coup, relations of Copei with the regime had very much deteriorated and a substantial number of their people were being jailed. By two years after the coup, relations were quite bad and Copei was demanding an immediate new election. They were finally called, but at that point Delgado Chalbaud had been murdered, and so everything was in suspense.

Once Pérez Jiménez was in charge, after the death of Delgado Chalbaud, Caldera was very closely watched by the police. There was round-the-clock surveillance of him in three places. One policeman was placed at the street corner near his house, who kept track of everyone who went in and out there. Another kept constant track of his office and kept a record of everyone who visited him--I was probably noted down the times that I went to see him, although Caldera doubts that they knew who I was. There was a third policeman who always followed him wherever he went, although he lost track of Caldera once in a while. After Pérez Jiménez fell, Caldera was shown the record the Seguridad Nacional had had on him, and it was five feet tall.

He was arrested for short periods various times. Then in August 1957 he was jailed, held incommunicado, because there were rumors that he would be the candidate of the united opposition in elections which were supposed to be held, and he was jailed to avoid that eventuality. His wife was told that he had suddenly been taken ill and was in very serious condition and had been taken to a hospital. But when she went around to various hospitals with an associate in his law office, she found no trace of him. So they went to Seguridad Nacional, which professed to know nothing about his whereabouts. So she went to the Papal Nuncio, and he went to Seguridad Nacional. He told Pedro Estrada that he didn't come to ask for Caldera's release, because Caldera had asked him never to do that, but he did think it right to come to find out Caldera's whereabouts and how he was, so that his wife and family could know. Finally, Pedro Estrada told the Nuncio that he could tell Caldera's wife that he was in perfectly good health.

He was held for four months, until, after Pérez Jiménez had decided not to have an election but a plebiscite on his continuing in power, and that had been held. Caldera was finally released in the middle of December 1957. He stayed at home until January 1, the day of the frustrated military uprising against Pérez Jiménez. That day, he was warned that the police were coming to pick him up and that they had orders to kill him. He immediately went to a friend's house, in front of which were some Seguridad Nacional people, but got into the house without them stopping him. Then he slipped out the back door, going to the house behind that one, which also belonged to a friend. From there, he was picked up by a car and taken to still another house. There the Papal Nuncio came, urged him to come to the Nunciatura. When Caldera said that he didn't think that he should seek asylum yet, the Nuncio said that he was merely inviting him to lunch. He stayed on for the afternoon, for dinner, and then for eighteen days in all. He was finally given safe conduct on January 19. He went to New York, where he was met by Betancourt, Jóvito Villalba, and others, who had read in the New York Times that he was arriving. It turned out that Tad Szulc, who was in Caracas for the Times, had thwarted the censorship by the simple expedient of speaking in Polish.

In New York City, the day after his arrival, he and other Venezuelan political leaders that were there--Betancourt, Jóvito, and others--were invited by Ignacio Luis Arcaya to lunch at the New York Athletic Club. That is where the first agreement with Rómulo and Jóvito was reached, and they agreed on a kind of non-aggression pact. As yet, Pérez Jiménez had not fallen, but it was apparent that his fall was imminent.

Later, in a meeting in Caldera's hotel, where Rómulo and he and a few friends of each, but not Jóvito, were present, he spoke very frankly to Betancourt. He urged Rómulo not to be a candidate for president, that there was still too much resentment in some quarters against him, that he was anathema to much of the armed forces, and that the chances of establishing a real democracy would be weakened if Betancourt tried to become president again. However, Betancourt insisted that he did not intend to run again, and his only worry was establishment of a strong basis for democracy in the country.

The 1958 presidential campaign was quite confused. They had all agreed to try to find a common candidate whom all three parties could support. Copei and URD urged nomination of Martín Vegas, but the Adecos rejected his name. Thereupon Larrazábal proposed a very dangerous idea, that there should be no single president for the next term, but rather a five-man presidency, presided over by him, in which would be included Betancourt, Caldera, Jóvito, and another person, an independent chosen from the business community. There was some mention of Eugenio Mendoza, although he had retired from the Junta de Gobierno by that time. Betancourt and Jóvito provisionally accepted this idea, although they both hinged their acceptance on Caldera's also accepting it. He was in Maracaibo, where he had been sick, and he was subjected to a great deal of pressure to accept the idea. However, he refused to do so, arguing that Venezuela needed a president who could assume the responsibility for the hard kind of decisions that had to be made.

With Caldera's rejection of Larrazábal's idea, the URD suddenly launched the candidacy of Admiral Larrazábal. Soon thereafter, Rómulo was chosen by AD, not by a convention for which there was not time, but by some intermediary body of AD. He was not named without opposition. Caldera was also named by Copei. The campaign was a very short one, getting started only late in October, the election being early in December.

Betancourt proposed the Pact of Punto Fijo. It had that name because that was the name of Caldera's house, where the agreement was signed by representatives of the three parties. In it, the parties agreed to govern together, even though they were running separately. Betancourt remained loyal to that, and so did Copei. The URD quit the government after the OAS Conference of San José, where Arcaya refused to sign the resolution condemning the Castro regime.

Copei was very loyal to the alliance with Acción Democrática. They were so because they wanted to stabilize the democratic system. He thinks that they made a major contribution to the success of the Betancourt regime and generally to stabilizing democracy.

He had various disagreements with Betancourt during the five years of Rómulo's administration. However, he always discussed them frankly with Rómulo, and usually they were smoothed over without too much difficulty. However, there were a few which were more difficult.

One of his most serious disagreements with Betancourt was in October 1962. Betancourt proposed at that time to deprive the Communist and the MIR congressmen of their constitutional immunity and throw them out of Congress. Caldera argued extensively with Betancourt about that, saying that the basis of Copei's and his personal support of the Betancourt government was the fact that it was a constitutional regime, and that was what the Copei was backing rather than any man or group of men. He added that if Betancourt violated the Constitution by doing what he proposed, the basis of Copei's support of and participation in the regime would disappear. However, Betancourt was not convinced and seemed ready to do what he had proposed.

Therefore, on October 12, the Día de la Raza, Caldera made a radio and television speech to the nation discussing the accomplishments of the regime and emphasizing that the basis of Copei's backing it was the constitutional and democratic nature of the regime and stressing the necessity for its continuing on that course. At first, he didn't know what AD's and Rómulo's reaction to this speech would be. However, he soon received a telephone call from Juan Pablo Pérez Alfonso saying that the speech was very good for the regime, and for AD as well. Although Rómulo didn't say anything about the speech, he did not bring up the matter again.

Of course, a year later, in October 1963, Betancourt did throw the Communist and the MIR congressmen out. But by that time, Congress had held its last meeting, and elections were only a few weeks away. His action then did not arouse any particularly hostile reaction.

Another disagreement was over devaluation of the bolivar. Copei was opposed to devaluation. Betancourt said in this case that he would not act if Copei disapproved. So he didn't do so then, although José Antonio Mayobre was forced to resign. Later, circumstances forced devaluation, and at that time, Copei did not oppose the measure.

In the 1963 election, Caldera hoped that there could be a candidate whom both parties could support. He proposed to Betancourt that it be Ramón J. Velázquez. However, Rómulo told him that Acción Democrática could not back an independent, and that it would have to support an AD nominee. Betancourt proposed with AD that there not be a single candidate selected by AD, but rather a list of five possible names, with Copei being given the right to decide which one would be the candidate whom both parties would support. He apparently ran into great opposition to this within AD because it was never made a concrete proposition to Copei. AD ended up name Raúl Leoni, whom Copei could not support.

Caldera understands that Betancourt's first choice for AD in that election was Pérez Alfonso, but that Pérez Alfonso turned Rómulo down. Betancourt didn't want Leoni because he felt he would arouse too much resistance, and because he doubted that Leoni, who was a compromiser and sometimes vacillated, would be able to take the kind of hard and rapid decisions which would be necessary in what Betancourt saw as still being likely to be a very difficult situation. In fact, Leoni had a fairly placid situation and ran into no particular difficulties.

Caldera was in a particularly peculiar position during the 1963 campaign. Copei decided that it would not withdraw from the government until the end of the Betancourt administration, even though it was running candidates against those of Acción Democrática. Thus, Caldera, the Copei presidential candidate, was both part of the government and was running against the nominee of the major party in the government. Some people claimed that there were two government candidates, and to some degree that was true.

Leoni was supported for the AD nomination by the labor people of the party. Also, there was the fact in favor of his nomination that he had always been recognized as the number two man to Betancourt in AD, just as Lorenzo Fernández was always recognized as the number two man to Caldera in Copei.

There was never any kind of formal suggestion that Caldera be the candidate, and he does remember that the old Adeco Ricardo Montilla came up to him one day, gave him an abrazo, and said how bad it was that Caldera was not an Adeco, so that they could support him for president.

He remembers that about that time a certain Yankee college professor named Bob Alexander told him that he would certainly be president, but after Carlos Andrés Pérez. The professor's prediction was almost right, except that he was president just before Carlos Andrés, not just after him.

He has not been active as a lifetime senator, speaking only on special occasions, on matters of major importance. Thus he spoke on oil nationalization, and recently on the bill to enact a new basic law on municipalities. At the time of the oil nationalization debate, he urged Betancourt that he too ought to appear and speak. However, he hoped that Betancourt would speak first, and he would be able to speak after Rómulo. But it turned out the other way around.

He supported and urged certain modifications in the situation of the lifetime senators, which were adopted. For one, a provision was accepted that they will not be counted for determining a quorum unless they are present. Second, they were given prior right to speak on any issue in the Senate.

The provision on lifetime senators adopted in 1962 was that all democratically elected ex-presidents would have that status, as well as others who have been constitutionally installed if they serve more than half a term. This latter provision covers situations in which the president disappears from office and, according to the Constitution, the successor is chosen to fill out his unexpired term by Congress.

* * * * *

LETTER FROM RAFAEL CALDERA, JANUARY 17, 1979

Your letter of December 10 is not really very enthusiastic or even too cordial, but I don't want to fail to satisfy, even if only partially, your curiosity. Perhaps the material which accompanies this letter will contribute to that end.

An attentive greeting for your wife and for you.

* * * * *

LETTER FROM RAFAEL CALDERA, MARCH 9, 1979

I acknowledge receipt of your letter of January 27, late because it came when I had left for Europe to receive an honorary degree from the University of Louvain. I was, to be sure, in Philadelphia, participating in some meetings in the University of Pennsylvania, with people from there, from Harvard and Cornell.

Don't worry about the annoyance in my previous letter. As a saying goes, "The love is the same." What happened was that I hoped that you would tell me that in spite of being an Adeco, you saw with sympathy (or least not with displeasure) the triumph of Copei, or at least that you would use the routine words "I congratulate you."

However, I can assure you that you will continue having in me the same friend and maintain the same relationship of the years in which we have known one another.

Receive, with your wife, a cordial greeting.

* * * * *

CONVERSATION WITH RAFAEL CALDERA IN HIS HOME IN CARACAS, AUGUST 21, 1979

The letter which Enrique Tejera Paris brought him from Betancourt in 1957 was just an incident in the process of AD and Copei reaching an accord. Early in the dictatorship, Copei had to make a decision: either to collaborate with the dictatorship as some of their members wanted to do, or to become increasingly critical of it, for what it was doing. They decided on the latter course, which some of those in the dictatorship itself could not understand. Valenilla Lanz, for instance, asked Caldera why he and Copei were so critical of the regime, that they had much in common. But having decided as they had, they sought to defend the human rights of the Adecos, and then of the URDistas, who also became persecuted by the government, and to fight against the dictatorship and for the restoration of democracy. He sought to conduct himself so that he would not get expelled from the country, because he had psychological value here, all modesty aside, as a symbol of the Resistance. But Pérez Jiménez finally got around to expelling him in January 1958, and when he got to New York, Kennedy Airport, he was greeted there by both Rómulo and Jóvito, with various of their associates. There followed the agreement of New York, which laid the foundations of the Pact of Punto Fijo.

The Pact of Punto Fijo was Rómulo's idea. At first, there was strong sentiment in favor of a joint candidate, but Betancourt was opposed to it, although not necessarily publicly. Caldera was told by one important Adeco that Betancourt felt that he had to be the candidate of AD, not only because he stood the best chance of winning, but also because if he were not the AD candidate, he would lose control of the party, since the future MIRistas as well as the ARSistas were fighting against his control of the party. So Betancourt finally proposed that each party run its own candidate, but that they agree on a minimum joint program, and that they agree to govern together. That was the Pact of Punto Fijo.

As we know, URD was loyal to that for less than two years. Then they felt that they had more to gain by being in the opposition. But the Copeyanos felt that the stability of the government at that point, which was very much in danger, required that they stay in the coalition, and they did so. It assured the government a majority in both houses of Congress, and generally gave the government a much broader base than it would otherwise have had. Betancourt, of course, strongly wanted them to stay in the government. It may be that one of his calculations was that that would not only strengthen the government, but would strengthen Copei, and that a strong second party was needed.

Copei had come in third in the 1958 election. This was the only time this happened, since they had been second in the Trienio and were always second or first after 1958. He thinks many people were surprised by how well Copei did in the 1963 election, particularly in view of their difficult position in the election of not being either in the government or in the opposition. They increased their votes from about 400,000 to about 600,000, while AD fell from the 1.2 million Betancourt had gotten, to 900,000. Some of the Adecos, such as Jesús Paz Galarraga, who was then AD secretary general, were very annoyed at this. For them, it was something like junior partner who steals some of the patrimony of the senior partner.

Leoni wanted Copei to enter his government. His first coalition was a very difficult one for Rómulo to swallow, since it included followers of the Jóvito Villalba and of Uslar Pietri, who had violently attacked AD and Betancourt. But even then, Leoni still hoped Copei would join the cabinet and gave the three posts which he had offered Copei--Fomento, Communications, and Justice--to three pro-Copei independents. But Copei decided not to enter the government, and the rest is history.

In the months that it has been in power, the new Copei government has been trying to clean up the mess which was left by the government which preceded it. Caldera's last budget was 15 billion bolívares; Carlos Andrés's was 50 billion. Caldera left a registered debt of 7 billion bolívares and what the Adecos said was a floating debt of another 12 billion. Even if one accepts that total of 19 billion, it compares with the registered debt when Carlos Andrés left of 50 billion, and a floating debt of another 50 billion. But more than this is the fact that Caldera's budget covered the government's development projects, whereas Carlos Andrés's covered only current expenditures and payment on the debt. Thus to even continue the large projects which Carlos Andrés started, but none of which he finished, they will have to further expand the debt. The budget will go up, but it won't go up enough to cover all those expenditures.

There is also the question of corruption. There are exceedingly persistent rumors of corruption in very high places under Carlos Andrés, of the "twelve apostles," intimate associates of the president who engaged in all kinds of corrupt deals. These rumors may be exaggerated, but he is sure that there is a good deal of substance to them.

Corruption may be inevitable when there is so much money around, but Gunnar Myrdal commented that although corruption is inevitable, it will not be damaging to a regime if it does not touch the top people in the regime. But Caldera is certain that it did touch some of the top people in the Pérez regime, and this is what makes it so serious.

There is also the problem of the police. The Metropolitan Police of Caracas, which is 50 percent understaffed, has become exceedingly corrupt, the police very widely demanding bribes to perform their duties. But even worse, there are problems with the Policía Técnica Judicial [PTJ], established in 1958 after the fall of the dictatorship, and a well-trained and disciplined force. Before Carlos Andrés went out of office, a scandal broke when a man sued a relative of the head of the PTJ, and even though he was a good Adeco, Carlos Andrés had to order his arrest.

There are very sharp disagreements between AD and Copei now. But he does not think that they represent at this point a danger to the regime. They are the more or less normal quarrels in a democracy. Furthermore, military regimes in Latin America are rather discredited. The Peruvian model is virtually dead; the Brazilian model is in grave difficulties. He thinks that the drift back to democracy in a number of countries is helpful.

The situation in Nicaragua is very disquieting. He thinks that the United States waited too long to intervene in the situation. When Viron Vaky was still Ambassador here, Caldera had discussions with him about it, and Vaky kept saying that the United States didn't want to intervene, to which Caldera replied that they had been intervening for forty years, and if they didn't now, it would be held against them. He thinks that what he said is being borne out now.

He was recently in Washington for a week, and Vaky asked him if he would like to see President Carter, and he said that he would. Vaky sent a memo of strong endorsement, but Carter did not receive him, various excuses which were quite thin being offered.

In a way, the next presidential campaign is under way already. One preliminary is the contest of both parties for their secretary generalships. But, of course, a potential candidate needs a good deal more than the support of the secretary general to get the nomination.

He wouldn't say that it is impossible that Copei would turn him down for the nomination if he should want it. Strange things happen in politics. It is too early for him to say whether he will want to be the candidate next time.

There is, to be sure, much talk about the Calderista and Herrerista or Pablista wings of Copei. But the strange thing is that many of those who are credited with being in the wing of Herrera or Pablo Aguilar are good friends of his and keep telling him that he is going to be president again.

There is considerable resistance to Carlos Andrés in Venezuela now. He thinks this is true in AD too. He thinks that Carlos Andrés's strident campaigning in the municipal elections helps explain the extent of AD's defeat in them.

*   *   *   *   *

TALK BY RAFAEL CALDERA AT CENTER FOR INTER AMERICAN RELATIONS IN NEW YORK CITY, NOVEMBER 4, 1981

Andrés Bello is one of the outstanding figures in Latin American history. His career falls into three periods. The first was his early years in Venezuela, when he represented the best cultural aspects of colonial Latin America. The second period was his nine years in England, which was during the period of the struggle for independence in Latin America. So far as Caldera can find out, he spent virtually that whole time in

London. He didn't even venture into other parts of Great Britain, and the stories about his having been in Paris are not true, so far as he can find out.

He was offered appointments as a diplomat in Europe by Bolívar, but turned these down. Rather, he accepted an appointment in the Chilean civil service, and he was in Chile for thirty-four years. There he wrote the country's civil code, which became the model for most of the rest of Latin America; he founded the University of Chile, to take the place of the university which had existed in colonial times; he wrote poetry which was good; and he was a student in a great variety of other fields. He was a truly extraordinary man.

Bello is a standing answer to the feeling in the United States that the Latin American intellectuals tended to be primitives. Andrés Bello, whose two hundredth birthday they are celebrating, was an intellectual of world standing in his time. He is someone of whom Latin Americans can be proud, and who can be a bond in strengthening the relationships between America and the United States.

Caldera has been here for several days and has been speaking about Andrés Bello and presenting busts of him to a number of United States universities. There is an active interest in this country in Andrés Bello and his significance in the history of the hemisphere.

*   *   *   *   *

CONVERSATION WITH RAFAEL CALDERA IN HIS HOME IN CARACAS, FEBRUARY 3, 1984

Copei lost the last elections for many reasons. He tried to sum these up in a recent speech which he made to the Copei Convention. He thinks that the party did much better because he ran for president than it would have done if someone else had been the candidate.

He of course heard the argument that he shouldn't have run because he should have remained in the background as the "reserve of democracy" in the country. He thought a great deal about the argument before deciding to run again. But he felt that the country and the party were in a very bad state and that he could serve both best by running. Anyway, he doesn't like the kind of passive role that this criticism implies that he should have. He doesn't relish living in an ivory tower.

He thinks that this last candidacy didn't weaken his personal influence and prestige. At least, a survey was conducted by a firm friendly to AD a week after the election showed that this was the case. Also, strangely, it showed that those who answered the questions were almost equally divided between him and Jaime Lusinchi when asked, "Who can best conduct the nation's affairs?"

One factor in the defeat of Caldera was the actions of the far Left. For one thing, it went into the election divided, so it didn't seem to present a viable alternative to the two major parties. For another, MAS had a lot of money (he suspects from AD) and carried on a great deal of propaganda on the subject of "change," emphasizing the need to get rid of Copei's government. Certainly many who were influenced by this propaganda ended up voting for Jaime Lusinchi of AD, the most viable opponent of the Herrera regime.

He has recently received the file Seguridad Nacional kept on him during the Pérez Jiménez regime. However, all that he received was the material of the last two years. It is several feet high. He knows that the Seguridad Nacional had round-the-clock watch on him by three people. One watched his home, another watched his office, and the third followed him around by car, wherever he went.

*   *   *   *   *

LETTER FROM RAFAEL CALDERA, AUGUST 9, 1989

I received your letter of July 12. I understand perfectly your permanent curiosity about the affairs of Venezuela, where you have so many friends.

In the impossibility of sending you a detailed and complete report, I tell you that the situation of the country, as I see it, continues being difficult. There are many and constant conflicts, including even in sectors such as the doctors and Metropolitan Police. The cost of living has risen excessively, and although wages increase, they fall much behind. The problem of the debt continues in that laborious process of conversations, without the creditors taking account of the urgency (one could say the extreme urgency) of a solution and the need to make effective concessions.

The president makes undoubted and continuous efforts to maintain a hopeful view, and that offers relative tranquility. In any case, the crisis is serious and a good part of the media of social communication veer toward a permanent criticism of the democratic system, toward an accentuated attack on the prestige of the political leadership.

To recognize these difficulties does not imply that I have renounced my optimism. I have faith in the future, but I am aware that in the short run there are worrying prospects.

I renew the security of my friendship and esteem.

*   *   *   *   *

CONVERSATION WITH RAFAEL CALDERA IN HIS OFFICE IN CARACAS, AUGUST 24, 1993

Venezuela is in an anomalous position now. There is a feeling of uncertainty about what is happening. According to the Constitution, when Carlos Andrés Pérez could no longer exercise the presidency because of charges brought against him in the Supreme Court, the cabinet chose someone to serve until Congress could elect an interim president. Congress chose Ramón J. Velázquez. But Pérez is still perturbing the situation. At first, he was discreet, but then he came back fighting as much as he could. For instance, at the July 4 reception at the United States Embassy, Velázquez came with his military aides, and Pérez came with even more military aides, as if to overshadow Velázquez. Tomorrow the papers will carry a Caldera article on this problem, saying that an end should be put to the situation, by Congress declaring Pérez's presidency is vacant and Velázquez is the undisputed president. Velázquez is a very good president, is a calming factor in the situation.

So here is Caldera at seventy-seven, running again to try to help the country to get out of its situation. It looks as if he has a good chance to be elected president. The people at Miraflores yesterday gave him the results of a poll that they made, which showed that only one of the four main candidates' support had risen from June to July (with 38 percent in July) and whose negative votes had fallen from June to July, and that was Caldera. Polls are not always reliable but if they show a steady tendency in one direction, they probably indicate a real trend.

It was painful to him to separate from the party which he had founded, Copei, but he hopes that the separation will be temporary. If he wins with a substantial vote, he hopes that there will be a reorganization of Copei and it can join forces with Convergencia, the dissident Copei group now supporting him. Convergencia is not strictly a political party, but only a way to participate in the campaign. The only way to participate was to organize as a party, but it is more realistically a list of candidates. It remains to be seen after the election if it will be organized as a regular political party.

There is a great variety of people supporting his presidential candidacy. The only parties of any significance are Convergencia and the Movimiento a Socialismo [MAS]. There have been long negotiations with MAS, and it has been agreed that in some legislature candidates, they will run separate lists. In most cases, they will have joint lists. The other parties which are supporting him are small, with two or three members of Congress. There has been agreement that the coalition behind Caldera will support all incumbents who are candidates.

There are a number of members of Acción Democrática who are supporting his candidacy. Three former members of Pérez's cabinet are among these and there are quite a few other Adecos as well. Dissident Adecos who are supporting him have organized a party, Avanzada Popular, but it is not yet clear if it will be formally recognized as a political party.

He is not afraid of running for president at such an advanced age, seventy-seven. He is in good health. Then there is the case of Arturo Uslar Pietri, who is ten years older than he and is still going strong.

He doesn't think that there will be a military coup before the election, although one can never be sure. He thinks that the top military figures have fear that if they overthrow the constitutional regime, they might be like Naguib in Egypt and Farrell in Argentina, and be pushed aside quickly by younger military men. He thinks that his candidacy is a pacifying factor. Many of those who are now lieutenant colonels got their original commissions from him when he was president. They remember the stability of that period.

Colonel Chávez, the leader of the February 1992 coup attempt, was put on television to urge rebels in Maracaibo and elsewhere, who were still in revolt, to give up. But in two minutes he said that "for now" they had been defeated, and would wait for a better day. As a result of that talk, he became a "phenomenon," and is now an unknown factor in the situation.

If elected, he will have serious problems to face. There is a budget deficit of 8 percent of the gross domestic product, a huge foreign debt, rampant inflation, and decline of the international value of the bolivar. These problems will have to be faced. But he thinks that the first need is to restore confidence in the presidency. There has been a great lack of confidence in recent years.

He knows that the International Monetary Fund will have to be dealt with. A small group from the World Bank was recently here, and they met with Caldera and his people. They said that the Bank was concerned with the growth of poverty here as a result of the economic program of the last five years. That is a new line for them. The visit of the World Bank group here means that at least the dialogue has been begun between the Venezuelans and the international institutions. However, so far there have not been any overtures from the IMF.

Insofar as corruption has been concerned, the first requirement is that those guilty of it be thrown out of the government. He will see to that. He will also bring in younger people (in their forties and fifties), who are so far not tainted by corruption.

The next Congress will probably be much divided. No party will have a majority. But he thinks that with strong leadership from the president, that situation can be handled.

Admittedly, the Venezuelan constitutional system is peculiar. But he thinks that it is better than having a vice presidency. Vice presidents in Latin Ameica are too often a source of perturbation. There are the cases of Vice President Barrientos who ousted President Victor Paz Estenssoro in Bolivia; Argentine President Frondizi had to oust his vice president, Alejandro Gómez; today the Nicaraguan vice president is the main leader of the opposition to President Chamorro. Even the United States has had trouble with its vice presidents. Nixon had to get rid of his first one. Also, he doesn't think that Lyndon Johnson had anything to do with the assassination of President Kennedy, but those who were responsible for the murder knew that Lyndon Johnson would become president.

Causa R (which stands for Radical), started as a trade union group in the largest union in the country, that in the steel company. The union had been very corrupt under its previous leadership, and the Causa R group defeated the incumbents. Then, under Carlos Andrés Pérez as president, the CTV intervened the union, and put in charge an Acción Democrática demonstration, but it was also very corrupt, and the dissident group regained control of the union. Then they went into politics as Causa R. They won the governorship of the state of Bolivar, and then to everyone's astonishment, won the mayoralty of Caracas. The Alcalde is a very intelligent black man. Andrés Velázquez, the Causa R candidate for president, was for a short time a member of the Unión Republicana Democrática.

* * * * *
* * * * *

CONVERSATION WITH CARLOS ANDRÉS PÉREZ IN HIS HOME IN SAN JOSÉ, COSTA RICA, SEPTEMBER 1, 1952

Táchira was the state in which Acción Democrática was always weak. This was due to the nature of the economy and social system there. This is an area of minifundio, of many small farmers with very small landholdings. These farmers think that they are masters of their own destiny, in spite of the fact that they are really head over heels in debt for everything they own. However, they are ambitious to send their sons to school. They don't have money enough to send them to most schools, and the only free ones in the country--where the student gets paid while he goes to school--are those of the Army and the Church. Hence, most of the military men, the officers, come from the state of Táchira. And the number of priests in Táchira is four or five times as great as in other parts of the Republic. The priests have much political influence, and they it is who told their faithful to vote for Copei, which was the majority party in the state.

During the last fifty years, virtually all of the rulers of Venezuela have been from Táchira. Hence, when the AD regime began trying members of the old regime for the things they had stolen from the nation, the adverse effects of this were felt more in Táchira than anywhere else, and those who were being tried found more sympathy there, which is another reason for that state not being friendly to the AD. In general, the AD had some 27,000 votes in the state, and Copei had 50,000.

Armando González, the head of the AD in Valencia, returned to Venezuela to participate in the Underground. He has been in jail for about a year and has recently been reported as being sent to the concentration camp of Guasina.

There has recently been a wave of arrests of Acción Democratistas, perhaps in preparation for the election.

*   *   *   *   *

LETTER FROM CARLOS ANDRÉS PÉREZ, APRIL 11, 1953

Before Rómulo left for Bolivia, he asked me to write you a few lines. He wanted you to know that he received all your correspondence; also we have received and read the clippings of your latest articles on the situation of Venezuela. Magnificent, and with the interest that you know how to put on the things of our unhappy Fatherland.

Rómulo will write you on returning from his trip, possibly April 20. Meanwhile, he left me a memorandum to help prepare for you ample information on the PCV [Communist Party] which we shall send you after he revises and amplifies it.

I write you under the sad impression left with us by the discouraging news we receive about the health of Alberto Carnevali. As you know, jailed since January 18, he was transferred to the Penitentiary of San Juan de los Morros--the capital of the state of Guárico--and there, incommunicado in a cell where they are not submitting him to physical maltreatment. At the beginning of April he began to feel light intestinal problems which were getting progressively worse. He asked for and did not obtain adequate and timely medical attention. On the 6th or 7th he suffered a grave crisis. It was then that the authorities of the jail acted. Given his grave situation, there was convoked a Medical Board which prescribed an immediate operation; he already suffered peritonitis infection due to intestinal obstruction; the operation was dangerous and so far he has not recovered from it, being maintained by blood transfusions. The diagnosis of the doctors who operated is that he has cancer of the stomach. And this news horrifies us. In the place where he is, there are no better medical facilities and an illness of that gravity requires all the resources of science that certainly not even Caracas has. In other words, the dictatorship is coldly assassinating Carnevali. In his grave state, they still keep him imprisoned.

Perhaps you could contribute to the freedom of Alberto. We are initiating an international campaign to see if we can get him transferred to the United States. We are trying to interest various foreign offices of friendly countries. You knew Carnevali and know the value of this great Venezuelan. We shall try to save him if it is still possible.

Your letter of April 7 for Rómulo came after his departure on the 6th. In any case, tomorrow I shall send a small memorandum of news that perhaps can serve for your article in the <u>Manchester Guardian</u>.

*   *   *   *   *

LETTER FROM CARLOS ANDRÉS PÉREZ, MAY 9, 1953

I received your letter of the 24th of April in reply to mine of the 14th. A strong attack of grippe has made it impossible for me to answer before this. Now I have fresh news about Alberto that I am going to give you.

I am sending a clipping from the newspaper <u>El Nacional</u> of Caracas. It is very interesting. With the title "North American journalist etc.," the censorship office--author of all those notes--tries to give the impression to the public that AC [Alberto Carnevali] is receiving the most careful medical attention; as if this would be proven by the fact that Jules Dubois, President of the Committee of Freedom of the Press for Latin America of the Inter American Press Association, has been permitted to visit the penitentiary and the bedside of the patient.

Thursday, by a cable of AP we learned that Dubois arrived that day, proceeding from Ecuador to Panama. By telephone we communicated with a Venezuelan comrade exiled and living in the latter city, to ask Dubois about the note of <u>El Nacional</u>. Yesterday we had a direct account of the result of those conversations. Mr. Dubois responded to our comrade that it was true that he had visited Carnevali for a few minutes in the San Juan de los Morros Penitentiary; that there he had encountered the mother of AC, who had informed him that all of the efforts they had made to obtain the transfer of her son to the United States or to a good private clinic of Caracas had met an absolute negative from Pérez Jiménez. His imprisonment in the penitentiary is not, then, as the government claims and as it forces the press of Caracas to publish, because the doctors oppose his being moved from the infirmary of the jail. And the strange thing about the activities of Mr. Dubois is that having been used intentionally by the dictatorship, he refuses to make any statement about his visit. Our comrade asked him in Panama for a few declarations for the press, and the reply of JD [Jules Dubois] was that he would not make any statement about the matter. It is worth while remembering that Alberto Carnevali is also a journalist, ex-editor of the important Venezuelan daily <u>Panorama</u> of Maracaibo, which makes the attitude assumed by Dubois the more inexplicable.

There is little more to add about the painful drama of Alberto Carnevali. He continues in a grave state. The doctors told Dubois that the cancer has been extending progressively and that there is no hope of saving him. Another report obtained by the Resistance, from a doctor who is attending him, predicts at most two or three weeks of life for Alberto. The time has passed when he might have been operated on successfully.

By means of Valmore Rodríguez you will have been informed of the days of terror through which Venezuela is living. Pérez Jiménez has unloosened on the country a frightful and bloody repression. More than twenty citizens are being tortured in the torture chambers of Seguridad Nacional. Among them are prominent Venezuelans, such as Dr. Eligio Anzola Anzola, Secretary General of AD, detained on April 24 in the streets of Caracas. He is a distinguished lawyer, a politician of national renown, who has been Deputy in the Venezuelan Congress, governor of a state, member of the judiciary of the Republic. He was also the Minister of Government in the cabinet of don Rómulo Gallegos; Ramón Quijada, Trade Union Leader who brought about in 1944 the separation of the majority of workers and their unions from a Trade Union Federation which had been cleverly controlled "from above" by the Communist Party. Quijada is Agrarian Secretary of the Confederación de Trabajadores de Venezuela and acting President since the imprisonment of Pérez Salinas three years ago. He carried on four years of clandestine struggle. Others tortured are doctors José Ángel Ciliberto (lawyer), Héctor Alcalá (engineer), Guaimare Rojas (lawyer) all national leaders of AD: Víctor Peñalver and Tomás Alberti, both members of the Executive Committee of the Peasant Federation of Venezuela; Víctor Olegario Carnevali, brother of Alberto Carnevali; Dr. Alirio Gómez (medical doctor). And many more. Among those recently jailed are Sr. Juan Francisco Rodríguez, President of the Venezuelan Chamber of Radio Broadcasting and Director of Radio Continente. And Sra. Doña Hortensia de Anzola Anzola, wife of Dr. Eligio Anzola, submitted to brutal interrogation.

But the government of Pérez Jiménez is far from achieving stability in spite of the terror. Right now, it has internally a very grave situation. He has not been able to name a Cabinet, in spite of the fact that one of his Ministers, that of Public Works, was named by the "Constitutional Assembly" as Comptroller General of the Republic. The fundamental difficulty that PJ [Pérez Jiménez] has had to reorganize his cabinet is the open opposition of high officers of the Army to Pérez Jiménez continuing as Minister of Defense. And as fomentor of discord has come his old colleague of the Junta, Lieutenant Colonel Llovera Páez, who decidedly appears to wish to accomodate himself in the Ministry of Defense. AD, on the other hand, filling the posts left vacant by recent jailings, continues the resistance struggle.

I wish to ask you a favor. That you send me whatever can be published about the moves made on behalf of Alberto. By your letter and from what Valmore writes us, we know all that you have been able to do.

Rómulo has not yet returned. He is in Chile, and will spend shortly some days in Uruguay. His trip has been very succesful. Now in Chile he has succeeded in uniting around the dramatic situation of Venezuela, all of the parties, from the Conservatives to the Socialists. He will be returning between the 20th and 25th of this month. Your last two letters to him have been sent to Uruguay, where I am sure he will get them on the 12th or 13th when he gets there.

*   *   *   *   *

LETTER FROM CARLOS ANDRÉS PÉREZ, OCTOBER 8, 1953

By airmail I am sending the little book of Rómulo Panamericanismo y Dictadura which contains the work that you know already, from the September issue of the review Cuadernos Americanos and now published separately. From Mexico they must already have sent you a copy. But it doesn't matter. The extra one you will know to put in the hands of some North American friend interested in our struggles.

Did you receive No. 21 of Informaciones Venezolanas? Its content is merely a palid sketch of the dramatic situation in which my country finds itself. Now, the prisoners of the Carcel Modelo are being transferred to the Concentration Camp of Ciudad Bolívar. Outrages and crimes continue the order of the day. The latest victim was a merchant of Barquisimeto,

José Antonio Roldán, sixty years old. He was arrested on September 3, and on the fifth expired at nine in the morning. They broke his head with a torniquet. In Maturín in Eastern Venezuela, there has been mounted a violent and savage repression. The Resistance rescued the most important prisoners from the jail, heading the list of those liberated Dr. Jorge Yibirín, and Pedro Estrada has personally gone there to direct the reprisals.

Receive a cordial greeting from your friend.

* * * * *

LETTER FROM CARLOS ANDRÉS PÉREZ, OCTOBER 7, 1954

These lines have the purpose of presenting again the situation of the Venezuelan exiles in the British island of Trinidad. We are informed about, and very much thank you, for what you have done about this last March which ended with an interpolation by a Labourite deputy in the Commons, of the English Minister of Colonies. Even if until now no positive result has been seen from these efforts, it is important that they know about the situation in London and that this problem has been addressed.

Vicente Gamboa Marcano had to leave last March. Other exiles, who were dumped later on that island by the Venezuelan dictatorship, have been met with all kinds of hostility, and in this month--those who have not yet left have been given a deadline to abandon the English possession on the menace of being sent back to Venezuela. These exiled comrades have not been able to leave for lack of resources and it would not be strange, given the close friendship of the governor of the Island with Pedro Estrada, if they would be taken again to Venezuela.

I send you various clippings from the press of Trinidad. One very important (Trinidad Guardian of August 25, 1954). This editorial makes clear the dirty negotiations between the dictatorship and the authorities of the Island of Trinidad. Those offers not fulfilled (and perhaps others, in cash, YES fulfilled) were made in exchange for the expulsion of Doctor Jóvito Villalba, Lieutenant Colonel Edito Ramírez, Lieutenant León Droz Blanco (assassinated months later in Baranquilla, Colombia, by an agent of Seguridad Nacional of Venezuela), and Vicente Gamboa Marcano.

I think that if this editorial comes into the hands of the Labourite friends, it may serve to reopen the problem. And this is the service which we wish to thank you for.

* * * * *

LETTER FROM CARLOS ANDRÉS PÉREZ, OCTOBER 18, 1954

I received your lines of the 11th. We thank you very much for your permanent interest in our Venezuelan affairs. I am sure that your good offices with the English Labour Party will be decisive in aiding us to resolve the problem created for our exiles in Trinidad by the manifest complicity of the colonial authorities with the dictatorship.

Today I send clippings which are more important than those sent the last time. As you will see after reading them, what is happening there is monstrous. Various exiles of AD are in very grave danger of being placed in the hands of the sanguinary police of Pedro Estrada. Among them the leader of the Venezuelan teachers René Domínguez; the dentist Miguel Ángel Rubio, who is in bed with a grave heart condition after four years in prison in San Juan de los Morros, and whom they are now trying to force to leave the Island; the worker Evangelista Fontalva. The unusual thing in this case is that they were accomplices of the dictatorship in accepting them as exiles, then calling them the next day to the immigration offices and giving them only a few hours to leave the Island. This has been going on since July; but now they have given a definitive deadline after which, if they have not left the island they will be placed on Venezuelan shores. And the most scandalous case is that of Ernesto Zamora, a merchant, and Juan Hernández, a worker, who arrived in Trinidad as exiles last June and then after receiving asylum were forced to go to another British possession in the Antilles, the Trinidad authorities giving them assurance that in Barbados or Grenada they would be received. The result was that, embarked in the ship Orion, they have gone to all those islands and in none of them have they been able to set foot on land, and so they have lived for several months on the ship, without going ashore and with the friends among Venezuelan exiles who still are in Trinidad not being permitted to go aboard to visit them. They are accused of nothing, nor have they even carried on political activities because they have been on shipboard since they became exiles.

We are planning to arouse a continental scandal over this situation, disgraceful for America, on the part of a colonial power. In this connection I ask that as soon as you receive these clippings and information you send them to friend Daines. In London also there are two exiles of AD, to whom I am writing to present the case to the Minister of Colonies.

Many thanks, friend Bob, for your generous aid.

*   *   *   *   *

LETTER FROM CARLOS ANDRÉS PÉREZ, DECEMBER 8, 1954

Tardily I read your correspondence of October 24. I was out of San José for several days.

It is very interesting that you write that article on the situation of the Venezuelan exiles in Trinidad for the Manchester Guardian. We are very grateful for this collaboration. And if you write an article on the same subject for Latin American periodicals, your help in this matter would be very efficacious. I must tell you that in Uruguay and other countries there is being mounted a campaign to bring pressure on the English government to change its policy of being hostile to Venezuelan exiles in that colony. Your article for El Tiempo, Excelsior, etc., would help us a great deal in this task.

I send a photo of comrades Juan Hernández and Zamora Arevalo, taken on the dock and in the street, where they were allowed to go on one occasion; also I send the notes of immigration ordering that Zamora and Hernández not come ashore. These two things will help you to illustrate and give more verification to your article. If you send articles to other periodicals, perhaps you could make copies of the photo and the immigration papers. If you don't use them, I would be pleased if you would return them. Soon Informaciones Venezolanas will reappear and we can use them.

Indirectly I have heard that you wrote a letter to the New York Times about the unusual decoration by Eisenhower of Pérez Jiménez and the subsequent invitation of State to blood-thirsty Pedro Estrada. For the first time our comrades in the U.S. did not send the clipping or it got lost in the mail. We are asking them to send it so as to give it due publicity and send it to Venezuela. From the clandestine command we are waiting for a document that was published on this scandalous "diplomatic" event which has caused true indignation in the country and is connected with the granting to the petroleum companies of the petroleum reserves still in the hands of the Venezuelan Nation. You certainly know that the Venezuelan dictatorship has agreed to give new concessions to the petroleum trust, which has in its power TWELVE MILLION hectares and is exploiting only TWO HUNDRED THOUSAND.

On the history of the CP [Communist party] in Venezuela, I will with pleasure gather the data which you request. But it would help this work very much if you could send me a memorandum or questionnaire on the questions which interest you concretely. I'd appreciate if you would send me that so I can proceed to order the data which is required for your book.

Your friend cordially greets you.

* * * * *

LETTER FROM CARLOS ANDRÉS PÉREZ, FEBRUARY 11, 1955

I received your lines of January 2 giving an account of the result of your efforts with the British Labour friend with regard to the Venezuelan exiles in Trinidad. Thank you very much, friend Bob.

I write now to tell you again about the same matter. I send a copy of a cable of INS [International News Service] which says there has begun another offensive of the colonial authorities to expel the Venezuelan exiles from the Island of Trinidad. Last year, your efforts, the protests of the Trinidad papers, and other influences that we mustered at least got the authorities not to molest the exiles. One sees that this year the dictatorship has given more money to certain English functionaries and has begun to pressure the government of the Island with the menace of taxes on its merchandise.

We, hoping for results from your efforts and those of other friends in Uruguay and other countries, have remained silent. But now, in view of the failure of those friendly efforts, we are going to initiate a press campaign in all America denouncing the collaboration of the English government with the Venezuelan dictatorship and arouse protests of all the democrats of the continent to the Embassies of England.

Could you help us with the article that you offered to write for the Manchester Guardian? And with its Spanish version for El Tiempo, Excelsior, and another copy for us to send to many papers in Latin America? We will be much obliged for this new service to the cause of Venezuelan democracy. In my last letter to you of December 8 I sent more information on the situation of the exiles. You have enough information to document your article.

Something more. In London we have an exiled comrade, a student, of much talent and qualities as a writer. He can carry out there direct efforts with the authorities and the Labourite friends to collaborate in this effort to change the policy toward the exiles in Trinidad. Perhaps his verbal and documented exposition to the Labourite friends and to the English authorities would impress them favorably. But he needs good connections to fulfill this work more effectively. Could you do us the favor of giving a letter of introduction to the Secretary of the Labor Party Mr. D.H. Daines? The exiled comrade in London is Francisco Sucre Figarella.

* * * * *

LETTER FROM CARLOS ANDRÉS PÉREZ, MARCH 1, 1955

Many thanks for your letter of February 15. Certainly comrade Sucre Figarella will by now have entered into contact with the British Labourite friends in London.

And our efforts have had some favorable results. Because the comrades of Trinidad write us to tell us that the hostility has ceased and there is the impression that they have received orders from the Metropolis. If this climate of tolerance is stabilized, we can attribute it in large part to your generous cooperation.

I'm interested in knowing when Tribune published the article a copy of which you sent me. We have it translated and want to reproduce it in some of the Latin American press, when we know when it appeared in Tribune. Has the one sent to Manchester Guardian been published yet?

We suggested to Rómulo your magnificent idea of a letter to the Times of London. I am sending to Miss Grant clippings of the press of Trinidad and we are asking her to present in Hemispherica the situation of the exiles in that English possession.

What do you think of the report in Time Magazine on Venezuela? For me it has a characteristic smell of gasoline. Although they say hard and just things about Pérez Jiménez and his sanguinary acolyte Pedro Estrada, there floats over all the long article the vapor of the marvelous essence, the "beneficent philanthropy" of the petroleum cartel. In the popular refrain of my country there is a saying: "the same smoke from a different pipe." That's the way the decoration of PJ, the invitation to Pedro Estrada of the S.D. [Seguridad Nacional], and this report of Time appear to me. Each of these, made to impress, or better, to flatter, different sectors of public opinion, or different interests. But together they are intended to justify the scandalous surrender of the rest of the petroleum reserves of Venezuela to the "Trust."

* * * * *

CONVERSATION WITH CARLOS ANDRÉS PÉREZ IN ACCIÓN DEMOCRÁTICA HEADQUARTERS, CARACAS, JULY 3, 1969

Acción Democrática has recovered pretty well from the MEP split. In terms of organization it is in good condition. They have had an extensive reorganization of the top leadership, and they are regaining ground after their narrow defeat last December.

They suffered particularly in the trade union field, where the labor group was divided in this split as it had not been in the two previous ones. Right afterwards, they were left with virtually no leaders in the petroleum federation, but they have been slowly recuperating these, while a number of MEP people in that region have been leaving MEP. The curious thing is that although some of them are coming back to AD, others are going to Copei and URD. None has gone to the Communist Party.

In general, there has been a considerable return of local people in the interior to AD. There are some nationally important leaders who would like to return, but AD wants to wait for the convenient occasion to have them do so. In any case, he thinks that MEP is definitely on the decline. This was shown by their vote last December, and they have gone down further since then. They have serious internal difficulties as well.

He doubts that AD will "learn" from the disastrous consequences of this last split when it comes time to choose a candidate for the next election. Parties don't "learn" in this way. But he would point out that the MEP split was one which in a sense had been incubating since 1948. In the 1948 Conference of the party, Domingo Alberto Rangel, Raúl Ramos Giménez, and Jesús Paz Galarraga formed a faction within the leadership, saying that the party in power had not moved rapidly enough to put its program into execution, and other things. As a result, they were removed from the top leadership by that conference. But then came the overthrow of Gallegos, and in face of government persecution, these differences were forgotten for the time being. However, it is notable that these were exactly the three men who led the MIR, ARS, and MEP splits. He doesn't say that this means there won't be any other split, but he does point out the historical facts.

A group of Rómulo Betancourt's friends have gotten together to buy him a house, since he is a man who has no material possessions to speak of, and lives from his senatorial income. They don't know yet whether Rómulo will accept this house, but they hope so, because the party needs Rómulo back here, and he needs to come back. He misses Venezuela very much.

The current situation is somewhat confused. Caldera won by the narrowest of majorities. He does not have a majority in Congress; in fact AD is the largest single group there. At this point, the Copeyanos don't want to cooperate with anyone. However, he thinks that what will probably emerge is some kind of a program on which AD can give its support to Copei without forming any kind of coalition with it, agreement on particular points and nothing more than that.

AD has lacked a youth movement since the MIR split, at least one of any consequence. It was hard to recruit one while they were in power, because in view of the subversion which existed through most of the AD regimes, the government did have to resort to repressive measures against the extreme Left and extreme Right, and those measures were antipathetical generally to young people, particularly here in Venezuela, where the young people have the tradition of opposing all kinds of repressive measures. However, now that AD is in the opposition, they have a better chance to recruit youth, since opposition is more congenial to them than being in the government. The AD is recovering somewhat in this area.

Copei, incidentally, is having considerable difficulty with its youth. When it was announced that Nelson Rockefeller planned to come here, the first people out to protest, even before the Communists, were the Juventud Revolucionaria Copeyana. Also, recently, when Fedecamaras was going to hold its twenty-fifth anniversary congress, it was programmed first for a liceo here in Caracas, but the JRC came out strongly against that, saying that "the exploiters of the people" should not be able to hold their meeting in a school. Fedecamaras finally had to meet in the Círculo Militar. Copei's problem with the youth is something like that which AD had with the MIR in 1959-1960.

The URD is now working very closely with AD. It is a party which took a bad beating in the last election, and is distinctly on the decline. The policy of AD now is to try to bring into AD their leaders in the provinces who are worthy of membership in AD. They may acquire also a few of the national URD leaders, but he cannot see Jóvito Villalba ever joining AD.

The Communists are now functioning quite legally. They are quite "pacifist" at the moment and are trying to reestablish themselves in organized labor and elsewhere after the terrible beating they took as a result of their participation in the guerrilla war. They have decided to liquidate their trade union group, the [United Confederation of Workers of Venezuela] CUTV, and to have its members join the [Confederation of Workers of Venezuela] CTV. It has not yet been decided in the CTV whether to accept these people. The MEP favors accepting them, because they figure that the Communists will support them in the CTV. The Copei also, curiously enough, supports their entry into CTV, for reasons which he does not understand; they just talk about "labor unity," without thinking of its consequences. In fact, government pressure is being used to try to bring the CUTV people into the CTV.

AD is strongly opposed to permitting entry of the Communists. They feel that the Communists will be in the CTV in order to cause trouble, that they will be there to favor a strike on every occasion that one is discussed, to undermine the economy, rather than to push the welfare of the workers. AD does not want the CTV to be turned into an element of subversion, and if the Comunists were there they might well be able to do this, being expert maneuverers and very loud talkers.

AD has tried to point out to Caldera and other Copei leaders the dangers of having the Communists in the CTV. He has talked personally to Caldera about this, saying that although AD is in the opposition, it does not want the labor movement to become a focus of subversion, and pointing out that although AD might be hurt by the Communists coming into the CTV, the party which would be most hurt would be Copei, both within the balance of forces in the CTV and in general, because of the dangers which Communist influence in the labor movement would represent. However, the Copeyanos continue to agitate for the incorporation of the Communists.

What is likely to happen was shown in the recent May Day demonstration. In the past, the CTV has held a huge demonstration, and the CUTV a tiny one. This time, the government, Caldera personally, brought pressure for there to be one May Day meeting. There was, and, of course, it was dominated by the Communists. There was a group of guerrillas right in front of the platform, and Caldera himself had to retire from the platform because of the hostility of the Communists.

The strength of Pérez Jiménez in last year's election was based on several things. One was the fact that he pictured himself as the one who was for law and order, and made much of the claim that under him there were not the crimes that there have been in the last ten years. That, of course, is false; there were the crimes, but the press could not report them. Second, the people of Caracas, or many of them, remembered that Pérez Jiménez had built a great number of things here.

This last election was the first one in which AD used surveys in its campaign. An early one, last March, before there were candidates named, but after the AD split, showed Pérez Jiménez was very strong in Caracas. It showed that those who favored him used the two arguments he has given. It showed, also, that most of those opposed to him cited his dictatorial regime as the reason, with only 1 percent of them saying that they were opposed to his corruption. This was disturbing because it indicated that there was a widespread belief that all governments are corrupt, and that Pérez Jiménez was nothing special in this regard. A further survey made in August showed that Pérez Jiménez was running far ahead of anyone else in the Senate race in Caracas. Most Adecos did not take these poll results seriously, but he did. He was therefore not surprised when Pérez Jiménez got the largest vote for his party in Caracas.

Many people have thought that it was a mistake for Pérez Jiménez to be denied his seat in the Senate. However, Pérez doesn't think so. First of all, if Pérez Jiménez were to have been allowed to become a senator, this would have acted as a stimulus to anyone in the military who might be contemplating a coup d'état because he could say that Pérez Jiménez, after being brought back here, kept in jail for five years, was after all allowed to take a seat in the Senate among the cheers of his followers, and so nothing was to be really lost by a coup.

In addition, one could have been sure that Pérez Jiménez would not have returned to take his seat in the Senate in order to serve in the Senate. He would have returned so as to gain the parliamentary immunity of a Senate seat, from which he could conspire, much the way that Batista did when he returned to Cuba as a senator. Furthermore, the government would have had to offer him protection. They couldn't have had him come back to be killed. They would have been forced to delegate this job to some military men, since few civilians would have taken it, or the government would not want to allow the kind that would to do so. Through these military men, Pérez Jiménez could have reestablished his contacts with the military, and this would have facilitated his conspiring.

Hence, it was by all odds better that he not take his seat. AD had tried to oppose his running at all, but had been overruled in the Supreme Electoral Tribunal by the representatives of the other parties. But when he was elected, AD took a legal case to the Supreme Court, which decided against him. The upshot is that he will not come back. He is a coward and he is not going to set foot here without parliamentary immunity and protection. He will remain abroad, living very well, causing scandals from time to time, but will not be the constant source of agitation and subversion which he would have been had he returned. Pérez suspects that by the next electon, he will be largely forgotten.

He thinks that one of the real dangers to the democratic constitutional regime is the nature of Congress. The institutions of democracy have not kept up with the fact that this has become an industrial society, and that the problems they have to deal with are much more complex than they used to be, call for much more study, much more expert opinion, than used to be the case.

First, the electoral law needs to be revised. They went entirely too far in the direction of proportional representation, so that the net effect is to stimulate the growth of a myriad of "partitidos." Some kind of a revision should be made in the law, to set at least a minimum vote for a party to gain representation in Congress. Also, the Electoral Tribunal should be changed, keeping the representation of the parties, but not allowing them to dominate the tribunal as they now do.

Second, Congress itself needs to be revised. Some limit should be put on the number of congressmen and senators. There are now 216 members of the Chamber of Deputies and 55 senators. Over thirty deputies had to be added this last election because of the increase in population. The number of voters represented by each deputy is too small, with the increased population, and Congress is getting unwieldy as a result. The upshot is that it spends most of its time on political maneuvering, instead of on really constructive legislative work.

Also the system of the Directive Board of Congress has to be revised. At the present time, there are fifteen members of the Board, which is supposed to plan the work of the Chamber. Every party has to have representation, so that the really substantial parties--AD, Copei, MEP, URD--are a minority in the Board. The miniscule Partido Socialista Venezolano, which has one deputy elected by the national quotient, has representation, of him, on the Board.

Something should be done fairly rapidly to change this. It will take considerable political courage, and it can only be done if the large parties, which means fundamentally AD and Copei, get together and push through the kind of changes which are required in the electoral law and in Congress itself. There has been a god deal of discussion of this possibility, but so far no concrete steps toward doing anything have been taken. But if something is not done, this might well prove to be the Achilles heel of the constitutional democratic system.

*　　*　　*　　*　　*

LETTER FROM CARLOS ANDRÉS PÉREZ, SEPTEMBER 7, 1971

I reply belatedly to your correspondence of July 20 because I have been on trips to the interior of the country. In the few days in which I have stayed in Caracas it has not been possible for me to put aside the time to dictate a reply.

I am going to answer, with pleasure, the questions you raise, from our point of view.

1. Problem of Pérez Jiménez.

This is really the greatest preoccupation we have in Acción Democrática. It is evident that the Pérezjimenista movement has been gaining more force than that it demonstrated in the last electoral process. Very diverse factors join in creating this incredible situation. In the first place, it is a sociological reality in all democratic countries that there exists an anti-system, negative, vote, although it is always the minority. And the anti-system in Venezuela is represented not by Communism or by extremism but rather dictatorship.

The middle classes are an actor in the Pérezjimenista advance. In a developing country like ours these classes are growing rapidly. The apparent contradictions of the system, their apparent weakness, generate in them conservative sentiments in which the concept of security generates the instinct of self-conservation. The presence of a political regime which is vacillating and demagogic in the face of the extremist sectors and the extraordinary expansion of the criminal class, a product among other things of the phenomenon of urbanization in our principal cities, gives to the national collectivity the sensation of instability and a vacuum of power. In the year 1970 there were committed in Venezuela

75,000 criminal acts. Expression not only of the common criminals but also of political violations. Strikes and other acts promoted with subversive interest and intention, as well as violent student actions, create a climate of confusion and disorientation which, mistakenly but definitely, makes many think that dictatorship is necessary to conserve and defend oneself. It is not by accident that the surveys show with the highest percentage of justification for the vote for Pérez Jiménez the phrase "because he had a government of order."

It is painful to admit it, but the complicity of important sectors of the national collectivity collaborates in creating this situation. With the exception of Acción Democrática almost all the political groups are conquetting with Pérezjimenism, hoping that the cowardice of the ex-dictator will keep him from accepting the presidential candidacy and they can capitalize on his votes. The "Third Force" says that it would not make a pact with Cruzada Cívica Nacionalista but would not find it inconvenient to accept the votes of the Pérezjimenistas. Copei and the government are clandestinely making offers. Political opportunism, that is, immorality and corruption, puts the circumstantial and fortuitous ahead of doctrinary and moral considerations.

Acción Democrática has tried and is trying to form a broad national front against this menace, but we must confess that we have not obtained the hoped-for results. The struggle appears as a confrontation between AD and Pérezjimenism. And as if we were acting out of vengeance and retaliation.

We consider that not only a possible victory would be a true national catastrophe about which no comment is necessary, but so would be an increase in his seats in Congress. We might see seated there the Pedro Estradas, the Vallenilla Lanzes, and all the multitude of henchmen who dishonored this country for ten years. Nothing is more damaging for the prestige of democracy and its institutions. Certainly the country could not endure this demoralizing attack.

However, we are not pessimists. We are carrying out and planning various activities to confront that influence. At this time we are awaiting the results of a national survey to determine the nature of the phenomenon and have our manner of combating it conform to that analysis. The tolerance and pandering of the government will be difficult, very difficult, to overcome because it constitutes a very great stimulus to the action of the Pérezjimenistas.

2. The candidacy of Acción Democrática.

There is not the remotest possibility that the choice of the candidate of Acción Democrática could bring within the party a serious conflict and even less possibility of a new split. The picture of the previous party conflicts has had such a psychological impact that it favors the thesis that the AD might push itself into a new divisionist process, above all when it proceeds to designate the presidential candidate. This view is incorrect. The fractionalist activity in Acción Democrática was due to deep and old causes. I am sending you a little book which has a talk of mine to the leaders in Caracas a little after the last split. There I analyze that process. Also, I'm sending my report to the National Convention. It is confidential, but a friend such as you should know about all of our internal affairs so as to judge better. It is rough, but it points out truths and is based on a secure optimism that we can overcome our weaknesses and difficulties, as we are in fact doing.

Personalism is the factor responsible for the great failure of democracy not only in Venezuela but in all Latin America. In the parties we have it and it is the cause of many problems on all levels of the organization. But now it is not mixed with the factionalist activity which plagued Acción Democrática since 1948.

We shall select our candidate certainly in the middle of the coming year 1972. The candidacy of Rómulo Betancourt depends more on his decision than on anything else. But if it is not he, that will in no way signify that the selection of the candidate will constitute a grave internal problem.

3. Acción Democrática vis-á-vis Copei.

As you can read in my report to the National Convention, we have inaugurated in Venezuela a new system of carrying on opposition. We have not allowed ourselves to be taken into systematic opposition. We act like a party with the vocation for power, keeping always in mind the national interest. Sometimes we are little understood and it is claimed that we are a party too close to the government party. However, we know that this conduct is not only the most appropriate one to national reality and the stabilization and expansion of the democratic system, but that, also, and from the practical point of view, it brings us respectability and prestige.

The relations between the two parties are difficult. The actions and procedures of Christian Democracy are very peculiar. It would seem that with them there is a special mentality. Examining the Chilean process which culminated in the triumph of Allende we see that it is bit by bit like what is happening in Venezuela. They seem to want to skip over the legal and conventional limitations which are part of the democratic system, insofar as the relations between opposition and government are concerned. They abuse official propaganda and the reins of power for partisan advantage. They create dangerous situations of lack of confidence and political instability. Rather than running the government, they wish to take advantage of it. However, we understand that from the opposition we must be a factor of democratic equilibrium. In accordance with this criterion, we move with discretion, tact, and prudence to maintain the solidity of the democratic regime.

4. Reasons for the weakness of the government of Caldera.

It is intrinsically a weak government because of its demagogic characteristics, the internal contradictions within the Copei Party, where we see develop the same tendencies which precipitated the defeat of Chilean Christian Democracy. They are carrying out a vacilating and complacent policy, wishing to conciliate all sectors. In conformity with that orientation is the famous pacification of the extremist sectors and which even includes Pérezjimenismo. On the economic front decisions are not taken and the industrial process is suffering very grave confusion because of the uncertain situation in which sectors of private enterprise exist.

5. The Third Force.

They want to copy the Chilean model. Something impossible, because both the social circumstances and the political structure itself are very different. However, they constitute and will constitute of factor of perturbation, particularly because of the very marked tendency toward radicalism. The problem of the presidential candidacy is undermining the possibility of consolidation of that Third Force. There already exists an evident antagonism between URD and MEP. It is foreseeable that the appearance of understanding will be broken between them very soon.

The Communist Party is making offers to those two parties in the alliance. However, they have not succeeded in unifying very much--the groups, tiny groups and personalities which maneuver around the Left influenced by extremism.

6. The Division of the Communist Party.

The situation of the Venezuelan Communist Party is very precarious. The MAS, Movimiento al Socialismo, left it practically in bankruptcy. All the youth and the basic cadres of the Communist Party now belong to this new movement. The most embattled people, those who structured the guerrilla and urban action are also in the MAS. The influence of the CP among youth is now absolutely null.

The definitive orientation of MAS is still unknown. They are going through a process of progressive radicalization. Approaching more and more, once again, subversive action. They do not form part of the Third Force.

I hope that the information I have given you will be of some utility for your analysis of our political life.

*　　*　　*　　*　　*

CONVERSATION WITH CARLOS ANDRÉS PÉREZ IN ACCIÓN DEMOCRÁTICA HEADQUARTERS, CARACAS, MAY 29, 1972

Acción Democrática is in very good shape. It will win the next presidential election without difficulty, hopefully by a larger margin than the last election was won. Some Adecos are not as confident as he is, but he is quite confident.

The bad aspect of the situation is that the voters will not be polarized between Acción Democrática and Copei, but between Acción Democrática and Pérez Jiménez. Pérez Jiménez's support comes partly from the marginal groups in the barrios. But also it comes from elements of the middle class, who are afraid of the expansion of crime which has come with the rapid growth of the big cities in recent years. They think that a strong government is needed to curb this crime, and that Pérez Jiménez can provide it.

AD has backed a bill to establish that no one can be eligible for elective office who has been convicted of certain kinds of crimes concerning the public administration. Such a law would disqualify not only Pérez Jiménez but many of those whom he hopes to take to Congress with him. The problem is not whether Pérez Jiménez will win, he won't, but that he will take to Congress a large enough element to make it very difficult to govern. However, AD hasn't found much support for this kind of a law.

He thinks that if Pérez Jiménez were to win the election with perhaps only 25 percent of the vote there would be an institutional crisis. He thinks that there would be a coup d'état.

Betancourt is very likely to be the AD candidate. However, it is not yet settled. But it is certain that there will not be a new party split over the issue of the candidacy. The rumors in the press over this are based on what happened in the past, not on the present situation.

There are internal problems in the party. But they are on a regional and state level, and they have nothing to do with one another. There is not the kind of national problem that there was before the MEP split.

The MEP is declining. A number of its secondary figures have returned to AD. There are several in Congress who have separated more or less from MEP, such as Mercedes Fermín, who didn't follow the MEP line in the recent University elections. José González Navarro has broken openly from MEP and has his own group now. If he had handled matters better, he would have taken more trade unionists with him. The MEP still has strength in Zulia and in Caracas, but elsewhere in the country it is very weak.

The Frente Democrático Popular is for sale. Jorge Dager keeps pretending he is a candidate, but this is for the purpose of making a better deal with Copei, getting a few more congressional seats.

The New Force will probably split up. If Jóvito Villalba is the candidate, MEP will withdraw from it. If Paz Galarraga is the candidate, the URD will withdraw. They are planning a congress to name their candidate, but MEP is constantly putting up issues to postpone the congress, because they fear a deal by the URD and the Communist Party at their expense.

The Communist Party is in a very bad situation. It has lost most of its youth and many of its secondary leaders in the MAS split.

AD is near to a clear majority in the CTV. For some time now it has been the largest single political force there. Recently it has won a number of important union elections. The split of González Navarro from MEP has undermined it very much in the labor movement, to AD's advantage. MEP has lost control of the metal workers' federation, the textile federation, electric federation in the private industry sector, and of several in the state-owned industries as a result of González Navarro's split.

Raúl Leoni is fatally ill. They are going to try to get him back here in Venezuela before he dies.

There are for practical reasons two MIR's now. One is headed by Américo Martín and Simón Sáez Merida and operates legally without giving up all underground activity. The other still is engaged in urban and rural guerrilla activities, which have revived recently.

He agrees that AD hasn't been active recently in the Socialist International. He thinks that they should become more active.

*   *   *   *   *

CONVERSATION WITH CARLOS ANDRÉS PÉREZ IN ACCIÓN DEMOCRÁTICA HEADQUARTERS, CARACAS, JUNE 25, 1973

All indications are that this campaign is going very well. It is like one of the AD campaigns of the early days, with the same drive, enthusiasm, and optimism. The polls, three of them, all indicate that he is at least twelve points ahead of Lorenzo Fernández, the Copei candidate. The real battle is between these two.

He thinks that the reasons for this good state of the campaign are several. First is the discontent which undoubtedly exists with the Copei government, which really has been inefficacious and has engendered widespread opposition.

He thinks that another reason for the success of his campaign is the way he is conducting it. In contrast with campaigns of the past, he is going on extensive walking tours in various parts of the country, talking with people in the streets, going into their houses, and thus building up a feeling of personal association. Also, he has overcome the taboo of the barrios of Caracas and other cities, and has climbed up and down the hills where the barrios are located, talking with people, finding out their complaints and their problems and asking for their support. He is the only presidential candidate who has been doing that. In general, his campaign has been quite different from that of the other candidates.

He doesn't think that MEP will do well at all. The party is in full disintegration, and many of its people are coming back to Acción Democrática.

In his campaign he has been very critical of the strategy of development which Venezuela has used so far. He has even been critical of the way in which the AD governments of which he was a part carried out development. He is the AD candidate, for sure, but this doesn't mean that he must defend the mistakes of the past.

The fact is that the process of development which has gone forward in the last fifteen years has not been successful. Poverty still exists; the great concentration of wealth and income still exists; unemployment is an ever-present and growing problem. As a result, there must be a fundamental shift of policy. First of all, there must be a shift to giving more emphasis to agriculture, which has not gotten the attention which it has deserved. This will be a means of limiting the encouragement of people to drift to the cities, particularly to Caracas. A great deal more resources must be put into agriculture.

Then something must be done to lessen the congestion of Caracas. Real pressure, through taxation and through incentives, must be brought on industrial firms to move out of Caracas. In any case, this is not a good place for industries and they would do better in the interior. This would become one of his first moves. He would also geographically decentralize the government. With modern transportation, there is no reason why all government branches should be here, and he would move some of them to provincial towns.

Something must also be done about the barrios. First, they must be provided the public services they need. Second, the government must very actively sponsor the establishment in them of artisan shops and small factories, so as to give additional sources of employment. This will help raise the levels of living of those people.

*   *   *   *   *

TALK BY CARLOS ANDRÉS PÉREZ TO YOUNG BUSINESSMEN AND "TÉCNICOS," IN CARACAS, JUNE 25, 1973

He thinks that youth is of particularly great importance in this country, if for no other reason than the extreme youthfulness of the population. Well over half of the Venezuelans are under twenty years of age. Their needs are certainly of primary importance in this country.

He thinks that the first need of youth here is education. As now organized, it is badly oriented. It doesn't instill objectives in the youth, or prepare them adequately for their later life. He intends to change secondary schools and the universities, to orient their courses of study more in conformity with the needs of the society and the economy. Also, he intends to introduce real education planning, to look forward to the needs of the educational system, and of society in general, and coordinate the growth of education with the growing and changing needs of Venezuela. Unfortunately, very little has been done so far.

One injustice which is done to many youth is done through the system of compulsory military service. It is not, in fact, compulsory military service to which all are subject. Rather, it is those who are poorest and worst off who are really the ones who have to do their military service. He will change this, by devising ways by which all youth of the appropriate age have to render their service in one way or another. A more flexible procedure will have to be worked out.

He is also very much concerned with sports and physical education. Sports are not just entertainment, they are part of normal growing up, and he intends to expand very substantially the facilities for young people to participate in sports. Physical training, in turn, will be stressed more in the schools.

Drugs in this country have not yet reached the level of a problem of major concern, but they are a growing problem, and one which must be dealt with. He thinks that it is wrong to deal with the addict as a criminal; he should be dealt with as someone who is sick, and this will be the kind of policy which Pérez will seek to follow. On the other hand, those who push drugs, particularly those who handle them on a large scale, will be dealt with with all of the strength of the law. They must be caught and punished severely.

Women's rights are another subject which is beginning to be talked about much more. The fact is that this is a male-dominated society, and that is not as it should be. However, he would like to suggest that in part at least this is the fault of women themselves, who do not take advantage of the opportunities which are available to them and to do new things, to undertake responsibilities equal to those of men. However, he will make it a policy to choose people for positions on the basis of their qualifications, and not on the basis of their sex. In the past, there has admittedly been too great a tendency to choose the man over the woman just because he is a man, even if she is more talented and capable. He will not do that.

He thinks that it is necessary to end the alienation of a sizable part of the youth from the regime. He thinks that the best way to do this is to prepare them adequately to play an important role in the building of Venezuela, and this he will seek to do.

He is asked about the question of what he will do if he lacks a majority in Congress. He can answer that by saying that he will have a majority; he will work with those forces in Congress which can provide a majority. He will not seek to govern only with members of his own party.

One of the major problems in Venezuela is certainly the parlous state of the family as an institution. In many places it hardly really exists, in the sense of the father, mother, and children living together in the same home. Often, this is financially and economically impossible. He thinks that the answers to the problem are full employment and a more equitable distribution of wealth and income in the country, and his government will have those two things as primary objectives.

He would stress the key importance of the first year of the next government. During that time, the fate of the democratic system in the country may well be sealed. The government will have to come to grips seriously with the problems which have been accumulating, and to broaden the basis of support for the democratic system, and demonstrate clearly that it can adequately deal with the problems which the country faces.

He has not thought it wise to lay particular stress on the weaknesses of the present Copei government. He has thought it wiser to make a positive rather than a negative campaign, to stress what he intends to do rather than what the present regime has not done.

There is great need for a new agricultural policy. In recent years, agriculture has not gotten enough attention. Much more resources must be turned into agriculture, to provide the products that the country needs, and to generate new exports. With the growing food crisis in the world, it will not be as easy as before to purchase outside the things which Venezuela does not grow for itself.

Of course, petroleum remains of key importance to Venezuela and its economy. However, what is done with the oil industry cannot be just the decision of Acción Democrática; it must be a decision which represents a wide consensus in the country. Some things seem clear. The future of the oil industry here does not rest in the traditional areas in which the oil industry is located. They are exhaustible in the foreseeable future. The real future of the industry lies in the Orinoco Valley, where it is known that vast reserves exist. However, the development of those reserves is a matter of time and of large sums of money, and resources and technical knowledge. He frankly does not think that Venezuela has the financial resources or the technical knowledge to do this job alone. He thinks that it is necessary to have the help of the international companies, but that help must be gotten on Venezuelan terms. The old type of concessions is dead, forever, new techniques must be adopted for opening up this great potential wealth. Meanwhile, it is very necessary to train Venezuelans to participate much more in this process than they have done in the past.

*   *   *   *   *

CONVERSATION WITH CARLOS ANDRÉS PÉREZ IN RÓMULO BETANCOURT'S HOUSE, CARACAS, JUNE 26, 1973

Acción Democrática has introduced the idea of having a single ballot in the December election. This is very necessary. The present system provides for the voter to get two different colored cards for each party--one for president, the other for other offices. He also gets an envelope, in which he places the two ballots which he wants to cast, throwing away the rest. But this can lead to abuses: for instance, if the card for the candidate of one party is missing, and the voter comes out and asks for it, he runs the risk that his vote will be declared null and void, since by asking for this card he has indicated for whom he is voting. The system worked all right when there were only three or four parties, but with the superfluity of them that there is now, it is exceedingly clumsy and subject to abuse.

However, there are problems with regard to introducing the single ballot, which the voter would then mark, presumably with a pencil. If he were to be asked to write an X on the party's color which he wanted, this would work fine for white or yellow, but not well at all on black or dark blue or brown. If they were to put a white box next to each party's color, with the voter supposed to place his mark on that box, the other parties wouldn't like this, since the AD color is white. All of this must still be worked out.

The expansion of Caracas must be stopped or slowed down. He will seek to forbid any new real estate development in the Caracas area, at least until a thorough study has been made of the feasibility of such new developments.

It appears to him that the Allende regime in Chile is on the way to failure. Marxism-Leninism can only be imposed by force. If Allende had had a Democratic Socialist program, he would not have had his present problems. But the Allende regime is determined to push forward a Marxist-Leninist regime at all costs.

It is fairly easy here to get one's name on the ballot. To be a candidate for president, one needs only 5,000 signatures, and for lesser offices the number is considerably smaller.

* * * * *

CONVERSATION WITH CARLOS ANDRÉS PÉREZ AT HIS HOME, CARACAS, JUNE 27, 1973

Copei is very jealous of power and is using all kinds of means to stay in power. The government is openly spending a lot of money to further the Lorenzo Fernández candidacy. Copei is also attacking Carlos Andrés violently for his role as Minister of Interior under Betancourt, accusing him of having been too harsh, but at a time when they were in the government and shared responsibility for what was going on.

There is very widespread corruption in the Copei regime. It involves not just politicians in the regime, but goes down through the public administration. There are two Copei politicians who have more or less retired from active politics and instead are engaging in all kinds of shady business deals with the government.

Lorenzo Fernández, the Copei candidate, and President Caldera have a division of labor in the campaign. Fernández doesn't talk about Cuba, Caldera does; Caldera doesn't talk about immediate nationalization of petroleum, Fernández does.

Copei has tried to give a Leftist and Nationalist tinge to their campaign. They attack Carlos Andrés by alleging that he is the candidate of the oil companies and Fedecamaras.

In terms of oil policy, he thinks that nationalization of oil before the concessions expire in 1983 may be necessary. But it shouldn't be the subject of electoral demagoguery in a presidential campaign. Also, it is still true that the Venezuelans will need help from the outside to develop the Orinoco field, which is estimated to take fifteen years really to get into production. They must seek the way for developing that field through some new arrangement with the oil companies.

In this connection, when Secretary of State William Rogers was here, he was seeking a decision on the issue of the Orinoco field. Caldera said that he would not discuss the issue. Carlos Andrés thinks that is silly; one should be willing to discuss anything but only agree to what is in one's own best interest. He also thinks that the implication given by the government that to discuss anything like this with the United States is unpatriotic is wrong. Of course, there are other possible sources of help. The government will have to decide which one is most convenient, or which combination of sources.

There is great need to give a new impetus to agriculture. There is a need for agricultural products. Also, agricultural development is the only way to keep down the drift to the cities, particularly Caracas. The peasants are conservative, they don't want to leave their land. They do so because of their poverty and their inability to make a decent living.

Acción Democrática has been virtually reunified. The great mass of the MEP rank-and-filers have returned. Also many of the of middle-rank leaders--an area in which AD was particularly badly hit by the MEP split. Some top leaders are now again aligned with the party, such as Manzo González of the ARS group. González Navarro and others, although they may not yet have done so, will rejoin the party. Also, Luís Augusto Dubuc, who has been inactive for quite a while, has returned to activity again. Of course, Luis Beltrán Prieto will never return. His attitude is a sad one.

The MAS is attracting all of the far Left. This is good, because it gets them involved in regular political activity. The MAS will get 10 percent or less of the vote, which would perhaps give them 25 members of Congress. This is certainly better than any Communist group has done before.

The MIR has been relegalized. This is good. However, the element which has gotten legal status is only a fraction of the old MIR, that headed by Simón Sáez Merida and Américo Martín. The MIR is split into a number of rival groups.

None of the minor candidates has a chance to win in this year's election. However, their presence in the campaign is convenient for Acción Democrática. They take votes from Copei. This time, Germán Borregal, the perpetual candidate, won't come in last, as he has done in the last three campaigns.

He hadn't realized the seriousness of the Watergate scandal in the United States, and that it might mean the impeachment of President Nixon. One bad thing in this, he thinks, is the way government secrets get to be common knowledge, particularly with regard to international affairs. This will make foreign governments very cautious about dealing with the United States, fearful that soon everything agreed to will be published in the United States press. A Great Power such as the United States must be able to do some kind of things for its own national security which won't immediately become common knowledge.

*   *   *   *   *

CONVERSATION WITH CARLOS ANDRÉS PÉREZ IN HIS OFFICE IN CARACAS, AUGUST 20, 1979

He thinks that it would have been difficult to prevent the fall of Rómulo Gallegos. He just was not the man for the position; he was not a politician. Furthermore, he did not like the military men. Also, he was separated from Rómulo Betancourt at that time, hardly ever saw him. This was a matter of jealousy on Gallegos's part, rather than any plotting by Gallegos's relatives.

Gallegos should not have been AD's candidate in 1947. A stream of people came to Miraflores to urge Rómulo Betancourt that Gallegos not be the candidate, including not only Delgado Chalbaud and Mario Vargas, but also Valmore Rodríguez, Gonzalo Barrios, Raúl Leoni, and many others. But Betancourt's response was always the same: that the party had a historical commitment to name Gallegos.

It is, of course, impossible to say whether, if Betancourt had been president, the coup could have been avoided. But what is very clear is that Gallegos was not the man for the job.

Carlos Andrés was Betancourt's private secretary when Betancourt headed the Revolutionary Junta. Then he had the same position for some period in exile. He was the executive head of the exile committee, which was first in Havana, then in San José. The committee kept in close touch with the underground AD in Venezuela, through a radio connection, over which they broadcast in code, and through messengers who went back and forth. The radio contact was maintained until the middle of 1957, when the police here finally located the transmitter.

In 1953, when the Pérez Jiménez regime rounded up the top leaders of the AD underground, there was the end of having a single top figure in the Underground, one of the major figures of the party before the dictatorship. In the last two years, the persecution was particularly concentrated on Acción Democrática. The Communists were the next most persecuted, but this was concentrated principally against a few top leaders who were well known. The basic Communist apparatus in labor, among the teachers, and elsewhere was not touched. The regime persecuted the top leaders to keep up the front of anti-Communism, but they didn't touch the rest of the Communist apparatus, because they knew that among the workers, students, and so on, the Communists were the chief rivals of AD, and they figured that the Communists would seriously weaken AD, and at the time they did not really fear the Communists. It was not that the Communists were particularly supporting the regime, although the Black Communists did, but that it was convenient to the government not to do anything really dangerous to the Communists.

The upshot of this was that younger Adecos still were taught by Communist teachers and professors, and tended to acquire their ideas. There was no leading Adeco figure here in the country at the time, who might have counteracted this. As a result, these Communist-inclined young people were the ones who had command of the bureaucratic apparatus of the party just after the fall of the dictatorship. It was a delicate situation for a while, since they challenged the right of the old timers to return to control of the party, even Betancourt's right to do so.

There was definitely a change in AD strategy after the end of the dictatorship. One of the causes of the fall of the Gallegos was that the bitter attacks of the parties on one another had prepared an atmosphere propitious to a coup, and they were determined to prevent that in 1958, and this was shown in the Pact of Punto Fijo.

There was no rejection of this new line in the party. Indeed, it tended to be turned against Betancourt, and his presidential candidacy. It was argued that his candidacy would motivate the military to make another coup. Ramos Giménez, Paz Galarraga fomented this idea, but even Gonzalo Barrios and Raúl Leoni were led, out of fear of the possible consequences, to urge Rómulo not to run. It was not that they had any enmity against him, but that they were afraid of what would happen if he ran.

But Betancourt cultivated the military men. He had always been good in handling them, both in the 1945-1948 period and in 1958 and afterward.

The only split in the party which had an ideological basis was that of the MIR. The other two were fights over the party's presidential nomination, and for personal positions of power within the party. He thinks that the split of 1968 was not provoked by Betancourt's famous letter. It was caused by the effort of Paz Galarraga and his friends to seize control of the party. Luis Beltrán Prieto was just their tool in this. However, Prieto did not have the qualities necessary to be President of the

Republic.

During Carlos Andrés's administration, he took advantage of a happy conjunction of circumstances such as Venezuela will probably not enjoy again. One, of course, was the increase in oil prices, which gave them resources such as had never been available before. Second was the world recession, which made it possible for them to get the services of technicians whom they needed from all over the world, including the United States, where there were quite a few highly trained people out of jobs. They could get technicians and even pure scientists, whom they needed under circumstances which would not have obtained except for the recession. The third thing was that there were tremendous amounts of money available in the banks, because of the oil situation and the recession, which made it possible for Venezuela to borrow funds abroad at very good terms, at less than 8 percent interest. They had to borrow, because even with the increased oil prices, they did not have enough resources for the huge projects which they were undertaking. For both the Guri Dam expansion to 7 million kilowatts and the steel plants, they needed $5 billion apiece, for instance.

He thinks that his government achieved many things. The most notable, of course, was the nationalization of the oil industry. It is running quite well under Venezuelan control and is providing the government with more revenue, even discounting the price increases in oil, than it did under private ownership.

He understands why the opposition should criticize the contracts that the government oil firms signed with foreign companies. They couldn't criticize the nationalization as such, and so they chose the contracts. That is understandable. But their criticisms were wrong. Compared with contracts of the same kind signed by any other oil-producing countries, they were favorable. Furthermore, they were only for two years, and then could be renewed, changed, or cancelled. A number were cancelled and others were modified.

His government undertook some gigantic projects. One was the steel industry, with the original plant of SIDOR being increased to 5 million tons a year. They've built up a large aluminum industry, the single largest plant of its kind in the world. They have contracts for its output for the next ten years, with the provision that as national needs grow, the contracts will be cut back, to give priority to domestic needs. In a world in which expansion of the aluminum industry has practically halted, and shortages are not foreseen in the future, this is a very useful enterprise. In addition, they undertook a very large expansion of the electric power industry.

The government also pushed very much the expansion of agriculture. This included a substantial expansion of irrigation, with the building of quite a few irrigation dams. The upshot was that agricultural production grew about 5 percent a year, which meant that it outran the increase in population of about 3 percent a year. For long this had not been the case.

There were also extensive social efforts. They built many hospitals; in fact, the country has sufficient hospitals and the problem now is to see that they are well run. They much expanded education, so that now there are four million kids in school. Expenditures on social security tripled under him. They achieved virtually full employment, with the unemployment rate being under 4 percent. As a result of all of this, the division of national income shifted from 51 percent to capital and 49 percent to wages when he came in, to 70 percent for wages and 30 percent for capital when he went out.

It is true that he sought to weaken the position of the "monopolies," the big family of conglomerates like the Mendozas and the Vollmers. He did this through the government's credit mechanism. Of course, Venezuela is unique in the degree to which the national income is channeled through the government, and this is what made his policy possible. He set up the Development Corporation for Middle and Small Industry. He established the Fondo Industrial. He organized a new agricultural bank. All of these institutions extended funds principally to the small and middle sized industries. He also decentalized public works contracting, requiring that in each region of the country, contracts be given with the priority to contractors from that region, and that they be given to national contractors only when local ones definitely could not do the job. As a result, thousands of new contractors were put into business or brought into relationship with the government. All of this helped them to reach the full employment situation.

During his administration, state capitalism really came into existence. This is because government ownership of key things like oil, mining and some new industries came to supplement the tremendous role which the government had already had because of its huge tax revenues.

They are starting work on trying to find ways to exploit the tar sands of the Orinoco. New technology is needed for this, and the cost of oil from them will be considerably higher than production of oil here now is. But the higher the price of oil goes, the more feasible it will become to exploit those large reserves.

During his government, he was much worried by the situation in the English-speaking Caribbean. Those countries need a great deal of help to build up viable economies. So far, the industrial countries have not shown much interest, and he fears that if no one else steps in, Castro will virtually have the place to himself. This is beginning to happen now in Grenada, and only because the industrial countries and Venezuela didn't step in. He is sure that the new group there, which overthrew a very corrupt and oppressive regime, would have been happy to accept Venezuelan overtures to extend help, but they were not forthcoming, and now they have turned to Castro, who is eager to help.

He warned Henry Kissinger of what was likely to happen in the English-speaking Caribbean when Kissinger was still secretary of state, but Kissinger wasn't interested. He found Carter much more receptive when he talked to him about it. He proposed to Carter a $1.5 billion program of aid spread over five years, $300 million a year. He suggested that it be patterned after the Marshall Plan, with some joint agency of the Caribbean countries being set up to present the needs of the countries of the area, and present these to the contributing countries, and be the channel through which the aid would be given. As a result of Pérez's suggestion to Carter, Carter suggested to the World Bank that it set up a group to study the possibilities of such a program, and to sound out possible contributing nations, such as Japan, the EEC and others. This was set up, but it found little receptivity from the donor countries, and the move seems to have died.

It is true that Barbados is in a better situation than most of the others. But it also has serious economic difficulties, and if it is not helped, it may well slip into the situation of the others. He helped them out at the time of one particularly acute crisis, and one of the last trips which he took as president was to Barbados.

He also made strong overtures to Jamaica. At the time he came to power, the only country which was giving aid to Jamaica was Cuba. He had the Venezuelan government give Jamaica some aid and got Carter to change the policy of hostility towards the government of Michael Manley. Jamaica is very important because Manley has very considerable influence, not only with neighboring Caribbean countries but also with a number of key African leaders such as Julius Nyrere.

He thinks that the loss of last year's election by AD is quite puzzling. Opinion surveys which AD had made by the Gaither agency showed that well over 50 percent of those polled were basically satisfied with his administration, felt that real progress had been made by the country during his government, and felt optimistic about the future. In spite of that, AD lost, and he doesn't quite know why. The difference in the candidates may have had something to do with it, but that is not enough of an explanation. He doesn't really know why they lost.

He doesn't think that the loss of the municipal elections was as serious as the opponents of AD are claiming. Copei did not get any more votes than they got in December. Neither did the Left. In the presidential election, there is no doubt that the Left voted substantially for Luis Herrera Campins, the Copei candidate--in the previous election between 80 and 85 percent voted for AD and Copei, this time 90 percent did, and the margin is the votes of the Left which went to Herrera. In the municipal election, the Left voted for their own candidates. What seems to have happened was that large numbers of AD voters abstained, not having too much interest, once they had lost the presidential election.

He doesn't think that the leaders of MIR and MAS are really converts to political democracy. However, they have concluded that preaching Marxism-Leninism is going to get them nowhere, and that they made a mistake in taking up violence. So now they are trying a kind of AD approach to politics, hoping to be sure, to destroy AD in the process. But there is a positive side to this, because any converts they are making are not being converted to Marxism-Leninism but to something quite different.

He did not take any part in the internal struggle over the party's presidential nomination this time. However, the struggle got rather bitter, and certainly was one of the factors explaining the defeat by Copei. The Lusinchi supporters either did not or were not allowed to play much of a role in the campaign. The same thing would have been true--in the opposite direction--had Lusinchi won the nomination.

There is no truth in the rumor that there is a split between himself and Rómulo and his position in AD. On the other hand, he and Rómulo are very different people. Also, Betancourt is very set on certain ideas such as the Betancourt Doctrine and the need for a very hard line toward the Castro government. He will never change his ideas on these subjects, and Carlos Andrés did not follow these ideas when he was president. But there is no danger of an open break between them. The split resulting from such a break would mean the end of Acción Democrática, and they both know that.

AD parliamentarians boycotted the last part of the recent session of Congress. This was because the Copeyanos, together with the smaller parties, violated the regulations of Congress. He cannot say whether, when Congress resumes, the Adecos will be back there or not. Negotiations about this are under way now.

During the Caldera administration, there was a parliamentary agreement between AD and Copei. He thinks that this is desirable this time, too. President Herrera has said publicly that he doesn't need such an agreement, and Caldera has said that it is very necessary. This difference of opinion is indicative of the struggle now going on in Copei between Caldera and Herrera Campíns. Herrera was not Caldera's candidate for the Copei nomination in the 1978 election.

The Herrera administration has taken the position that the Venezuelan economy is overheated. They have therefore tried to cut back on some of the programs he had under way. If they persist with this, they will provoke a recession here. Also, this policy has not served to slow down inflation. In fact, inflation is running at a higher rate now than when he left office. During his period in office, he was able to keep inflation at about the rate it had in the industrial countries, that is, about 7-8 percent.

They did not have any particular problems with Domingo Alberto Rangel during the exile period. He was not at that time of any considerable importance. He gained importance when he returned and aligned himself with the young people who ultimately formed the MIR.

*   *   *   *   *

CONVERSATION WITH CARLOS ANDRÉS PÉREZ AT RUTGERS UNIVERSITY IN NEW BRUNSWICK, NEW JERSEY, OCTOBER 1, 1982

He thinks that Acción Democrática will win the next election. The present Copei regime is very discredited. However, the next AD government will have to take over a disastrous situation. The Venezuelan economy is in terrible condition as a consequence of this government's policies.

During his administration, the government launched a number of development programs, using the increased oil resources for that. But the Herrera Campíns government has either cancelled all those projects which were still in the planning stage or has suspended those which were under way. This is particularly the case with industries in the Guyana area. If they had gone forward, the country would be producing a wide range of things which would have gone far toward dealing with the present economic situation.

However, not only has the Herrera government not gone on with the development programs of his administration, it has dramatically increased the national debt, both in foreign exchange and bolivares. Although in his presidential election campaign Herrera violently attacked Carlos Andrés for increasing the national debt, Herrera has more than doubled it. But there is nothing to show for it. It is not at all clear what the Herrera government has spent all that it has borrowed for. It has just totally mismanaged the economy.

*   *   *   *   *

CONVERSATION WITH CARLOS ANDRÉS PÉREZ IN NEW YORK CITY, MAY 2, 1984

The next presidential election campaign has not begun yet. This is fortunate, because there are very serious economic and other problems to be resolved in the country, and therefore it is too early for there to be the kind of political tensions which are involved in a presidential campaign.

President Jaime Lusinchi is doing quite well so far. However, he is faced with very difficult problems and he needs all the support which he can get. Of course, Carlos Andrés is supporting him completely, since this is his duty.

Municipal elections come up at the end of this month. At present, it looks as if Acción Democrática will win those elections. It is possible that the Leftist elements will slightly improve their situation, since they are entering these elections together--there is no problem of the relative positions of the top leaders of the various Leftist parties. However, AD is likely to do very well in the elections, better than last time.

Venezuela has problems with its foreign debt and its general economic situation. However, Venezuela, fortunately, is not now engaged in any kind of negotiations with the International Monetary Fund.

He is keeping very active. He is dividing his time between Venezuelan internal affairs and his international activities. He is here to consult about the problems of Central America.

The Contadora Group is much more than four countries which are trying to act as intermediaries in the crisis in Central America. It had its origins in the Malvinas Crisis. That taught the Latin American countries that although they should develop good relations with the United States, the countries of Western Europe, and all the free world, they could no longer depend on some international organization outside of their own area to defend their security.

So the Contadora Group is an effort of the Latin American countries to solve a problem which is a Latin American problem. In doing this, the four countries of the Contadora Group--Venezuela, Colombia, Panama, and Mexico--have the backing of all of the democratic countries and countries moving toward democracy in Latin America. For instance, they have the strong support of the Brazilian government, which since the Malvinas incident has moved very close to the other Latin American countries, in spite of its long history of being apart from them. Also, Argentina, which seems so far away and so much more a European country than a Latin American one, is also strongly behind the Contadora effort.

There is no difference of opinion among the four countries of the Contadora Group concerning what they should do with regard to the Central American crisis. It is true that Venezuela and Mexico have long had different approaches to the Castro regime in Cuba. All democratic elements in Latin America agree that the Castro regime is a Communist regime at the service of the Soviet Union; there is no question about that. But they also agree that, like it or not, the Castro regime exists, and there has to be some kind of coexistence between it and the other Latin American regimes. But the Mexicans have had an unbendable and incomprehensively exaggerated belief in non-intervention, and this has guided their relations with Cuba, and the Venezuelans have not agreed with this. However, this disagreement has in no way brought any difference in their attitude within the Contadora Group.

The first thing the Contadora Group did was to draw up a list of twenty-one points for resolving the crisis of Central America. All five governments of Central America have agreed with those points, and to try to work to carry them out. However, after that had occurred, the Contadora Group came up against the fact that there are elements in the

Central American situation over which the countries of the Contadora Group have no control.

On the one hand, there is the arming of Nicaragua by the Soviet Union via Cuba, which is very extensive. The other is the attitude and actions of the present administration in the United States. The U.S. has converted Honduras into a militaristic country and a military base for the United States armed forces, while at the same time using Honduras as a base for attacks on the Sandinista regime in Nicaragua.

These forces outside the control of the Contadora Group have very much curtailed the further development of its intermediary efforts. He thinks that the only rational solution to the problem is that which the Contadora Group is trying to develop, that is, negotiations for a political solution to the problem. However, so far, the United States although formally expressing support for what the Contadora Group is trying to do, has not borne out such support.

For instance, the Nicaraguan regime said that it would be willing to remove all foreign military advisers now in the country. It is without question that there are advisers there from the Soviet Union, Cuba, and the East European countries in considerable numbers, and that the commander of the Nicaraguan armed forces now is a general with extensive experience in Angola. However, the Nicaraguans said that they would be quite willing to get rid of all of those if the United States would withdraw its advisers from Central America and its troops from Honduras. However, the United States has refused to talk about this offer, saying that they would only begin to withdraw their advisers and troops after all foreign advisers were gone from Nicaragua. This is in spite of the fact that the Nicaraguans had agreed to have the withdrawal of advisers from their country out under international supervision.

In discussions he has had recently in Washington, he has talked about all of this both with members of Congress and with officials of the State Department. In his talks with the State Department people, they always raised the issue that one could not trust the Sandinistas to carry out their promises. But when he went on to ask them what they thought should be done instead of taking the risk of seeing whether the Sandinistas would fulfill their commitment, the discussion always got quite vague.

He thinks that the only other alternative is a military one. That can certainly not be successful without extensive United States armed intervention in the area. The success of such intervention is by no means assured, and a defeat of the United States would also be a defeat for Central America, for all of Latin America, and a major strategic victory for the Soviet Union. He thinks that the risks in that direction are also very extensive and should be weighed against those involved in seeing whether the Sandinistas would carry out their agreement to get rid of their foreign military advisers.

He doesn't have to place himself ideally in the position of being president of the United States, which is clearly impossible in any case. to pass judgment on what would be a proper policy for the United States to pursue. He can say in this connection that if Jimmy Carter had been president during the last few years, the Central American crisis would have been resolved, and would have been resolved in a way satisfactory for democracy in the area and in the hemisphere generally.

He thinks that as part of the solution of the Central American crisis it is essential for economic problems of the region be dealt with. The

Kissinger Report bore out this need, and it is certainly absolutely necessary that the economic development of the area be pushed forward, to deal with the factors underlying the crisis in Central America.

During his visit to Washington he commented to someone that there were two major crises which were facing Latin America. One of these is the Central American crisis about which he has been talking. The other is the debt crisis.

One doesn't any longer have to talk in theoretical terms about the dangers in the debt situation. The International Monetary Fund-type prescription for depressing the economies of the debtor countries is a time bomb which is waiting to explode. It has already exploded in the Dominican Republic in recent days, where rioting against the International Monetary Fund program there has resulted in the death of more than fifty people, several hundred more people wounded, and four thousand people arrested. The net result is that a democratically elected regime is very much in danger of being overthrown.

Nor is this kind of crisis confined to the Dominican Republic. At the present moment the democratic government of Costa Rica is in serious danger also of being overthrown for the same reason. This may seem impossible, but it is in fact the case.

In fact, the danger is even more widespread. Venezuela, Brazil, Argentina, or almost any of the democratic or near democratic regimes of the region may be subject to the same kind of danger. In fact, the kind of situation is beginning to appear in Africa, so that it is a world wide problem, not confined even to one region.

He thinks that what is required is that the governments of the creditor countries, the governments of the debtor countries, the financial community of the creditor countries, and that of the debtor countries get together to work out the details of a solution to the problem of the debt. The solution involves the establishment of a fixed interest rate and one at relatively modest levels; and the spreading of the debt over a longer period, so that the amortization payments per year be smaller. Finally, it also involves the fact that the debtor countries will not be able to continue to pay their debts unless they are able to earn the foreign currency necessary to pay them by selling their goods in the industrialized countries, and so there has to be a reduction of the protectionist measures in the industrialized countries, which limit the ability of the developing countries to sell their goods to the industrialized ones.

He thinks that it is time that there be recognition that both parties share the blame for the present situation. The banks in the industrial countries were certainly lacking in responsibility in misjudging the ability of the developing countries to pay back the debts that they were incurring, and the governments of the developing countries were also lacking in responsibility in judging their nations' abilities to pay their debts. So since both sides share the responsibility for the present situation, both sides should share in solving the problem.

However, nothing is being done at the present time to resolve the situation. This is highly dangerous, because the whole situation could break down at any time.

*   *   *   *   *

CONVERSATION WITH CARLOS ANDRÉS PÉREZ IN NEW YORK CITY, APRIL 18, 1988

He did not have a great deal of difficulty in getting the presidential nomination of Acción Democrática. There was a semi-primary, in which various thousands of local officials of the party participated, to name the party nominee. He got about 70 percent of the votes of those who participated.

The Copei candidate is Edmundo Fernández, but he has very considerable problems. One is that Rafael Caldera is not supporting him. In spite of the fact that Fernández had been a protegé of Caldera, there has developed a very strong antagonism between them in the last year or so, so Caldera is not helping Fernández in the present campaign.

There are various other candidates. Teodoro Petkoff is running as nominee of MAS, again. There is no doubt that MAS has gone through a significant transformation. It says that it is no longer a Marxist-Leninist Party. However, Carlos Andrés doubts that they will do very well in the election campaign.

The Communist Party has its own candidate, the chancellor of the Universidad Central de Venezuela. However, the Communist Party has been reduced to a very minor factor in national politics. The MIR is equally impotent.

Jóvito Villalba's wife is the candidate of the URD. However, Jóvito himself is very ill, mentally very much deteriorated, and virtually dead physically, and certainly dead politically.

Luis Beltrán Prieto is still alive. A few months ago, he was virtually dead, but he recovered and is now vigorous again. He is still active in writing and passing judgment on what is going on. However, MEP is virtually non-existent, although it officially still exists.

In addition, there are several independent candidates.

One can say that Pan Americanism began with the Monroe Doctrine, which proclaimed America for the Americans. However, in time it developed into a claim for preeminence and dominance by the United States in the hemisphere, and particularly for United States firms with influence in Latin America.

However, with the Good Neighbor Policy, and cooperation during World War II, relations changed, giving rise in 1948 to establishment of the Organization of American States. We are now celebrating the fortieth anniversary of the OAS.

Subsequently, there have occurred three very significant events which have changed relations between Latin America and the United States. These were the Castro Revolution, the Sandinista Revolution, and the Malvinas War.

The Malvinas War was particularly significant. Until then, the theory had been that America was one region, with common interests and common purposes. But this was challenged in the Malvinas War. At that point, it became clear that the United States had a greater commitment to the North Atlantic Treaty Organization [NATO] than it had to America, since it gave strong support to the British. That was so in spite of the fact that the Latin Americans were strongly in support of Argentina in the conflict. But that made it clear that the old idea of Pan Americanism was no longer really valid.

During the 1970s and early 1980s, there was a victory of democracy in the Latin American countries. However, at the present time that victory is in serious danger, particularly as a result of the Panamanian situation and the debt problem.

Insofar as the Panamanian situation is concerned, there was intervention by a group of Latin American leaders, specifically himself, Alfonso López of Colombia, and Daniel Oduber of Costa Rica. They negotiated with General Noriega with regard to his exit from the situation there. They had reached agreement with him that he would leave the scene in May of this year, and that before that there would be a new electoral law agreed to by the regime and the opposition, and they had gotten the regime and the opposition to agree to this, with international supervision of new elections, after the National Assembly agreed to change the electoral law in conformity with the demands of the opposition. They had gotten agreement from Felipe González, Prime Minister of Spain, who made an informal visit to Costa Rica, to accept Noriega in Spain if there were no charges against him in the United States, which might raise the question of extradition.

However, right when they had reached this agreement, they got the sudden news that Noriega had been indicted in the United States. As a result of that the whole thing collapsed, and Noriega took a very hard line, which he is still continuing to maintain. Also, the United States took an increasingly hard line, leading to the crisis which now exists.

The effect of this crisis on Panama is devastating. As a result of it, the international financial system which Panama has had during recent years has completely collapsed, and the future of the Panamanian economy is very dim indeed. Therefore, the situation in Panama amounts to a major crisis.

However, the Latin Americans have to recognize the strategic interests of the United States in the present situation. The situation is more urgent than one might first think. It is not an issue of what will happen at the end of 1999. The fact is that at the end of 1989, although the Canal will be governed by a joint board, the majority of the board will be in Panamanian hands. So the issue is one of considerable urgency.

At the present moment, there is a deadlock and crisis. He thinks that the United States may not have any alternative but a military intervention in Panama, since he does not think that much of anything else will dislodge General Noriega from his present position. He would not be surprised if there was a military intervention.

In that connection, it should be recognized that none of the democratic governments of Latin America presently supports Noriega. However, it should also be recognized that military intervention by the United States in Panama would arouse an almost universal revulsion in Latin America.

The other major problem is that of the international debt of Latin American countries. It has reached the point that the debt situation puts the whole democratic development of Latin America in grave danger. This is illustrated best perhaps by the case of Venezuela. It is the only country which had been paying off not only the interest due on the debt but its amortization as well. However, the fact is that Venezuela has been using half its earnings in foreign trade to pay the debt, and this cannot possibly continue.

The situation of other countries is even worse. In the case of Argentina, for instance, it is questionable how long the democratic regime there can continue to exist. The economic crisis there is such that the whole regime is in peril.

In the case of Brazil, it is true that it didn't pay on its debt for almost a year, and that it spent a good deal of what did not go abroad to pay the debt on internal expenditures. But it was forced to do that because the economic crisis provoked before by its trying to pay the debt was so great that there was danger of a social explosion if funds were not spent on dealing with social problems. But this situation cannot continue for very much longer now that Brazil has begun to pay on the debt again.

The case of Peru is another example. Alan Garcia didn't pay except a minimum part of the debt payments, and what he didn't pay abroad he used to stimulate the development of the economy; the result has been an increase in demand for imports, and so Peru is back in the same situation as the other debtor countries now.

He thinks that it is absolutely necessary that there be real negotiations among the bankers, the governments of Latin America, and the governments of the creditor countries to work out a solution to the problem. There has to be a reduction of the amounts which Latin Americans themselves have to pay, but it is clear that the banks in the developed countries cannot themselves make such arrangement; the governments must be involved as well. It is true that Secretary of the Treasury James Baker made overtures to solve the problem, but what he proposed was not sufficient, and there must be wider negotiations.

He thinks that a new approach to Inter American relations has to be reached. It will involve the recognition that there are in fact two different regions involved, although they have certain interests in common. He thinks that the OAS could be the forum through which these two regions--the United States and Latin America--could negotiate. It exists and doesn't have to be created.

*   *   *   *   *

CABLE FROM CARLOS ANDRÉS PÉREZ, JANUARY 13, 1989

Thank you for your cordial message of felicitations on my election. I have pledged my word to rescue the country from the crisis and in that I shall put my decided efforts. Believe me that I shall not defraud those who put their confidence in me. I use the occasion to send you my New Year's message.

*   *   *   *   *

CONVERSATION WITH CARLOS ANDRÉS PÉREZ IN PRESIDENTIAL PALACE, CARACAS, JULY 23, 1992

When he came into office this time, there was a terrible economic situation. There wasn't any question as to whether he should or should not go to the International Monetary Fund. He had no choice. Inflation was at 80 percent, there was a terrible balance of payments crisis. The growth of the economy had stopped.

He has liberalized the economy. He ended a number of policies which had held for many years and which were wrong. Thus, he reduced tariffs and freed prices. He adopted a floating exchange rate. He began limiting subsidies to weak firms. He also reduced a variety of other protective devices.

These policies have been successful. The growth rate of the GNP last year was 9.5 percent. This year it is estimated at 4-5 percent, not as good as last, but still one of the highest in Latin America. Real investment by Venezuelan firms and foreign ones already here is growing, although new foreign firms are still cautious. Inflation is down to 40 percent and is still falling. Foreign reserves have been built up. Most important, confidence has been restored; both foreign and domestic investors are happy.

He realized that liberalization policies would cause trouble for many, particularly the poor. So he established a system whereby they surveyed all families, their incomes, the number of children in the families. There were then instituted both money grants and grants in food to the poor. This cannot be continued indefinitely, but it is necessary now. They also instituted free meals in the schools. Unemployment fell last year from 9 percent to 8 percent, and is still falling, so the need for such aid should begin to decline.

It is true that corruption is a serious problem. They have set up a commission to investigate all aspects of it. Yesterday the head of the Confederación de Trabajadores de Venezuela had his parliamentary immunity lifted by Congress, so he can be prosecuted. Carlos Andrés thinks that he is a sacrificial lamb for those who are shouting about corruption. The case against ex-President Jaime Lusinchi is still pending.

There is no doubt about the fact that the last two administrations were bad. They were very bad in the administration of public affairs. They did nothing to curb corruption, and inflation got out of hand. He has tried to change that situation.

The February 4 coup attempt was serious for him. Miraflores was surrounded. There was some shooting into the building. They wanted to kill him. He got the idea of going on television to address the people and the rebels. He drove out of the palace in a car, and they didn't prevent him, and went straight to the television station. He addressed the people, and the soldiers, loyal and rebel. When the rebels heard him on television, they gave up.

He had been in telephone communication with the Minister of Defense, whose building was also surrounded. When Carlos Andrés told the minister that he was going to talk on television, the Minister arranged to rig up television screens facing the rebels, and when they saw Carlos Andrés on television, they turned in their arms. The great bulk of soldiers stayed loyal. The top military commanders are loyal to democracy. The group which led the revolt were men who had infiltrated the armed forces after the Betancourt-Leoni period, determined from the start to organize a military coup. They planned their coup very well. It is true that the principal leaders of the coup were all from the same graduating class in the military academy, but they had recruited others from other classes. He doesn't think that there will be another coup attempt.

It is true that after the coup Rafael Caldera and Arturo Uslar Pietri took advantage of the situation to call for his resignation. But, like Rómulo Betancourt, he said that he would have to be taken out of office dead before the expiration of his term. Then they came up with the crazy idea of a referendum on whether a president, members of Congress, etc., should stay in office after the first half of their term, with 5 percent of the electorate enough to call for such a referendum. Fortunately, that idea was defeated.

Unfortunately, the political parties have been discredited. People judge them as being responsible for all of the country's problems. That is a very dangerous situation.

Apparently, Rafael Caldera wants to run for president again. Rumors have been that he is negotiating to be the candidate of Movimiento a Socialismo. But Edmundo Fernández controls the Copei party machinery, and he intends to run again. So there may be two candidates out of Copei in next year's election. The return of Caldera to the presidency would be disastrous.

* * * * *
* * * * *

CONVERSATION WITH LUIS HERRERA CAMPINS IN MARACAY, VENEZUELA, APRIL 25, 1960

Copei is doing all right. It has recovered from its defeat of 1958. Being in the government has not discredited the party, has given its leaders administrative experience, and has generally raised the prestige of the party. They are gaining ground in Caracas and elsewhere.

The recent revolt of General Castro León was a triumph for Copei. It occurred in Táchira, a Copeyano state and the home of all of Venezuela's militarists. But the party reacted marvelously against the revolt and was in the lead in suppressing it. The peasants who arrested Castro León were Copeyanos.

The Copei is making progress in the labor and student movements. In the University Federation of Caracas, they got 40 percent of the votes recently. In Andrés Bello University they lost by fifty-seven votes, against all of the other parties combined.

* * * * *
* * * * *

CONVERSATION WITH JAIME LUSINCHI IN ACCIÓN DEMOCRÁTICA HEADQUARTERS, CARACAS, JULY 30, 1962

The situation here at the moment is calm. However, the Peruvian coup d'état is very disconcerting. It is not the first in Latin America. There has been the Army's insistence on conditions for Goulart's taking over in Brazil, the Argentine coup which overthrow President Frondizi, the Ecuadorean one against Velasco Ibarra, the situation in Guatemala. The Brazilian case doesn't have any immediate repercussions here because the links between the Brazilian and Venezuelan armies have never been close, but those in Argentina and Peru are more serious. He hopes that nothing will happen here, but there are certainly civilians who would like to see something tried by the military.

The ARS split in Acción Democrática did not do much damage insofar as the rank and file members of the party are concerned. However, it did take a number of leaders of the secondary rank who are a loss to the party.

* * * * *

CONVERSATION WITH JAIME LUSINCHI IN ACCIÓN DEMOCRÁTICA HEADQUARTERS, CARACAS, APRIL 1, 1963

The situation here is basically good. The government is strong. There is no danger from the military now, since they are generally under control.

He thinks that Acción Democrática will win a good deal more than one and a half million votes, out of a total of three and a half million. He thinks that Jóvito Villalba is not likely to get more than 350,000 and that Admiral Larrazábal will not get much more.

Acción Democrática hasn't named a candidate yet. It wants to have a party man as the coalition nominee. Raúl Leoni and Gonzalo Barrios are the chief candidates for the AD candidacy. However, the convention, which will be held in May will make the final decision. There are now talks under way between AD and Copei about a coalition candidate.

He doubts that the opposition will be able to put up only a single candidate. Jóvito Villalba wants very much to run, and so does Admiral Larrazábal, and he presumes that both of them will do so.

The ARS is now supporting Arturo Uslar Pietri, which is peculiar. However, they want to back Uslar Pietri, an independent, because ARS is very weak, and they want to hide this weakness by backing some "independent" candidate, who might get more than just the ARS votes.

AVI, Asociación Venezolana Independiente, is a pressure group. It is the same old Venezuelan oligarchy wanting to save itself in a situation it cannot change basically. It talks of a candidate of "agreement" among the AD, Copei, and AVI, but they want an independent, not a member of any party.

It would be good to have an extreme Leftist candidate as another opposition nominee. But as of now the Communist Party and MIR cannot participate in the campaign with their own candidates. However, the Communists are seeking a means of having a nominee.

The labor and peasant situation is o.k. The new labor confederation, the CUTV, is a fraud. It has no base in rank and file unions.

The AD will receive the delegation of the Socialist International. However, he doubts very much that AD will join the International. It is not convenient now that the AD join any international organization.

* * * * *

CONVERSATION WITH JAIME LUSINCHI IN ACCIÓN DEMOCRÁTICA HEADQUARTERS, CARACAS, MAY 28, 1968

The AD presidential campaign is going very well. The party has recovered to a large degree from the defection of the supporters of Luis Beltrán Prieto. The reception which Gonzalo Barrios is receiving has been very good, and he is sure that AD is going to win again this time.

Barrios and other national leaders go out of Caracas to campaign on Thursday through Sunday. During the early days of the week they work here in Caracas. They are carrying on a strong campaign in Caracas, both in the barrios and in the urbanizaciones. He thinks that the party is going to do much better in Caracas than it did last time. In fact, he thinks that the party is going to win a bigger percentage of the votes than it had last time.

* * * * *

CONVERSATION WITH JAIME LUSINCHI IN THE CAPITOL, CARACAS, JUNE 9, 1971

He thinks that the chances are very good that Acción Democrática will win the next election. He is sure that the party will not split over the presidential nomination this time, as they have done in the past. They have learned the difficult way the result of doing this. None of the possible candidates would split the party. The party has an advantage in this now.

There are bitter struggles within Copei. Among other things, there is no doubt that there is a struggle between Opus Dei and the Jesuits for influence in the party. The chief representatives in the government of the Opus Dei tendency are Calvani, the Foreign Minister, and the Minister of Defense.

President Caldera has proposed the promotion of Minister of Defense General Martín García Villasamil from a brigadier general to a major general. However, it is not likely that AD will support this. The Minister of Defense is a very disagreeable man, a martinet, who is very much disliked by his subordinates. He also has tended to take an insolent tone when he is interrogated by Congress. Lusinchi thinks that it is very unlikely, therefore, that AD will support this promotion, which is in any case somewhat premature.

The youth of the Communist Party were very much upset by the Czechoslovakia crisis of 1968. This is one of the reasons that the great majority of the youth of the party went with the dissident group, the MAS. At the same time, the Communists are reported to get $85,000 a month from abroad, and he suspects that with some of the leadership who went with the MAS, it was as a result of differences of opinion and quarrels over how this money should be used.

The New Force has been trying to attract the MAS to its ranks. However, the MAS has refused to join it. This does not mean, in Lusinchi's opinion, that they don't want any contacts with other parties. For instance, one of the MAS leaders, Gustavo Machado's son-in-law, approached Lusinchi, as leader of the AD bloc in Congress, and said that he wanted to talk with him about the problem of the University, which has been closed.

He thinks that the position of MAS is similar to that of the Trotskyites. They accuse the Communist Party of having betrayed the struggle for the Revolution. However, the MAS people are horrorized by the mention of Trotsky. Nevertheless, they represent an anti-Stalinist reaction.

He thinks that there are grave dangers in the United States withdrawal from Vietnam. He was in the United States for some time recently and was disconcerted by the evident frictions which he found there. He thinks that many of those who are for complete withdrawal don't understand the importance of what they are advocating. He thinks that if the United States withdraws, the Communists undoubtedly will win in South Vietnam.

*   *   *   *   *

CONVERSATION WITH JAIME LUSINCHI IN ACCIÓN DEMOCRÁTICA HEADQUARTERS, CARACAS, MAY 29, 1972

Acción Democrática has difficulties with Copei in Congress. The Copeyanos are very hard people to get along with, make it very difficult to cooperate with them. Now there is a debate in Congress in which AD is criticizing the wide use of government funds during the recent campaign for the Copei nomination for president. The use reached outrageous proportions.

The Copei government has given the appearance of great weakness. This is the result of its trying to please everyone. They appear not to know just what it is that they want to do, which is another thing that makes it hard to work with them.

The AD trade union situation is getting better. There has been a split in the MEP trade union following, with the exit of José González Navaro, although MEP is still a power in the unions. The Communist Party hasn't been able to recuperate any of the trade union support which it once had before it went into the guerrilla campaign.

The dissident Communist group MAS is supporting José Vicente Rangel for president. Lusinchi doesn't think that Rangel will get very many votes, but what he does get will hurt the MEP and the New Force, not AD. The MAS had a good meeting for Rangel in the Nuevo Circo last week.

Copei has serious internal difficulties. Apparently there is no open split, but there are very serious tensions within that party.

* * * * *

CONVERSATION WITH JAIME LUSINCHI IN ACCIÓN DEMOCRÁTICA HEADQUARTERS, CARACAS, JUNE 25, 1973

The Acción Democrática campaign is going very well. All of the polls indicate that Carlos Andrés Pérez, the AD candidate, is going to win. Of course, one doesn't know how much faith to put in polls, but they are an indication.

In any case, the race is between Pérez and the Copei nominee, Lorenzo Fernández. The latter is not a very good candidate. He is an employer, owner of the EFE ice cream company. But he is going around the country telling the workers that they should get ready for participating in running their firms, because that is what his administration is going to introduce. Lusinchi would ask him whether he intends to introduce co-participation in the EFE ice cream company. He doubts it very much.

MEP doesn't stand a chance. Their party is in the process of full decline, with many of their people coming back to AD. The party is still there, but it is no longer a major factor in politics.

* * * * *
* * * * *

CONVERSATION WITH RAMÓN J. VELÁZQUEZ IN HIS OFFICE IN CARACAS, JUNE 25, 1954

Fortunes here have all been made from the government. Some of the generals who took over the control of the government got rich. For instance, the Guzman Liberal Revolution here was designed to turn over to Guzman and his family the lands of the Church, which had been the largest landholder. More recently a Minister gave his own company contracts for importation, construction, etc. under Medina Angarita. Some of the friends of the dictators have had monopolies. For instance, under Gomez there was one known as Pan Francés, because he had the monopolies of water, salt and flour out of which the kind of bread known locally as Pan Francés is made. Until ten years ago all alcoholic products were the monopoly of one man. Each dictatorship leaves a few more rich families. This one has been particularly prolific. In the last six years, fortunes of from two to three hundred million bolivars have been made, compared with the twenty million Gómez left when he died. The present prosperity has been thus largely confined to the top group. The poor man remains very poor.

In the next two or three years there must come a crisis among the military. It will be much like the one which was resolved in 1945. At that time the group of young officers who made the revolution were discontented with their positions, feeling that the road was stopped by the generals who had taken over when Gómez died. Just so, now, there is a younger generation of officers who feel that their progress is stopped by the colonels who took over in 1945

The political parties will know better how to take advantage of the situation this time. They have past experience as a guide. The parties are all intact underground, and will be willing and anxious to take advantage of any breaks in the unity of the military men. This in spite of the tremendous persecution to which the political parties have been subject.

Democratic Action did not build up the civilian forces sufficiently when it was in power. At the time, he thought that certainly the AD had armed militia who could confront exactly the situation which arose in November 1948. But they had no such thing.

Betancourt counted too much on his ability to handle the military, his cleverness, and didn't use enough force to keep them in line. He had a perfect opportunity in December 1946 when there was a general plot headed by Pérez Jiménez to oust Acción Democrática, but Pérez Jiménez got cold feet, so that though the Maracay garrison rose, that of Caracas did not, and the thing was suppressed. Pérez Jiménez's brother who headed the plot in one state, said that he had moved on orders of his brother Marcos. This was all published in the press, but in spite of it Betancourt left Pérez Jiménez in his post. There would have been no opposition within or outside the Army to a thorough purge at that moment. Then, from January 1948 the army chiefs were openly plotting against the regime, and they could have cracked down on them at any time. But they left them alone.

Gallegos confided too much in Delgado Chalbaud. Delgado Chalbaud was completely disloyal, but Gallegos thought him to be completely loyal to him, Gallegos. The whole life and background of Delgado Chalbaud, his father's unsuccessful attempts first to shoot Gómez, then to revolt against him and take the presidency, convinced Carlos Delgado Chalbaud that he must right his father's wrongs and become president. He was in on the plotting from the beginning.

In general, the Acción Democrática people forgot the first thing about the Venezuelan Army, that it exists to support a dictatorship. If they had taken that more into account, they would probably have lasted longer in power. He doesn't think it would have made much difference if Betancourt or Gallegos had been president in November 1948.

He fears that Venezuela is going to be much like Manaos. The oil boom will end sooner than most people here think. Then they will have giant cities, but no base for them. The iron mines will not be a substitute for oil, because the contract this regime has made with the iron companies is worse than Juan Vicente Gómez's first contract with the oil companies in 1919.

The government has done nothing to build up other industries or agriculture. The Acción Democrática regime had a program of agrarian reform, but this one has not continued it. Its "agrarian reform" consists of cutting forest areas, settling immigrants from Eastern Europe there at gigantic cost. They have a showplace there, but they do not have a program which means anything for the country at large.

As to the proposed steel plant, they have brought in an "expert," a general, from Brazil, to advise them. He would have thought they would have gotten someone from Germany or Sweden or someplace else, but not from Brazil. A number of new industries have grow up, but not due to the government. They are due to the oil boom, and most of them are more or less artificial and will collapse when the boom collapses.

The government has no economic program. Today it is free enterprise, tomorrow socialistic, today it is protectionist, tomorrow free trade. The only program the govenment has is that of tremendously wasting the country's resources.

They are trying to build up an aristocratic military caste here. For instance, even the sentry box in the new officers' club is made of marble. The same day they opened the 40 million bolivar officers' club, they opened a 4 million bolivar housing project. That is about the general prpportion in the country. The officers' club here is the most aristocratic anywhere in the world. There are others like it in the provinces. This all sits very badly wih the people.

There is no doubt that there are numerous recently ex-Communists in the government. Whether they are turncoats or sent there by the party, he cannot tell. That they are ther is certain; and that there have been no official Communist publications of their expulsion is equally certain.

The Communists, with their position before the November 1948 coup and now include the following: Rafael Heredia, secretary general of the Communist Party [CP] in the Federal District, senator; Antonio Seijas, Communist leader in the teachers federation, deputy; Monte Santander, secretary general, CP Estado Lara, deputy and in 1952 chairman of the government party's national campaign; Vaugh Salas Lozada, member of the Central Committee, CP of the Federal District, in charge of public relations in the Ministry of Public Works; Nelson Luís Martinez, director of the Communist periodical Aqui Esta and member of the Central Committee of the CP in the Federal District, now public relations chief in the Ministry of Education; Angel Delgado, Communist leader in Caracas, now deputy; Luís Garcia, Communist leader in Caracas, now a deputy; Ramón Pinedo, Communist trade union leader, now head of the government's trade union group, the MOSIT; Rafael de Leon, Communist student leader and leader of party in Caracas, now head of the government's political party.

There is no control of foreign exchange here, and immigrants are sending gigantic amounts of money to Europe. They are virtual transients, here to earn money to go home, to Sao Paulo or to Buenos Aires.

He has faith in the people's understanding the situation. The urbanization which the oil boom has brought has made people more politically conscious. They showed in December 1952 that they knew what the score was, when they voted against the government.

*   *   *   *   *

CONVERSATION WITH RAMÓN J. VELÁZQUEZ IN OFFICE OF SECRETARY GENERAL OF THE PRESIDENCY, IN MIRAFLORES PALACE, JULY 27, 1961

He is editing a series of books on the political thought of Venezuela during the nineteenth century. One of the recent volumes has reports and speeches by the man who was virtually prime minister of Paez over a hundred years ago, and it is astounding to what degree the problems which he reported on are the same ones which the country is wrestling with today.

The country is facing a tremendous problem of readjustment to democratic life. The fact is that in its hundred fifty years of independence, Venezuela has had a democratic regime only a bit more than a half a dozen years. There was the dictatorship of Paez, followed by Monagas, who was much fiercer; followed by a short restoration of Paez. There then followed a more or less democratic period, of weak government, followed by another long dictatorship, followed by four years under two doctors who were more or less democratic, followed by the thirty-eight years of the Andina generals, Castro and Gómez. Then came the regime of Lopez Contreras, who allowed certain freedom of expression, followed by the Medina regime, the three years of the Revolutionary Junta, culminating in the worst of the modern dictatorships, that of Pérez Jiménez. So Venezuela just hasn't had much democratic experience, and it is something which requires adjustment, whether upon the part of himself, General Briceno, the Minister of Defense, the porter or the taxi driver.

Unfortunately, this democratic experiment started at exactly the moment when the economy had reached its apogee and was starting to decline. During the Pérez Jiménez period, the regime had had tremendous wealth passing through its hands, as a result of the Korean War, the Cold War, the Suez Crisis. As a result, the budget ran to 5 billion bolivares a year. When they started to give new oil contracts, this rose in one year to 10 billion bolivares.

The investment which the government made of this fabulous wealth was put 90 percent in Caracas. The dictators tend to have a pharaonic attitude in this regard, and everything is done to decorate their capitals. As a result, here, there was transportation, housing, jobs, schools and health services in Caracas, while the interior was starved of all of these things. So the people of the provinces came in hundreds of thousands to the capital city, which became the terribly inflated head on a virtually paralytic body of the nation.

In addition, the provisional government after Pérez Jiménez made some terrible errors. On the one hand, it greatly inflated the bureaucracy, by 200 to 300 percent, which it has been very hard for the government of Betancourt to change, due to various political pressures. In addition, the Provisional regime had had the so-called Plan de Emergencia, which was virtually a dole, but given the name of a wage. The present regime has had to try to do away with this, by putting these people in actual work, which is outside the regular budget. The government has had a good deal of progress in this, but the job is not completed yet.

All of this adds up to tremendous economic and social problems. With these hundreds of thousands of people having come to Caracas, the government has had to try to provide them with the minimum amenities, has had to provide jobs and other things, which means spending more on Caracas than they would like to have to do.

However, there is a relatively stable situation now. This is not to say that there is not still a menace from both Right and Left. However, the events of last October and November demonstrated this stability. Although the students in the liceos, including one two hundred meters from Miraflores, and in the university caused street disturbances, and actually fired guns from the universities, the people of the cerros did not join them, although thousands of throwaways circulated there, urging them to do so last year. This is partly due to the fact that the people are very tired of these continuous street demonstrations for political purposes, and partly because the people honestly did not want to demonstrate against the constitutional regime. However, all of this demonstrated that the left-wing extremists are largely confined to the University.

The problem of establishing democracy here is demonstrated by the degree to which the people are used to a regime in which the president decides everything. Under the various dictatorships it was customary for a citizen to read in the paper how the president had resolved all of the pending problems. The citizen didn't have to bother his head about thinking about them; and this attitude has tended to persist to a considerable degree.

This is typified by the type of letters which are addressed to the President and which pass Velázquez's desk. Some go so far as to ask the President's permission to get married; they ask him to pave a short street in some small town, they write to report some robbery which has been committed in some outlying district. Velázquez refers many of these to the proper authorities involved, but also writes the people to explain to them that the president cannot and will not do everything, and that their requests or complaints should be addressed to those parts of the government which are empowered to deal with them. This is a long process of education of the people. It indicates that the process has just begun.

The law provides that his office should serve as the intermediary between the president and the ministers. However, in addition, it serves as intermediary between the president and the twenty or more "institutos autonomos" which have flourished in recent decades and which, although theoretically depending upon some ministry, seek direct access to the president for themselves. It is his job to sift all of this out, and to deal with as many problems as he can, sorting out those with which the president must deal directly.

* * * * *

CONVERSATION WITH RAMÓN J. VELÁZQUEZ IN HIS OFFICE IN CARACAS, JANUARY 3, 1978

He was not of the generation of 1928. He became a first year law student in 1936. He first met Rómulo when Rómulo gave two lectures in the headquarters of the Federacion de Estudiantes de Venezuela on oil. This was the first that the oil problem had been analyzed from the anti-imperialist, anti-company, and anti-Rockefeller point of view.

One had to have lived under the Gómez dictatorship to understand how much it had cut Venezuela off from the rest of the world. It raised a veritable wall around the country. It once banned the importation of an anti-Marxist book, for instance, because it thought that Marxism was something which should not be discussed at all, pro or con. As a result, it was the exiles, those of the 1921 generation of Gustavo Machado, and those of the 1928 generation such as Betancourt, Leoni, Jovito, Otero Silva, who had read about Marxism, anti-imperialism, and so on, who brought these ideas back to Venezuela.

Betancourt was not the first exile to arrive after Gómez's death. Jovito was here in December a few days after Gómez died. The Communists were back before the end of December. Betancourt was not here until the end of January 1936. He returned with the idea of forming a party and began work immediately to establish groups for that purpose. He never paid much attention to the Students Federation, left the Communists and Jovito control it. It was really a matter of the Communists controlling it, since Jovito had no group of his own, although he was the hero of 1936, and Betancourt was still relatively unknown. Betancourt concentrated immediately on organizing political groups and unions. Also, he immediately showed interest in organizing the interior of the country, whereas the Communists were largely concentrated in Caracas, leaving only Juan Bautista Fuenmayor and a small group in Zulia. Those who were to form Accion Democratica had the help of Valmore Rodriguez in Zulia. He was the key figure there at that time.

Various groups emerged. ORVE was under Betancourt's leadership, as its Secretary General. The Partido Republicano Progresista [PRP] was pro-Communist, the Partido Democrático Nacionalista [PDN] was the group of Valmore Rodriguez in Zulia. They functioned for a year and a half, until Lopez Contreras suppressed them. An order was issued for the arrest of Betancourt, among others, but he was betrayed or gave himself up and was captured and spent a year in Chile. For some time, he collaborated with the Communists, but finally broke with them. He had the Partido Democrático Nacional [PDN], of which he was Secretary General.

In the election of 1941, the PDN put up the symbolic candidacy of Rómulo Gallegos. Of course, the election was determined before it was held, and General Isaias Medina Angarita was elected. He liberalized the regime considerably, legalizing the PDN as Acción Democrática, the Communists and the Union Popular and Union Municipal.

AD sought to get a common candidate with the government for the 1946 election. There was agreement on Diogenes Escalante, Ambassador to Washington. However, he had a nervous breakdown,which ended his candidacy. The agreement with the government therefore fell through and Betancourt and AD joined forces with a young military group which was very unhappy because of the many semi-literate generals who were sanding in the way of their professional advancement. Betancourt didn't make the Revolution of October 18, 1945, the military did--no civilian in Latin America organizes a military coup.

Betancourt had the great political capacity of being able to take advantage of the military coup to bring about profound changes in the country. As a result of this, the old Venezuela died on October 18, 1945. Betancourt became president of the Junta Revolucionaria, but all of the other members were also ministers, and as a result, Betancourt remained the de-facto President of the Republic.

Betancourt supported Gallegos for President of the Republic, although he was well aware of the dangers of an inexperienced intellectual like Gallegos becoming president. Betancourt had previously pledged his support for Gallegos and could not turn back from that pledge.

With the entry into office of Gallegos, there developed a wide gulf between him and Betancourt. This was due to a group around Gallegos, who were all related. They included Lopez Gallegos, Luís Lander, whose grandfather was a Gallegos, a Minister of Education who was married to a sister of the wives of Lopez Gallegos and Lander. These people sought a separation of the two Rómulos because of considerations of the presidential succession.

The whole Gallegos period was one of great tenseness. There was unremitting criticism of the regime by Copei, which accused the AD of having a party militia, which they did not have. There were also administrative failures, simple things like gaping holes in the Caracas streets about which the government seemed incapable of doing anything, as well as the same kind of conditions on the Caracas-Maracay highway. Within six months of the overthrow of the Gallegos regime, the holes somehow or other were all filled in. One of the contractors who carried out this work under the Junta Militar was the man who had been Public Works Minister of Gallegos and in that capacity had seemed unable to do anything about the bad condition of the streets and highways.

The epic of the Resistance was a long one. At first, the Resistance consisted only of Acción Democrática. However, later there was some participation by the Communists, and in the last years also by Copei. Everyone of the AD leaders was in jail. Velázquez himself spent four years in jail, was only liberated on January 24, 1958. Betancourt was the real leader of the Resistance, giving it guidance through his letters, his proclamations, his speeches and so on.

So long as Delgado was in charge it was a dicta blanda, as the Spaniards say. But after December 1952 it was one of the worst dictatorships that Venezuela had ever had. It was more a police dictatorship than a military one. Its really key figure was Pedro Estrada. He was virtually a kind of prime minister, superior in power to his supposedly hierarchical superior, Minister of Interior Vallenilla Lanz. Pedro Estrada had dossiers on every one. Velázquez saw many of them after the fall of the dictatorship. Estrada had them not only on Betancourt, Jovito, Caldera, and so on, but also on Vallenilla Lanz and other ministers, top military men of the regime, and so on. He had extensive records on the corrupt deals of various figures in the Pérez Jiménez regime, enough data to prosecute all of them.

Pérez Jiménez alienated two key groups. One of these was the Army. He governed alone, without any Junta such as now exists in Argentina, Brazil, Bolivia, and Peru. The military as such had little power, real power was in the hands of Pérez Jiménez, Estrada and Vallenilla Lanz. There developed the same kind of discontent among the colonels, captains, and majors as had existed before 1945 against the generals, this time because the generals were all corrupt.

Pérez Jiménez also alienated the old economic groups, that is, the Mendozas, the Vollmers, the Zuloagas, and so on. He created a group of new rich to whom he gave the public works contracts, credits of the Corporacion de Fomento, the Agricultural Bank, and the Industrial Bank. The old groups resented all of this. However, in the beginning they all paid court to Pérez Jiménez and to Pedro Estrada. The country club crowd felt flattered to have Pedro Estrada sit down with them at lunch.

The crisis of the Pérez Jiménez regime arose because of the economic situation beginning in 1956. The government couldn't pay its debts, the boom declined and the situation got very serious by 1957. In these circumstances, the plebiscite on whether Pérez Jiménez should stay in power served as the last straw, ultimately bringing about the collapse of the Pérez Jiménez regime.

*   *   *   *   *
*   *   *   *   *

Further Reading

Several of the people dealt with in this volume have themselves written books of interest to those wishing to know more about them. Others have been the subject of biographies. In still other cases, somewhat broader-based studies contain relevant material on the Bolivarian presidents who are interviewed and corresponded with in the present volume.

There are entries on most of our subjects in the _Biographical Dictionary of Latin America and Caribbean Politics_, edited by Robert J. Alexander, and published by Greenwood Press, Westport, CT, 1988.

BOLIVIA

The two standard studies of the Bolivian National Revolution, in which most of our Bolivian presidents played roles of greater or less consequence are Robert J. Alexander's _The Bolivian National Revolution_, published by Rutgers University Press in 1958, and James Malloy's _Bolivia: The Uncompleted Revolution_, put out by University of Pittsburgh Press in 1971. The story is extended through the 1960s and 1970s by _Bolivia: Past, Present and Future of Its Politics_, by Robert J. Alexander, Praeger Publishers, New York, 1982. Finally, James Dunkerley's chapter on "The Crisis of the Bolivian Revolution" in _The Latin American Left from the Fall of Allende to Perestroika_, published by Westview Press, Boulder, 1993, deals with the second periods of Víctor Paz Estenssoro and Hernán Siles in power in the 1980s.

The only published biography of Víctor Paz Estenssoro of which I am aware is that written by José Fellman Velarde, _Víctor Paz Estenssoro, El Hombre y la Revolución_, published in La Paz in 1955, during Paz Estenssoro's first administration.

PERU

Fernando Belaúnde Terry published a short book, _La Conquista del Perú por los Peruanos_, Ediciones Totantinsyn, Lima, 1959, in which he elaborated on his view of his country's needs. Pedro Pablo Kuczynski's _Peruvian Democracy under Economic Stress: An Account of the Belaúnde Administration, 1963-1968_, Princeton University Press, Princeton, 1977, dealt in detail with President Belaúnde's first administration. Two more general books which deal in part with Belaúnde are Eugene Chang Rodriguez's _Opciones Políticas Peruanas_, Centro de Documentacion Andina, Lima, 1985, and Carlos Albert Astiz's _Pressure Groups and Power Elites in Peru_, Cornell University Press, Ithaca, 1969.

ECUADOR

Two of our Ecuadorean presidents are themselves authors. Galo Plaza published _Problems of Democracy in Latin America_, University of North Carolina Press, Chapel Hill, 1955; and Osvaldo Hurtado's _Political Power in Ecuador_ was published by the University of New Mexico Press, Albuquerque, in 1980.

Other books which deal in more or less detail with the periods in which our presidents were chief executive include James Levy's _The Challenge of Democratic Reform in Ecuador_, University of New Mexico Press, Albuquerque, 1981; John Martz's _Politics and Petroleum in Ecuador_, Transaction, New Brunswick, 1987; and David Corkill's _Ecuador: Fragile Democracy_, Latin American Bureau, London, 1988.

COLOMBIA

Eduardo Santos published a book about the suspension of his newspaper by the Rojas Pinilla dictatorship, _La Crisis de la Democracia en Colombia y "El Tiempo_," Gráfica Panamericana, Mexico, 1955. David Bushnell wrote about the Santos administration in _Eduardo Santos and the Good Neighbor, 1938-1942_.

Other books deal to some degree with the roles of the Colombian presidents dealt with in the present volume. These include John D. Martz's _Colombia: A Contemporary Political Survey_, University of North Carolina Press, Chapel Hill, 1962; _The Political Dimensions of Change_, by Robert H. Dix, Yale University Press, New Haven, 1968; and Richard Sharpless's book, _Jorge Eliécer Gaitán of Colombia: A Political Biography_, University of Pittsburgh Press, Pittsburgh, 1978.

VENEZUELA

Among the books dealing with the career of Rómulo Gallegos there are Harrison Sabin Howard's _Rómulo Gallegos y la Revolución Burgesa en Venezuela_, Monte Avila, Caracas, 1976; and Simón Alberto Consalvi's _Auge y Caida de Rómulo Gallegos_, Monte Avila, Caracas, 1991. Other books which deal with Gallegos and the other Acción

Democrática presidents of Venezuela include *Cuatras Figuras Blancas*, Focon Serrano Producciones, Caracas, 1975; and *40 Años de Acción Democrática: 4 Presidentes*, Ediciones de la Presidencia de la Republica, Caracas, 1981 (Volume I includes Rómulo Gallegos, Volume II deals with Raúl Leoni and Carlos Andrés Pérez).

A book dealing with the career of Rafael Caldera is Gehard Cartay Ramírez's *Caldera y Betancourt: Constructores de la Democracia*, Ediciones Centaura, Caracas, 1987. Donald Herman's *Christian Democracy in Venezuela* is a history of the Copei Party and as such deals extensively with Caldera, and to a much lesser degree with Luis Herrera Campins.

More general books which also have information about the presidents dealt with in the present volume include John D. Martz, *Acción Democrática: The Evolution of a Modern Political Party in Venezuela*, Princeton University Press, Princeton, 1966; John D. Martz and David Meyers, *Venezuela: The Democratic Experience*, Praeger Publishers, New York, 1977; David Eugene Blank's *Politics in Venezuela*, Little, Brown & Co., Boston, 1973, and his *Venezuela: Politics in a Petroleum Republic*, Praeger Publishers, New York, 1984; and Daniel Levine's *Conflict and Change in Venezuela*, Princeton University Press, 1973.

Index

Acción Democrática:
achievements of discredited by
Copei government, 165;
alliance of with Copei, 201;
arrest of some of its trade
union leaders under AD
government, 155; attacks on
by Communists, 151; attitude
of, towards the Army, 246,
247; boycott of Congress
session by, 233; breaks up
Copei meeting, 198; change in
strategy of, after fall of
Pérez Jiménez, 230; commitment
of to Rómulo Gallegos, 198;
congressional accord of with
Copei in Caldera
administration, 233; contacts
of Caldera with, before
October 1945 Revolution, 171;
criticisms of its 1945-1948
regime by Caldera, 171, 172;
didn't build up civilian
forces enough in 1940's
regime, 246; electoral decline
of, 204; establishment of,
151; experience of in
power,190; failure of to
continue coalition with Copei,
146; favors union affiliation
with ICFTU and ORIT, 177;
impact of MEP split on AD

trade union following, 216;
imposes 50/50 petroleum
formula, 156; improvement of
trade union situation of,
245; internal situation of,
according to Leoni, 163;
kinship of, with Bolivian MNR,
9; kinship of, with Democratic
Left of Ecuador, 115; lack of
youth movement of, 217; last
minute expenditures of its
regime, 186, 187; legalization
of, favored by Caldera, 173;
Leoni's hopes for its third
electoral victory, 165; loses
1978 election, 144; loss by of
1978 municipal election, 273;
members of in Revolutionary
Junta, 141, 142; names
Betancourt for President in
1958, 200; number of members
support Caldera in 1993
election, 208; opposes entry
of Communist unions into CTV,
218; opposition in, to
Betancourt 1958 nomination,
230; opposition of, to general
amnesty for guerillas, 159;
outlawing of, 181; overthrow
of, 167; pays attention to
interior of country, 159;

266

of unity with PRA, PRIN and
Christian Democrats, 76, 77;
radicalization of during
Sexenio, 16, 38; and rebuilding
Central Obrera Boliviana in
early Banzer regime, 72;
refusal by of joint ticket with
Falange, 78; relations of with
Army, 46, 61; relations of with
Falange Socialista Boliviana,
62; renews contact with miners,
47; reorganization of in early
Banzer regime, 64, 65, 69;
reunification of, 29; role of,
as representative of peasants,
workers and middle class, 20;
role of, in Villarroel regime,
14, 38; splintering of, 2, 19,
26, 54; split in remains, 29;
split of with Banzer regime,
74; still largest Bolivian
party, 60; and student
movement, 28; supports
reelection of Lechín
as head of Miners Federation
and COB, 59; sympathy of miners
for, 13, 37; treatment of its
exiles by Perón regime, 15, 16;
various phases of its
government, 90; violations of
human rights by its regime, 87,
88, 91; wins power in April
1952, 17, 38; withdraws from
Banzer government, 3; women
deputies of, 92
Movimiento Nacionalista
Revolucionario de Izquierda, 77
Movimiento Popular Cristiano, 23
Movimiento Republicano
Progresista, 181
Movimiento Revolucionario
Pazestenssorista, 26, 29, 32
MRL. See Liberal Revolutionary
Movement, Colombia
MRP. See Mouvement Républicain
Populaire
Myrdal, Gunnar, 204

El Nacional, 211
Naguib, General, 208
Nass, Raúl, 152
National Civic Crusade, 190, 196,

221
National Front, Colombia, 128,
129, 130, 135
NATO. See North Atlantic Treaty
Organization
Natusch Busch, Alberto, 3
Naziism, 53
Neruda, Pablo, 109
New Force, 149, 150, 169, 192,
194, 222, 223, 224, 244
New Leader, 183
New York Times, 200, 214
1952 Revolution. See Bolivian
National Revolution
Nixon, Richard, 54, 148, 209
Noriega, Manuel Antonio, 239
North Atlantic Treaty
Organization, 238
Nueva Fuerza. See New Force
Nyrere, Julius, 233

OAS. See Organization of American
States
October Revolution, Venezuela, 155
Odría, Manuel, 54, 97, 98, 100,
105, 106, 129
Oduber, Daniel, 239
Ojeda, Fabricio, 177
Olaya Herrera, Enrique, 127
Ongañía, Juan Carlos, 111
OPEC. See Organization of
Petroleum Exporting Countries
Operación Triangula, 2, 24
Operation Pan America, 82
Order of the Condor of the Andes,
5
Organización Regional
Interamericana de Trabajadores,
177
Organización Venezolona, 250
Organization of American States,
114, 120, 146, 147, 162, 201
Organization of Petroleum
Exporting Countries, 190
ORIT. See Organización Regional
Interamericana de Trabajadores
ORVE. See Organización Venezolana
Ospina Pérez, Mariano, 128
Otero Silva, Miguel, 171, 250
Ovando, Alfredo:
establishes tin refinery, 68;
introduced to Argentine
"gorillas" by Paz Estenssoro,

282

38, 57, 58, 62

UN. *See* United Nations
Unión Democrática del Pueblo. *See*
   Unión Democrática y Popular
Unión Democrática y Popular, 3,
   85, 86, 90, 93
Unión Municipal, 250
Unión Popular, 250
Unión Republicana Democrática:
   attitude of to military regime,
   174; in Betancourt government
   coalition, 178; experience of,
   in power, 190; has Jóvito
   Villalba's wife as 1988
   presidential candidate,
   238; lack of control over by
   Jóvito Villalba, 157; in Leoni
   government coalition, 160;
   names Larrazábal as candidate
   in 1958, 142, 200; in New
   Force, 194; in 1968 election,
   184; possible support of for
   general amnesty for guerrillas,
   159; pretensions of to be a
   mass party, 164; represented on
   Concejo Supremo Electoral in
   1951, 173; rights of defended
   by Copei, 203; role of, as
   part of New Force, 149, 169,
   222, 224; role of, as possible
   coalition partner under
   Caldera, 196; role of Luís
   Miquilena in, 157; status of in
   1969, 218; supported by Acción
   Democrática in 1952 election,
   142, 175; supports Martín Vegas
   for President in early 1958,
   200; supports single
   candidate for 1958 election,
   176; wins 1952 election, 174;
   withdraws from Betancourt
   government, 142, 143, 201, 204
United Confederation of Workers
   of Venezuela. *See* Central
   Unica de Trabajadores de
   Venezuela
United Nations, 34, 75, 120
United States Embassy, 31, 91, 207
United States Government, 31
United States Steel Corporation,
   156
University Council, 72

University of California at Los
   Angeles, 82
University of Chile, 206
University of Louvain, 203
University of Santo Domingo, 119
University of Texas, 105
URD. *See* Unión Republicana
   Democrática
USAID, 24
Uslar Pietri, Arturo, 143, 159,
   160, 163, 184, 204, 208, 241,
   243

Vaky, Viron, 205
Valenilla Lanz, Laureano, 203,
   221, 251
Vallejo, César, 109
Valtin, Jan, 87
Valverde, Sr., 78
Vanderslice, Lane, 62
Vargas, Mario, 198, 199, 229
Vegas, Martín, 200
Velasco, Juan, 34, 35, 56, 79,
   102, 103, 111, 114
Velasco Ibarra, José María, 113,
   114, 117, 123, 124, 242
Velázquez, Andrés, 209
Velázquez, Ramón J.:
   author's contacts with, 150;
   chosen as President in 1993,
   150, 207; conversation of
   author with, June 25, 1954,
   245-248; conversation of author
   with, July 27, 1961, 248-249;
   conversation of author with,
   January 3, 1978, 250-252; first
   meeting of with Rómulo
   Betancourt, 250; jailed four
   years by Pérez Jiménez regime,
   251; position of, on Acción
   Democrática regime of 1940's,
   246, 247; position of, on
   Communists' role in Pérez
   Jiménez regime, 247; position
   of, on corruption of Pérez
   Jiménez regime, 246; position
   of, on difficulty of
   Venezuela adopting democracy,
   248; position of, on 1958
   Provisional Government, 248,
   249; position of, on October
   1945 Revolution, 250, 251;
   position of, on role of

About the Author

ROBERT J. ALEXANDER is Emeritus Professor, Rutgers University. Over his long career he has published 34 books and more than 700 articles.